ACROSS ISLANDS AND OCEANS

*A Journey Alone Around the World
By Sail and By Foot*

JAMES BALDWIN

Atom Voyages • Brunswick, Georgia

Contents

1   First Steps to a Voyage..1
2   Non-stop to Panama.. 22
3   Link to the Pacific...36
4   West Sets the Sun... 49
5   A Savage on Hiva Oa...70
6   Bora Bora..90
7   These Friendly Isles... 100
8   Tikopia Unspoilt.. 119
9   Adventure Country... 141
10 On the Kokoda Trail... 160
11 In the Shadow of Sumburipa................................ 177
12 Highlander... 191
13 A Mountain Too High...204
14 Surviving New Guinea..221
15 The Sheltering Atoll... 230
16 Solitary Sailor.. 245
17 To the Peaks of Reunion.......................................269
18 Trek Into Zululand..285
19 Cape of Storms... 306
20 Emperors and Astronomers....................................322
21 Martinique Revisited...346
22 The Blue Highway.. 362
    Table of Passages..370

Introduction

*To be truly challenging, a voyage, like a life, must rest
on a firm foundation of financial unrest. Otherwise, you
are doomed to a routine traverse, the kind known to
yachtsmen who play with their boats at sea..."cruising"
it is called. Voyaging belongs to seamen, and to the
wanderers of the world who cannot, or will not, fit in. If
you are contemplating a voyage and you have the means,
abandon the venture until your fortunes change. Only
then will you know what the sea is all about.*

- from Wanderer by Sterling Hayden

The voyage I wish to tell you about took two years to complete,
and though I've described bits and pieces of it before in short articles,
some 25 years have passed before I got around to telling the tale in
more detail. My story takes place between 1984 and 1986 when I was
in my mid-twenties, as close to broke as I dared to be and hungry for
the adventure that is only provided by a long voyage.

The basic premise is not so unusual: a young man on a quest for
adventure, knowledge, romance, his fortune – strikes out to see the
world. It has taken me these many years and thousands more miles
under the keel to give me a more balanced perspective on that life-
changing first voyage alone around the world.

The nature of cruising in sailboats has changed dramatically since
1984. Today's sailors are typically older and retired, their ventures
well-financed with larger and more expensive boats. For both better
and worse, new labor-saving devices and safety equipment, at more
affordable prices, has reduced the physical and technical challenges of
voyaging, and reduced along with it, the rewards gained by hard
physical work, self-sufficiency, and the heightened awareness of risks
inherent in true adventure. Perhaps most disconcerting, the popularity
of world cruising has made the search for unspoilt islands more
challenging than ever.

I write this narrative now, in part, to provide a glimpse into a style
of exploration to which the modern traveler may not have been
exposed, and to remind them that, for the most part, they can still
voyage now, as I did then, living close to nature and filling their lives

with discovery, on their own terms. Compared to a simple boat, a backpack and my boots, the thought of fussing around with airlines, taxis, buses, hotels, restaurants and all the other trappings of typical tourist travel, leave me as uninspired as a purposeless voyage.

The point of my journey was not to be first or fastest in any category, but to venture beyond my old world and self. When I began, I didn't realize that along the way my growing commitment to walk across each island and climb their highest peaks was to be as big a part of the adventure as the sailing. Like a richly lived life, as a voyage unfolds it evolves and carries you where it will.

Twenty-five years after that voyage I find my life has changed. The sharp edge of my hunger to explore has been sated somewhat by the banquet of decades of roaming under sail. I awoke recently to discover I'm fast becoming an old sailor, and what better task for an old salt than to share his stories before they're forgotten.

While reading my saltwater-stained journal and tattered log book, and flipping through the faded photo albums, it seems almost as if it were someone else's life depicted there. Was I really so rash that I set out across oceans possessing only a few hundred dollars, on a boat with sails so old you could push your finger through them? Surely it was not me that had been so dimwitted to walk into a dark cave in New Guinea and tumble into its deep, black pit? Was it foolish and selfish to seek the love of an island girl when I knew I would soon sail away from her forever?

While there turns out to be no perfect plan, I learned some things on this imperfect voyage that shaped my life in the best ways possible. Beginning with a world-view as small as my boat left me with no room for passengers. Alone on the oceans, I learned how to live in isolation. Hiking across the islands with near-empty pockets and well-worn boots, dependent on the generosity of the inhabitants, taught me how to live in society. What richer reward for a passage of two years?

There is room, now, to bring others aboard for my journey.

May you also avoid a "routine traverse."

James Baldwin
Brunswick, Georgia
May 2009

ACROSS ISLANDS
AND OCEANS

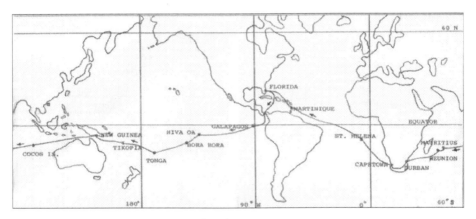

Atom's route map

The radiant goddess Circe sent a sail filling wind behind us, a good companion for a voyage. We made all shipshape aboard and sat tight: wind and helmsman kept her on her course. All day long we ran before the wind, with never a quiver on the sail; then the sun set, and all the ways grew dark.

- *Homer,* The Odyssey

PS_BX04531323

CreateSpace
7290 Investment Drive Suite B
North Charleston, SC 29418

Question About Your Order?
Log in to your account at www.createspace.com and "Contact
Support."

04/13/2015 09:37:59 AM
Order ID: 87807388

Qty.	Item
	IN THIS SHIPMENT
1	Across Islands and Oceans 1470004615

1 First Steps to a Voyage

A sailor's worst fear arrived before dawn. Under gray twilight I knelt on a shore of coarse pebbles and scattered black boulders and faced a crazed sea. Surf crashed on rocks, filling the air with wind-driven spray that streamed down my face and soaked me through. Numb with fear and cold, I watched my sailboat, my home, now half-submerged, breaking up on the sharp talons of an inshore reef. Waves hammered the boat, grinding away years of work. The mast collapsed with a shudder. I felt sick with fatigue and helplessness.

It seemed my solitary voyage around the world had come to an abrupt end on this uninhabited coast. If my course had been another mile to the south I would have sailed clear of this ship-killing island. Curling up behind a rock, I closed my eyes and gave way to overwhelming physical and mental exhaustion. The ceaseless thundering of waves breaking on the reef filled my semi-consciousness.

When I opened my eyes again I was somehow back aboard my boat, wedged face down into the thin vinyl-covered cushion of the leeward bunk. I turned over to focus on the scene around me while the sound of surf shook the cobwebs from my mind. Was the shipwreck real and this now a dream or the other way around? "Idiot!" I cried as I bolted up the companionway steps....

* * *

The series of events leading me to that fearsome island encounter likely began with childhood days watching sailboats gliding across the flat waters of Michigan's Lake St. Clair. I used to imagine they were all bound for distant adventures. Our little lake, deep within the Midwest watershed was, after all, connected by hundreds of miles of rivers, greater and lesser lakes, canals and locks, to the roiling waters of Niagara Falls and on to the sea. Ocean-going ships plowed up and down our lake's deep-water channel daily – proof of our connection to the larger world.

A family trip in our single-engine airplane to the Out Islands of the Bahamas in my early teens gave me a taste for travel among tropical islands. On that trip my father had me sit in the back seat next to the life raft with an open knife in hand with instructions to puncture the raft if it should accidentally inflate inside the cabin. My father taught me to fly small planes by the time I was sixteen, but I gave up the sport soon after, when an electrical fire filled our cockpit with smoke and we made a terrifying emergency landing. Suddenly, sea-level travel seemed more appealing.

Looking back, I can't recall a time I hadn't dreamt of running down the trades on a sailboat to the fabled islands of the South Pacific. I held these yearnings in check, finishing high school and vocational courses, before moving into an apartment shared with friends and scratching about to "earn a living" while searching to discover my purpose in life. I was nearly sidetracked into marriage until my girlfriend concluded I was of the wrong temperament to have children underfoot and a mortgage over my head.

Though motor boating was occasionally involved in a few of our early family vacations, we never had a sailboat of our own. The first boat I almost launched was a 12-foot rowboat, more rot than wood, that a neighbor gave me in exchange for hauling it away. It took six of us kids to carry it down the street to my backyard. We worked for a month on the boat during our summer vacation, rigging a crude rudder and patchwork sail, dreaming of the day we would launch her. My parents thought it unsalvageable and tried everything to discourage me from drowning myself in it. Still, we patched her up.

The day before our proposed launch I found someone had knocked new holes in the bottom. My buddies and I were crushed as it was now beyond saving. At the time we blamed the older bully down the street but in retrospect, my father was not bothered at all about the tragedy and rather too soon appeared with a can of gas and said, "Burn it." The case of the sabotaged boat remains open.

Looking back now I see that, in time, we become more learned and less wise. So it was at the wise young age of eighteen I chanced to read the recently published biography *To Challenge a Distant Sea* about the life of French sailor Jean Gau. Beginning in the 1950s, he twice sailed alone around the world in his 29-foot Tahiti Ketch, named *Atom*. Gau lived great adventures – encounters with hurricanes and cannibals, shipwrecks, a love affair with a beautiful Tahitian *vahine*. Each time he returned to sea was, for him, a coming home. Did Gau's world still exist out there? I was determined to find out.

At the time I didn't know the course I would ultimately take, nor did I dare imagine I would travel across oceans alone. I was no Jean Gau and had no reason to believe I ever would be. Yet, from that time on, dreams of tropical seas and exotic landfalls never ceased. Through his book's pages, I saw myself rediscovering the world from the deck of my own sailboat.

Why I was so permanently affected by this book I couldn't say. It certainly awoke the nagging notion that the promise of a full life was not to be found in my hometown or even on any single continent. What better siren song to capture an innocent youth than romantic visions of being aboard a stout boat anchored snugly in a palm-fringed lagoon, then putting out to sea and running before the warm trade winds to a new landfall where perhaps some vahine awaited.

Like all aspiring sailors of my generation, I had also read the book *Dove*, about Robin Lee Graham, who sailed alone around the world between the ages of sixteen and twenty-one. His story, too, inspired me to undertake a voyage, but an inward one, an entirely different type of journey. It seems his father and publishers pushed him to continue a voyage he grew to hate, filled with perpetual loneliness and lovesick self-pity. Too much anguish and loathing made Graham's story, in many ways, the antithesis to the path I sought. By the time I got underway, I had the advantage over Graham of a few more years maturity – yet I was still young enough to believe in my own invincibility.

My faraway dreams took on a glimmer of life on one of those frigid Detroit winter evenings when my equally bored, broke and quietly desperate teenage friends gathered around the kitchen table for yet another Saturday night poker game. We'd all had a few beers when I started daydreaming aloud about islands in the South Pacific. I told them condensed and not strictly factual accounts of what I had read; that in those warm tropic seas far to the south were countless volcanic islands and coral atolls peopled by gentle brown-skinned natives who never worked a day in their lives because ripe fruit practically dropped into their hands. And that this paradise lay within easy reach of even a small sailing yacht.

Carried away by my own enthusiasm, I went on to tell them of the unequaled charms of the Tahitian women. "Pure goddesses!" I claimed, adding how they were not too pure to literally throw themselves at visiting sailors. To make up for lack of first-hand experience and make my vision more compelling, I recited descriptions of island girls from romantic stories of the South Pacific by Herman Melville, James Michener, Paul Gauguin and others. Fact or fiction, we believed what we wanted, and needed, to believe.

Staring at me over empty bottles of Detroit-brewed Stroh's beer, my friends appeared spellbound, or possibly just in their normal stupor – it was hard to recognize the difference. "Tell us more about these native girls," someone said when I paused long enough to drain another bottle. After a few more of these Saturday night sermons, they claimed to be as convinced as I that we must go to sea and go quickly. Dying of boredom was the only apparent alternative. Their passions proved shorter-lived than my naivety. Life interfered, as it commonly does.

There were real obstacles to overcome before my shanghaied crew and I set sail. We had no boat, no money and we knew nothing about sailing or the sea. We didn't even know any sailors. And these, I admit, were not our weakest points. Like typical American teen-aged boys, we were impulsive and erratic and lacked the degree of forethought the sea demands.

As a first step we laid out a plan, agreeing to work at our various jobs for one to two years with the goal of saving at least $10,000 each. We would then pool our money and buy the largest, old wooden sailing boat we could afford. Sixty feet long, not counting the bowsprit, sounded about right. To learn about boat building and to save money, we would refit it ourselves, teach ourselves to sail and then set out to voyage around the world together. Knowing the outcomes of teenage schemes better than I, my parents warned me it was another doomed venture, but it seemed doable at the time.

For my part, after finishing metalworking vocational school, I labored almost three years at factory jobs, moving on several times whenever a new position offered better pay. For months I assembled and welded metal cabinets on a production line until my mind went numb. The next job paid better as I made heavy braze repairs on cracked punch press frames. This job required I operate a propane torch the size of a mini flame-thrower while standing on a scaffold atop a half-ton of flaming charcoal – stoking the fires of hell. Through productive labors and self-denial, each week I put away at least one dollar for every two earned. In later years I had the luxury to discover that the only worthwhile work is the kind you would choose as charity work, if circumstances permitted, which has become my goal now and forever.

Back in my apartment I'd lose myself each night in nautical books borrowed from the library; reading whatever I could find, from *Elementary Dinghy Sailing* to *Two Years Before the Mast*. Yet there is only so much a book can do. As the Chinese proverb says: "To walk one thousand miles is better than to read ten thousand books."

My first real step to getting under sail was when a friend and I bought an old 12-foot sailing dinghy. Together we sailed most Sundays and holidays on Lake St. Clair, paddling about in the calms and capsizing in any wind strong enough to fully stretch the sails. Because our little boat's overly tall rig carried a mainsail that couldn't be reefed or lowered once underway, we spent windy days clinging to the bottom of the upturned hull.

Eventually, through books alone, I became familiar with the rudiments of boat design, navigation and ocean weather patterns – at least the bookish version, which is far from the real thing. After nights dreaming of narrowly escaped shipwrecks and exotic landfalls, I awoke to the rude buzz of my alarm clock. On autopilot mode I plunged into another winter day's toil in a depressing smoke-filled factory. In my beat-up 1961 Volkswagen Beetle, I slid along ice-covered streets on bald tires in pre-dawn rush hour traffic.

The morning commute brings out the savage in those of us actually awake at the wheel as we drive bumper to bumper, 70 miles-an-hour in all weather – icy streets traveled by ice-encrusted souls. It was not lost on me that most of the people on the roads at that hour were on the way to build even more motorized metal boxes for already-crowded American roads. We were a society of movers. We moved frantically, if not purposefully.

In the factory's smoky welding pit, the days dragged on. I moved like a misshapen gear in a machine determined to ultimately mash my rough edges into a kind of tortured conformity – if I stayed long enough. I recognized it on the faces of the men around me: with each passing year their own hopes and plans faded slightly more into the barely remembered dreams of their youth. Physically, I was here working alongside them, but I was not one of them.

I had confided to a co-worker that I would soon quit this job, buy a boat and head for distant lands. "Sure you will," he told me and passed my secret to the rest of the shop which earned me the ridicule, pity and suspicion usually reserved for the mad. The day my bank account reached the $15,000 goal I had set for myself, I broke free, walking out of that soul-crushing hellhole for the last time. I knew that was as close to rich as I'd ever be in Detroit. It couldn't have felt better if the whole shop had walked alongside me cheering, instead of just following me with quiet stares, the kind that said, "You'll find nothing better out there, fella."

It should have been no surprise that, one by one, my friends lost their enthusiasm for our joint venture. Their lives had moved on in other directions. One of them was said to have dropped out in the drug-cult of California, a lost soul to us and himself. The others had made safer, more practical plans for their futures. One longtime friend, whom I hadn't seen in a year, was engaged to be married and had already signed a mortgage on a new house in the suburbs. He turned his head away when I stood before him as a resurrected ghost of a dream he had quietly buried long ago.

I was now twenty-one years old. I had never owned a real boat and had never even stepped foot on a sailboat larger than a dinghy. Though little problems and discouragements came at me from all quarters, they were nowhere near enough to dissuade me. I decided to buy the best second-hand boat I could afford. If necessary, I'd travel alone, as long and as far as my meager talents could take me.

Through the coldest months of that winter I searched through lifeless boatyards and poked my head under countless snow-laden tarps. Finally, a boat caught my eye as it lay despondently under a blanket of snow, gripped in the ice of a frozen canal. I had no patience to wait for the ice to break up so the boat could be lifted out of the water and properly inspected. In spite of my haste, the marine surveyor reported that this 28-foot Pearson Triton, built of fiberglass in 1963, was solidly constructed, although somewhat neglected and minimally equipped. Though I had some initial doubts due to its small size, I was reassured by its long keel and admired the low sleek profile and handsome lines of the hull.

"You can sail this boat anywhere in the Great Lakes," the broker assured me. Yet these Great Lakes were still only lakes: fine for cruising or beginning a voyage but too familiar to satisfy my growing lust to explore.

"And beyond, I hope," I added.

My parents thought it reckless to spend my limited savings to buy a boat, but they didn't mind at all my plan to sail around the world – because I simply didn't tell them until I was halfway across the Pacific. You can talk about doing a thing until everyone finally talks you out of it or you can actually do the thing.

The Triton had a good reputation among sailors in the U.S. She was designed in 1959 by the skilled Swedish marine architect, Carl Alberg, who was known for his seaworthy designs based on earlier proven sailing craft of northern Europe. Equally important, she was beautiful to my eyes and I could imagine us bound together for exotic places. It was as if the boat spoke to me: "I've been waiting for you. Take me somewhere far away from here and we'll look after each other just fine."

At some point during a boat search you have to put away the formulas of sail area/displacement ratios and the like and follow your gut. A boat, like a woman, has to excite and incite you to dream. If it doesn't, just walk away. Even the name, *DOCTOR'S ORDERS*, ridiculously taped onto both sides of the white hull in four-inch high black letters did not dissuade me. A name change was the first job I'd see to, regardless of popular nautical superstition. You don't sail into Tahiti and moor alongside world cruising yachts in a boat with a name like that.

Atom on ice in Michigan

After some offers and counteroffers, we agreed on a price of $12,000. This was a fantastic fortune to me since it represented four-fifths of my savings and three years of hard work. The owner later told me he was reluctant to sell but his wife had ordered it. A fair deal some might say; he temporarily saved his marriage and I had my boat.

That first winter I tried living aboard my nameless new boat as she lay trapped in the frozen canal. Soon the constant rain of condensation from the underside of the non-insulated fiberglass deck, caused by using the boat's alcohol stove for heat, forced me back to my apartment. The heady daydreams continued however: with nose pressed against the frosty apartment window, watching snow blow into drifts around my car, I envisioned my little VW as a ship fighting her way around Cape Horn in a mid-winter storm.

The spring thaw brought relief and I recall taking Maria with me on our first sail. By the way, never take your girlfriend with you on your first sail – unless, that is, you want to terrify her so much with your stupidity that she never wants to go sailing again. Since no sailing book had told me this, we went blindly ahead as I helped her fit a raincoat over her jacket and sweater in an attempt to ward off the effects of below freezing temperatures.

A light snow fell from that Michigan-gray sky as we chopped away at the ice in the slip with an ice-fishing spud, then used the inboard gasoline engine to motor out the canal. Once clear of the breakwater, I silenced the rumbling beast then raised the full mainsail and the largest jib. Trimming the full sails to take us close to the wind caused a slight heel and the boat began to glide along effortlessly. Clusters of snowflakes swirled in the air currents around the sails. Now and then I made a sharp turn to avoid the scattered ice floes. It felt good to be the only boat on the water. We were probably the first boat sailing that year, even attracting the attention of a Coast Guard helicopter that buzzed past us. Everything felt fine, yet Maria did not trust my untested sailing skills and looked at me apprehensively as I tacked upwind. Within a few minutes the wind picked up, causing the boat to heel over sharply until waves were spilling over the leeward side of the cockpit and splashing around our feet. Maria demanded to know what the hell was going on as I tied a life jacket around her and told her to go below and close the hatch. I let the boat round up into the wind, pulled down the flogging sails and motored back into the marina, thoroughly chastened.

Safely back at the dock, I wondered why the boat had seemed so unstable. When the wind came up she felt almost as tender as my old sailing dinghy. This was my home: a four-ton boat to carry me across the oceans and here it was, about to roll over and sink in Lake St. Clair! Either this boat had been robbed of the three thousand pounds of lead in her keel or I had not paid attention to the sailing books I'd read.

Later, sitting at a bar next to the marina, a couple of relative old hands at sailing assured me it's the nature of sailboats to "put the rail under" while carrying full sail in a fresh breeze, particularly a boat like mine of a low freeboard design. We were in no danger of rolling the boat over in anything short of hurricane conditions – something unlikely on our 20-mile-wide lake. Once the boat is heeled to about 45 degrees the wind is spilled from the sails and the lead ballast in the keel forces the boat upright. All we needed to do that morning was reef the mainsail and set a smaller jib to maintain balance. Those books I had read discussed reefing sails, I just hadn't realized reefing was required in such moderate winds. Also, the technical words on the pages of ten books were not half as impressing as one minute under sail. What I needed to be told was: "When your ass gets wet, it's time to reef, boys."

Maria remained unconvinced I would make a competent sailor and before long I faced the same choice as the previous owner – the girl or the boat. I thought I loved Maria, but I knew I loved the boat. As painful as it was, the choice was obvious.

The next summer I convinced one of my footloose friends, who had not found employment elsewhere, to escape the coming Michigan winter by joining me on a voyage to Florida and the Bahamas. The second member of my little crew was an older fellow, found through a pay-by-the-word *Detroit News* advertisement I placed containing these economical words and nothing else: "Sailing south. Share expenses. No experience necessary." None of us had more than limited day-sailing experience, but I figured the best remedy for this was to set aside the sailing books and make our way to the open sea.

The two-man crew I'd managed to enlist made it clear that merely having a boat was not the woman magnet I had imagined. Maria had forced the issue when she told me, "You're going to have to sell that boat so we can buy a house." She had visions of marriage and a $12,000 down payment on a house in the suburbs with a 30-year mortgage. I couldn't understand, and still don't, how people could chain themselves to a house, a job, a bank loan and a discontented spouse when they are still young enough and uncorrupted enough to appreciate the wonders in this wide-open world. Prisons come in many different guises, the most common being filled to capacity by the self-committed.

By September we reached the Atlantic by sailing through Lakes Erie and Ontario and motoring through the New York Barge Canal system to New York City. We reached Florida through a series of short offshore passages and longer detours inland through the Chesapeake Bay and Intracoastal Waterway (ICW).

Like East Coast disciples of Huck Finn, we followed the connected bays, rivers and canals of the waterway on its meandering course south. One misty evening at anchor in the Carolinas, returning fishermen tossed a basket of live crabs into our cockpit for a free dinner. Our journey continued, past the industrial back doors of big cities and the river-facing fishing port towns; past plantation homes set in green forests, primeval cypress swamps and the Georgia salt marsh where slaves once dammed the creeks to harvest rice and King Cotton along the river's muddy banks; and past the shadows of concrete apartment towers lining the canals of southern Florida.

A significant portion of our time was occupied with various schemes to refloat the Triton after running aground when straying from the marked channel. Impatient bridge tenders and road traffic were apparently more annoyed than impressed as we'd try to pass through the opened bridges, under sail, during the frequent stalling fits of the old and cranky Atomic Four gasoline engine. First, the carburetor wasn't getting gas, then it flooded and backfired a ball of flame that singed my eyebrows. Another time it lacked spark. The trouble-shooting and cursing became routine. Living alongside an old engine on a sailboat means you either become a proficient mechanic and a half-assed sailor or a half-assed mechanic and a frustrated sailor.

While on a thirty-six hour offshore passage from Cape Fear to Charleston, I nervously plotted our course and speed each hour as I made wildly inaccurate first attempts at celestial navigation. My first position fix by sextant observation of the sun placed us firmly ashore in mid-Kentucky. I didn't share that with my crew since even they may have noticed a slight error in longitude. A happy ship requires the crew must never lose confidence in their skipper. Keep 'em in the dark if you must. Why advertise your incompetence? Much of it will come out soon enough on its own.

Despite our near total ignorance at the beginning of the voyage, it culminated with an idyllic winter of gunk-holing across the shallow turquoise banks and among the myriad sandy islands of the Bahamas. When the sack of potatoes and three cases of discounted macaroni and cheese we had bought in Miami ran out, we anchored for a while off an uninhabited island, named Great Stirrup Cay, where we fished and collected the leathery meat from conch shells with an intensity tweaked by hunger. Twice each week we walked across the island to where a cruise ship set up a barbecue on the beach. There we mingled with sun burnt vacationers, returning to our boat with bellies and pockets stuffed with hamburgers. Missing our families, girlfriends and a well-rounded diet finally caused us to sail back to Florida where my slimmer, sea-weary friends made their way home.

Back in Ft. Lauderdale I worked a few months part-time apprenticing in repairing and fitting out sailboats around the marinas, but there was a shortage of paid work for inexperienced hands. Here I spent most of my remaining funds on a new, $1,500 Aries self-steering wind vane. During the past year, I had experimented with balancing the sails and various sheet-to-tiller arrangements with mixed success. No matter what I tried, the boat would not remain balanced for long periods with the wind from behind and I dreaded the idea of crossing an ocean with one hand tied to the tiller. With the new wind-vane there was no longer any need for the mind-numbing drudgery of hand steering. Now it seemed possible to sail alone into the South Pacific, even going around the world alone, which I quietly set as my goal.

First, however, I needed to replenish my cruising funds and better equip the boat. With a job waiting for me in Detroit, I decided to make my first long offshore passage alone by sailing the thousand miles nonstop from Ft. Lauderdale to New York City. That ten day autumn passage held some anxious moments as I trained myself to sleep in brief naps and keep a vigilant eye out for shipping and weather changes. On this trip I became moderately proficient in celestial navigation which greatly increased my confidence. Before that passage I had renamed the boat *Atom*, in the sense of the ancient Greek definition: small, powerful, unbreakable. It was also in tribute to the late Jean Gau, owner of the original *Atom*, whose writings of adventure first inspired me to challenge my own distant seas.

Back in Detroit, I returned to the daily tedium of heavy repair welding in another smoky shop. For fifty-plus hours a week my lungs were poisoned by toxic fumes and asbestos dust that hung in the air like permanent smog – a far cry from the pure cool winds of the Bahamas Out Islands in winter. My co-workers looked like co-zombies, the older hands wheezing and hacking themselves into early retirement or an early grave. I thought of something I had read about men that are sick of living but too frightened to just lay down and die. They go numbly on about their routines, the forgotten, fiery lust for life turned to ashes. They went on working for the promise of a pension and their "health benefits," which was ironic in that almost any other job would benefit their health better than any doctor's pills. Eventually, their purpose for living disappeared when their jobs moved to China. It's possible I judged them unfairly – expecting others to feel as I do. As for me, between the "In and Out" punches on a time card, I existed somewhere between yesterday's memories and tomorrow's expectations. The time allotted by the gods to a sedentary man with a sedentary mind can be too much; and yet, for a seeker, it is never enough.

In the hours after work and on Sundays I made modifications and repairs to *Atom* to make her more comfortable and seaworthy. There was little time for sailing. For nearly a year, *Atom* rested on a trailer in my parents' backyard as I disassembled and refit her from the rudder on up to the mast rigging, or at least as much as my limited experience and resources allowed. Using plywood, epoxy resin and fiberglass cloth, I added bulkheads and reinforced several areas of an already strongly-built hull and deck. Any experienced shipwright would have rightfully pointed out my flawed and inadequate work.

Meanwhile, my parents asked if they would ever have the use of their backyard again. A small crisis came when, without asking, I chopped down one of their beloved trees that crowded my work area and its overhanging branches dripped a red, staining sap on my freshly painted light-blue decks. *Atom* was then, and remains, a work in progress; transforming, as I do, along with her.

During this time I kept my plans for a solo world voyage to myself. I told friends and family merely that I was planning a trip to the Caribbean and maybe later towards the Pacific. It would be better to quietly get started with the voyage than to worry them or invite more questions than I could answer.

After two years back in Michigan I again quit my job and cleared the decks for adventure. My earlier trip through the Bahamas had taught me that beating down that "Thorny Path" against trade winds and currents in a small boat wasn't the best way to go. Boat and crew took a terrific punishment with progress slow and uncertain. There was no way I could make it around the world unless I followed a carefully planned route, running, for the most part, with the trade-winds at my back. As a last test before the solo voyage, I planned to sail through the lakes back to New York, and from there sail offshore to Trinidad with a stop in Bermuda where I would island hop back to Florida for final fitting out.

After talking my hometown buddy, Mathew, out of enlisting in the army, the two of us set off from Detroit in the autumn, hell-bent for warmer climes like the honking Canadian Geese passing overhead. A northerly gale caught us a few days out of New York harbor, kicking up a surprisingly high breaking sea as we crossed the Gulf Stream current. The motion was as lively as an endless roller coaster — as if we were on tracks running downwind, the wind vane holding her course. Not once did we turn sideways in a broach as boats will do when hard pressed and badly helmed. We rode *Atom* like a horse, gaining more confidence in her as she charged up and down the hills without stumbling. Sitting inside with hatches secured, I could block out the breaking waves landing on deck and mute the moaning of the wind in the rigging. I believed I was invincible in my cocoon.

Unfortunately, my crewmate saw it differently. Where I was absolutely liberated to be galloping over hills on my steed, Mathew complained he felt he was riding a tire as it rolled and bounced down one rocky hill and up another in an endless dizzying procession. He was also terrified we would be sunk by the high waves that broke harmlessly onto the afterdeck and filled the cockpit with their light foaming crests. Worst of all, he seemed to be terminally seasick. During those seven days he rarely left his bunk other than when I dragged him up on deck, clipped him into his harness and wedged him into a corner of the cockpit. Mostly, he sat crouched down or bent over on his knees with chin over the rail as if in supplication to Allah. Otherwise, he sat in his bunk still wearing his green Army surplus rain gear with a bucket held between his knees and cursing involuntarily. After a few days without eating he heaved up nothing but bits of yellow slime and still, he couldn't stop convulsing. It was remarkable that someone could be that sick and still be alive.

Having never felt mal de mer, I have a bad habit of treating the seasick with heartless contempt. I gave less than helpful advice like: "Pull yourself together, man." Usually I coax and cajole seasick crew into taking a spell at the tiller. This sometimes works because it's hard to concentrate on seasickness when you're trying to follow a compass course and not jibe the sails while getting face-slapped by constant sea spray. Seasickness becomes lost amongst the general fear and misery of the helm.

Strangely, within minutes of arriving in Bermuda, Mathew made a miraculous recovery. Within an hour of mooring alongside the quay in St. George's Harbour, Mathew was sitting up at the table with raised knife and fork as I dished up a sticky pot of macaroni and canned tuna spiced with two heaping spoons of black pepper. That night at the pub he described the trip to the other sailors there as "The Hell Voyage," adding with exaggerated drama: "The storm was incredible! The first couple days I was afraid I would die. After that, I wished I was dead."

In a few days he was on a plane back to Detroit, a place that looked a whole lot better to him than another trip offshore. But time heals a sailor's bad memories just as surely as a new passion cures a jilted lover. I took some satisfaction in hearing that Mathew purchased his own sailboat for use on the lakes a few years later.

By now I had enough basic sailing skills to continue the trip. Still, I wasn't yet entirely comfortable with the idea of going solo and attempted to find replacement crew to share the watch-keeping and travel expenses. While moored along the quay in St. Georges, I hung a sign low in the mast rigging that read: "Sailing to West Indies. Crew needed. Share expenses."

A week later, as I was about ready to depart alone, I awoke to knocking on the cabin top. I stuck my head out the hatch to see a thin young man with stubby black hair staring down at me from the quay. He pointed to my sign and said, "I'm your man. Jon Clark from Manchester."

Jon was on vacation in Bermuda visiting his brother who worked here as a gardener. His sailing experience was limited to some short passages along the English coast. He did have two important qualifications: he had the money to share expenses and his was the only serious response I got. I practically yanked him aboard before he could reconsider. Jon proved to be a great sea companion on the 15-day nonstop passage to Trinidad. Though he was seasick for a few days and doubtless in some misery, you would hardly have known it. He stood his watches without complaint, ate my peppery meals, and then quietly went on deck and spewed them over the side, answering my queries with, "Feeling much better now, thank you."

For two months we sailed the Windward Isles of the Caribbean and climbed the volcanic peaks of nearly every island between Trinidad and Martinique. Our timing was not so lucky when we landed in Grenada in October, 1983, and found ourselves ducking bullets as the Americans attacked to retake the island from a Cuban-backed regime. On the first day of the battle a Grenadian policeman came out to our boat in a small launch and demanded we surrender our weapons. He seemed disappointed to hear we had none. It was unclear whether he was pro-Cuban, pro-American, or as confused as most of the locals. Probably, like most people, he was wisely not going to commit himself until there was an obvious victor. Before leaving he advised us to keep our heads down and not move until the shooting stopped. That is just what we did for three long days.

We weren't much bothered by anyone after that encounter with the police, aside from the U.S. Navy helicopters circling overhead several times each day. At night we watched small arms tracer fire decorate the hillsides like berserk fireflies. In our minds there was always the chance we might be boarded by Cuban soldiers aiming to hijack our boat to sail home. When the fighting was over we sailed north through the islands of the Grenadines and on to Martinique where Jon caught a flight back to England. With new confidence in my sailing skills and my boat, I sailed alone back to Ft. Lauderdale with stops along the way at Guadeloupe, the Virgin Islands, Puerto Rico and a single stop in the Bahamas.

Over several years of sharing my boat with all manner of crewmates, it became apparent that having crew aboard was generally more work than not having them at all. A crew must be fed, consulted, depended upon, humored and catered to in countless ways. Compared to sailing alone, the experience when shared was somehow diluted, less vivid, less memorable. Although I was an only child who had long ago learned how to fill solitary hours, I had never been accused of being anti-social. Still, sailors who choose to go alone on the sea go there to stand apart from society, if only briefly. To those considering a long voyage alone, it should be heartening to know that among the inevitable trials and miseries there is also much to be gained. Only absolute solitude can sharpen the senses and develop a deep appreciation of simple pleasures otherwise lost to the distractions of a companion. In any case, the time of a sailor alone at sea is brief compared to the time he shares with friends in port and ashore. And when he does come ashore from his solitary sojourn he surely can appreciate his friends all the more after experiencing their absence.

That first solo voyage introduced me to a life cruising under sail that suited me perfectly and strengthened my resolve for the ultimate adventure – to sail alone around the world. If you've never felt the lure of Jack London's *Call of the Wild,* or Herman Melville's romance of the South Seas, or Henry David Thoreau's quest for essential living and self-examination, then there is little I can write now to inspire it, or even explain it.

While enjoying the mild winter climate of Florida, I made final preparations to *Atom* for the voyage ahead. The thing that concerned me most was the lightly stayed mast, which I watched vibrate and bend a bit more than I thought was safe while beating against heavy seas. The existing rigging was twenty years old and marginally sized as well. I couldn't afford new rigging at this point so I left the original wires in place on the fractional rig and added extra rigging going to the head of the mast that I scrounged from cast-offs in the boatyard dumpsters. This rig would never win a race to windward because of the extra weight and windage aloft, but my voyage was primarily downwind with long stretches far from repair facilities. I was willing to do whatever it took to prevent the mast coming down and leaving me adrift in mid-ocean.

With a hull as solid as the Triton, I didn't let the lack of a life raft worry me, especially since I couldn't afford one anyway. My 6½-foot plastic dinghy had built-in flotation that could be used in an emergency, but only in fairly calm conditions. Underneath the dinghy stowed on deck, I kept a grab bag of survival gear with a jug of fresh water, a jar of peanut butter, fishing gear and flares.

Although a short-wave transceiver was way beyond my budget, I did have a short-range VHF radio for contacting nearby boats or shore stations, and a cheap short-wave AM receiver so I could hear news and get accurate time signals required for celestial navigation. It was just as well that I had no long-range two-way radio since it would have given me a false feeling of security. In U.S. coastal waters, people have gotten used to the idea of instant rescue. In the far Pacific or Indian Ocean, you are on your own and you'd better face that fact right at the start. Besides, I wasn't going to sea to chat with other people. As I mentioned before, there was time enough for that in port where the contrast from the soul-cleansing isolation of being alone at sea gave me reason to appreciate human contact all the more. Confronting myself and my fears alone would lead me towards that liberating state of self-sufficiency I was seeking.

Since I was making such a drastic change in my lifestyle, I chose this opportunity to purge the toxins from my body. I had already quit smoking, drinking alcohol, even coffee, as well as all other kinds of subtly mind-numbing drugs. Gone, too, would be the excessive fats, sugars and meats, and most of the additive-laden foods of my past life. In place of that, I committed myself to at least two years of a vegetarian diet of mostly unprocessed foods consisting mainly of whole grains and vegetables.

This was not a way for me to try to add years to my life – I wouldn't be sailing across the oceans alone in a small boat if that was my goal. I sensed that something in my lifestyle was keeping me from being as fit as I knew I could be, and would need to be, to live the life I imagined.

The major items on my initial provisioning list were: 20 pounds each of whole wheat flour, corn meal, brown rice, dry beans, dried fruit, non-fat powdered milk and oats. I also bought alfalfa and mung beans for sprouting, potatoes, onions, cabbages, limes and an assortment of other foods that keep well without refrigeration. I would bake my bread and grow sprouting seeds onboard to supplement the fresh vegetables available at the native markets along the way. For snacks I had baked enough homemade, toasted granola in the oven at a friend's house to fill a garbage bag. I bought only a few canned goods such as tomato paste and carried none of those expensive meat products. As a protein supplement I took several pounds of brewer's yeast to mix with milk and some dried soybean product called TVP (texturized vegetable protein), which is a good high-protein meat substitute.

I did not entirely forsake modern technology. My most useful electronic gadget was the depth sounder, followed closely by the radar detector alarm I used for collision avoidance. One item that I might have been better off without, but was too unsure of myself to believe it then, was that cranky old Atomic Four inboard engine that, by frequent tuning, I was able to coax into assisting me when entering ports on windless days and to get me through the Panama Canal. When the inboard engine, with its generator, was not being used, a small, home-made wind generator, eventually replaced with a solar panel, kept the single 12-volt battery charged. Later I concluded that a small outboard motor kept in a locker until needed would serve me better. For offshore navigation, aside from a faulty mechanical boat speed indicator, I had only the traditional methods of celestial navigation: a sextant, a compass and a clock. Through necessity, my sense of guessing speed, drift and leeway improved with every passage.

Now that the boat was ready, my biggest concern was that I had only $500 in savings remaining. I didn't expect this would get me around the world. I did hope it would see me across the Pacific. From there I planned to work my way around the globe, taking temporary jobs wherever I found them. Thankfully, I was wise enough, or reckless enough, to refuse delaying the voyage another year or two by returning to work. After all, if lack of money stopped me this year, then other insecurities could just as easily keep stopping me until my instinct to explore faded into that cursed life of regrets I was so eager to escape.

I worked out a budget that allowed me to spend less than $100 a month. This might seem impossible today, but it was not then. It did require a large dose of rashness and ingenuity and just a little in the way of what others might call hardship. An example of this was that a new set of charts for all the oceans and harbors along my proposed track would cost me several hundreds, if not thousands, of dollars. Even photocopying borrowed charts was beyond my micro-budget and copy machines were still rare in distant ports. I solved the problem by buying a roll of tracing paper for $5 and traced copies from charts borrowed from fellow sailors in ports I visited along the way. Later, I found that sometimes other sailors would pass on charts that they no longer needed. Not that I would recommend this for prudent navigation – just a solution for a desperate young man unwilling to be delayed by excuses.

My plan was to sail direct for Panama, transit the canal and cross the South Pacific to Australia, or perhaps New Guinea, where I would wait out the Southern Hemisphere's cyclone season. The following year I'd cross the Indian Ocean to South Africa and round the Cape of Good Hope during the summer months. The alternative route up the Red Sea and through the Med was out because of the contrary winds and expenses involved. From South Africa's Cape Town it was more or less an easy downwind run across the Atlantic and the Caribbean Sea to return to Florida where I'd begun. I expected to make only ten to fifteen stops along the way, partly as a way to reduce expenses, and also because I looked forward to some long, uninterrupted passages. I had already picked out most of these likely stops from research I'd gathered by reading every account I could find of travelers before me. The time limit of a two-year circumnavigation suited the seasonal weather patterns and gave me a goal with a foreseeable end.

2 Non-stop to Panama

I STRUCK the board and cry'd, "No more;
I will abroad!
What? shall I ever sigh and pine?
My lines and life are free, free as the road,
Loose as the wind..."

- George Herbert

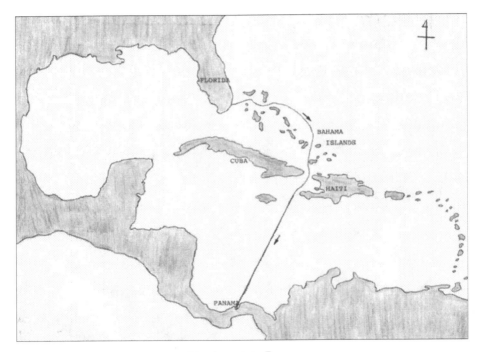

Atom's route to Panama

A handful of friends and relatives waved goodbye to me from the dinghy dock in downtown Fort Lauderdale as I hoisted anchor and raised the mainsail. I motor-sailed *Atom* between the concrete breakwaters of the river's outlet to the ocean, where I hoisted my largest light-air jib and shut down the noisy engine. Our full sails caught the afternoon sea breeze, carrying us 30 miles southward along a shoreline beach backed by continuous concrete high-rise buildings. That evening I anchored off a sandy islet next to a marina in Miami's Biscayne Bay.

The next day at high tide, I brought *Atom* up to the beach and secured mooring lines to the palm trees. As the tide dropped, *Atom* rolled onto her side like a wounded whale drawing her last breath. Though she looked in distress, the intentional grounding was actually a poor-man's haul-out. For two days, working in shifts to match the six-hour rhythm of the tides, I scrubbed the rough beard of barnacles, shells and grass off the bottom and applied new anti-fouling bottom paint. Her old bottom paint had lost much of its effectiveness and needed quite frequent scrubbing – I did this every couple of weeks by diving overboard, while at anchor, with snorkel and fins and a stiff brush in hand. With fresh bottom paint the scrubbing routine could be postponed for a few months. It's essential to begin each passage with the cleanest hull possible, since even a slightly foul bottom makes a boat sluggish, particularly in light winds or headwinds.

Sitting in the cabin at night, while the boat tilted and righted to the tides, I restudied the *Pilot Charts* depicting prevailing winds, currents and assorted meteorological and oceanographic information gathered from over a hundred years of ship reports on all oceans around the world. As I pondered the course ahead it sunk in, that here I was, finally ready to cast off, with *Atom* as my ticket to anywhere in the watery world.

The average yachtsman is basically a tourist on a boat who associates mainly with other yachties. That's alright for them. My aim was different. My distant seas held the promise of a boundless spiritual empire; an empire lying within reach of even the poorest vagrant sailor, provided he has a capable boat. To make the most of this precious gift, my quest from the start was about experiencing other cultures, which meant getting off the boat and living among the islanders whenever possible.

With a freshly painted boat bottom, a rising tide lifting and beckoning us on, I hoisted anchor May 2nd, 1984. Ahead lay a distance of 1,500 nautical miles to Panama, a passage requiring navigation through the numerous reefs and islands of the Bahamas against prevailing winds, before turning south to the fabled Windward Passage. From there I could sail free with the wind at my back, or so the *Pilot Charts* promised.

Our voyage began with *Atom* eagerly pushing her way into the Straits of Florida with a fair south wind on the beam. Full sails, strong heart and open mind – I was on my way! Here and there, patches of cumulus clouds cast shifting shadows on the indigo sea of the Gulf Stream. As Miami's jagged skyline dropped from view, within me rose the lone voyager's familiar state of calm, yet heightened, awareness.

The genoa, largest of my four headsails, set like a smooth curved sheet, funneling the air aft into the slot between it and the full mainsail. Standing on the side deck between the sails, I could feel the wind accelerate giving us more lift than either single sail alone could provide.

Not long into the afternoon the wind eased until finally we sat becalmed. Without the steadying effect of wind on sail we rolled and pitched, more or less together, the boat and I, as the Gulf Stream carried us inexorably off our course, northward, at about three miles to the hour.

As often happens, one minor misfortune is compounded by another. When a breeze did return it was light and from ahead, which had me barely holding our position as we tacked against the wind and the flow of the current. Meanwhile, the radar detector sounded its alarm several times an hour as other ships passed. Our first few easy miles had turned into the frustrating beginnings of a long voyage.

By the next day I had coaxed *Atom* through light, shifting headwinds across the 50-mile-wide straits to enter Bahamian waters at the Northwest Providence Channel. The first island I sighted was the barren, uninhabited rock with the grand name of Great Isaac Cay. A mile long and a couple of stone's throws across, the truly "Great" thing about the island is its lighthouse that casts a beacon visible for 25 miles.

For the next few days I threaded a course through small, low islands, some palm-covered and others barren limestone, plotting my position from one to another by compass bearings and dead reckoning (a rough guess of the effects of course, speed and time). For example, if I sail at 5 knots for two hours to the east, I can use the compass rose and parallel rulers on the chart to advance my position 10 miles east where I place an X on the chart and note the time. It can be as simple as that or it can get complicated by frequent course and speed changes, unknown currents and darkness. On a good day it's simple geometry – on a bad day it's all intuition and guesswork until your position can be fixed by compass bearings off points of land or celestial observations.

When near land I kept an attentive watch, and if tired, slept lightly between rings from a kitchen timer set to 15 minute intervals. Most nights I sat in the cockpit, straining to see the land I knew lie out there somewhere and listening for the alarming sound of surf crashing on a reef. Throughout these flat Bahamian islands, unpredictable currents threatened to carry the unwary to destruction. The island of Great Stirrup Cay drifted by during the night as a dark, shaded outline: its non-functioning lighthouse rendering it less than Great, at least for a sailor passing in the night.

Next on my course was the one-to-two-mile-wide by 90-mile-long, Eleuthera Island. After its serpent-like shape fell astern I had a few days of clear sailing in deep water.

Pressed over by the wind, *Atom* charged ahead, gathering speed as she climbed the face of a wave, then flung her bow into the air, only to protest with a bang and a shudder as we landed in the next trough. My old, patched-up sails were stretched taut as we pushed into the strong trade wind. As the bow speared the next wave crest, water swept the deck from bow to stern. Leaks in the cabin sprouted from straining thru-bolted deck fittings.

The builders of fiberglass boats typically place a core material sandwiched between two layers of fiberglass on the boat's deck and coach roof to gain strength and save weight. Within *Atom's* fiberglass deck was a waterlogged balsa wood core, which, at the time, I attempted to repair with the half-measure of caulking up the obvious leaking ports and fittings. My boat and I were still in the stage of learning each other's faults and weak points. Correcting and accommodating them would take some time. Now, my make-shift-repair mentality caused old leaks to reappear and kept me bailing cupfuls of seawater out of the leeward lockers at all hours. Anything not well sealed in plastic bags became wet and then moldy during these few days pounding to windward. To keep even more water from getting below I kept the hatches dogged shut, causing the inside of the cabin to become miserably hot.

I stayed on deck getting salted and sunned like a piece of dried beef, retreating down below only after sunset to escape the stifling cabin. Lack of a companionway hatch spray cover, aptly called a dodger, caused me some suffering during the thousands of miles to come, but a dodger and a bimini awning over the cockpit were two of many "non-essential" items struck from my fitting-out list in favor of a more immediate departure. I just had to tough it out until turning downwind brought some relief from the elements.

It's impossible to overstate the difficulties of taking a small, ill-equipped boat to weather against the trade winds. Ocean racing boats are designed for good windward performance, if not comfort, but a small, heavily-loaded cruising boat that tries to slog long distances to windward will eventually shake itself, or its crew, to pieces. Because I had doubled up the rigging wires on the mast, and carried a heavy load of supplies packed aboard, I noticed some lost sailing efficiency. At best, I could make 50 degrees off the wind. In stronger winds, about 70 degrees was all I could manage as course made good, taking into account the sideways slip of the boat through the water, which increased as the boat heeled. To buoy my spirits, I reminded myself that once I cleared these islands, 90 percent of the remainder of the world voyage would be with the relative ease of a downwind ride.

As I made progress along the windward side of the Bahamas, I altered course more to the south. At sunset I passed the long and low Mayaguana Island and by morning approached Great Inagua, the last of the "Great" (and less than great) islands of the Bahamas. Sailing close along the leeward side of Great Inagua, the only visible activity was a mechanized conveyor loading a Canadian freighter from a mountain of salt gathered from the island's extensive salt drying ponds.

I had good reason to delay at Great Inagua: my calculations showed I was still several hours early for a daylight arrival at the

Windward Passage between Haiti and Cuba. I hove-to by back-winding the foresail, easing the mainsheet then lashing the tiller to leeward, and drifted like this for a few hours behind the shelter of the island.

With sunset approaching I trimmed sails for a close-reach at 60 degrees off the wind and resumed my journey. It was a sleepless night of pounding into heavy seas that seemed to drop the boat on solid earth instead of the liquid sea that streamed down the cabin windows and dripped onto my bunk. Conscious of currents pulling me towards a light visible on Cuba, I pressed on at a good speed, knowing that the less time I spent in these waters the less effect the current would have. While the wind vane held her on course, I wedged my body into the lee-cloths of the drier windward bunk and eased the long hours of the night reading about the voyages of Columbus by the light of my gimbaled kerosene lamp. It was an appropriate book for these waters as my little boat crossed the wakes of Columbus' three caravels, all of us setting out to discover a world new to us. About twice an hour I set the book aside and climbed out of my bunk to check the horizon for ship traffic and to bail water out of the leeward bunks and lockers.

At daylight the wind dropped and a few hours later the sea became calm. A line of position from a sextant sight of the sun showed I was in the center of the 40-mile-wide Windward Passage. At a speed of barely one knot, the Triton's motion was easy. There being no apparent danger, I went to sleep. I awakened not long after to the deep pulsing howl of a helicopter hovering close overhead as if attempting to perch on our masthead. A crewman leaned out the open door, took a photo of me fighting to lower sails in the rising tornado of his rotor wash, then they turned to skim along the water to the east towards Haiti. Two hours later a U.S. Coast Guard ship was beside me, launching from her deck a boat nearly the same size as *Atom*.

As the launch approached the young officer in charge shouted across the water, "We are going to board you. Maintain your course and speed." I hand-steered in the light wind as they came alongside and two of the armed, uniformed teenagers clambered aboard. "Why didn't you answer our call on the VHF?" the young officer asked.

"I didn't feel much like talking – since I was asleep," I replied.

After a cursory look through some of my overstuffed lockers, I noticed my two guests losing their focus and swallowing deeply; sure signs of impending seasickness. My familiar pleasure of tormenting seasick guests got the better of me as I told them: "There's more gear stowed under the forward berth you haven't checked yet." Then couldn't resist, "Also, there's a locker behind the toilet if you don't mind the odor."

Back on deck and apparently feeling better, they radioed their captain who asked my destination. "Bound for Panama and then around the world, alone, he says," was relayed over the radio with just a hint of disbelief. The captain apparently had heard even less plausible stories on his sea ventures and in reply simply asked if I needed anything. Since they had intruded uninvited on my sea of solitude, I thought they might as well do something useful and told them I could use some fresh water to top up my tank and a detailed weather forecast for the Caribbean Sea. They returned to their ship and sped back minutes later with several jugs of water, an armful of satellite weather charts and a two-day old Miami newspaper, all compliments of the captain. I wondered if I should have ordered lunch and a bag of ice as well.

"Can you guys come back in a few days?" I asked one of the guardsmen. Thinking I was serious, if a bit mad, he patiently explained they were too busy searching vessels passing through the Windward Passage for drug smugglers and Haitian refugees trying to make their way to Florida. Why they searched me, a southbound vessel clearly not fitting either profile, he didn't say. He did tell me they had picked up 30 Haitians that morning, apparently heading towards Florida on a battered old fishing boat, and were on their way to "repatriate" them to the Haitian capital of Port Au Prince when they intercepted me.

Because I consider myself a man with an independent conscience, unlegislated by either the left, right or center of politics, I had mixed feelings about the right of refugees to travel at will between countries. Still, I was annoyed that the U.S. Coast Guard felt it had the right to patrol international waters and other country's coasts, forcibly removing people from their boats because they might intend to land later in the United States. Even back then, a man need sail long and far to get beyond the reach of the government's minions. I held back any open criticism since I didn't want my trip declared a "manifestly unsafe voyage" whereby they might haul me back to Miami in leg irons. Thank God there were no Cuban gunboats around to "repatriate" me to Florida.

The plight of the Haitian boat people was, and still is, a sad story any way you look at it. Largely because of deforestation caused by poor conservation, the farmlands of Haiti are eroding into the sea, leaving the land scarred and bare. As families grow, their small plots of land can no longer support them. Birth control was unheard of and, without any type of government assistance, many were starving. Often a father decides to gamble everything by selling his barren land to pay a smuggler for passage for one of his sons to America. The young man joins a crowd of others who have paid up to $2,000 each to board an open wooden boat for up to a 30-day ordeal at sea. If he survives to reach Miami, and if he can find employment, he'll try to send money back to his landless family, who now live in a tin and cardboard shack in a shantytown. Many Haitians never make it to the U.S. They get shipwrecked or duped by skippers who have been known to drop them in the Bahamas, telling them they are in Florida. Others have been thrown overboard to drown off the Florida coast because the nervous captain saw a Coast Guard boat approaching.

I was struck by the contrast of these desperate people to my own privileged cruise. The Haitians picked up that morning were pulled from their boat and dumped ashore back to the misery of Haiti; I was given water and a newspaper and wished bon voyage. Where I could move freely about the world by flashing an American passport, the Haitians were usually picked up before they got far from their native shores. Forced to return home, some were jailed and tortured. Others simply disappeared. Around the time of my voyage, there had been repeated popular uprisings in Haiti as the island teetered between brutal dictatorship and a communist takeover, as happened across the straits in Cuba.

As the Coast Guard ship steamed away on its unhappy mission, I looked to the west and spotted the rough outline of Cuba's 12,000-foot high Sierra de Purial. I was now becalmed and drifting close to the 12-mile territorial limit where Cuban gunboats at the time were known to haul in foreign yachts for lengthy interrogations. Not far away, on Cuba's south coast, is the U.S. Naval station at Guantanamo Bay. This thorn in Castro's side was also off-limits to yachts. Now was one of those times to put the engine to use and burn up some precious gasoline. For three hours I motored south towards the open sea to put a few more miles between myself and international politics.

Despite my eagerness to reach less troubled waters, for the next three days I averaged only about 50 miles a day. With a fair wind I could easily sail 100, or sometimes as much as 145 miles a day. The weather charts given to me by the Coast Guard indicated a deep low-pressure area passing to our north. So at least I had an explanation for the slow going. Here, where trade winds are the rule, I had calms and vexing, light, shifting winds instead. A weather map may explain the weather. Unfortunately, it does nothing to change it.

The sun, standing straight overhead at noon, shot its blazing yellow arrows that reflected in a metallic glare off the rolling sea. In the tropics, if you can't find shade on a windless day, you will soon mark the sun as your constant enemy. Yet, even as I sat becalmed under this torpid sun, staring until the sea morphed into a pulsing desert of sand dunes, through meditation I momentarily escaped to the remembered perfume of a cool autumn day by my favorite fishing stream in a northern Michigan pine forest. When I needed something more than illusion, I doused my naked body with buckets of tepid seawater.

At night I found relief from the heat by sleeping on deck where I could detect, and get up to trim sails to, any faint aspirations of wind. During the long hours sitting motionless at night, I watched the parade of stars rise and set, and thought about the distances and oceans ahead. Would *Atom* be overcome by a storm and be driven ashore or broken up on a reef? Thankfully, those thoughts occurred less and less as the days unwound. Somewhere along the way I lost the feeling of lurking danger and started sleeping soundly, even if only for an hour or two at a time. I was gradually learning to let unproductive worries slip away in my wake and live in the present moment. For the past week, navigating through the Bahamas, I had not slept more than an hour at a time. Either it was a wind shift that required a sail adjustment, an intruding ship that triggered my radar alarm, or the need to stay alert for islands and reefs that demanded my attention. The beauty of calms at night was the glorious deep sleep they allowed.

Stepping on deck one morning, as casually as stepping onto the front porch at home to pick up the morning paper, a scan of the horizon caused me to catch my breath. Not more than half a mile off the starboard bow sat a three-masted square-rigged sailing ship frozen still under clouds of limp canvas. I thought I'd drifted into the pages of *The Voyages of Columbus*. I knew there were very few large sailing ships still making ocean passages and certainly none that would lay becalmed without carrying on under auxiliary diesel power. The ship's captain and I eyed each other through binoculars until a light wind filled in and they set to hauling their braces to get underway. I hoisted my bright orange and red spinnaker to take advantage of the new wind. The captain hailed me on the VHF and told me they were en route to Bermuda, their engine had broken down and, like myself, they'd been drifting and making little progress for the past several days. The ship close-reached ponderously to the north with barely enough way for steerage while *Atom* headed south under spinnaker, cleaving the calm waters at a speed that made the sluggish square-rigger look like it was sailing through molasses while dragging an anchor.

During the day the erratic trades slowly strengthened and the seas began to build. From every wave that slapped *Atom's* side, a burst of fine spray flew up and the sun turned each into a brief rainbow. A small migratory bird perched on the stern pushpit rail and rested there through the night. As I got up each hour to check course or adjust sails, my guest flapped his wings once to acknowledge my presence and settled back down when I retreated to the cabin. Sometime before dawn I looked out expecting to see him there and he had flown off.

I had been in the habit of taking a noon sextant sight, which gave me my latitude, and another sight later in the afternoon to give me a line of position to cross with my latitude line for a position fix. This technique was simple, but prone to error, as it depended on the accuracy of my dead reckoning during the hours between the two sights. Now that the sun was passing directly overhead on its annual springtime journey north, taking a noon sight became awkward as the sun viewed through the sextant mirror appeared to jump around the horizon on all sides. From here on I seldom bothered with the noon latitude sight, preferring to take morning and afternoon sights and later to make morning or evening twilight star and planet sights.

Preparing for twilight sextant sights

The island of Jamaica was not far away and made a tempting landfall but, as I was well-provisioned and enjoying being at sea now that I had a fair wind, I maintained a course for Panama. With the full force of the Northeast Trade Winds set in we ran free on our 140-mile per day sleigh ride. In a rush we made up for those motionless days. The waves rose to gently nudge *Atom's* stern as they hissed by. For the next two days I didn't touch a sail as we rode the waves under the singing wind.

In the mornings I would make my topsides inspection to check for chafed lines and sails, or rigging working itself loose. As I moved around deck I disposed of the bodies of flying fish that had hurled themselves aboard during the night. The remainder of the morning I usually exercised my mind by reading from my library of more than 100 increasingly salt-stained books. I had heard Thoreau's books critiqued as "a verbose treatment of the commonplace." That may be true to a reader harried by the pace of modern city life, but I savored his observations of nature, man and self with all the attentiveness and boundless consciousness of a sailor alone on the sea. In the afternoon I exercised my body. I knew from experience that if I relied only on the activities of handling the boat to keep me in shape, I would arrive at the next port with limbs as weak as a baby.

Sailing alone is exhausting at times but, on the whole, it is a series of brief activities followed by long periods of rest. To build up stamina and general good health for my shore excursions, and to combat the feeling of lassitude that easily creeps up on the lone sailor, I exercised every day, vigorously, with few exceptions. I did sit-ups, push-ups and deep knee bends, working my way up to sets lasting two hours. I also practiced a few yoga forms that can be managed on a less-than-stable platform. After the exercise, a saltwater bucket shower in the cockpit, followed by a rinse with a cupful of precious freshwater in the solar shower bag, completed my afternoons.

At night I studied the stars, memorizing the sky charts by penlight and then locating them in the real world planetarium reeling overhead. Where one man sees emptiness, another man sees his world bursting with fullness.

No matter what I was doing, if there was steady wind, the Aries wind vane took care of the hard work of steering the boat day in and day out. I had merely to get the boat settled on her course with sails balanced, then feather the wind vane's thin plywood vane into the wind and attach the steering lines. *Atom* would hold a course more accurate over the long term than any helmsman. When the boat naturally tried to fall off course, the slight change in apparent wind direction tilted the horizontally pivoting wind blade which caused the wind vane's small rudder to turn and kick up from the flow of water against its side, pulling one or another of the steering lines connected to the tiller. Back and forth it endlessly kept up its pendulous bowing from side to side. Lacking a sense of compass direction, when the wind shifted it was up to me to make an adjustment, and the wind vane would again carry on. It's an ingenious and simple device and was responsible, more than anything else, for the increasing number of solo sailors on the world's oceans in the 1970s and 80s. This was before the flood of instant navigators was set loose on the seas by the availability of inexpensive GPS satellite receivers in the 1990s.

Atom triple reefed in squalls near Panama

As I approached Panama, unsettled weather moved in turning completely overcast with frequent squalls and thunderstorms that kept me jumping to the sails to reef, or unreef the main, or haul down and replace the jib with one larger or smaller. It was a routine that I became so practiced at over the years, I could literally do it blindfolded. For two days now I had been unable to confirm my position by celestial observation due to the clouded skies. At least I knew I was still on the canal approach as ships were passing by more frequently each day. Most shipping passed me unseen, behind sheets of continuous rain. I knew of their close presence by the radar alarm's insistent "Beep-beep!"

Another long night of dodging ships and straining to see land through the blackness brought my reward at dawn, when the dark mountains of Panama stood outlined against a misty gray sky. It took the remainder of the day to make the last ten miles to harbor as I sailed against a four-knot counter-current running along the coast.

When my anchor hit bottom in Cristobal Harbor, I ran up the yellow quarantine flag and fell happily exhausted into my bunk. For the next 12 hours, until a customs launch arrived to clear me in, I lay in the deep unconscious state that few non-sailors will ever know. The passage of 1,500 miles in 15 days had been a small personal triumph. Tiring, yes, but without mishap.

My confidence in successfully completing the world voyage was growing. Next step: test my skills at navigating the greater shoals of Panamanian and U.S. Canal Zone bureaucracy.

3 Link to the Pacific

An age will come after many years when the ocean will loose the chain of things, and a huge land lie revealed; when Tiphys will disclose new worlds and Thule no longer be the Ultimate.

- Seneca, Medea

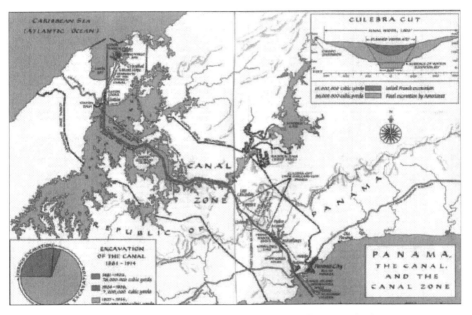

Map of the Panama Canal from The Path Between the Seas

Until I looked more closely at the charts of the Caribbean for the planning of this voyage, I had assumed the Panama Canal was located not only south, but also west of Florida. It turns out the entrance to the Panama Canal lies east of the 80th meridian of longitude, which puts it east of Florida. It became odder still when I looked at a detailed map of the S-shaped landmass of Panama. As the isthmus twists itself in a curve to the north, from certain points in Panama the sun is seen to *rise* over the Pacific and *set* over the Atlantic.

The closest Columbus came to the great ocean holding his elusive Indies was on his fourth voyage when he sailed along the Caribbean

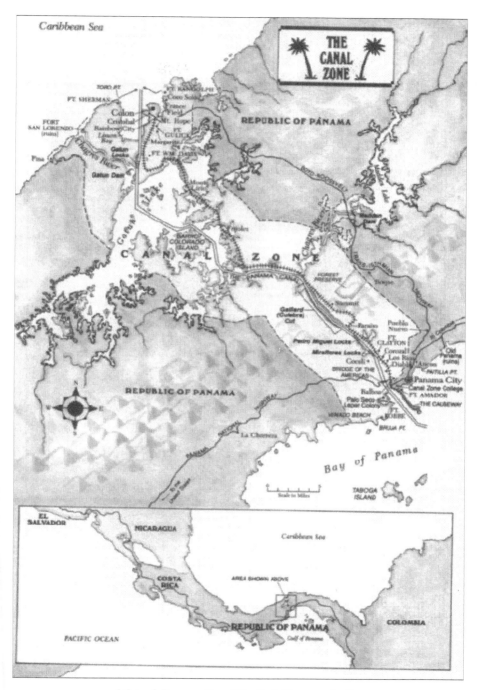

Map of Panama from The Path Between the Seas

coast of Panama, which he named simply Tierra Firma. In the local Indian dialect, Panama means "an abundance of fish."

Ten years after Columbus passed this way, Indian guides led Vasco Nuñez de Balboa and a group of Spaniards on a three-week trek over the low mountains of the Continental Divide and through Panama's disease-ridden jungles. Upon reaching the Pacific shore, which in this region lies south of the Caribbean Sea, Balboa christened the waters El Mar Del Sur (The South Sea) and claimed all lands and peoples within this ocean now belonged to the monarch of Castile. Although Balboa's reach far exceeded his grasp, he was among the first to imagine a canal between the Atlantic and Pacific. That dream obsessed explorers, politicians and engineers for the next 400 years. Thanks to their work, today's circumnavigating sailors can bypass the ice and storm hazards of Cape Horn far to the south. This thickly forested country has hundreds of enticing bays and coastal islands that make it a worthy cruising ground in itself, but with visions of Polynesia burning in my brain and the anxiety of organizing the canal transit, and knowing the reputation for thieves in the main canal ports, I wanted mostly to be out of there as quickly as possible.

Once the customs launch cleared me in, I lowered the yellow quarantine flag and rowed my plastic dinghy over to the "yacht club," which resembled nothing more swank than a friendly small-town marina. Stepping past a pair of four-and-a-half-foot Kuna Indian women hawking decorative hand-sewn *molas*, I set out on foot for the various offices holding the permits for a canal passage. Thus began three days of shuttling between the offices of Immigration, Port Captain, Admeasurer and Berthing Department. Each gave me a stack of paperwork to fill out or sent me somewhere else to get this stamp or that receipt. I kept scribbling on forms and handing over money. When all documents were finally placed in the correct files in the proper offices, *Atom's* total charge for a canal passage was $130, including a $60 security deposit to be refunded six months later by mail – provided my little boat did not damage the great locks.

In a perfect example of bureaucracy gone mad, small yachts were treated here as if they were miniature commercial ships. Skippers are faced with pages of cargo forms and pest control officers spraying insecticides below. Even an "admeasurer" came aboard one morning with a bagful of forms, tape measure, calculator and slide rule, to determine my cargo capacity. I was stupefied at this gross inefficiency as the admeasurer led me around *Atom's* deck and cabin at the end of his tape measure. Did they not realize the cost of these ridiculous labors exceeded my fees? It would have meant less work for them, if not lower charges for small boat owners, if they had eliminated the pointless paperwork.

After 1999, when the Canal Zone was handed over to Panama, the delays in waiting to get through the canal are typically weeks and sometimes more than a month. Even more objectionable are the new fees, which were raised more than 1,000 percent. As idiotic as the old system was, the new one makes the Cape Horn route look considerably less disagreeable.

The city of Colón, located at the Atlantic entrance to the canal, is as bad as its name implies – truly the ass end of Central America – which is not an easy distinction to earn. From all I've heard since I was last there, this tough town is little improved. Colón citizens either rob or get robbed, or do both, as circumstances require. Even the Panamanian Consulate staff in Miami, who issued my visa, warned me of the troubles. "The muggers work the streets in gangs, so don't go out by yourself, even in the daytime," she said as she leaned forward to whisper through the bullet-proof glass. As I gathered my papers to leave, I overheard her tell her assistant in Spanish, "Such a nice young man. I hope he won't get killed."

A gringo couple from one of the sailboats in the harbor told sailors gathered around the yacht club bar that they had just been robbed by a couple of knife-wielding thugs who followed them into a supermarket and relieved them of their cash and watches in front of the store's armed security guard. "You must understand," the guard told them, "it's my job to protect the store, not the customers."

While I was in port, another man from a sailboat waiting to transit the canal was pulled off Colón's main street at high noon and dragged into an alley where his wallet, watch and shoes were removed. Then he was stabbed, perhaps just for being a fat-cat gringo. It doesn't help matters when the thieves know sailors have pocketfuls of cash to buy provisions and pay off officials for their canal permits.

I couldn't afford to put any more money into Colón's economy than was necessary. As a defensive bluff against the scavengers, whenever I ventured beyond the walled compound of the yacht club, I emptied my pockets and turned them inside out, stuffed my money into a waist belt hidden under my shirt, and hung a large diver's knife conspicuously from my belt. I kept one hand threateningly on its hilt as I walked fully alert with head twisting in all directions. I must have appeared somewhat crazed, but the security guards and police I passed must have thought I fit in well enough, since none of them looked twice at me.

Everywhere there were beggars who followed and harassed nervous gringos down the streets. Other unemployed Panamanians sat hunched over in the shadows as if trying to make themselves disappear from a hostile city. On the way to Colón's outdoor vegetable market, a trail of beggars and would-be muggers followed me as I walked quickly from one police-guarded corner to the next. In a futile attempt to blend in with the darker-skinned locals, I growled Spanish expletives at anyone who stepped out of the filthy side streets and approached me. Some of these criminals may have had more money than I did and I was not feeling at all charitable. The "sharing of cultures" part of my journey would have to begin somewhere more hospitable.

At the yacht club bar I met a tall Texan, named Jim, who worked as an engineer for the Panama Canal Company. He took me in his Chevy to see firsthand how the thousands of Americans who operated the canal lived barricaded within the U.S. zone. As we drove through the gates into the U.S. side of Panama, where local laborers kept the lawns well-manicured, he pointed out the supermarkets, movie houses, a Boy Scouts Club – a whole North American hometown transplanted into a cleared patch of Central American jungle. "Many of these Americans never leave the U.S. zone, since they have everything they need right here," Jim said. "Going outside is getting too dangerous for most folks."

Outside that fence was the other Panama, a fearsome place best avoided. Many Panamanians, particularly aspiring politicians and half-educated university students, were rancorous patriots. They held an ironic disgust for the American imperialists who handed them their independence from Colombia more than one hundred years ago and were the main employer in the country, paying Panamanian workers a fair wage. In 1984, Colón was a powder keg on the verge of all-out anarchy awaiting the upcoming elections. General Noriega was still in power and the American invasion was just a few years down the road.

Despite the acrimony, the day-to-day street crimes were not politically motivated. Visiting sailors, American canal workers and Panamanians alike, faced the same criminals lingering in the dark corners. With a thriving American colony right in its center and joint ownership of the world's greatest canal, Panama should be an economic and social success story. Technologically, the canal is a huge success – the social side, sadly, a great failure. Who's to blame, the gringo "oppressors" or those who won't help themselves?

Of course, I can only describe what I saw around the big cities at each end of the canal. From what little I saw of the rest of the country, the rural villages and their uncorrupted inhabitants live in a world apart. The world over, a poor man raised in the countryside is courteous and respectful to all. Put the same man in the squalor of a broken city and, as often as not, he becomes sullen and vicious. Large, capital cities, whether New York or Paris or Panama City, were of no interest to me on this journey.

The horror stories of damaged spars, and even the sinking of a yacht in a canal lock when a tugboat broke loose and crushed it against the lock wall, made me expect a scary passage. I had been through dozens of locks in the Great Lakes system but the scale of things here dwarfed those. As it turned out, I had less trouble actually passing through the canal than I had complying with the complicated regulations. Each yacht, no matter how small, must have, in addition to its captain, a canal-company-appointed pilot/adviser and four line handlers, each with 125 feet of heavy mooring lines. Instead of hiring extra crew, I transited the canal twice: first as a line handler for another yacht whose crew then reciprocated by helping me when my boat's turn came.

On my first transit through the canal, I was a line handler on a 50-foot yacht from France. After this passage I returned to the Atlantic coast via the transcontinental railway, the first of its kind in this hemisphere, built almost 60 years before the canal opened. This railroad was financed by American businessmen looking to cash in by providing an alternate route, other than the three-month voyage around Cape Horn, to the newly discovered California gold fields. Thousands of imported African, Chinese and Indians labored in the tropical heat to finish this first rail link between the oceans. Many of these immigrants stayed and contributed to present-day Panama's rich racial mix.

Some railroad workers, exhausted by poisonous insects, reptiles and rampant tropical disease, were driven to suicide by the intolerable conditions. After several instances when the bodies of workers were found swinging from trees behind their barracks, guards were posted outside the laborers' quarters to prevent more from hanging themselves before their contracts were up. Finally, in 1855, the railway was completed and passengers rode in comfort across the isthmus in three hours at the then incredible ticket price of $25 in gold. The human cost to complete the track is estimated at 12,000 dead – their ghosts said to be forever pounding spikes on the bloodstained track.

Under Panamanian control since 1979, the railroad, which had been so convenient for local commuters, commerce and travelers alike, was in sad decline for a number of years, becoming inoperable at one point. After significant modernization in 2001, the Panama Canal Railway of today is reportedly once again thriving.

The French couple, and their two crew from the yacht I had assisted through the canal, offered to return to help me bring *Atom* across. The five of us re-crossed the continent by train in two hours for less than $2 per person. Arriving the night before our scheduled transfer, my French guests, each with a long mooring line thrown over their shoulder, managed to find bunks inside *Atom's* small salon and even smaller forward cabin. I slept that night on deck tucked into a cockpit seat until dawn when the pilot came aboard and we motored upriver to the first set of locks to await the opening of the 800-ton iron doors.

The 50-mile canal of today takes ships from the Caribbean port of Colón through locks, a dammed-up lake and a cut in a low saddle in the Continental Divide to the Pacific port of Panama City. From the Atlantic side, three double locks (allowing two-way traffic), raise ships 85 feet to the level of Gatun Lake, which is crossed to reach another set of three locks that lower ships back down to the Pacific. It's a deceptively simple-looking system but the design and construction problems took the world's best engineers about 25 years to overcome. What a sight this would have been for Antonio Cerezo, a humble priest I'd read about who constructed a canal-like ditch connecting Colombia's Caribbean-flowing Atrato River to the Pacific-flowing San Juan River. Incredibly, this Atlantic-to-Pacific canoe canal was dug by Colombian Indians under the priest's direction and completed more than 200 years ago.

The Panama Canal, in turn, was started in 1881 by a French company that began the dredging under the direction of Ferdinand de Lessups, the genius builder of the Suez Canal. Full of self-assurance and the backing of thousands of French stockholders, he proposed a sea-level canal by either tunneling under the mountains or making a 300-foot deep cut through them. Nine years later, after completing about a third of the digging, the bankrupt French company gave up. It had become obvious that a sea-level canal, incorporating the wild torrent of the Chagres River, was impractical. Proving its impossibility took the lives of nearly 20,000 men who died of malaria and yellow fever, which doctors of the time blamed on "mephitic vapors," or swamp gas.

When the United States took on the enormous project in 1904, the first obstacle was how to deal with the fractious Colombian government who held Panama as one of its provinces. The Colombian Congress dragged out the debate over the terms of the canal treaty so the U.S. declared Panama independent, installed a local government and wrote their own terms for the canal project. With the U.S. flush with confidence over their recent easy victory in the Spanish American War, they were not interested in making concessions. Within a year of taking control of the project, U.S. engineers had brought the disease-carrying mosquitoes under control by filling in swampy breeding grounds, fumigating and burning large areas of grasslands. The Chagres River was dammed to form Gatun Lake, six sets of double locks were constructed and mountains of earth were moved in the 10-year project. A century later and it's obvious that building the canal today would be an impossible task. Politics and environmental concerns would stop it cold before the first shovelful of dirt could fly.

Like a minnow dropped in a swimming pool, *Atom* entered the first 1,000-foot-long lock and we made fast to a tugboat lying against the lock wall. Several other larger yachts were tied two and three abreast, held in the center chamber by mooring lines pulled up by line handlers on top of the walls. The steel gates slammed shut and the lock began to fill from below as cavernous aqueducts in the floors poured in millions of liters of fresh water, fed by gravity, from Gatun Lake. As the water level rose, the tug adjusted its mooring lines with squealing hydraulic winches that stabilized us in the turbulent waters. When cables break under this kind of tension the whiplash of wire has cut men in half. It was a parting cable that sank a yacht when the tug careened across the lock, crushing the sailboat as it smashed up against the opposite wall.

Despite the increased risk, at the second and third locks our pilot again arranged for us to raft next to the tugboat so we would not have to take a center-chamber position and tend four lines of our own. In the third lock a Russian container ship was hauled in behind us by steel cables connected to four locomotives, called mules, riding on tracks at the top of the lock walls. I watched nervously as the ship seemed to tower directly over us before inching to a stop. Once the waters raised and the doors began to open, we cast off from the tug and shot out the lock before the Russian ship's thrashing propeller and the four mules could push its bow over us.

From the third lock we entered 23-mile-long Gatun Lake. This huge man-made lake is fed almost entirely from the moisture-laden clouds coming in from the Caribbean during the rainy season. For *Atom's* passage, the lake poured a phenomenal 200 million liters of fresh water into the locks that was then dumped into the sea. A rough calculation, based on three gallons of freshwater use per day, meant I could sail for the next 48,400 years before using that amount of water again. This thought put my notions of resource conservation in a new perspective. Despite man's enormous efforts to shape the forces of nature, it is the nine months of tropical rains each year that is keeping Gatun Lake's level up and thus the Panama Canal in operation. A slight change in the climate of the region could close the canal with more finality than a hundred terrorist's bombs.

Locking through the Panama Canal

Though the canal is not in immediate danger of running out of water, an equally serious threat comes from the local farmers, called *campesinos*, who have encroached on the canal zone and are continually burning large tracts of forest within the canal watershed in order to plant their crops. This fragile jungle forest is the only thing keeping the soil from running into the canal and choking the locks with sediment. These days, dredges work continuously to clear mud from the canal. If a solution is not found, the canal could be choked to death long before climate change shuts it down.

As we approached the lake our pilot was informed by hand-held radio of a one-hour delay at the next lock. With the pilot's agreement we dropped an anchor at the edge of the lake and leapt from the sun-fired furnace on deck into the warm lake-water bath. Our French crew took turns keeping an alligator watch from the boat as the rest of us, pilot included, swam leisurely under the shade of moss-laden trees overhanging the flooded valley.

As we got underway again, we passed through a swarm of bees flying in rapid nervous circles around the boat. They pressed in closer and the pilot warned us not to swat at the bees or make any sudden movements. "Killer bees," he said softly. "They particularly don't like anything colored red." We all looked at one of our crew who was already wrapping a white towel around his bright red shorts. One of the bees was hovering in front of my face and I had an almost uncontrollable urge to swat him away. I asked the pilot, "What should I do if this killer bee lands on my nose?"

"Nothing," he said. "Just try to make him as comfortable as possible."

Our pilot had been stung before and knew from whence he spoke. When one of these bees feels threatened it releases a scent into the air which sends the rest of the swarm into a rage and they attack with a fury. These Africanized bees had recently arrived in Panama on their relentless migration northward. It was hoped the bees would become less aggressive as they interbred with laid back Latin American bees, but as of now, their temper seems just as bad as when they first got off the boat from Africa.

We approached the opposite end of the lake where the dead trunks of trees emerged from the shallows like drowning totem poles. The passing ships seemed strangely out of place in this flooded tropical forest.

For two hours we motored through Galliard Cut, gouged through the mountains of the lowest point in America's Continental Divide. Cutting through a few hundred feet of elevation occupied 6,000 men working day and night for seven years. The scars of the digging are now mostly covered by jungle growth, although the tiered layers carved into the mountainside to prevent landslides remain clearly visible. At the end of the cut we entered Pedro Miguel Lock, where we were lowered, along with millions of liters of freshwater, to the mile-long Lake Miraflores. Across the lake we descended the final two locks to the level of the Pacific Ocean. Moving down the final stretch of the canal, we passed under the Bridge of the Americas, the single road link between North and South America. Along shore I saw it was now low tide; the high water mark was visible 20 feet above. On the Caribbean side the tidal range was small enough to be barely noticeable.

My line handlers and the pilot disembarked during a one-minute pit stop at the Balboa Yacht Club dock. I was told that mooring fees here were $25 a day and that yachts were prohibited from anchoring anywhere else in the harbor. This clever bit of corruption sent me scurrying out of the harbor to Taboga Island, where I anchored freely just as darkness closed in.

A small white-washed village of red-tiled roofs greeted me as *Atom* slipped into a horseshoe-shaped bay alongside local fishing boats and six other cruising yachts riding at anchor. This little island in the Gulf of Panama lies within sight of the rolling green hills of the mainland. Here was a peaceful place to base myself for a few days and gather fresh provisions for the passage ahead. The next morning I went ashore and watched from the public square as fishermen hauled their boats out of the water on a steep cement ramp. At the village store I bought half its meager supply of bread, onions, cabbages and oats. There was little else available. Fortunately, I was still well-stocked with provisions from Miami and Colón supermarkets and I had hardly made a dent in the 10-kilo bag of granola I had prepared in Miami.

Part of the old-world quality of Taboga was the absence of cars disturbing the peace. The roads are just wide enough to allow pedestrians to brush by the overhanging branches of hibiscus and fragrant oleander blossoms. While walking around the hilly island, I looked down a cliff face to see the battered hull of a steel sailboat fully exposed on a reef at low tide. She was washed up on the rocks, as rusted and abandoned as her owner's dreams.

Atop the highest hill in Taboga I scanned the scattered islands stretching across the horizon like stepping stones to the misty slopes of

Panama. Here, captured by the contrast of mountain and sea, began, in a small way, my relationship with the mountains of each island I was to encounter.

I looked down on the harbor and the little dot that was *Atom*. From here she seemed so small, so suited to her name. Held back by her two anchors, her bow sniffing the open sea, she seemed to be saying, "Don't delay. This great ocean holds the treasures you are seeking. They lie there to the west, just over the horizon." With the last of the great lock doors clanging shut behind me, the long, watery road ahead beckoned.

4 West Sets the Sun

...tossed on the billows of the wide-rolling Pacific – the sky above, the sea around, and nothing else!

- Herman Melville, Typee

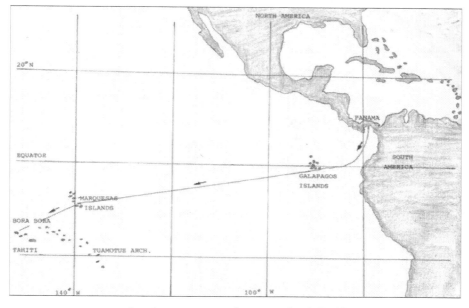

Atom's course across the eastern South Pacific

From the world map laid out on the bunk in front of me, I could see the total water area of the Pacific is far greater than all other oceans – even larger than the world's total land area – an expanse of one hundred million square kilometers. With barely five months left for me to navigate some 9,000 miles before the beginning of the cyclone season in November, I planned only a few stops while crossing the Pacific, then I'd choose a spot to layover till the cyclone season passed the following year.

My first goal was to reach the Marquesas Islands in French Polynesia about 4,000 miles to the southwest. For most of that distance I would ride firmly harnessed to the southern hemisphere's Southeast Trade Winds that lift and tumble the waters of the southern winter all the way across to Australia. To reach the trades, I must first sail a thousand miles to get clear of the windless Gulf of Panama and its unsettled weather until south of the equator.

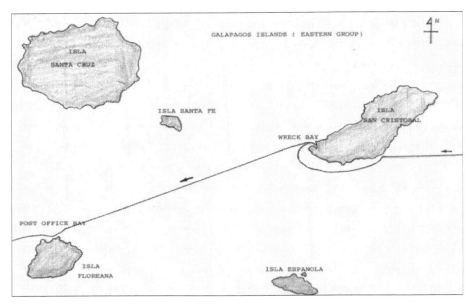

Course through the Galapagos

With my provisions, dinghy, water cans and a hundred other items stowed and ready for sea, I pulled up my two anchors hand over hand and slowly left Taboga Island on the sultry breath of an uncertain wind. True to predictions, I logged only a few miles before the wind deserted me altogether. From then on I played hide and seek with a fitful breeze that seemed to be pulled in all directions at once. We glided on a sea so calm I appreciated why Magellan had named it *Pacífico* (Peaceful). As we drifted south on the languid and erratic current, I was inclined to rename at least this part of the ocean *Paciencia* (Patience).

On the advice of my photocopied *Pilot Charts* and a well-used *Sailing Directions* book, I laid a course south from Panama until near the equator where I would turn west to pass close by the Galapagos and then on to the Marquesas. In that way, I should avoid some of the calms and headwinds prevailing on the more direct route.

Pacific calm

As expected, the Pacific approaches to Panama were as thick with shipping as the Atlantic side. At times I watched up to six ships passing on either side of me, some close enough that I hand-steered to stay clear of them. Sleep was again reduced to the brief moments between glances at the compass and the familiar but annoying beeps of the radar alarm. The wind, when any could be felt, continued in light puffs from every quarter. Rarely did I sail more than a mile in any direction before the wind suddenly vanished, only to spring up later from some other direction. On that first night at sea I watched faraway storms produce ominous silent flashes of light, the kind we called "heat lightning" back on my grandparent's farm in northwest Minnesota. Later I learned that all lightning produces thunder. What is commonly called heat lightning is actually lightning as far as 50 miles away, still visible, yet too far to hear its thunderclap.

The next day I watched successive banks of dark clouds drag veils of rain across the horizon. That night I entered into an area where lightning flickered low, and thunder cracked, as though armies of artillery were battling on all sides of me. Looking out the cabin windows was like staring directly at an arc welder flickering its cold light into frozen images on my retina. With the light display came torrents of rain – rock-heavy, vertical drops turning abruptly into cutting horizontal sheets during fits of short, but violent blasts of wind.

It seems remarkable to me now that I was not struck by lightning that night, or anytime, in all my years sailing on a boat completely ungrounded or in any way "protected" from lightning. Against most professional advice, I held onto my "groundless" theory: no lightning protection at all is better than an insufficiently grounded rig. A perfect ground for extreme voltages is hard to design and expensive to install and might merely serve as a lightning attractor. The theory has worked – at least so far. An even less demonstrable theory of mine holds that the degree of lightning attraction to a vessel is in direct relationship to the amount of expensive, vulnerable electronics it contains. In this regard, *Atom* was well-protected from lightning by her poverty of electronics.

At first when these storms approached I dropped all sail, cowering in the cabin until they passed. But not every rain cloud brought strong winds and it became clear that this strategy was hampering any progress in this mishmash of winds and was only prolonging my stay here. To take advantage of the gusty winds, I began testing my nerve by sitting at the tiller with reefed or even full sail spread throughout the squalls.

For the first time in my young sailing career, the sea took on a malevolent persona. Every mile I wrestled with this devil by constantly changing sails and reefing only after the boat was laid over on her beam ends by sudden gusts of wind. Typically, these squalls arrived at night when they could bring the most menace. I'd lie in my bunk debating whether to take in a reef until it was too late. Then I'd rush to pull on a raincoat, connect my harness and get on deck while the boat plowed on at various courses and crazy angles of heel – sails and rigging shuddering in protest. As often as not, *Atom* was back on her feet in a near calm by the time I made it to the mast. If I was not sitting becalmed, I was sailing on the point of blowing out my sails and it exhausted me mentally as much as physically. With each squall I might advance a single mile or sometimes not at all.

Bigger yachts with diesel engines typically avoid much of this drama by reefing the mainsail and motor-sailing on a more direct course. This is the choice: test your resolve one-on-one with nature's dark side or burn up a tankful of diesel as the nonstop day and night thumping of the motor numbs you into insensibility. Living so close to a diesel motor is like being stuck with an annoying crewmate. You may not like him much, but his familiarity is easier than the unknown wrath of nature.

One of my route planning books, *Ocean Passages for the World*, declares conditions here "vexatious" (some would say maddening) for sailing craft. This is an area within the Intra-Tropical Convergence Zone (ITCZ), more aptly called the Doldrums. This belt encircles the earth near the equator where the Trade Winds of the two hemispheres meet and struggle for dominance. *Ocean Passages* warns ships to expect long periods of calms, light shifting winds, and continuous rains and thunderstorms. The heat energy released from the center of the tropical seas is what spawns hurricanes and fuels the wind systems of the earth. To clear the Doldrums, I held my southerly course until I neared the coast of Ecuador where the skies cleared somewhat and I turned to the west. Here I came across an oil drilling platform 200 miles off the coast of Colombia. At first I mistook it for a ship until I passed close by and clearly saw it rooted to the seafloor like a giant steel spider.

In this area one morning, as I was below preparing a bowl of oats with granola and powdered milk for breakfast, a sudden jolt and lurch of the boat sent my meal spilling to the floor. It sounded like a hole was knocked in the hull and the rudder was getting ripped off. As I scrambled up the companionway steps my mind raced through the catalog of possibilities. Had I sailed onto the back of an irate whale or uncharted reef? Should I stop to collect my emergency grab bag or inspect the bilge for an inrush of water? Could I stuff a cushion into a hole in the hull from inside or rig a makeshift collision mat from outside? I had a six-foot plastic dinghy but no life raft. I was up on deck just in time to see an enormous uprooted tree trunk rise behind us. We had ridden up and over the entire floating tree. I checked the tiller and was relieved to see we still had steering. Back down below I reached into every corner of the bilge and the lockers below the waterline and found no leaks or visible damage. The next day, during a spell of calm weather, I gathered my nerve to enter the water to inspect the hull for damage. I lowered the sails and hung a rope swim ladder over the side and extended the line on my safety harness. Even after looking for the shadowy figures of sharks under the hull and satisfied they were absent, I still had an unreasonable dread of leaving the security of *Atom's* deck and plunging alone into mile-deep waters. I was relieved to see only some deep scratches in the paint and fiberglass and no serious damage. While in the water I took a few minutes more with snorkel, mask and fins to scrape off the newly-grown barnacles and weeds clinging to the hull with a stiff brush and putty knife. The partial collision bulkhead I had installed in the lower section of the bow while refitting in Florida was reassuring, but this encounter later persuaded me to add the extra insurance of several watertight bulkheads fore and aft. *Atom* was essentially my life raft and she must remain afloat for me to survive.

One morning, about 80 miles off Ecuador, I awoke to the deep throbbing of a diesel engine nearby. A fishing boat, about 50-feet long, was following me just off my port side. When I came on deck, two fishermen stood at their railing staring back at me. Perhaps they thought they were about to claim an abandoned boat until I disappointed them with my appearance on deck. Unsure of their intentions, I made mine known by tacking sharply away at right angles to their course. If those Ecuadorian fishermen were looking to try their hand at piracy, I was more or less defenseless, unless you consider poverty the best defense.

I hadn't carried a gun aboard since I'd had my own gun pointed at me by a lady in Savannah, Georgia. She had been invited aboard *Atom* by my crewmate Tony on one of my trips down the Intra-Coastal Waterway. This nearly 40-year-old hippy had answered my ad in the *Detroit News* seeking crew to share expenses on a trip to Florida. Tony had been a committed hippy (he preferred to call himself a hedonist) for his entire not-so-adult life. He certainly looked the part of the hedonist, with his curly brown hair flowing into a long curly brown beard, his rounded Buddha-like belly and knobby-kneed bird legs. I liked him immediately, but reminded him, "No drugs on the boat. I can't afford to have the boat confiscated." He said he was fine with that and kept his stash hidden from my view.

The single most amazing thing about Tony was, that as we made our way through the Great Lakes and down the east coast, no matter where we stopped, Tony came back to the boat with a new girlfriend in every port. It was unbelievable! I could almost never convince a strange girl to "come visit my yacht" for the night. Tony scored every time and each time it made me a little crazier. He had a technique the women loved. Several times I watched him work his magic. He would go to a bar or restaurant or supermarket and pick out the loneliest looking girl he could find. It didn't matter if she was somewhat fat or even plain ugly. If they looked at all neglected and were genuine females, they suited Tony. Once he zeroed in on his prey he chatted them up until inevitably getting around to discussing his acupressure technique for relieving their stress. He had a huge picture book on the subject back on the boat. Once he laid his hands on their shoulders and indicated their "stress points" they were like zombies, which he then led straight back to the boat and closed the forward cabin door behind them. In the mornings I would tap on the door to tell Tony it was time to shove off and he'd appear with some poor, disheveled girl scribbling down her phone number and desperately sad to see him leave. I told him he really needed his own boat to practice this fine art of his.

On our stopover in Savannah, I struck out at the bar as usual and came home alone. Tony was already occupying the forward cabin with a guest and working his magic from the sound of it. Early the next morning, and anxious to catch the falling tide down river, I tapped on the door, "Tony, it's time to get sailing." Nothing. I knocked again. There was some grumbling. A few minutes later I knocked a bit harder. The door flung open and a short, heavy woman in black leather pants held up with a belt of motorcycle chain, stood there pointing a huge revolver at me with two meaty hands around the wooden grips. "Shut up and get the hell outta here or you're a dead man," she growled.

I eased my way out on deck and went for a long walk. That gun looked familiar. The filthy wench had found my .44 Magnum Smith & Wesson Dirty Harry Special hidden behind a false panel in the hanging locker. It was a leftover from my teenaged hunting and target shooting days. When I came back an hour later she was gone and Tony was cooking scrambled eggs in the galley. "Wow man, you really pissed her off," Tony said.

"Sorry about that Tony. I'll try to be more considerate." I sold the gun before my next trip and haven't carried anything heavier than a flare pistol and a spearfishing gun since.

To ensure no one would ever find *Atom* sailing along without her crew, I always wore a safety harness with a line secured to a fitting on the center of the coach roof. The line was of a length that permitted me to travel from bow to stern and no farther. During calms I would at least clip the line around my waist if not wearing the full harness. On a boat with only a two foot freeboard in the aft section, it's easy to pull yourself back aboard when it would be impossible on a higher boat. This is one of those seemingly minor, but critical points, that make a small boat far safer in many respects than a large boat. What could be worse for the solo sailor than to watch his boat sail away from him after making one careless step? It has happened often enough before and will happen again as long as sailors go to sea. I had no desire to test my ability to "drown like a gentleman" as one English singlehanded sailor put it when asked what he would do if he ever fell overboard. So, I proceeded to sail around the world bound to my boat, not only spiritually but physically as well. It may have been an inconvenience, but it was reassuring not to need to consider each moment if conditions warranted a safety harness – it was always on.

At 84 degrees west longitude I dipped south across the equator, but held no ceremony to mark the occasion as crewed boats did in earlier days. Surprisingly, here on the equator, the bright sun overhead did not generate as much heat as it had a few days earlier. I found out why when I took my daily saltwater bucket shower. The bracing cold water confirmed I was in the chilling grip of the Peru Current, originating in Antarctic regions, and now carrying me along to the west.

That day I sailed into a patch of dancing water where an upwelling current broke through to the surface with thousands of little sharp vertical wave tips accompanied by a hissing turbulence. In these waters oceanographers discovered a powerful current 300 feet below the surface running at three knots opposite to the surface current. Under this is a third current, again running parallel to the surface current. Here, and around the Galapagos Islands, these currents meet in a conflict of great swirling eddies. It's these currents, and others in every sea, that interlink all oceans. A drop of spray falling on *Atom's* deck that day may also have flowed on the other side of the globe thousands of years before.

Ever since leaving Panama I noticed the Aries wind vane becoming progressively more sluggish and unresponsive in light winds, first under-steering and then over-steering. I compensated by daily applying light oil on the bearings and reefing sail more than I normally would, in order to slow the boat and increase the apparent wind across the wind blade. Finally, it got so bad I had to attempt a repair, which is a daunting task when you consider I had the entire Pacific to cross and if I dropped an essential part into the sea, I would be doing a lot of grueling hand-steering before I could get a replacement. Leaning over the transom, ever so carefully, I unbolted the frame and heaved the seventy-pound vane gear up and into the cockpit. Since the wind vane was nearly new, I could hardly believe what finally became clear. The nylon bearings that fit so well had not worn, but swollen, from the effects of water and sun and were binding the free movement of the rudder shaft. It was a design fault and poor choice of materials that I later learned had caused the same problem on many other boats. Aggressive work with a file gave it the clearance needed and we soon resumed our journey under full sail.

Two weeks out of Panama the daily positions recorded in my logbook, and the X marks stippling my homemade chart, showed I was nearing the Galapagos Islands. On my present course I expected to clear the easternmost island, San Cristobal, by 30 miles sometime during the early morning hours. Even so, I set the alarm and dropped into an uneasy sleep. I felt little cause for worry since I trained myself to sleep lightly and awake to changes in the wind and wave patterns. This unusual sleep pattern, as well as the effects of isolation, had always given me more vivid dreams at sea than when in port. A good portion of my sleep time was more like drifting in and out of a dream world just below the surface of consciousness.

This was the night of the nightmare I wrote of earlier, where I stood watching helplessly from shore as my boat broke up on the rocky coast of some unknown island. The surf surged in around me, roaring as it broke against the car-sized boulders scattered on the rocky beach. I opened my eyes and noticed the gray twilight of dawn entering the cabin. I lay there in my bunk, still drunk with my overindulgence of sleep after weeks of building exhaustion. The sound of the dream's surf still pounded in my head as I slowly perceived the shipwreck had been a dream. Thank god, it was just a dream and we were still afloat! I turned in my bunk to look at the telltale compass mounted on the bulkhead. The course was off by ninety degrees. Finally, I realized the danger we were in. I leapt from my bunk to the deck and could hardly believe the sight. Dead ahead, only a few boat lengths away, was a shore strewn with black rocks where the waves crashed angrily. In a scene terrifyingly identical to that of my nightmare, *Atom* surged ahead to her foretold fate. For one long second, perhaps the longest second in my life, I stood frozen in disbelief and thought: "Christ, what to do?"

A wave breaking next to me broke the spell. With tiller in one hand and jib sheet in the other, I tacked the boat to windward away from the shore as quickly and with as much concentration as I have ever tacked a boat. On both sides of me the sea heaved and broke on submerged reefs. I held my breath and willed the boat to pull away, to skip between the foaming breakers filled with hull-cracking rocks just below my keel.

Once clear of the danger I felt my legs and arms tremble. "Damn, that was close! You almost lost it there, boy," I said out loud and then chuckled to myself. I rarely spoke aloud while alone because of the unnerving hollowness to the sound. Now that the shore was no longer a threat I hurled a string of insults its way, then smiled smugly. One minute more of sleep and we really would have been dashed to pieces on that desolate coast. Besides sleeping through the wind-shift, which is something I rarely do, I had underestimated what must have been a four-knot current setting me towards the island during the night. As spooky as it seemed at the time, I can't credit my premonition to any extrasensory cause. Possibly the sound of the surf was not enough to waken me in my fatigued state, but it did trigger a dream, disturbing enough to wake me in time to prevent the disaster. I wonder, though, about the striking near-reality of the dream and close resemblance to the rocky features of the actual shore. I still shudder a bit, deep inside, whenever I think of it. In any case, when you need to believe in rational explanations, you can find them.

Spanish mariners of the 17th Century had no doubts about the mystical nature of these islands, calling them Las Islas Encantadas (The Enchanted Isles) due to their apparent change of location as strong, changeable currents swept the ships past as they floundered about in light winds.

Numb as I felt, at least I had caught up on some much needed sleep. With twelve hours of daylight ahead of me, I sailed around to the opposite side of the island to look at the possibility of anchoring in Wreck Bay. After dropping our sails we drifted near the two other yachts there while I debated whether to release my anchors. On all sides of me, squadrons of blue-footed boobies dived vertically into the water in hopes of scooping up a small fish.

The skipper from a Belgian-flagged yacht rowed over in his dinghy and gave me the lowdown on the clearing-in procedure. Since I had no visa, officials would allow only a three-day visit for which they charged $30. Before leaving Florida I had applied for a visa but received no reply. I took that as notice that cruising yachts were not welcome in Ecuador's National Park of the Galapagos. I didn't intend to make just a three-day stop at any port along my route. To get the boat dried out and back in shape after a rough passage, and then prepare it for sea again, would take two days itself and leave little time to see the island. Besides, I had spent a good chunk of my $500 traveling fund in Panama and I saw no point in plundering the cruising kitty here. It was a tough decision since as far as I knew, this could be my last chance to see the islands. As it turned out, I did return to these waters again three years later and made my shore explorations then.

The Encantadas were probably first discovered, though not permanently colonized, by Chimu Indians from coastal Peru several centuries ago. Since Europeans entered the Pacific the island group has hosted a procession of explorers and buccaneers, scientists, pioneers and even a convict colony. Given that they were not worth fighting over by Western powers who claimed most of the Pacific islands, Ecuador was allowed sovereignty over these islands, straddling the equator 600 miles off its coast.

Charles Darwin, the English naturalist who visited these volcanic isles prior to forming his *Theory of Evolution*, wrote:

> *These islands at a distance have a sloping uniform*
> *outline, except where broken by sundry paps and*
> *hillocks; the whole black lava, completely covered by*
> *small leafless brushwood and low trees. The fragments*
> *of lava are reddish-like cinders, the stunted trees show*
> *little signs of life. The black rocks, heated by the rays of*
> *a vertical sun, like a stove, give to the air a close and*
> *sultry feeling. The plants also smell unpleasantly. The*
> *country was comparable to what one might imagine the*
> *cultivated parts of the Infernal regions to be.*

Despite Darwin's somber description, I would later discover these islands to be rich in its strange creatures, both animal and human. At the time I had little choice and didn't much know what I was missing as I handed the Belgian sailor a previously written letter to home and a dollar for postage. Then I hoisted sail and resumed my journey.

Offshore I picked up an escort of several porpoises gamboling under the pressure wave of our bow which they love to ride like surfers catching a wave. Watching them from on deck at the bow, their movements appeared as effortless as sleek torpedoes. Throughout the day this or that gang traveled alongside me, now and then taking to the air in leaps and back flips as if from pure love of flight. Were their high-pitched squeaks resonating through *Atom's* hull meant to call me back on deck? Thoreau tells us in Walden: "According to Greek mythology...Bacchus made the Tyrrhenian mariners mad, so that they leapt into the sea, mistaking it for a field of flowers and so became dolphins."

Several miles offshore I encountered a lone seal on the surface with his back towards me. As I sailed silently past, I caught his attention with a shouted, "Hello!" Startled, he turned and lifted his head revealing what appeared to be an elderly man's whiskered face. Having looked me over, he grunted as a startled old man might do, then dove out of sight.

In these waters the upwelling of the Equatorial Undercurrent brings cooler, nutrient-laden waters to the surface, which supports the enormous schools of fish I watched racing past in underwater clouds. By some secret signal each fish simultaneously changes course to elude the dark shadow of an approaching predator. Overhead, the albatross, shearwaters and petrels glided with masterly grace over the waters. The majestic waved albatross breed on only two islands in the world, one of them nearby Hood Island, and spend the rest of the year soaring over the empty southern oceans. If in human terms I was alone, there was too much life around me to feel lonely or bored.

Sunset gazing has always been a fixed daily ritual. One particular night, among these enchanted islands, I soaked up a sunset no artist could reproduce. Multiple layers of wispy clouds stacked in rows above the horizon were colored in soft yellow and red brush strokes on a blue sapphire sky canvas. In front of this scene, a half mile off the bow, a pair of porpoises repeatedly jumped clear of the water forming smoothly arching silhouettes on a sea painted metallic orange.

That same night I sat becalmed as currents pulled me westward at two miles to the hour. Our slow speed suited the moment. Stars burned bright from high overhead down to near the water's edge. Where the stars left off, a brilliant display of phosphorescence took over. Looking straight down into the inky water I could not tell it apart from the sky as the star-like pinpricks of light from luminous creatures mixed with real stars reflected from overhead. The gentlest of rolling seas merged to become one with the sky. The lack of a discernible horizon added to an effect that nearly overturned all sense of direction. Then the plankton-rich waters exploded with a bright bioluminescent glow outlining my old gang of porpoises from head to tail; the radiance of cool flames washing their bodies as they raced through the water. Around them piercing flashes marked small fish darting here and there to elude the hunters.

With morning's faint breeze, *Atom* sailed close along a bay on the north coast of Floreana Island and then slid away to the west, gathering speed as the wind freshened. After passing the last craggy sentinels of the western Galapagos Islands there lay over 3,000 miles of wide-open ocean before I would see another island break the surface. The effect of the emptiness ahead suggested I might sail off the edge of my world as soon as it got dark.

On the next day, my 26th birthday, the trades filed in with certainty. The wind strengthened and for a week blew consistently from the east to east-southeast. As I settled into my sea routine I recorded days of 140 mile runs in the log book. On and on we sailed, west-southwest, always reaching for some unknown place hidden behind the setting sun.

I was eating pasta and tomato sauce out of a bowl in the cockpit one evening, enjoying another sunset and the brisk sailing, when suddenly, "Bang!" the entire jib was flying loose out to leeward. The original inner forestay had parted from the deck taking the jib with it. I almost choked in fear, thinking the mast would come down next. Then I remembered I had doubled up the rigging wires in case of such an event. I reeled in the thrashing sail and made temporary repairs to the forestay with shackles, thimble and bulldog clamps. We were sailing again within the hour.

The final insult of that day came when I went below and found my bunk soaked by a wave that had snuck aboard through the open port. The sea began to pile up and once or twice a day the different wave patterns overlapped, creating a wave high enough to climb over the stern and splash into the cockpit. One of the few disadvantages of a small and low riding boat is the near constant wetness of living so close to sea level. I never knew when I'd get dumped on, so these occasional sloppy waves discouraged me from sleeping out in the cockpit during nights of otherwise pleasant weather.

A slow day on the Pacific under reefed sails
when the wind vane needed repair

For another two weeks I sailed without incident in a moderate
southeast wind. As *Atom* plowed on towards the rim of my visible
world, the days became a collage of patching sails, baking bread in a
skillet on top the single-burner kerosene stove and reading books. I
even relaxed enough in the unchanging weather to sleep up to four

hours at a time and I found my strength building and my spirits soaring.

During the day I focused on the moods of the sea and a world composed of the whites and blues of clouds, sky and sea. At night, as always, the stars, planets and moon held my attention. Polaris, the navigator's North Star, whose altitude above the horizon is always equal to the observer's latitude in degrees north of the equator, had dropped below the horizon long ago. It was replaced by its less-precise southern hemisphere counterpart; the Southern Cross, which swings in an arc around true south. As I ventured farther south, the familiar star patterns of the northern sky appeared upside down. In the southern sky, new stars, previously unknown to me, rose higher every night.

While sailing west the new moon appeared later and fuller every night until one evening that white balloon floated free from the ocean, directly astern. Of all the days at sea, this was the time most looked forward to, when once each month a full moon rises opposite the setting sun, and in turn the following morning, the sun rises in the east just as the moon is extinguishing its light in the sea's western horizon. I stood as a mere atom between two luminous beings locked in an eternal dance.

On darker, moonless nights it was easier to observe the orbits of the five visible planets – Venus, Jupiter, Mars, Mercury and Saturn – as they drifted in the grip of the cosmic currents. Occasionally, four planets were visible during one night. Jupiter, with its attendant four moons, one or two of which seemed to me were just visible through my 10-power binoculars, was rising in the east during evening twilight. When low in the sky it was bright enough to cast a path of silvery light across the waters. Mars and Saturn were there also, not as bright as Jupiter, or so easy to pick out without a planet chart, but still firm allies marching side by side.

At night, while standing braced in the companionway with head and shoulders above the hatch, I craned my neck back to stare at the mainsail as it swept out a pattern against the stars. With bow pointed west, surfing swiftly down waves on an eastward turning earth, I momentarily felt as if the planet were spinning beneath me while the boat was held immobile by some unseen force. It was an illusion similar to a memory I had of sitting in a stopped car next to a train that began to reverse. For a moment I felt I was moving forward and pressed down harder on the brake.

During this long isolation at sea I startled myself with unexpected flashes of memories of insignificant events I thought long lost. I sometimes mentally replayed a period of my life – a long ago chat with a friend, a childhood incident, all with remarkably complete recall. At first these lifelike views into the past made me uneasy. Then they grew familiar and even welcome. Where my mind roamed I willingly followed. This heightened awareness into the past only happens when senses normally numbed with the anesthetic of our intrusive society are reawakened and laid open. Out here, even the clock became absurd, with its breaking of time into meaningless seconds and minutes. If not for the requirements of celestial navigation I might have thrown my clocks overboard, followed by the calendar as well.

For the solo sailor to remain on good terms with the sea he needs to balance his blind romantic love with a good dose of fearful respect. She will send you subtle messages like an underlying swell pattern or halo around the moon, which you need to be aware enough to read and act upon. For instance, I learned from experience that a change in wind direction often foretold an imminent change in the wind's strength as well. Waves of chaotic shape indicated the nearness of land or surface currents, and their set, or direction of flow relative to the wind. Swells from distant storms will ride under the local wind, wave and swell patterns and tell you something about weather coming your way. The whispers of light wind passing over sails and rigging and the gurgling of water along the hull are sounds so ever-present and hypnotic they are only really noticed when they change their patterns or are absent. The slightest unrecognized sound, like waves slapping the hull at a different angle, served as my replacement alarm clock when far from shore. However, as in the past, I would continue to be caught by surprise from time to time.

One night while sleeping a bit too soundly for my built-in alarm to be heard, *Atom* was laid over flat by a rain squall that crept up out of nowhere. The wind gusted at gale force for a brief time as I struggled naked, but for my harness, to lower the sails before they were torn apart. The night was so black that lacking functioning deck lights, I worked entirely by feel, relying on memory for the position of each line and cleat. In the morning I found an open seam in the mainsail that required restitching by hand. Also, I found another of the original mast shroud wires had a growing crack in the lower swage fitting and I reinforced it with wire and clamps. Later, in port, I replaced it from a roll of second-hand wire and end-fittings from my spares locker.

This was the main problem of sailing on the cheap. Those expensive rigging fittings that should be replaced at the first sign of wear, needed to be used until they actually started to fail and then replaced with other, questionable, used spares. The only option was to over-strengthen everything and use redundant systems. Nowadays, with more knowledge and better finances, I shudder at my makeshift approach, but it did see me through.

Sure, you can stay home and work towards the day when you have the perfect boat, perfectly outfitted, as most people try to do. You might even wait and do your cruising as a retired person clutching a fistful of platinum credit cards on a finely fitted boat filled with expensive gadgets needed to maintain your increased demands for comfort and security. But by that time you are somewhat lacking in the robust health and enthusiasm to fully engage in your long-postponed adventure. If I chose to sail as a young adventurer, poorly equipped in the material sense, I make no apologies. I was well-fitted out in health and spirit. As all sailors ultimately learn, it is easier to prepare a boat for sea than to clear the decks of your life for a voyage into unknown waters.

At least the rain shower that night allowed me to take on a tankful of fresh water. To catch rainwater I had installed a valve on each side under the deck drains that diverts all rainwater hitting the deck to a hose inside the main cabin that I used to fill water containers and the built-in water tank. As the winds eased, I let the rain rinse the salt off the decks for a few minutes and then opened the valve to fill my shower bag and every bucket and container I could lay hands on. I tasted each container for salt before pouring it into the main water tank because occasionally a wave would land on deck and contaminate the water for a few minutes until it had a chance to rinse off again.

Most of my fresh vegetables were eaten or turned rotten within a month of departing Panama. After that I still had some onions, squash, potatoes and the alfalfa and mung beans ready to eat after three days in the sprouting tray. A few limes wrapped in foil also lasted about a month. I later learned to rinse some of the vegetables and fruit in a bucket of water with a couple spoons of bleach added to kill the mold-starting bacteria and extend their life in the tropics. One of my favorite dinners was a cornbread prepared in a covered frying pan on the stovetop and ate as a sandwich with sprouts and mustard. This cornbread was filling and delicious hot from the skillet. Leftovers were still edible later the same day. By the second day it felt and tasted like a rock hewn from the cornbread quarry, perhaps because my basic recipe contained no eggs, sugar, oil or preservatives.

While laying my track across this immensity of open horizons, I became more and more impressed by what I'd read of the seafaring abilities of the ancient Polynesians. Western ethnologists think of the Pacific as being divided into three regions classified loosely as Polynesia (Many Islands), extending in a great triangle from Hawaii to New Zealand to Easter Island; Micronesia (Small Islands), containing most of the atolls and smaller islands of the tropical northwest Pacific; and Melanesia (Black Islands), extending from Fiji to New Guinea. By the time European explorers arrived almost every habitable island in the Pacific was, or had been, inhabited.

The Pacific Islanders certainly arrived in some type of voyaging canoes, but how and from where? Norwegian anthropologist, Thor Heyerdahl, suggested that Polynesians, at least originally, descended from American Indians who drifted across in large rafts from South America. To support his theory, he led the famous expedition in 1947 on a balsa raft, the *Kon-Tiki*, which sailed over the same waters I was now crossing. Most anthropologists reject Heyerdahl's theory today. They believe that about 50,000 years ago, Polynesians began a series of slow, eastward migrations by sailing canoe from points in Asia, and by AD 1000, had settled as far east as Hawaii, the Marquesas and

Easter Island. They may even have gone on as far as the west coast of South America in a kind of reversed Heyerdahl theory.

I wonder how many of those experts who skippered nothing more than a car or office desk can imagine the difficulties of taking canoes of vine-lashed logs against the prevailing trade winds for thousands of miles. Even with a modern designed sailing vessel, I would no more try to cross the tropical Pacific from west to east than I would consider swimming across. Yet it apparently is possible to make fitful progress east during those rare seasons of El Niño when the trade winds abate to be replaced by variable and temporary west winds. That seems to have been the principal way they managed to make such long passages to the east. In fact, the year previous to my Pacific crossing had been an El Niño year and yachts making passages across the Pacific had reported unusual headwinds and out of season cyclones.

Perhaps it was a combination of migrations from Asia as well as from South America that peopled the islands in the eastern Pacific. However the Polynesians arrived, they did navigate their craft between the various island groups without a compass, using their knowledge of stars, wind and wave patterns, currents, seabirds and doubtless some other methods now lost to us.

It remains nothing short of a miracle to me how those ancient navigators made long voyages into unknown territory and then were able to find their way back and forth between the newly discovered lands and their home islands. By contrast, I need do little more than unfold my chart, set some sail, point the bow of my boat downwind, set the self-steering and let nature take over. The blessed, timeless quality of the sea is that, while man has conquered the continents with a lasting presence, at sea, the evidence of our passages, ancient and modern, are erased in the moments of a ship's vanishing wake.

From a mid-ocean perspective, the islands of the Pacific are only a minor intrusion on the bosom of a boundless sea. Charts of the Pacific, particularly those showing a few hundred of its thousands of scattered islands, distorts our perspective. Say we had a chart whose scale depicted a one-mile-long island as a speck just one millimeter wide (less than the thickness of a penny). For it to include the entire Pacific, that chart would be longer than my 28-foot boat. In spite of

Western charts appearing crowded with islands, Polynesians know this is not reality. They live in a world comprised of 70 parts water to one part land. No wonder they were so at home on the sea until their fragile cultures were turned upside down by the arrival of Europeans. It takes a long voyage to get a feel for the true nature of this planet, to watch day after day the furrows of waves reaching out to the rim of the horizon, to sense the earth's rotation as stars wheel overhead at night.

I was, finally, fully at peace with the sea. At the same time, I was tremendously eager to make landfall once I sensed its approach. On my last full day at sea, I stood for hours on deck trying to discern an island from the island-shaped clouds. A three-star sight during that evening's twilight fixed my position 25 miles east of Hiva Oa Island. I reduced sail, hove-to, and kept both eyes open through the night.

5 A Savage on Hiva Oa

I have escaped everything that is artificial, conventional, customary. I am entering into truth; into nature...it is true; I am a savage.

- Paul Gauguin on Hiva Oa

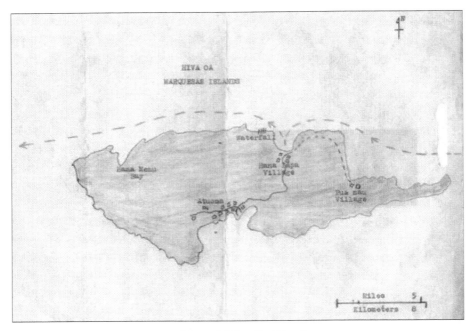

Map of Hiva Oa Island

At dawn on the thirtieth day out from the Galapagos and forty-five days out from Panama, I watched as the slender black thread of land began to solidify in the increasing light. *Atom* had sat out the night, drifting with jib backed and mainsail reefed, riding the waters as comfortably as a gull with folded wings. My mind had been focused on Hiva Oa Island for so long I might have conjured the island from a cloud on the horizon. Cloud or island ahead? Only one way to settle the matter: I adjusted sails and course for the cloud-shaped island.

Approaching the east end of Hiva Oa, I sailed recklessly close under high cliffs that threw back the trade wind-driven swells in thunderous fountains of spray. Unlike many of the sandy-shored, translucent, lagoon-filled isles of Polynesia, the Marquesas Islands lack a protective encircling offshore coral reef, and their weather-beaten shorelines take the full force of the Pacific rollers. Farther along the coast, lush and dark wooded shores led up furrowed valleys to jagged bare peaks pointing skyward like volcanic Gothic spires. Looking for better protection from easterly wind and swell, I passed by the first four slight indents in the coast that were optimistically referred to as "bays" on the chart – to a sailor, a bay implies some degree of protection, not merely small zigzags, particularly on an exposed shore filled with breaking waves.

Children of the Marquesas

Twelve miles down the coast, I entered the sheltered bay of Hana Iapa. It was comprised of a few visible grass-roofed huts at the bottom of a steeply rising valley, cloaked in a thick layer of green, floppy-topped coconut palms. On the far side of the bay, a silvery ribbon of waterfall fluttered down a vertical cliff into the sea. I passed a small islet whose weathered contour looked peculiarly like a stone carving of two profiled heads, back to back. A river of air descended from the valley, rippling the bay with the unmistakable flowered-scent of a tropical island. A single, gray cloud drifted across the bay, releasing just enough rain to form a translucent rainbow that touched the water, as it touched my soul, to complete a sailor's vision of paradise.

Tucked into the eastern corner of the bay, mostly beyond the reach of the sea swell, were three other yachts anchored a hundred yards off a short cement quay. I dropped sails, hoisted my yellow quarantine flag and motored into an open spot not far from where the other boats sat huddled together. The bottom was a mixture of sandy patches, sharp rocks and coral. Though only 15-20 feet deep, the bottom was just vaguely visible due to the run-off of sediments from the stream entering the head of the bay. I dropped my main anchor, a 25 lb plow-type with 25 feet of chain attached and another 100 feet of nylon rode shackled to the chain, onto a sandy spot surrounded by dark shapes of coral.

The problem was how to let out enough scope to get the anchor to hold while not permitting the nylon rode to chafe itself in two on the rocks as the boat swung to the wind shifts. Most cruising boats in the Pacific Islands use an all-chain rode, which partly solves the problem, but they still often get their chains wrapped around the coral heads, requiring them to dive and clear them at some point. Using my plastic dinghy, I set out my remaining two anchors in a triangle pattern: 13 lb lightweight Danforths, best used in sand or mud bottoms. Each line was fastened to the bow so the nylon rodes could remain taut and not wrap themselves around the coral where they would chafe through in a matter of hours.

A woman from a 40-something-foot Canadian-flagged boat, named *Lorelei*, waved at me and I rowed the dinghy over to meet them. Gwen Cornfield and her husband Mike had sailed from British Columbia and for the past several years cruised the islands of the South Pacific. The third member of their crew was Linda, who was about my age and had flown out to join them in Tahiti for a few months vacation before flying back to Canada. They invited me aboard and were surprised to find out this was my first stop after 45 days alone at sea.

"We thought you had just sailed around the island from the main port of Atuona and forgotten to take down your Q flag. Was it tough being alone all that time?" Mike asked.

"Well...umm, you're the first people...I mean...this is the first time I've spoken to anyone in a month. It is great...umm ... to talk to someone." I wanted to talk but couldn't put together a coherent sentence. I'm sure I sounded stupid at first, but I soon regained my speech and told them the highlights of my trip so far.

They confirmed what I'd heard in Panama, that all yachts arriving in the Marquesas are required to check in at one of the official ports of entry, the nearest of which was some 30 miles around the other side of the island at a crowded, open roadstead of an anchorage, at the main town of Atuona. There was also the not-so-little matter of an $850 cash bond sailors were required to post, to cover an airline ticket home in case a shipwrecked, or love-struck, sailor found himself unable, or unwilling to sail away when his 90-day visa expired. Not having $850 laying around, I adopted the simple ruse of avoiding the gendarme as long as possible while keeping the required Q flag up to comply with the only portion of the law I could afford.

After Gwen and Linda fed us a huge dinner, Mike got on his short-wave amateur radio and placed a radio link call back to my mother in Michigan, letting her know I'd arrived safely.

The crew of *Lorelei* planned to walk to a village a few miles along the north coast the following day to buy fruit and vegetables from the local farmers. After assuring me it was safe to roam this part of the island without running into any officials of the immigration type – the only road they could approach on had been washed out in a rainstorm a few days ago – I eagerly accepted an invitation to join them. As I was leaving to row back to *Atom*, I hesitatingly asked the lovely Linda if she'd like to "come visit my boat."

"Sure, let's go," she said and slipped her attractive, slender body into my dinghy. Back on *Atom*, the young solo sailor's hormones were raging, but I was so concerned not to act like a desperate dimwit that I bungled my imagined chance by sitting on my hands and talking at her nonstop for two hours. Now that I learned how to talk again, for some reason, I found it impossible to stop. She was kind enough to let me rattle on without letting on that I was making a bloody fool of myself. Sometime after midnight, she gratefully accepted my suggestion to take her back to *Lorelei*. I returned alone to *Atom* where I found a nagging shipmate called loneliness had crept aboard.

Early next morning, well before the sun had risen high enough to strike the uppermost coconut fronds in the central valley, we came ashore in *Lorelei's* dinghy, landing on a beach of bird's-egg-sized stones rattling in chorus with the incoming swell. Along shore was a row of open-sided huts filled with coconuts cut open to dry under the sun. A river, whose eroded banks showed that it ran deep and wide on rainy days, was now a shallow creek that flowed slowly down the valley under the branches of yellow-flowered hibiscus trees. The creek hesitated in a deep pool just before it seeped across a sandbar to mix with the saltwater of the bay. My boyhood dreams of the land of Melville's fictional South Sea adventure romance, *Typee,* were finally being realized and I was not disappointed by what I found.

We had no sooner pulled the dinghy ashore and started walking along the trail around the bay when a shirtless, teenaged Marquesan boy, heading the opposite way to work in his family's coconut grove, greeted us, and decided on the spot to become our guide for the journey to the village of Pau Mau. Our new companion, whose Christian name was Eric, led us up along the ruins of a road that had once been well-laid-out with hand-cut stones. Along the way, Eric told us the vowel-laden names of every craggy outcrop, or indent in the coast, from Hanapaoa Bay to Mount Ootua. For every spectacular basalt pinnacle that hove into view above the luxuriant green slopes, another fluid Marquesan name rolled from our guide's lips.

During this hike I learned that, on Hiva Oa, all paths that are not leading sharply downward, are leading equally sharply upwards. For several miles we followed the remains of the stone-lined road and passed moss-covered rock platforms in the shape of building foundations. These had once been the Marae temples where traditional religious ceremonies, including human sacrifice, took place.

Rounding a corner in the trail, we were alerted by the thumping sound of unshod hooves to a herd of wild horses breaking from their cover and racing over a sloping grass hillock flecked with fluffy white pods of flowering cotton. The cotton had been introduced here a century earlier in hopes of giving islanders a second cash crop to supplement copra. The Marquesans, who were wisely skeptical of adding another labor-intensive industry to their already-filled day, now let the cotton grow wild and abandoned to the wind.

The next narrow valley held the single house of a family who had emigrated from France two years previously. The young parents and two children, including a baby, lived in this remote homestead, the nearest road a two-hours walk. Their house was constructed in the native fashion using bamboo frames, palm-thatch walls and grass roof. They seemed pleased to have visitors and showed us around their home, all self-made down to the last stick of furniture and wooden serving bowls. As self-sufficient as they could possibly be, they lived with little contact from society, aside from the once or twice a month trek to town to get the few supplies that couldn't be made with their own hands, fished out of the sea, or grown in their garden. They could have built near a village or a road, but instead, they chose for neighbors the bougainvillea, croton, hibiscus, lofty mango and breadfruit trees, their vegetable gardens bordered with citrus and papaya trees, and an extended family of chickens and wild pigs. Because of the close proximity of their animals, compost pile and outhouse, there was also a healthy insect population. To live ashore in this part of the world is to endlessly endure flies trying to crawl into your eyes and nostrils. The children had numerous little sores from scratching at insect bites. While we visitors nervously swatted at the flies with our hands, our French host family were as unperturbed as cattle in a field. We were told that at night, every creature in the area is under siege from mosquitoes and the only refuge is found under mozzie nets draped over our hammocks and bamboo bunks.

Possibly worst of all are the lovely, sandy beaches nearby that beckon us, but which are rendered virtually off-limits to people due to the nearly invisible stinging gnats called nonos that inhabit the sand. We all knew when a sailor was newly arrived because his exposed limbs carried the red sores of the nono. You don't feel their bite until, a few hours later, itching red welts appear over all your exposed skin. The next time you would see the nono-bitten sailor approaching in his dinghy, he had learned enough to either be sprinting between the water and the tree line, or else he was wearing long pants, socks and shoes as he landed. Legend has it that these pests were released on the islands by a god intent on punishing the people for breaking one of his taboos. It also works well to keep developers away.

This tropical version of Thoreau's Walden Pond allowed our hosts to live as their own masters, seeking out the primitive and elemental aspects of life close to nature, though these rewards are hard-earned. The entire family were as thin and sinewy as birds compared to the fat most of us carry around. The island homesteader's relentless battle against insects made any pests associated with my own sea-steading seem trivial. When insects flew out for a visit on *Atom*, I was able to put up screens over the hatches or re-anchor a bit further from shore.

I wondered, but didn't ask, how they had managed to buy this well-located piece of land. Most property here is jointly held by members of large native families and they do not easily come to agreement to sell at any price. Though visitors are shyly welcomed, the Marquesans are not keen to have so many foreign settlers that they become a minority in their own land.

As our hike continued to the next bay, just far enough back from the beach to avoid those blasted nonos, was a small village of five simple houses built from the sawn wood and pleated fronds of the palm tree. We met several men working at producing copra from ripe coconuts. Fallen nuts were gathered into piles next to a sharpened iron spike driven into the ground onto which a man thrust the nut down to twist off the husk. Other men pried the oily white flesh from the inner shell and laid the pieces on slit bamboo racks to dry in the sun. Depending on the weather, after several days of drying, the copra is bagged and stored until the arrival of the government-subsidized cargo vessel − still locally called the "copra schooner" − from Tahiti. Much of the copra is refined and shipped overseas as cooking oil. Copra work is physically hard, though it has the advantage of allowing each man to work when he wants, for as long as he wants, and be paid accordingly. The trees are there waiting, each one producing some 40 nuts annually − 80 trees in a grove yielding a ton of copra each year.

While the men joked with us and continued working, a boy scrambled effortlessly up a tall palm and twisted a few immature drinking nuts until they dropped to the ground, where our guide Eric deftly sliced off the tops and handed them around. The workers watched approvingly as we slurped up the cool, slightly sweet water. In addition to the sightseeing, we had hoped to find farmers willing to sell us some vegetables, however, there was nothing to buy, just a gratefully accepted gift of a few oranges and bananas and all the husked coconuts we wanted to carry.

At this point, the crew of *Lorelei* turned back while Eric and I detoured inland to rejoin the main cross-island road and continued on into the village of Pua Mau. There, in a place overgrown with brush, Eric pointed out the ancient, 10-foot-high, lichen-covered stone idols, called tikis. My common language with Eric was French, he being far better at it than I, having spoken it since childhood at the island's French colonial school. I asked what he knew about the origins of these stone creatures. Eric made an indifferent shoulder shrug and said, "Je ne sais pas," which in this case means either I don't know, or maybe, I can't or won't say. That the current generations of islanders will admit to knowing nothing – and caring less – about this ever-present and not-so-long-ago practice, only makes it all the more intriguing.

Some archeologists theorize that the people of Easter Island originally emigrated from the Marquesas, and that these weathered stone monuments on Hiva Oa were created by those same people who went on to the similar and greater works on Easter Island's famous long-eared moai statues. As on Easter Island, forgotten generations of Marquesans quarried smaller, but still substantial, chunks of lava rock weighing over a ton, and shifted them miles across the tortuous terrain to their chosen resting places. They then carved them into mysterious forms and stood them upright using earthworks, levers and coconut fiber ropes.

Today's Marquesans may have been part of a second migration that arrived here several hundred years after the builders of the stone roads, temples and tikis. Another theory has the stone carvers arriving later and enslaving the local population to do the work for them.

Either way, at some point, a conflict took place in which the stone artisans, whose culture included sun worship (no, not your typical tourist's version) and human sacrifice, were themselves carved up and eaten. The victors, who were either slaves or invaders from other islands, knocked down the tikis and temples. The present population is mostly made up of the descendents of these cannibal tribes that survived the battles with the stone artisans. In Pua Mau, three fallen tikis, probably symbols of deified ancestors or other gods, have regained their feet. If not exactly in their full past glory, they stand as weathered, mute symbols of the Marquesan people's long struggle to survive invasions of other warring tribes.

The natives used to call these islands Te Fenua Enata, The Land of Men. The six inhabited islands of the group lay in two clusters of three each, spreading across 250 miles of ocean. The depopulation and cultural devastation of these islands began in 1595 when Mendoza – the Spanish discoverer sent by the Marquesa de Mendoca of Peru – got into a scuffle and slaughtered several hundred of the natives.

Until Captain James Cook's rediscovery of the islands in 1770, the Marquesans had gone about their cultivating of food crops and occasional raids of neighboring islands to pick up guests for their human feasts, with little outside interference. Despite their savage state, Cook noted the Marquesans were "without exception the finest race of people in this Sea." Cook traded nails, cloth and hatchets for hogs, fruits and vegetables to nourish his ailing crew. One of Cook's officers recorded that the heavily tattooed men were "exquisitely proportion'd" and the women were "very beautiful" with long hair "worn down their backs in a most becoming and graceful manner."

Within 50 years of Cook's visit, the population he estimated at over 100,000 people was reduced by four-fifths. The guns of European raiders claimed far less than the insidious European diseases and the consequent famines. Others were carried off as slaves to work till death on the dry guano islands along the South American coast. The ensuing social turmoil resulted in even more devastating intertribal wars and the end to their seafaring expeditions.

When the French took control of the islands in 1842, they nearly succeeded in exterminating the remaining population. By 1936, the one-time Land of Men contained only 1,300 people, a population reduction of some 98 percent. In recent years, through better governance, or at least less-bad governance, the main islands are slowly being repopulated.

The French missionaries did succeed in wiping out nearly every trace of the islanders' original culture, with a special emphasis on eradicating the wildly erotic fertility dances described by the South Seas whaler turned writer, Herman Melville. In his fictionalized book *Typee*, based on his very real visit to the Marquesas in the 1840s, Melville states:

The term 'savage' is, I conceive, often misapplied, and indeed when I consider the vices, cruelties and enormities of every kind that spring up in the tainted atmosphere of a feverish civilization, I am inclined to think that so far as the relative wickedness of the parties is concerned, four or five Marquesan islanders sent to the United States as missionaries might be quite as useful as an equal number of Americans dispatched to the islands in a similar capacity.

We returned to Hana Iapa and *Atom* where I heard that the road to Atuona was open again and I thought I'd better turn myself in to customs and immigration before they decided to come looking for me. A long coastal navigation around the island would surely have been dogged by periods of calms behind the mountains. *Atom's* ailing engine might get us through the calm bits if it felt like working, but it would not help once I turned the corner along the south coast and came face-to-face with a brutal beat against wind and current for several miles. Instead of making that risky passage around the island to anchor in a marginal harbor, I decided to report my arrival by walking across the island carrying my passport, boat's registration and clearance papers from my last port.

As I walked up and away from Hana Iapa, a fresh wind swept down the valley, rustling the coconut fronds and breadfruit tree leaves overhead. Across the bay on the exposed shore, a blowhole at the base of the cliffs timed the pulse of the sea to eject fountains of spray with a deep bass "boom" of a distant cannon shot. On my side of the bay, men paddling two canoes dropped a long semi-circular net into the water and then brought lines tethered to the ends to another group of men and women standing in the surf. The two groups at either end of the net exchanged instructions and encouragement as they pulled the net up the stony shore where shouting children picked out its few small fish and dropped them into baskets. To suit the occasion, the fish might be marinated and eaten raw as *ika tee*, or baked in banana leaves in an earth oven.

I was barely out of the village when the rain began. Within minutes the dirt road became a steep mass of mud and earth-stained rivulets. Grabbing a banana leaf as a disposable umbrella, I sloshed my way up the island's backbone of black lava, basalt and red tufa. In most places this island's rock foundation was so overgrown with vegetation that from a distance the crenellated land looked to have a gentle rolling form. Up close, its bony structure showed deeply scored cliffs, the naked scars of recent landslips and bare peaks so sharp that the lush tropical growth fell away in a losing battle against gravity and the erosive forces of wind and rain. Away from all signs of human existence, under a veil of cloud and rain, somewhere near the abandoned stone tiki quarry, the dark forest undulated with water and exuded something foreboding.

The higher elevations resembled a temperate zone forest where the ragged pandanus trees gave way to troops of close-ordered ironwood trees guarding a ridge. In the pre-Christian era, the ironwood or toa trees were carved into skull-crushing war clubs. At the crest of the ridge the rain lifted, the clouds blew away and I looked out over the windward coast beyond the vegetation-choked valley for several miles across a white-flecked blue sea to another brown and green volcanic upheaval – the sister island of Tahu Ata.

In half the time it took to climb the north side of the mountain, I ran and occasionally slid by the seat of my pants, down the equally muddy southern side. In Atuona, the harbor was crowded with a supply ship sitting as Mother Goose to a flock of some dozen yachts rolling uneasily and pecking at their short-scoped anchors. Down the road, shimmering red bouquets of poinciana and yellow-flowered hibiscus trees bordered the main street and its brick homes, general goods store, bank and the gendarmarie.

There are a couple of different ways for an English-speaking sailor to transact his business with a truculent French official. You can adopt the Englishman's habit of insisting the Frenchman speak, or at least understand, English. The idea being to wear our Frenchman down so that he submits to the indignity of speaking English, which he usually knows, more-or-less, but is loathe to use, as if each incident were a replay of Waterloo. That approach may not work so well if your papers are not entirely in order. In my case, I decided on the tactic of the hopeless groveling fool (one that I can play perhaps too well), with a smattering of incomprehensible French pulled from a phrase book.

My knock at the door of his residence caught him in the middle of a late lunch or early dinner or perhaps an extended lunch/dinner. The gendarme looked fresh off the plane from France, only a few years older than myself, and no doubt still in shock over his good fortune at landing this coveted Polynesian post. When he saw me on his stoop covered in mud and carrying a backpack, he stepped outside and led me at arm's length back down to the lawn to speak with me. He seemed truly amazed, and then a little irritated, to find out I had walked across the island to check in. Once we established my boat was not in the harbor, he proceeded to tell me I would have to move the boat here and then visit the bank next door to post the required $850 cash bond.

Back and forth we went, with the gendarme insisting I move my boat and pay the bond, and myself pleading ignorance and penury and a broken engine thrown in to settle the point. Being a reasonable man (and what could he do about it anyway?) the gendarme finally agreed I could remain two weeks to make repairs and then must sail directly to Tahiti to arrange bond payment there. Fortunately, "passing the buck" is as alive in colonial Polynesia as anywhere else. The terms of our truce were especially agreeable to me because they could be safely ignored. In later years, sailing through Asia and Africa, I learned avoidance is the best tactic with some officials. The gypsies of both the land and the sea know the rule: never ask permission, never be denied.

The Marquesas, like all of French Polynesia, are ferociously expensive. They are not a welcoming sort of place for a low-budget traveler. I noticed that a single bottle of Tahiti's Hinano brand beer at the grocery store cost six dollars. I made one necessary indulgence and bought a baguette and some cheese for the better part of ten dollars, converted at the counter into francs by the Chinese shopkeeper. In fact, my entire budget for an expected two months of cruising among the French Isles could easily have been blown here in two days.

At the cemetery above the bay, I sat down to enjoy my baguette and cheese at the overgrown grave of the French painter and sculptor, Paul Gauguin, who spent the last two years of his life here on Hiva Oa. Years ago back in Detroit, I had been captivated by his stunning paintings of Polynesian life and I had determined then to make a pilgrimage to his final island home – and perhaps catch a glimpse of the Polynesia he had painted.

When Gauguin left his wife and young children in Paris to go to Tahiti in 1891, he told a friend, "I'm leaving to live in peace, to be rid of the influence of civilization. I only desire to create very simple art. In order to achieve this I must immerse myself in virgin nature, to see no one but savages, to share their life and have as my sole occupation to render, the way a child would, the images formed in my brain, using exclusively the means offered by primitive art, which are the only true and valid ones."

Gauguin fantasized about the approaching day "when I'll flee to the woods on an island in Oceania: there to live on ecstasy...there on Tahiti with a new family by my side far from the European scramble for money. In the silence of the beautiful tropical nights I will be able to listen to the soft murmur and music of the movements of my heart, in harmony with the mysterious beings around me. Free at last – without financial worries. Able to love, sing, and to die."

Gauguin moved into a Tahitian-style hut a good distance outside the capital of Papeete and took for his new wife a teenage vahine, named Tea'Amana (Giver of Strength). His numerous paintings of her became the embodiment of his South Seas fantasy. Of her Gauguin wrote: "She seemed to love me, but did not tell me so. I

Two Tahitian Women, 1899 - Gauguin

loved her and told her so, which made her laugh. She knew it very well. Naked, she seemed clothed in an orange-yellow garment of purity – a beautiful golden flower...which I worshipped as an artist and a man."

Two years later, Gauguin returned to France with dozens of paintings of a of dream-like, idealized Polynesia, but his inspired, unconventional genius went largely unrecognized at the time. He returned to Tahiti where he continued painting and began writing anti-government editorials in local publications.

Gauguin had listened to the islanders' stories of wrongs done to them: a girl trying to report a rape who was then raped by the magistrate who dismissed the case, gendarmes arresting girls for indecency after searching out their bathing places, natives wrongly accused of all sorts of crimes merely because their culture was not the French ideal – and Gauguin himself was threatened with expulsion from the islands when he tried to intervene.

Tahiti had become too civilized and corrupted for his tastes so he moved to the more remote Marquesas. He built a home and art studio here in the center of Atuona village that he called the House of Pleasure, and carved on its wooden frames his favorite maxims, "Soyez mysterieuses" (Be mysterious), and "Soyez, amoureuses vous serez heureuses" (Be in love, you will be happy).

Having been rejected by Tea'Amana after his return to Tahiti, he took here a new 14-year-old vahine he had lured away from the local Catholic mission school. This monstrous behavior, and his continued public protests against the colonial government and church, soon made him the enemy of the local priests and police. The European colony shunned him as a heretic and salacious traitor. The islanders on the other hand, loved Gauguin and saw him as the only European who never tried to exploit them or treat them as inferiors. But the villagers were soon forbidden by the priests and gendarmes to visit the home of the white painter. Only Tioka, the island's old witch doctor, refused to be scared away. Since Gauguin had interceded and gotten Tioka's prison sentence reduced after his conviction for cannibalism, the fiercely independent old man spread the word among the islanders that here was one good white man who could help them.

Between increasingly serious bouts of illness, Gauguin completed several more paintings that he sent back to his art dealer in Paris. A degree of recognition and money began to trickle back to him. His running feud with church and state was exacerbated by his published newsletters railing against the intimidation, ill-treatment and denial of elementary justice done to the natives. For his trouble Gauguin was convicted of libel against the government and sentenced to a large fine and three months in prison. Before the sentence could be carried out, he died alone in his house from heart failure complicated by his various ailments. As the hated priests removed the body of their adversary for burial, it was reported the old Tioka cried "Gauguin is dead: we are lost!" and then sang the Marquesan death chant.

The islanders were said to miss seeing their odd friend, barefoot with colored *pareo* around his waist and an astonishing silver-tasseled green beret pulled over one eye, traipsing off to some lonely part of the valley to capture the tropical scenes on canvas. Speaking of his legacy to art and not necessarily about his behavior, Gauguin said he wanted to provide future generations of artists with "the right to dare anything." If there were similarities between Gauguin and myself, they were mainly limited to a mutual distrust of the minions of bureaucracy, and perhaps a desire to cultivate the savage within.

By the time I rose from Gauguin's grave (not that I actually rose from his grave in any metaphysical sense), it was too late in the day to return all the way back to Hana Iapa. On the edge of Atuona, I pitched my one-man tent alongside a shallow stream next to a fruit orchard. Entering my thin fabric tent, which was held open by two little fiberglass rod hoops, was more like slithering into a loose-fitting garment laid out on the ground. Soon after sunset, a rain began that continued through the night. I became aware I was too close to the river when it rose and wetted my feet inside the tent. Adding to my discomfort, a chill night air flowed down the mountain, forcing me to slog around in the unhappy combination of cold, rain and darkness as I struggled to relocate my tent to higher ground.

At dawn I attempted to drive the chill from my bones by marching briskly back up the mountain towards Hana Iapa. Along the way I passed an abandoned four-wheel-drive jeep stuck up to its axles in mud in the middle of the road. Where the road crossed a high ridge, I detoured onto a trail that took me up the chine to what could have been one of the island's highest peaks, but it was engulfed in a rain-filled cloud that blocked what surely was a stunning view. A series of sharply dropping trails, much harder on the knees than an uphill slog, brought me back to Hana Iapa.

During my absence, my friends on *Lorelei* had moved on to another island and two other yachts had arrived in the anchorage. I was relieved to see *Atom* appeared as I had left her. However, once I got on deck and checked the anchor rodes, I saw one of the lines was loose. When I pulled it in, there was no anchor on the end, just a frazzle where the coral had cut the line in two. Diving with fins, mask and snorkel, I located the missing anchor and freed up the other two rodes, which had also worked enough slack in their lines that they too were nearly chafed through on the sharp rocks. The rest of the afternoon I spent splicing the three-strand nylon lines and resetting the anchors with fender floats attached in an attempt to lift the slack from the lines above the reach of the rocks. This was not the last time a lack of all-chain rode would nearly cause the loss of my boat.

I became friends with a Hana Iapa family who lived above the stream in a simple home of bamboo, plywood and thatch, located on the sole road passing through the village. The father, Tehoko, almost daily paddled his canoe out to visit *Atom* with his children and to bring me food from their garden. In return, I gave him fishing tackle and an armful of T-shirts I'd bought by the bundle at a flea market back in Miami. Out here in the Pacific Isles, far from a clothing store, they were now worth something as barter goods.

Besides the garden around their house, many Marquesans have an inland garden on land they use, or ignore, according to their needs. Tehoko invited me to join him on a horseback trip to his second garden. My backside was relieved when I finally dismounted the hard wooden saddle. Sensing what would interest me most, Tehoko's cleared some vines away from a rounded Volkswagen-sized boulder revealing ancient carved symbols, the meanings of which were now lost, at least to words.

At the garden, Tehoko brought down a whole banana tree with a single swipe of his machete. Then he cut off a stalk of the rare and delicious red bananas. I smiled then as I always do whenever I see a banana tree cut down, remembering the first time I saw a man do this on Tobago Island in the Caribbean. This destruction of a whole tree for a single bunch of bananas seems a terrible waste to the uninitiated Westerner, but each tree produces its bunch of bananas only once. From the base of the cut trunk, another tree will grow and bear fruit again within a year. I still laugh as I remember what a fool I looked like when I ran forward and grabbed the man's arm to stop him from cutting the whole tree down to get me the bananas I'd asked for. He had a good laugh as he explained the necessity of it. He might be laughing still, when he gets together with friends to recount stories of the dumbest white men they ever met.

As we moved into a partly flooded stream bed, Tehoko showed me how to select and cut the potato-like tuber of the taro plant, which is a basic staple of the Polynesian diet. The purplish-white flesh of the taro is more dense and chewy than a potato – probably more nutritious as well – and became a favorite ingredient in my vegetable stews whenever I could get them.

Another incredible food found in the gardens of Hiva Oa is the pomplemoose, a grapefruit-like fruit nearly the size of a basketball and as sweet as a Mandarin orange. There are few pleasures like biting into a fresh, ripe pomplemoose, mango, papaya, or pineapple from a tropical garden. I'm not talking about the horrid Hawaiian pineapple grown on chemical feed, sprayed with insecticides, picked green, injected with chemicals to retard spoiling and then refrigerated for thirty days while being shipped to your antiseptic supermarket. For anything like the real flavor of a pineapple, you must snatch it from the dark volcanic soil at the peak of ripeness and eat it unrefrigerated.

We tied our sacks of fruit and vegetables on the horses and led them back to Tehoko's home where I was given a bagful of taro and other foods that would keep well, to take on the next leg of my passage west. Much of the so-called farming here is little more than plucking the food from the ground or trees. At least I saw no planting, just an endless cycle of harvests. This is part of the reason for the apparent indolence and carelessness that Westerners see in the native Polynesian – he needn't worry himself with our misplaced notions of "make hay while the sun shines." Winter never comes to Polynesia.

Nearly daily I went to visit Tehoko's home where I spent happy days with his family. Tehoko's wife and eldest daughter, Celestine, prepared meals for us containing the South Seas staples of roasted cassava, poached breadfruit and taro root baked in an earth oven and slathered with coconut cream, with side dishes of those fantastic little red bananas and papayas sprinkled with lime juice. Tehoko said, "It's a shame you just missed the July," as Marquesans call Bastille Day, which is celebrated throughout French Polynesia as their National Day. "We had a great feast with music and dancing."

Celestine was a lively teen-aged girl; a slender, beguiling beauty with dancing black eyes. Laughing at my flawed pronunciation but encouraged by my efforts, she helped me compile a short phrase book of the Marquesan language, which as she spoke it, sounded more like music than words. With my rough French, we strained at times to communicate with each other, sometimes by my pretending to understand when I could not. I thought now of extending my stay here, despite the gendarme's curt orders to leave.

Taking me into her garden, Celestine led me past bunches of white morning glories in full bloom. We passed under giant leafy breadfruit trees, slender trunks of the green mop-topped papaya trees, and over to the climbing vanilla orchids wrapped in a leafy embrace around the trunks of young kapok trees. In vanilla's native Mexico, pollen-questing bees help fecundate the orchid. On Hiva Oa, there is no bee enterprising enough to do the work and the flowers must be pollinated by hand. Showing me one of the delicate yellow-green blossoms, Celestine held the bloom in one hand, and with the other, transferred pollen between stamen and pistol with a sharpened twig. On another plant she lifted a dangling bunch of seed pods beginning to ripen. When fully ripe, she picks them and lays them out in the sun to dry. In America, a faint resemblance to vanilla flavor is extracted by steeping the pods in alcohol. In the islands, the women cut the dried pods into small bits and put them in desserts imparting on them the true, full vanilla flavor.

I followed Celestine through the garden and a short way into the forest to a waterfall so gentle and well-concealed by hanging vegetation that I did not even see it until we were standing knee-deep in the pool at its base. We sat on a smooth-topped stone with our feet dangling in the pool as the cool, misty air swirled around us. She picked some ripe yellow guavas and placed one in my mouth to eat whole – skin, pink flesh and tiny hard seeds all together.

Like most Marquesan vahine, Celestine wore only the pareo, a colorful printed or tie-dyed piece of light cloth wrapped sarong-like around the body once and tied behind the neck. Her long, silken black hair framed an Asian face, trimmed with the smiling eyes and lips of Polynesia. I felt the savage Gauguin whispering in my ear: "Ah, here is the essence and ecstasy of Oceania."

"Would you like to see the ancient burial site?" Celestine asked in French. At this point I'd follow her into a temple of human sacrifice without hesitation. We walked a short way further into a place of dark silence where the aerial roots of banyan trees pushed up through the flat-topped stones of what had once been a pyramid-shaped temple. At the center of the ruins, I looked down into a space between the rocks and spotted a human skull staring back at me through empty eye sockets. Looking farther, I saw complete skeletons entwined in the web of tree roots. Not so long ago, the tattooed witch doctors, like Gauguin's friend Tioka, had led islanders to place their dead on this sacred temple, much to the consternation of the Christian missionaries who insisted they bury their dead. Having your remains buried underground was considered a horrible fate to the Marquesans, though many have accepted it now. We spoke in hushed tones and as we left, I had the vague feeling that if we lingered too long the ancient skeletons would reach out and pull us back into their world.

My allotted two weeks in Hiva Oa had passed. The next day I untangled my anchor rodes yet again. As I lashed the dinghy on deck under the boom and prepared to hoist sail, Tehoko and Celestine came out by canoe to wish me "Bonne chance" and heave aboard another basket of fruit. Moments later, a light breeze wafting down the valley pushed me slowly out to sea. I said farewell to The Land of Men (and Women) with a long, deep blast from my conch shell horn.

6 Bora Bora

Atom anchored in Bora Bora's lagoon

Once clear of Hiva Oa's jagged coast, I set a southwest course to clear the rocky ramparts of Ua Pu Island not far to the west. Nine hundred miles off my bow lay Bora Bora.

When French explorer Louis Bougainville sailed through these islands in 1767, he described it as paradise on earth: "Nature has placed it in the best climate in the Universe, embellished it smilingly, enriched it with all its gifts, covered it with handsome inhabitants...she herself has dictated their laws." And so began the romantic myth of Tahiti.

In fact, when Captain James Cook arrived a year later, he recorded that the Tahitians stole anything that glittered, were constantly warring with their neighbors and practiced human sacrifice. By 1900, Tahiti had lost most of Bougainville's charm as well as any resistance to Western civilization, at least for Paul Gauguin who wrote: "It was Europe...under the aggravating circumstances of colonial snobbism, and the imitation...of our customs, fashions, vices, and absurdities of civilization. Was I to have made this far journey only to find the very thing which I had fled?"

Tahiti was not on my list of ports to visit any more than Honolulu or the American South Seas capital in Samoa. Those places might be magnets for credit card-toting tourists and high budget cruising yachts, but they held nothing for me and in fact represented "the very thing which I fled."

Then there is Tahiti's less developed sister island, Bora Bora. For me, that double-barreled name has always been a magical incantation, conjuring up images equally intoxicating as the name Tahiti. The flowing syllables of those two islands, more than any other, define the words exotic and sensual. Any fool would know Bora Bora was not now as Bougainville had described it more than two hundred years ago. Yet, I hoped Western civilization's heavy hand may have come down more gently on this outlying island of Tahiti. Even if I convinced myself Tahiti was ruined, I had more seamanlike reasons for holding course for Bora Bora: Tahiti lay a point or two too close to the wind for *Atom's* taste.

French solo sailor Alain Gerbault put it simply when he wrote: "Why go against the wind to certain islands if there are some equally beautiful ones to leeward?" Through the language and lore of sailors come metaphors apt to any man's life, such as a sailor's struggle to windward isles or his free flight to leeward. Enough windward destinations await us in life that we need not seek them out.

Between *Atom* and Tahiti lay a group of low coral atolls no solo sailor, equipped with only a sextant, should care to approach. From deep water, changeable currents can set you on the reefs before even sighting the sandy motus of the atolls. Even the chart boldly declares it "The Dangerous Archipelago" in case it was not otherwise apparent from the groups of tiny dots sprinkled over the chart like star constellations. True, some solo sailors have successfully passed through these islands, even in the days before GPS satellite navigation. Most of them had dependable engines to negotiate the currents in the narrow passes, and either God's own pilot looking over their shoulders, or the seamanship skills of a Moitessier or Slocum. Remembering my own near disastrous approach to the Galapagos, I wasn't willing to chance another near shipwreck and so held course a good distance off The Dangerous Archipelago.

For three days *Atom* bounded smartly over the waves, as if running a steeplechase, but the weather then deteriorated to a near gale and steady rain. As an atmospheric depression passed, the winds abruptly ceased. The seas still ran high, as they do for a time after the onset of a sudden calm. Without wind in her sails to steady her, *Atom* behaved like a rodeo bull gone berserk. Her head would lift to a wave crest, fall and bury itself in the following trough, then raise again to send a river of water streaming from her back. With the bow down, the stern kicked up so high the rudder lost its bite on the water. Then the stern fell until the afterdeck scooped another load of water to send rushing forward. Along with the pitching motion, *Atom* occasionally swung round to a sideways stance, rolling in her crazed way from toe rail to toe rail. With no wind, there was no way to hold a course, and nothing to do except lash the tiller amidships to prevent it beating itself to pieces against the side of the cockpit. After a half-day wedged in my bunk behind the lee-cloths, a fresh wind of about 20 knots from the southeast returned.

Atom now resumed her familiar steady, long strides over the waves. With a fair current assisting we covered 165 miles in one 24-hour period between two evening star fixes. Part of me wanted to slow down to save wear and tear on the sails, but the thrill-seeker urged me on until I noticed a seam beginning to let go in the jib. With the wind square on the beam – our fastest point of sail – the leeward toe rail and side deck was almost constantly under water, causing some new deck leaks to make themselves known. I went back to sponging seawater out of leeward bunks and lockers and pumping the rest out of the bilge several times a day. Going forward later to swap the number three jib for the storm jib, I noticed with some amazement how low the bow was riding in the water. As with any heavy-keeled displacement boat with a short waterline, our attempt to push the sea aside at seven knots boat speed resulted in our nearly plowing ourselves under.

The wind eased some and the seas gradually steadied to give us a more normal heave and roll. The strong wind that had so agitated the seas yesterday, now caressed it into lying low. Its soft touch produced an equally calming effect on myself as well.

About this time, I tossed overboard a full pot of vegetable stew due to an extremely strong acid flavor that I traced to the taro root I'd harvested from Tehoko's garden. It turns out I had not learned so well when he had shown me how to separate the edible from the non-edible roots. I then test boiled the rest of my taro stock and ended up throwing at least half of it overboard.

During the day, I'd watch flying fish take wing ahead of our bow. Those slow to lift off risked the slashing bite of the dorado fish who hunted under cover behind our keel.

At night, the flying fish were attracted to the soft yellow glow of my kerosene cabin light shining out the companionway hatch and bronze-framed cabin ports. Thump – one hit the side of the cabin house or flew into the mainsail and dropped on deck. A few times a fish would come flying, arrow-like into the cabin, once landing on top of me in my bunk. The next part some won't believe – I could barely believe it myself! As I reclined in the leeward bunk, with my head propped up against the galley cabinet, a flying fish shot through the companionway hatch, hit the cabin house side above the galley, and fell – yes – fell, right into the frying pan sitting on the gimbaled stovetop. We both lay as we were, momentarily stunned. I could have dropped a little oil in the pan, put on a cover, and lit the cooker. Instead, I dumped him back over the side – the first fish to go live from the frying pan back to the sea.

It reminded me of another memorable encounter with a flying fish as I sailed *Atom* in the Straits of Florida one dark night between Key West and Miami. A ship was overtaking me and I stood in the cockpit scanning her well lit bridge and deck with my binoculars. For a fraction of a second, I heard a fast approaching whoosh. Then, POW! I was hit square in the chest with a force and shock that sent me crumpling to the cockpit floor. My first thought was that someone on the ship had shot me. That lasted just a second until I saw a full-grown flying fish lying beside me.

Just before noon on my seventh day out of Hiva Oa, I sighted the craggy peak of Bora Bora rising from its coral base. Having spent my childhood in the flat, mid-western states, I've never lost my feeling of awe at the sight of towering cones of land emerging from the sea after days or weeks of anticipation. The first hint of Bora Bora was a clump of white cumulus clouds piled up on the horizon. They showed no sign of drifting away as they normally would over open sea. A few miles closer in, the clouds detached themselves from the sea and the top of the island's central peak became visible as it lifted above the curvature of the earth.

I sailed as fast as I knew how in a race to beat the setting sun. It would be foolish to attempt to enter a strange harbor after dark, particularly a narrow, reef-lined entrance. At sunset, when green slopes fronted by a frosty white line of surf battering the windward reef were clearly outlined, I was still six miles short of the lagoon entrance. The night passed easy as I turned about, backed the jib and hove-to in the sheltered lee of the islands of Tahaa and Raiatea. Fair skies and moonlight allowed me to see the dark mass of the islands and scattered lights ashore, and to keep clear of the reefs that wrap each island.

By dawn, I had reset the sails and positioned myself directly in front of the entrance. Bora Bora's central island, surrounded by the flat waters of an encircling lagoon, was backlit by the sunrise. The lagoon, in turn, was surrounded by a circle of barrier reefs and a necklace of low, palm-covered motus.

Wind and current were both spilling directly out of the narrow pass between the reefs so I started the engine to gain the anchorage. On both sides of me the surf broke in an unmistakable warning of shallow reefs. Midway through the pass, the engine failed. Now at the mercy of the current, I was ejected from the pass and in no time found myself a mile out to sea. It was a familiar routine, as if some mischievous ghost resided in this tired old engine. So happy in his former life, puttering around the safe harbors of Michigan's lakes, the old Atomic Four was now frightened into a seizure whenever we entered the swirling currents and hull-ripping coral heads in a tricky pass.

Along with the ghost, I guessed there was saltwater contamination in the fuel tank from the leaking deck fill fitting, which in turn led to a clogged filter and corrosion to the carburetor. With scraped knuckles and a back sore from hanging over the engine, I managed to strip and clean the carburetor and fuel filter without losing any essential bits into the bilge. On our second attempt, we entered the harbor and found it was deep, very deep: everywhere over 60 feet with hard coral bottom right up to the suddenly shallow shelf next to shore. This made it impossible to anchor securely with the puny ground tackle I carried. What I would have given then for my current setup of an anchor windlass and 33-pound anchor with 150 feet of chain, shackled to a ¾-inch diameter nylon rode!

After searching around for a suitable spot, I fortunately found an empty mooring buoy in front of the Oa Oa Hotel. Next door to the Oa Oa were the $200 a day thatch-roofed bungalows of Club Med. A topless French girl sailed past me on a windsurfer, confirming that I was back in civilization. Squeezed between mountain and lagoon, the village of Viatepe lay only a few minutes walk from the hotel's dinghy dock.

Any visions I had of being welcomed as the brave solo voyager in this particular corner of paradise were quickly dispelled by my visit to the local gendarmarie. As in Atuona, the gendarmes here serve as police, customs and immigration. Three officers, dressed in their sensible short pants tropical uniform, greeted me politely in French. Then one of them poisoned the atmosphere by bringing up that touchy issue of the $850 bond sailors are expected to hand over with the promise of having it returned by bank transfer when they leave the colony. As before, I replied in the negative, and unlike before, un petit crises ensued. Six arms flailed about like angry orchestra conductors, adding emphasis to the excited discussion, first facing each other, then me, and back to themselves again.

It was as if I were the first sailor to reach their blessed shores with less than $850 in his pocket. This went on until they conceded that since I had been forced into their fair harbor by the extraordinary circumstances of my tale (broken engine, navigational error, storms, imbecility, sea monsters no less) I could stay four days. I had asked for two weeks and got a definite "C'est impossible!" Even with my limited French I couldn't pretend not to understand that, particularly as it was spoken by three frowning faces swinging side to side. With some further grimacing and head-scratching we negotiated a one week stay with the familiar provision that I then sail directly to the bank in Tahiti. Let's see, Tahiti lies 200 miles dead to windward. "Qui, pas problem."

As it so happened, one week was exactly how long I had intended to stay. I was learning that to get along with French officials when you are not, shall we say, following the rules, you must first engage in a good, long, polite argument and never, never speak to them in English, no matter how poor your French is. The sadistic delight they take in watching you fumble with phrase book and dictionary, and then stand before you, teacher to dunce pupil, correcting your pronunciation, goes a long way towards pacifying the puffed up French bureaucrat. It's a matter of feeding their wounded pride. Play the game, humiliate yourself, and they will yield in the end.

Another thing that perhaps I should not keep harping on about was the outrageous prices of goods in the shops of French Polynesia, but it was a constant concern. There was almost nothing in the shops of Viatepe I could afford. It was fortunate that my needs were few. And then, my luck changed in an instant and it seemed I might even manage to depart Bora Bora with a few dollars more than when I arrived.

In one of the tourist boutiques I struck up a conversation with Philippe, the shop owner. Somehow, I mentioned to him I had new T-shirts I was trading for food with the islanders. Philippe was selling T-shirts in his shop for $15-$20 each. He came to the boat and picked out a bagful of my most colorful shirts picturing popular rock bands. He had no garden vegetables to offer, but cash was fine with me. "Will you accept eight dollars apiece, mon ami?" The next day my shirts from Miami were hanging in his shop's racks, ready to sell to tourists from Sydney or Paris, or perhaps even Miami. Imagining the pleasure the three stooges customs officers in the gendarmerie would have in locking me up for smuggling, I reminded Philippe, "Let's not mention this *gift* exchange to anyone."

The best way, really the only way, to see this island, if you want to avoid the rushed views of a rented tourist scooter, is to walk the island's sole circular road as it skirts the banks of the lagoon. The irregular-shaped island, some 20 miles around, is a bit far for a relaxed, single day walk, so I brought along my tent to camp on the opposite side of the island and then continue around back to Viatepe the following day.

What luxury to walk under the shade of the overhanging palms on the smoothly paved road paralleling the many beaches. Neat little homes were decorated as art on canvas with window boxes sprouting bright flowers. Pareos on clotheslines flapped in the warm wind like colorful flags of the various states of Oceania. Loaves of baguettes hung out of mailboxes next to the front gates, delivered daily from the Chinese bakery in Viatepe. I barely noticed the resort hotels, of which there were a few. Unlike the towering concrete eyesores of Waikiki or Miami Beach, these were one or two stories high at most, covered on the outsides with timber and palm thatch in the native fashion that's so easy on the eye. The road was so lightly traveled I wondered where the tourists were. It was Tahiti without the traffic. The vehicles that did pass me were mostly motor scooters, sometimes loaded with father, mother and three children in precarious balance.

How magical to share the road with beautiful, dark-eyed vahines, wrapped in pareo as they zip by on puttering Vespa scooters, bound for home with a basketful of baguettes. Many vahine wear the hibiscus flower in their flowing silky black hair. A flower above the right ear means available, left means she's already taken. If you're introduced to a local vahine, she'll ignore your offer of a limp handshake as she joyously plants a kiss on each cheek.

On the far side of the island, far from houses or hotels, I stopped for the night in a coconut grove along the beach. I knew enough not to sit down or pitch my tent directly under a tree pregnant with skull-cracking nuts. For a long while I sat up tending a small mosquito-deterring fire of discarded coconut husks. Over a palm-covered motu, I watched the moon rise, seemingly suspended in the lagoon between sea and sky. Surf breaking on the reef miles away became a visible white line. Warm trade winds stirred the palms, their long fronds waving and shadowboxing in the faint light. I felt I understood Gauguin when he wrote: "The lofty coconut trees lift up their plumes, and man does likewise." Deeply I breathed in the perfumed island air. This, at last, was my Bora Bora!

In the morning I was awake before the soft glow of predawn. The sun would soon rise over the same motu that birthed last night's moon. Before it did, I was on the road again. Though written for a harsher land and hardier breed of traveler than myself, I couldn't help but place myself in John Masefield's poem as I continued my trek around the island:

> There is no solace for us,
> For such as we,
> Who search for some hidden city
> We shall never see ...
> Instead there is only the road,
> The Dawn and the Wind and the Rain
> And the Watchfire under the stars,
> Then sleep...
> And the road again.

The walking was so effortless that I gave in to the temptation to climb the central mountain peak that loomed constant above my left shoulder ever since beginning my counterclockwise walk at Viatepe. A trail lured me up, and then disappeared. I continued moving up through thick brush. A vertical stone cliff face forced a detour. In another place, I entered a mass of hanging roots from trees seemingly rooted in air. Grasping suspended vines for balance, I stepped, then swung like an orangutan, from root to branch until I looked down to see I was well above the ground in a net-like tangle of vegetation. I went as high as the rocks and trees rose. I guessed I was on or near the summit, though I had no way of knowing, for the trees and roots had me completely boxed in.

Later that day, I gazed up at that broad perpendicular cliff face from the deck of my boat in the lagoon. The geologic story of this island was as clear as the scene before me — an epic of perpetual struggle between land and sea. This island, with its peak eroding into the lagoon, showed itself older than Hiva Oa, younger than the atolls of the Tuamotus. Ephemeral islands begin as newly born volcanic peaks pushing up from ocean depths, and like a man, make their stand for a time against the elements, before sinking again from erosive forces, to live and die in infinitely slow motion.

After seven dream-filled days in Bora Bora, I returned alone to the sea and once again set aside the shore-going mask we've all learned to wear in society. I laid a course for the islands of Tonga, 1,500 miles to the west.

7 These Friendly Isles

Few men who come to the islands leave them;
they grow grey where they alighted;
the palm shades and the trade-wind fans them till they die...

R. L. Stevenson

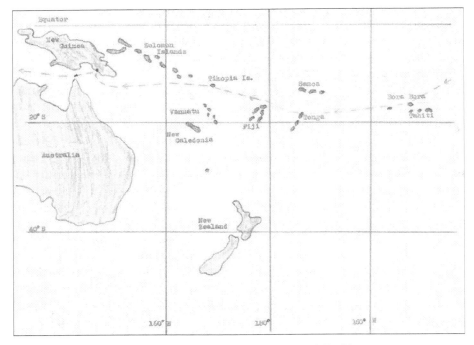

Atom's course across the western South Pacific

With wind, current and sun all behind her, *Atom* shot out the coral-guarded inlet and away from Bora Bora. A day later, we approached Motu One, a single, lonely low atoll directly on my course line for Tonga. In retrospect, I could have laid a course farther north to safely avoid it, but I hoped to sight the island during daylight to confirm my position; an island sighted and confirmed being worth more to a navigator than a supposed position on paper. In this case, I was counting on a couple of well-timed star sights to guide me past. Then, as the clouds rolled in, I put the sextant away for the night.

Vava'u Island, Tonga

I assumed the island was 20 miles ahead, yet I could not be sure. To be cautious, I hauled in the sheets, swung *Atom* into the wind, and reluctantly hove-to for nine hours. With this fair wind, I had given up 50 miles of easy progress during the night. Better the lost miles than to pile headlong onto an unseen reef. As it turned out, ocean currents combined with our drift to carry us halfway to the island during the night.

This leg of my Pacific crossing was to Tonga's Vava'u Island; the last stop before crossing the vague ethnographical line between

Polynesia and Melanesia. At dawn, I sighted a line of green marking an island so low that the coconut palms looked to be rooted in the sea. Passing this danger marked the boundary of French Polynesia, and I packed away my French dictionary until next year.

With the wind steady from the east, I set up my running rig. One reef in the mainsail, pushed all the way out to starboard, balanced with the number two jib held out to port on the spinnaker pole. This slowed the boat by about one knot from what she could do under full sail, but the wind vane steered a better course at this lower speed, and with less sail up there was more time to react to rising winds or a chance midnight squall. With *Atom* looking after herself, the hours and days drifted by as I tucked into my books, performed sets of deep knee bends and push-ups between the bunks, mended sails and generally got back into my sea-going routine.

I grew to appreciate the compact world within a small boat. Within two steps of my bunk I could reach all my tools and possessions. This was convenient living, everything within arms reach of everything else. When I felt the need for more space, I walked ten steps from the cockpit to the bow and clung with one hand on the forestay, scanning the wide-open western horizon.

I attempted a haircut on the foredeck with dull scissors and no mirror. Using my fingers to judge the evenness of the length, I kept snipping in corrections until I was mostly bald. With no crew on board I was not in the least embarrassed, and I would have nearly two weeks to sprout a less scary-looking head of hair before going ashore. It became a habit of mine to cut my hair nearly to the scalp at the beginning of each long passage. I saved water and shampoo and found this ritual shearing of the crew in some way symbolic of the rebirth and new beginnings each passage represented. I also took to wearing, if nothing else, a wide-brimmed straw hat to prevent sunburn.

The moon was waning, rising later each night and showing smaller slices of itself until, within a few days, it disappeared. As compensation for losing my lunar companion, the star watching was all the better without the competition of moonlight. The strange patterns of stars visible to the south were still new to me. To learn to recognize them in their constellations, I stayed up on deck many fair nights referring to star charts with a penlight held between my teeth.

Running down the Trades

A broach at seven knots jolts me back from my mental wanderings among the stars of the Southern Cross. Too much sail, tuck in another reef. *Atom* settles down on her course and I take seven hours of sleep interspersed with hourly peeps through the hatch to confirm all is well with course and sails and the unlit path ahead. By morning the winds were caressing the sea so gently that I hoisted all sail and we crawled along at two miles to the hour all the day through. The relative stability of our stance on the water gave a good opportunity for baking bread. I managed to turn out a lumpy loaf of oatmeal bread by placing a baking dish inside a large aluminum pot, strapped down on the kerosene stove rail as a makeshift oven. On most days, pan-fried cornbread was the easier recipe on a rolling boat.

During our slow crawl across the sea, I spent some hours lying flat on deck with eyes trained over the side, dangling a hand into the water and watching the ecosystem trailing under the boat. Small fish sought sanctuary close to the hull until chased away by larger tuna and dorado, which also kept station around the hull for days at a time. The

Spanish called them dorado (the golden ones) because their flanks flash gold among their many colors. They break away at a blinding speed to inhale an unwary flying fish, and then fall back in patrol formation under the shadow of the hull.

A year earlier, I would have set a lure or gone for my spear gun at the sight of this potential meal. For now I was an observer, not a hunter, and welcomed the shared company. When living alone on the sea and blessed with abundant stores of food on board, even fish became precious companions. Like using a fast to strengthen the spirit and purify the body, I felt stronger through my odd disciplines.

I had lived higher up the food chain and would do so again. For now, I lived a more passive coexistence in the world. There's no way to feel this state of being, alone in the sea-world, or even to understand it, if you spend most of your days and nights hidden within the walls and roof of a house, then take a car to an office or factory. Men have stood on the moon and told us about it, yet what do we really know of how it feels to stand on the moon?

After passing Palmerston Atoll – a tiny islet in an otherwise empty spot of the ocean – the barometer took a quick dip. Nothing to worry about since cyclone season is months away, I told myself, as the wind freshened and backed to the north. Cataracts of rain came down on us. The wind kept backing into the northwest, indicating the center of the disturbance would pass to my south. It was confirmed that night by lightning displays in the southern sky. At midnight the second squall line caught me asleep. *Atom* heeled sharply, then, overpowering her wind vane, turned into the wind as flogging sails shook her rig. Seconds after being comfortably asleep, I was battling a wildly flapping jib that nearly threw me over the side before I got it down to the deck. Try pulling a bed sheet off a clothes line in a hurricane at night, while walking on ball bearings, and you'll get an idea of the awkward ballet I performed.

The squall passed quick as it came but I didn't trust the weather and hove-to until dawn when the storm had visibly passed, replaced by a faint resemblance of the normal trade winds. For the next two days, there was only the lightest puffs of air from astern. By using the light spinnaker and some hand-steering, while constantly adjusting the sail trim to the fickle breeze, I made acceptable progress.

A flock of sea birds, probably terns of some type, kept me amused with their fishing antics. As *Atom* cleaved the calm waters, small fish scattered ahead of us. When a bird hovering at masthead height caught sight of a fish, he cocked back his wings in a vertical dive, hitting the water like a missile. They usually emerged with their prize clenched in their beaks. Tuna were also in high spirits for some reason, taking to the air in arching leaps and nearly landing on deck a few times.

The sunsets off the bow were, if possible, even more unbelievable than any before. The red, yellow and whites of the pulsing spinnaker cloth matched the shifting tones on the horizon behind it. To the north, spiked clouds indicated a distant mountain range that my charts told me were pure illusion.

Now and again, usually a few times on each passage, the earth's atmosphere struck just the right balance to produce the sailor's fabled Green Flash. But it's no fable, despite the claims of color-blind or otherwise unseeing sailors who claim it's a myth. In simple scientific terms, the atmosphere at the horizon acts on the setting sun as a filter for the rainbow spectrum contained in visible light. With red blocked by the horizon, and orange, yellow, blue and violet scattered by molecules and absorbed by the atmosphere, green is left as the last prominent wavelength for the observer. It takes a clear sky with the right amounts of moisture and pollution-free clarity of air to bring off a good green flash. Being near the tropics helps. To know a thing you must see it first, and to see you must look with an open mind.

The setting sun, having made its flashy departure, handed the sky over to Venus, which glowed low in the west next to a sliver of new moon. Arching back across the heavens were the familiar celestial lanterns of Saturn, Mars and Jupiter. I took a sextant shot at Jupiter, bringing her down to the water with the mirrors. A few calculations produced a satisfying line of position on the plotting chart. To add more certainty to the position, I shot three prominent stars as well, all done during the half hour of twilight while there was still a discernible horizon.

To the uninitiated, the practice of celestial navigation is both archaic and mysterious. A brief description will dispel some of the mystery. First, the star is identified, either through memory of its position in a constellation learned by referring to star charts, or by pre-computing likely visible stars referenced in a book titled *Selected Stars*. Then, the sextant is used to bring it down to a dimly visible horizon. This is done by rocking the sextant's arm and making final fine adjustments to the vernier screw knob to bring the mirrored image of the star down to touch the horizon during the single second that the boat crests a wave. The instant of this event is noted to the nearest second. And it is a meaningful moment, considering that a few seconds off could result in a position error of a mile or more.

The sight reduction tables are then referenced, using the sextant altitude reading in degrees, the exact time, and an assumed (guessed at) position in latitude and longitude. Using the tables and making some twenty sets of simple addition and subtraction, a position line is obtained. Two of these position lines make a fix. Three is better. The precision of a two star fix taken in average conditions cannot be assumed to be better than about three miles, depending on the accuracy of your clock and sextant, and your skill using it. The tight triangle of a three star fix may get you within a mile or two at best. And that is as good as it gets.

To those who know, celestial navigation remains a mark of competency that sets a true navigator apart from merely a satellite-guided sailor – one who wouldn't have the remotest chance of finding a not-so-remote island a few miles off their bow if they happen to lose their GPS. This, and lesser calamities, causes today's adventure-averse sailors to reach for the rescue beacon.

From my journal of August 28 comes the following entry:

> *I crossed the International Dateline last night and advanced from Tuesday directly to Thursday. So for me, Wednesday the 29th never existed. The strange part is that the time zone Tonga belongs to puts those islands geographically firmly in Tuesday. Yet by some creative bending of the dateline, Tonga declares they are in Thursday. Then they set their clocks to minus 13 hours from Greenwich Time, bringing them briefly to…Wednesday?*

Even though I understood the necessity of the date change, I was somewhat confused with the mechanics of it and was perhaps unreasonably mourning my lost Wednesday.

Thirteen days after departing Bora Bora, I approached the northern coast of Vava'u Island. The steep shoreline exhibited white scars of landslips here and there. On the western coast, I passed through deep passages between bold rocky islets and the main island in a scene looking more like a Scandinavian fjord, except these valleys were cloaked in sun-soaked grooves of coconut palms and tropical gardens. The channel wound around to a landlocked bay where I laid *Atom* alongside the concrete quay in downtown Neiafu to clear in with customs and immigration.

Two large Tongan officials asked only a modest three dollar fee for port charges, then returned to their card game as I moved *Atom* further into the harbor to the yacht anchorage off the Paradise Hotel. For four dollars a week I had the use of the Hotel's dinghy dock and freshwater tap, the swimming pool and showers, even a movie once a week in the lounge, all unexpected luxuries.

This last remaining Polynesian monarchy, which regally calls itself The Kingdom of Tonga, contains over 150 significant islands in three main groups, stretching 200 miles along Polynesia's western margin. To the south is the country's capital city, Nuku'alofa ("The Abode of Love"). Other sailors had warned me that Nuku'alofa was not so lovely as its name implied – more of a congregation of squatter settlements. Not an abode of love so much as the abode of natives who have migrated to the capital in search of things they wouldn't find, though they have seen enough of tourists bearing traveler's checks and unceasing demands.

The central group, called Ha'apai, is a cluster of dot-like islands where Captain Bligh stopped to take on water just before his crew mutinied and set him adrift. The northern group of Vava'u, where I landed, was seldom visited by Westerners before one of the better known visitors here a few centuries earlier wrote in his diary:

> [Because of] "the friendly behaviour of the Natives who
> seemed to vie with each other in doing what they thought
> would give us pleasure...this group I have named the

*Friendly Archipelago as a lasting friendship seems to
exist among the Inhabitants and their Courtesy to
Strangers entitles them to that name."*

Little did Captain Cook know, the local chief was craftily planning
to make them feel at ease, then catch them off-guard, murder the
sailors and capture their ships. Cook left his "Friendly Islands" just
before the plans could be carried out. And though this nickname is
still used and applies very well to today's Tongans, at least a few of the
early European visitors might have said that "The Treacherous
Islands" would better describe the natives' disposition.

The best known of the unlucky ships to visit these islands was the
500 ton, three-masted square rigger, *Port-au-Prince*. In 1806, the ship
was roaming the South Pacific indulging in a bit of whaling and
piracy when they headed to Tonga to make repairs. Unfortunately for
them, they anchored off the island of Lifuka, the same island Cook
had stopped at in the *Endeavor*, 30 years before. The islanders had
patiently waited and plotted for Cook's return. This time the Friendly
Islanders would not miss their chance.

As the crew repaired the ship's leaking hull, Lifuka's chief came
aboard bearing gifts, welcoming the captain to visit ashore.
Meanwhile, hundreds of Tongans armed with clubs and spears
climbed aboard the *Port-au-Prince*. Captain Brown refused to believe
they were in any danger because, after all, hadn't the great Captain
Cook himself named these the Friendly Islands? Captain Brown then
stepped into a canoe, was taken ashore, and clubbed to death. The
natives on board screamed *Maté! Maté!* (Kill! Kill!) and quickly
massacred most of the crew. The fate of Captain Brown should make
a cautious sailor a bit skeptical of island descriptions in pilot books
and cruising guides.

Since none of the Tongans knew how to sail their prize ship, they
beached it and stripped it of every piece of metal they could find. To
stone-aged Tongans, any metal was of such rarity and usefulness that
they burned the ship to collect the iron, bronze and copper bolts that
fastened her timbers. Of the few crew who were spared and kept as
slaves was 15-year-old Will Mariner. Chief Finau took a liking to
young Will, adopting him as his son and giving him the name Toki.

Will quickly learned the Tongan language and ingratiated himself with the chief by teaching his warriors how to fire the cannons salvaged from the *Port-au-Prince*. With Will's help, Chief Finau became ruler of all the Tongan Islands. In gratitude, Will was made a chief himself and given a plantation on Vava'u Island where he lived four years until a visiting ship picked him up and returned him to England. Today, white men are still referred to in Tonga as *Papalangi* ("Sky-Burster") after the incredible tall rigs of the sailing ships that rose over their horizon 250 years ago.

At the yacht anchorage, a man named Matoto watched my arrival from shore and paddled out in his canoe to welcome me to Vava'u. For $5 per person ($3 if you don't eat the lobster, he told me) Matoto organized a "traditional" Tongan feast at nearby Ano Beach. That Saturday, a small bus took ten of us from the visiting yachts to a secluded beach. When we arrived, a band of guitar, banjo, ukulele, wooden drums and a screechy violin were warming up.

We sat under the palms by the beach and watched a solo dancer as she played out an ancient story with intricate, graceful hand motions and subtle movements of her ankle-garlanded feet. Then she was joined by other girls also decorated with flowers, shells and beads over their pareos. Honey-colored skin shone with a generous coating of coconut oil. Their bodies swaying to the music captivated me like underwater coral sea-fans set in motion by surf passing close overhead. Hands and feet moved in a gentle wave-like motion, as hypnotizing to the sailor as the roll of the ocean. The women then performed another dance peculiar to Tonga, sitting cross-legged on the grass, their hands, arms and shoulders moving in precise unison.

Some of us swam off the beach while our hosts placed the food in a rock-lined fire-pit oven. Before sunset, we sat Polynesian-style, cross-legged on *pandanus* mats, while the unearthed food was carried out on long trays of plaited palm fronds. In front of us were heaped piles of lobster, octopus, fish, a whole roast pig, fruit salads of papaya, mango and pineapple with coconut cream. My hands quickly fell to the corn, taro, breadfruit, yams, cassava and sweet potatoes, all locally grown in the sun-blessed island of Vava'u. We ate, each according to his taste and capacity, until we fell back, one by one, in satiated bliss. It was noon the following day before I could think of eating again, and then it was from the basket of leftover vegetables Matoto insisted I take home with me. Poor Captain Brown arrived 180 years too early.

An itch to find the untouristed Tonga led me to fill my backpack with camping equipment and set out to walk to Longamapu Village located at the end of the road that wanders across Vava'u. I walked along a shady lane, past villages, hills and bays with dreamy, soft-sounding names like Taoa, Faleolo, Ha'akio and Feletoa. In the small villages, I never passed anyone without being greeted. If a Tongan who knew some English spotted me, I was obliged to stop and visit. They were the most socially inquisitive people I had ever met. If I responded to their, "Hello," with the Tongan version, "Malo E Leilei," they smiled hugely and asked all sorts of personal questions in a friendly way that came natural to them.

The standard questions were asked, in the same order everywhere, almost as if they were checking off points in a survey: where was I going, where was I coming from, my name, marital status, family size, and so on. Each greeting was conducted like a job interview and all the while I was scrutinized from head to toe, with a sympathetic smile. Actually, it was wonderful to partake in these interviews with total strangers, even if the questioning was mostly one-sided. It was a first step in being recognized as something more than a tourist.

As I walked through the village of Tefesi, a teen-aged boy with the Tongan curly mop of black hair introduced himself as Malakai and instantly decided to join me for the walk to Longamapu. He knew little more of English than I knew of Tongan, but by referring to my phrase book we had a type of conversation. More out of desire to practice Tongan than any real need to know, I asked in Tongan, "Are we close to Longamapu yet, Malakai?"

"Yes, close."

A mile farther down the road I tried, "Is it one more mile?"

"Yes, one more mile," was the smiling response.

So we walked at a fast clip for two and a half more hours. "That was some mile, my friend!"

Tongans, I learned, have an overwhelming urge to answer "yes" merely to be agreeable. Why disappoint the temperamental, demanding foreigners with a "no?" To Tongans, agreement is more highly valued than accuracy, which is maddening to tourists. After I got used to it, I learned how to phrase my questions more carefully and avoid inquiries that only showed my impatience.

As we walked, I saw that most of these gently-sloped hillsides were in cultivation with one crop or another. Wide groves of taro, cassava, yams and bananas bordered the road until it ended at Port of Refuge Bay by the village of Longamápu. We walked down to the seashore where I staked out my tent and Malakai built a fire on the beach. When the driftwood burned down to red embers, we tossed in a whole breadfruit to bake. A few minutes on each side to burn the skin black and we rolled it out of the fire with a stick and cracked it in half to eat the soft, bread-like center pulp. Actually, the texture and taste were like a combination of yam and bread. As we ate, several people from the village came to join us bringing papaya and oranges to share. Will Mariner had been chief with a plantation here, but not a single local person I spoke to had ever heard the story of the white Chief Toki. For all I knew my hosts may have even had a few drops of Will Mariner's blood in their veins.

A man in his early 20s, named Ilangi Vea, looked long at my tent and asked if I really was going to sleep in that "thing." He warned that the south wind would be cold at night so would I please stay with his family in the village. Nights in Tonga couldn't get cold enough for my liking but, seeing no clubs in their hands, I was happy to go along. The hospitality in the islands, like the solitude found at sea, increases as a direct function of your distance from the crowded cities.

On top of a hill overlooking the bay, Ilangi led me to a two-room thatched house that sheltered his family of nine. In the grassy yard was a single breadfruit tree that reached over to shade the house from the afternoon sun. Inside was not a single piece of furniture. The floor of crushed coral was covered with finely woven mats. These houses are light and airy, but must be rebuilt every second or third year as they weather and dry out. Last year's hurricane, called cyclones in the South Pacific, took many of the houses down early. Since then, some of the people here switched from thatch to tin roofs, which are less work, last longer, and are more secure, but make a horrible racket in a heavy rain. Some of the richer families have burdened themselves with homes built of cement blocks and tin roofs. These are both noisy in the rain and unbearably hot in the sun; their sole attributes being their longevity and the relative sanctuary of cement walls during cyclones.

The island's electrical grid had not yet reached Longamapu Village. As darkness fell, the kerosene lamps and cooking fires lit up the open doorways of each home. Ilangi and his brother unhooked a guitar and ukulele from the thatched wall and played Tongan songs with the rest of the family singing along. I don't know how long they played. I was tired from the five-hour walk and the sweet sounds sent me to sleep under a rough *tapa* blanket made from pounded tree bark.

I was awakened by the Polynesian pre-dawn concert of crowing roosters and barking dogs. This was replaced with the sound of chopping wood to fire the kettles for morning tea. From nearby homes came the sweet choral singing of Tongans joyously greeting a new day. We sipped tea brewed from the dried leaves of a neighbor's orange tree. Ilangi and Malakai took me to the community house where women were painting patterns on tapa cloth and gluing lapped edges together to form long sheets used for blankets, clothing and wall coverings. The cloth comes from the *haipo*, a type of mulberry tree, which are planted and carefully tended for two years until they mature. The bark is then stripped off and the soft, white inner layer is hung to dry in the sun. Then it is beaten flat and thin with a wooden mallet. Two of these pieces are fixed back-to-back with arrowroot glue. Traditional geometric designs, or the Tongan coat of arms, are then painted on using black and brown dyes from the sap of mangrove roots.

The women also weave handsome baskets and mats from specially prepared pandanus leaves. Tongans wear these mats, called *ta'ovala*, around their waists. Under that, the men wear a knee-length skirt of patterned cloth. Women's skirts were all ankle-length. It had surprised me to see the bank manager, wearing a white shirt and black tie, stand up from behind his desk to reveal the ta'avola mat around his waist on top of a skirt. This was the formal attire in Tonga.

A basket takes shape in a Tongan home

When I left Longamapu, Ilangi made a gift to me of the tapa blanket I had slept under the night before. I had made the mistake of openly admiring the blanket and now was obliged to take it, according to custom. I thanked him and presented him the only extra shirt I had with me and carefully folded the multi-layered cloth into my pack.

On the way back to Neiafu I traveled a different, higher route that offered a better view. Norfolk pines lined the ridges and family-sized plantations patterned the hillsides. I happily lost myself in the tonk-tonk rhythm of ironwood mallets sounding throughout the valley as women pounded the tapa over logs. Each hour or so a passing vehicle would stop to offer me a ride. It was as if they had never seen anyone walking long and far just for the enjoyment of it. I thanked them for the offer, answered their barrage of questions, and continued walking so I could better appreciate the slowly unfolding landscape. You can always drive to your destination, but a true journey is made on foot.

Over a century ago, King George Tupuo's Land Act gave each male Tongan a parcel of land upon reaching his 16th year. That piece of land was 100 *ofa* square, an ofa being the span of the king's outstretched arms. As long as the man farms it and pays a small tax, he can keep it. None of this land could be sold; in title it still belongs to the crown. Today, with the growing population, these land grants have likely been reduced, if not stopped altogether.

Although Tonga was a British protectorate for a time, mainly in order to keep it out of the grasping colonial hands of Germany and France, the country craftily managed to retain its sovereignty. The ruler at the time of my visit was King Taufa Ahau Tupuo IV, who took over in 1965 after his mother, Queen Salote, died. Tupuo IV is of kingly size, well over 300 pounds, and was reported to be a skillful surfer, at least in his younger and slightly leaner years.

A Tongan friend invited me to the Kava Club in Neiafu on Friday night. The mildly narcotic kava drink is made from the root of a pepper shrub, traditionally prepared by virginal maidens who chewed the roots to soften them. The saliva-soaked roots were then squeezed into bowls of water to extract the kava. Either kava-chewing virgins are now a rarity, or spit-flavored kava has gone out of favor. Today, the drink is prepared by beating them with clubs (the roots, not the virgins!) and the powder placed in a mesh screen and squeezed into a pail of water. It comes out looking and tasting like stagnant muddy ditch water – just as they like it. They drink this in a social way, much as we do coffee or beer. It numbs the mouth and its strange earthy flavor is, what we might call, an acquired taste.

The kava clubhouse held over a hundred men sitting on mats, in groups of five to ten, around huge wooden bowls that servant girls refilled with kava by the bucketful. A girl kneeled behind each bowl, scooping out a half coconut shell full of kava to one person at a time. Each man swallowed the brew in one gulp, and ritualistically threw the cup to the floor to be picked up by the server and refilled for the next person. With some effort, I held back from spraying the first mouthful all over my smiling hosts. I then threw the cup down with perhaps a little more enthusiasm than was called for. So we sat, hour after hour, the kava cup making countless rounds. Actually, I did count, and it tasted considerable better after the fifth cup when my mouth was completely numb.

I had read the story of a young American sailor who visited Tonga and was served kava by a girl named Foi'atelolo, meaning "fat liver full of oil." That is some flattering name considering the Tongans love of oily food, especially pig's liver. Tongans start out slender in their youth but grow quite large, sometimes enormously so, as they mature. A woman's beauty is measured in kilos, with those at the heavy end of the scale being most highly prized by Tongan men.

Between gulps from the kava cup, the men told stories and spread the latest gossip. As the only Westerner there, I was urged to use my numb tongue to tell our group about myself and why I was in Tonga. With one of the men acting as interpreter, they queried (you might say quarried) every nugget of detail from my story. My tales of sailing among the isles of the Pacific seemed to stir in these men some atavistic memories of their warrior ancestors who voyaged throughout the central Pacific to conquer or settle new lands. Sadly, the voyaging canoes are no more, though the faint longing for a voyage beyond their home island lives on.

After each ten rounds of kava, a collection was taken up for the evening feast with each group trying to outbid the others. The groups gave themselves names like The Fishermen, and The Sailors, and the amounts they donated were tallied and called out to keep the competition going. Some of the money would go to the local college, whose brass band was booming and blaring British marching songs right outside our door to insure we could not forget them at donation time. In my honor, our group chose the name Amerika, and I in return, emptied my pocket of its few coins and bills. They may have thought Amerika would be at the top of the cash donation list. Instead, when the speaker read off the fnal tally, it was The Fishermen over The Amerikans at $35 to $27. When I stood up to leave, I found the numbness had spread from my tongue down to my feet. As I left, my fellow Amerikans loaded me down with a basket of food to bring back to my boat.

That same weekend I went to sample another feast on the beach. This time a different group performed, the girls dancing wave-like in the center with athletic young men leaping about in frenzied accompaniment. Then the men alone performed the *kailao*, the Tongan war dance. Drums beat out a steady rhythm as the men stomped the ground, kicking up sand, grimacing and shouting, their leafy costumes rustling as they swung wicked-looking war clubs at their imagined enemy. Next, a long-haired man with a wild set of eyes and two twirling machetes leapt out in front of us. After dark, he came back and did some tricky juggling of flaming clubs.

This feast and dancing went on for six hours after which, we all piled into the back of a pick-up truck for the ride back to town. When the paid guests had filled the truck to capacity, the musicians squeezed in around us. Then the dancers, the cooks and the women selling handicrafts wedged their way in with their piles of gear. Those who couldn't get on top of us hung along the sides. As we bounced down the dark, rutted road, the Tongans sang at full vigor, even the old woman with a breaking voice tried to be heard above the rest. Leading the singers was the crazy-eyed fire dancer, who finding no other spot available, was sitting on my lap like an overgrown infant.

Matoto invited me to visit his church with his family on Sunday. Everyone on Vava'u Island was devoutly Christian. Even the smallest village had at least two churches. There are Mormons, Seventh day Adventists, Free Weslayans, Catholics and other more obscure groups represented. The Adventist church believes Sunday in Tonga is actually Saturday, despite the man-made deviation of the International Dateline (*Atom's* navigator agrees!) and so hold their services on Sunday instead of their usual Saturday meetings. It's not clear to me if they live the rest of the week twenty-four hours behind their neighbors or if the dual dates are only necessary for the religious calendar.

Introducing Christianity here had been a deadly task. In 1797, the London Missionary School landed ten missionaries on Tongatapu Island. They were welcomed at first and promised protection by the chiefs. They soon discovered the natives were more interested in stealing their supplies and tools than in saving their souls. Two years later, civil war broke out across Tonga and three of the missionaries were murdered by the natives. The rest were burned out of their houses and fled to the coast where they lived in caves for a year until a passing ship picked them up. Years later, they tried again and eventually they baptized the chief, giving him the name George, after the King of England. Following the royal example, Tongans flocked to Christianity, embracing it with the zealous fervor of the newly converted.

The missionaries have unquestionably brought peace and order to the islands. They have also reversed the natural and ancient customs of the Tongans. Even today, the women discreetly cover their bodies from neck to ankle, even when swimming. The Tongan dancing is mostly reserved for paying tourists. Men on this tropical island are forbidden to go shirtless in public! The liberal-minded Gauguin had no idea how good he had it in French Polynesia.

Church bells ring out to announce services for one denomination or another nearly every day of the week. Everywhere is heard the songs of practicing choirs. Sundays immobilize the island like a general anesthetic. No work or shopping is permitted. It is possible you might be arrested for fishing on a Sunday, and shame on the couple caught holding hands on any day of the week. When cultures as fragile as those of Oceania are overturned by a foreign civilization, these vigorous-hearted people may be inclined to take the instructions of the new deity to extremes. Not even Mohamed himself could have done a better job of straitjacketing a pagan culture.

My friend Matoto belonged to the Free Weslayan Church in the village of Pangiamotu. The wooden building's large open windows let in the light and air and let out the music of the choir. The congregation, wearing their finest clothes, sat barefoot on floor mats. When they sang it was like the angels of heaven in ecstasy. I'd never heard 30 mouths sing so loud with such rich voices and perfect timing without musical accompaniment, effortlessly holding a four-part harmony. During the sermon, the preacher slashed at the air with his arms to punctuate an emotional speech, but since his words, and the songs he directed, were all in Tongan, his passionate message flew over my head.

After the service, I shook hands with the entire congregation and then followed Matoto to his house for the big Sunday dinner they had begun preparing on Saturday. Again, I surprised myself by overeating and had to sit back to catch my breath and wonder if this gluttony was a sign that my own cooking was lacking something. But then, it could be that overindulgence in all manner of things is the natural state of a sailor on shore leave.

I asked Matoto about the abundance of food on this island. Plantations thrived everywhere. Sugar, flour, and tinned meats and fats were at the top of their imports. Many Tongans were obese and burdened with one of the world's highest incidences of diabetes. There were little, if any, crops exported and the island's sole vegetable market was overstocked. Matoto explained that this year they did have a surplus, though with the vagaries of the weather and the occasional cyclone, some years many of the crops failed. They could not predict what would happen from one year to the next. Judging by the size of the people, they had enjoyed some bountiful years recently.

In Matato's house there were four heavy sacks of taro roots harvested from his own garden. "Will you sell some of your surplus at the market?" I asked.

"No, this I will share with my friends," he said, then went on to explain, "The Ha'apai group of islands south of here also produced more than they needed this year. Because they are poor, we let them sell their crops here."

In Tonga, the essentials of life; from food, to spirituality, to friendship, are available in abundance.

8 Tikopia Unspoilt

*Fired by lust for adventure and the desire to see new
lands, canoe after canoe set out and ranged the seas. Fear
of storms and shipwreck leaves them undeterred. The
reference of an ancient song to the loss of a man at sea
as a 'sweet burial' expresses very well the attitude of the
Tikopians.*

-Raymond Firth – anthropologist, 1936

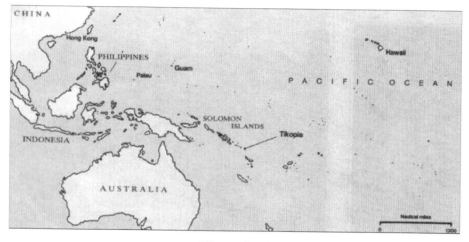

Western Pacific

I had settled on a course towards New Guinea, still some 2,700
miles away, with cyclone season approaching soon. My course was first
set northwest to avoid the labyrinth of reefs around the Fiji Islands.
Several days out of Tonga, I awoke from an afternoon nap to an odd
tapping sound on the hull. Visitors, here? On deck I saw we were
moving through a field of floating stones covering the ocean like a
blanket as far as I could see. I reached into the water to pull out a fist-
sized piece of pumice and examined its light, porous structure.

Thumbing through the *British South Pacific Pilot* gave me an
explanation. I read that in 1928, between Fiji and Tonga, several ships
reported encountering fields of floating pumice – lava rock – that later

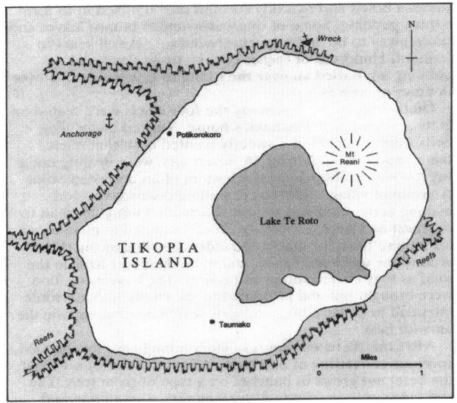

Tikopia Island

washed up in huge quantities on the eastern coasts of the Fiji Islands.
The *Pilot* went on to give this report by *HMS Veronica*:

> *The first large field encountered was fully three quarter
> mile wide. The effect on the sea was most marked, a
> choppy sea with breaking waves reduced by the pumice to
> a mere oily swell. The pumice was mostly the size of
> gravel, a few lumps up to two feet in diameter being
> observed. The swell caused it to make a noise like
> drifting sand. The field was not more than one foot
> thick, and it would only form serious resistance to very
> small craft. It removed all weed from the waterline,
> scrapped off some paint, and fouled the condenser inlet.
> The following day more fields were encountered, very
> thin and straggling, as far as we could see.*

It was clear the rock I held in my hand was recently molten lava, flowing deep within the earth, that had been ejected through an undersea vent. Because it was impregnated with numerous air pockets, it floated to the surface. Judging from the concentration of pumice I plowed through, one of these underwater volcanoes was not far away. I almost expected to see an island born before my eyes, but wherever it was, it remained hidden beneath the waves. Seeing the pumice was harmless at the slow speed we were moving, and was actually helping flatten out the waves, I carried on cleaving through this blend of earth and sea until breaking into clear water several hours later.

I learned later that, while I had been at sea, there was a huge volcanic eruption that transformed what used to be known as Tonga's Home Reef into the one-mile-long, 150-foot high, Home Island. There are uncharted islands out there, after all….

When well clear of Fiji's reefs, I breathed more easily and felt the familiar open ocean welcome me back to its endless empty horizons. We had sailed for seven days with the wind locked onto a single compass point – east by southeast. While the winds started feebly, they increased so gradually that I barely noticed the difference from day to day.

On day seven, I noticed a hole had chafed in the mainsail where it rubbed against the mast spreaders, and the jib was also starting to unravel at one of its seams. A half day working with leather palm and needle, pulling the thread through a ball of wax to make it slide through the stiff layers of sailcloth, brought things back in order. By easing off the mainsail halyard, I used the slack between the sail slugs as steps to get me halfway up the mast where I hung on with one arm against the boat's motion as I taped over the cotter pin that had chafed the sail. The side-to-side whip of the mast was more violent than I expected. It took all of my strength to keep from being flung off. As the boat rolled, I had to stop at times and just hold on, wrapping my arms and legs, vine-like, around the mast. This was the only work I recall doing the entire week, but such ease wouldn't last.

The next day the wind fell calm, the sky grew overcast, and a series of rain squalls passed over *Atom*. I reefed and tacked, always alert to any wind shift. In this latitude, at this time of year, these low-pressure

areas pass by once every two to three weeks. I had hoped to slip
between them since one had passed through just before I'd left Tonga.
By now, I was used to their pattern: first the trades go light and shifty
as the barometer takes a fall; there follows two days or more of short,
but vicious squalls and heavy rains; the wind veers to the north, then
backs to the west, and the sky slowly begins to clear as the wind hauls
back to the southeast. Knowing these storms' patterns and behaviors
reduced my anxiety until it became routine sail-handling.

On the eleventh day out, as the rain cleared away, I picked out a
dark lump on the horizon. Slowly it grew to a green fortress
surrounded by coral reefs and lashing surf – Tikopia Island.

I had been aiming for this particular island, among all the islands
of the western Pacific, since the beginning of my voyage in Miami.
There, I first heard about Tikopia while reading the unpublished
journal of another circumnavigator. He wrote that this island was the
most fascinating of all the places he had visited. The population of
about 1,000 lived a traditional lifestyle without electricity, motor
vehicles, or even a single shop to buy food or merchandise. The four-
mile-wide island has no police force or immigration officers (bless'em).
The four clans of the island are ruled by four hereditary chiefs. No
airstrip, and a reef-lined anchorage only suitable for settled weather,
meant tourists were almost as rare as tropical snowstorms. It was just
what I had been seeking, but feared no longer existed.

From two miles offshore I scanned the shore of Tikopia through
the binoculars. The entrance to the anchorage marked itself with a
white line of surf rolling along a fringing reef. To the crowd gathering
on the beach, I was merely a small speck of sail on the horizon. As I
got closer, I could see people waving their arms above their heads.
Outrigger canoes were launched into the surf, the men pulling hard
on their paddles.

I was soon surrounded by the eager islander's canoes. Several men
and boys climbed aboard, handing me coconuts and papayas,
apparently the first things that were within reach when they sighted
my sail. I returned the favor by handing out fishhooks, which they
welcomed with smiles and bright eyes. At first they tried to
communicate with me in Solomon Island Pidgin English, which they

had picked up from visiting teachers and missionaries. Pidgin is a simplified English, stripped to its basics and beyond, and then reconstructed with a generous sampling of local dialect. A few German words have been tossed in as a legacy from the Kaiser's Colonial period.

Slowly, my ears began to recognize the local Tikopian dialect's similarities to Tongan. I had already memorized a hundred-odd words and phrases of Tongan so I was well on my way to basic communication. They indicated the excitement ashore was because I was the first yacht to visit the island in months, and only the fourth boat they had seen that year, aside from the monthly mail boat from the island group's capital city of Honiera. With the sailing season so far advanced, I might well be the last boat to stop here this year.

Guided through the menacing brown coral heads by canoes on either side of the bow, I tacked into the empty anchorage. The man in the lead canoe directed me to stop over a narrow sand patch where I dropped the main anchor. As the anchor bit into the sandy bottom, my Tikopian guide called out, "Malo e Leilei!" (Welcome) then came alongside where I handed him a second anchor to set out to keep *Atom* from swinging into the surrounding coral heads lying under the shallow waters.

One of my guides through the reefs was a young fisherman whose Christian name he gave as Joseph Roto. Through a combination of Pidgin and Tikopian, he made me to understand that although there were no "officials" to take my documents to, the local custom called for *palangi* (that would be me) to ask permission of one of the *teriki* (chiefs) before exploring the island. A gift for the chief, he added, would be customary.

After a few minutes securing anchors and sails, I stepped into Joseph's canoe and we paddled through the surf to land among a curious crowd on the beach at Potikorkoro Village. Many of the women were bare-breasted with plain tapa cloth skirts and wore their hair cut short as jar-head Marines. The men also wore tapa cloth or the brightly patterned cotton sarongs similar to the pareo of the French islands. In Pidgin, they are called *laplaps*. Beyond the beach a narrow, level plain butted up against vegetation-lined cliffs, giving little hint what lay beyond.

As we made our way through the village shaded by coconut and breadfruit trees, Joseph and his friends gave me more advice regarding local etiquette: first in importance being to never turn your back to a chief, never walk upright in his house and take care not to present your retreating bum to His Highness. Moving around on hands and knees was an easy rule to follow since the entrances to the thickly thatched grass huts are so low you are forced to crawl in on your belly. Traditionally, this low entranceway allowed householders to dispatch any unwelcome intruders with a club to the head as they made a clumsy entry.

Chief Tofua

The long, low hut of the chief was built around a foundation of heavy, vertical hardwood posts sunk into the sandy soil, supporting a framework of bamboo to which were fixed rows of plaited sago palm leaves. Outside the knee-high, doorless entrance, we stepped over two live sea turtles laid helpless on their backs where they would remain alive until dropped into the earth oven at the next feast.

As I entered, Teriki Tofua motioned from across the room for me to come to him. From my crawling position, the old man certainly looked dignified as he sat Buddha-like in front of other members of his clan on a palm mat laid on the sand floor. His arms and chest were covered in tattoos (tattoo is Polynesian, meaning "to puncture"). As he puffed on a clay pipe stuffed with pungent locally-grown tobacco, clouds of gray smoke hung in front of his deeply-lined and weather-roughened face and long, salt-and-pepper-colored, curly hair and beard. As is their custom, he set aside my gifts of fishing tackle and kava roots without examining or acknowledging them – an attitude I nearly mistook for dissatisfaction or bad manners. Maybe he actually was disappointed, because he then asked if I didn't have any whisky to give. Imagine, the mad palangi sails clear across the ocean alone and neglects to bring us whisky? Despite my poor provisioning, after a few questions about who I was and what I came here for, they set before me a basket of baked green bananas, breadfruit and taro roots as well as a reddish-orange ripe papaya. Eat more, they urged, and I did. After I was stuffed to everyone's satisfaction, Tofua welcomed me to travel wherever I wished, apart from one sacred valley behind the crater lake, which was *tapu*, or forbidden, to the palangi.

As I explored the island that first day, I discovered four separate clans, each represented by their own chief. In order of rank were Teriki Kafeka, Tofua, Taumako and Fangarere. I passed through each of their territories, meeting each chief and presenting them with fishing hooks and line which they felt obliged to ignore. In return, they fed me to the point I could barely walk.

The leeward side of the island, called Faea, houses three villages and the bay containing the partially sheltered anchorage. The windward side of the island, known as Ravenga, is larger and consists of five villages and a freshwater crater lake called Te Roto, lying in the island's center. Each of the four clans claim to have arrived here from different island groups many generations before the first white men entered the Pacific. Between Tonga and Fiji, I had sailed over the ethnic and cultural line between Polynesia and the darker skinned, kinky-haired people of Melanesia. Both types were recognizable here.

Chief Kafika and Chief Fangarere

With the chief Teriki Taumako I struck up an immediate friendship. He ruled the clan on the south coast near the lake. His ancestors came from Tonga and he had a friendly and sympathetic manner. After our first meeting, he asked me to come back the following day for another meal and a longer visit.

"What time should I come?" I asked in the universal gesture by pointing at my watch and raising my eyebrows.

Taumako at first held out a hand with upturned palm to indicate it was up to me. Then, seeing me hesitate, he realized I was of the watch-owning-tribe who couldn't function without a schedule. He pointed over his shoulder to a point in the sky indicating the position of a late afternoon sun. On an island of few timepieces, the sun was their celestial clock. I never again wore my watch on Tikopia. With that simple gesture, I dropped out of the clock-crazy world where people parcel up time so as to fulfill the demands of their punctual neighbors.

Freed from the need to keep appointments, I arrived early the next day at Taumako's house to assist in preparing the food, or at least see how it was done. The previous day, maybe half the women, men and children from the village had climbed up to their clan's mountain gardens to gather taro and cassava roots, green bananas and breadfruit, which they piled into baskets made of woven palm leaves to bring back to the village. As I arrived, the *umu* (earth oven) was cleared of the ashes from the previous fire and dozens of stones pulled out of the pit. Dry leaves, sticks and coconut husks were thrown in, followed by chopped logs. When the wood was fully ablaze, the stones were tossed on top of the fire.

Meanwhile, I helped the men reduce a pile of about fifty coconuts into heaping bowls of grated coconut by splitting and laboriously grating the white flesh on a serrated piece of iron fixed to the edge of our wooden stools. To make cream from the grated coconut, we packed it into stripped hibiscus bark fibers and twisted the mass back and forth until all the cream was extracted through our hands into deep wooden bowls. We shook the dry gratings out for the dogs and chickens to eat and repeated the process until we had three bowls full of rich, oily cream.

While we were grating the nuts, the fire burned down to glowing coals and white hot stones. The women used sticks to spread the stones evenly around the bottom and sides of the pit. This was fiercely hot work and perhaps one reason the women wore their hair clipped so short. Green, spade-shaped taro leaves were then laid over the stones, followed by root vegetables and bunches of green bananas and papayas. All this was covered with more leaves and allowed to bake in its own moisture for a few hours.

When the woman in charge of the umu signaled it was ready, we uncovered the smoldering pile of leaves and vegetables. The intense smoke and heat forced me to stumble out of the cooking hut gasping for air. The women seemed immune to it and soon had the vegetables piled into giant wooden bowls where we pounded them into a mush with the blunt ends of cut palm fronds. While we worked this huge mortar and pestle, others poured the cream on top until we had a uniform cheese-like pudding called *susua*. It was then wrapped into packets in taro leaves. From time to time, some of this susua was taken away to be buried in leaf-lined underground pits and left for several years to ferment. Hundreds of caches of this pungent pudding, called *masi*, are buried around the island to tide the people over in times of crop failure due to cyclones or drought.

I had my doubts about masi, until I unknowingly ate some that was offered to me and asked what it was. Taumako assured me this particular batch of masi had been dug up from the sandy earth after sitting there for seven years. Its taste was unique and not entirely as bad as it sounds, being something like a strong blue cheese, with a tangy flavor, but best eaten in small amounts.

That day, we filled fifteen baskets with vegetables and packets of susua that were distributed among the families in the Taumako clan. Each basket contained two days supply of food for each family. This whole communal operation is repeated every second day among all the villages on the island. Today's leftovers hung from the ceilings in their basket for tomorrow's meal. The islanders work their independent garden plots and then distribute the food equally among their clan, so that none go hungry. Even then, in the mid 1980s, Western influence regarding working for individual gain had caused this type of communal effort, in gathering and preparing of daily meals, to mostly disappear from the lives of other Pacific islanders.

Back in Taumako's house, the chief and I sat down to eat. Despite my cries of "Enough!" Taumako's wife and daughters continued to set more food before me. It was not possible to visit anyone here without being stuffed like the Thanksgiving turkey. Tikopians eat by the stomach, not by the clock, and their mostly vegetarian diet encourages them to eat long and often. The custom of sharing a meal with every casual visitor that happens by meant I was never lacking for food. It was actually a problem of too much, too often. I had so many invitations to visit each of the villages that I began to plan my visits according to when I could tolerate more food. If there were several stops to make, I would soon be so completely overfed I could hardly walk. Fortunately, there was a scarcity of sugar and meats on the island; it's hard to become seriously ill on too many baked vegetables.

When I asked Taumako about the best route to climb Mt. Reani, which is Tikopia's highest peak standing a modest 1,200 feet above the sea, he called for a teenaged boy, named Tivoli, to guide me. The next morning, Tivoli, bare-foot and wearing only a laplap, led me along a path that wandered in and out of villages, then along a beach strewn with boulders and stones of all sizes. I nearly ran to keep up with his sure-footed strides as our path twisted among, and sometimes over, the large boulders.

We passed under a vertical cliff of bare rock that stood with its base along the high tide mark of the beach. As we squeezed past, the trade wind funneled around the mountain with accelerated force, blasting us with sand picked up from the beach. Leaving the coast, we ascended a vine-laced trail, stepping aside frequently to let heavily-laden farmers descend with baskets of vegetables destined for the earth oven. They moved in swift, balanced steps, their toes gripping the loose rocks and soil.

As the trail grew less steep, we entered cultivated lots of fruit trees, assorted vegetables and tobacco plants. Tivoli halted now and then and used his long bush knife to point out some remarkable features of an especially fine garden. I'd copy down the names of everything he described in my growing Tikopian dictionary and reply so far as my limited vocabulary would permit.

From our perch on the grassy peak of Reani, one sweep of our eyes around the horizon took in the entire island kingdom.

Pale green and still, Lake Te Roto reflected the cliffs and lush hillsides that rolled down to its marshy edges. A solitary fisherman paddled his canoe – a gliding waterbug – across the lake. Formed in the crater of an extinct volcano, the lake is continuously fed by freshwater springs and occupies nearly a third of the island's area. Beyond the lake, framed between jumbled peaks and a narrow strip of beach, a line of white foam marks the reef. Past the breakers lies the cobalt blue of the *moana* (the deep sea), and the unbroken horizon. Even at the top of Reani, you cannot escape the mournful muted thunder of Pacific swells ending their multiple thousand-mile journey on the reefs of Tikopia. The trees on the mountainside leaned seaward like concert-goers listening to the pulse of the waves. The endless heartbeat of the sea, and the wide open horizon, continually reminds the islanders of their profound isolation.

Looking over the empty sea, Tivoli said something like, "Friend, when you leave here in your boat I will go with you." For the native peoples of Oceania, nothing could be worse than traveling alone. To be away from the protection and care of your family and clan meant you were vulnerable, miserable with worry and loneliness. Every native person I encountered in the Pacific found it incomprehensible that I was crossing the oceans alone for adventure, and to focus, undistracted by travel companions, on the peoples and places I visited. In his innocence, he assumed that his courageous offer would be automatically accepted. He only understood my decline of his offer when I told him he had no passport to travel. He seemed more relieved than disappointed at the news. Perhaps, for a brief moment, he felt the urgings of his ancestors to recapture the freedom of voyaging across the watery highways of the Pacific. This speck of wave-lashed land may be all of the world he would ever know. We stood there, each contemplating a life other than the one we had. Paradise or prison? For Tivoli, Tikopia was some of both.

As we returned to the friendly stir of the village, a boy messenger told me Teriki Taumako wished for me to visit him before returning to the boat. His village, Bot sa Taumako, sat on the edge of the lake with its back to the ocean. Entering the village we saw fishermen standing in the shallows using hand-lines to catch pan-sized fish.

Inside Taumako's house were all four of the island's chiefs and several village elders sitting around baskets of food. They had been having a meeting regarding preparations for an important event planned for a few days later. A month earlier, Chief Taumako's father had died, passing his title to his eldest son. Since then the islanders had observed a period of mourning with many activities declared tapu, including dancing and certain social events, out of respect for the dead chief. The end of mourning was to be marked by a large feast and celebration.

In front of the gathered crowd, Taumako honored me with a gift of a shell necklace carved in a bird-like design, called *temanga*, which is worn only by the island's chiefs. Long ago, travel among the widely spaced islands of the Pacific was fraught with dangers and a high risk of never returning home. Because of this, by custom, the chiefs of

Tikopia are not allowed to travel outside of their island unless the Solomon Islands government requests them for a meeting in Guadalcanal. This happens rarely, so they are naturally curious about other lands and people they will never see. As I sat on a woven mat with my back pressed against the hut's main support pole, I answered their questions about my travels.

Judging from the amazed and satisfied expressions of the audience, my interpreter was a skilled storyteller. I suspect that whenever my own narrative lacked in exciting events, he embellished it with exaggerated claims. The man had been educated for a few years in the capital of the Solomon Islands and was one of only a couple people on the island who spoke some English.

"Ask the palangi sailor if he was ever bothered by sharks," asked someone.

My simple answer of "No" was translated something like – "Bothered? This man has killed many sharks, sometimes with his bare hands!"

At one point, Chief Tofua made a speech to all present, claiming that I (he called me "Samesi" as the closest approximation to James that their language allowed) was a "willing man" and must belong to a royal bloodline, and wished me to verify the fact by admitting to them that my father was a chief. "No young man of the common class could have come so far alone," he asserted.

If I told them the truth, that as far as I knew, I came from what they would call the caste of commoners, it would not go over well. Perhaps my head was puffed up with all the attention poured on me and I feared being stripped of my chiefly necklace and privileges, as unlikely as that would have been. Thinking quickly, I remembered my grandfather had held public office as sheriff. So, I told them the little lie that yes, I had descended from a chief – not a great chief – but a type of chief, nonetheless. Chief Tofua nodded his head approvingly and the tension of the moment vanished.

Then they wanted to know why I did not eat the fish when it was offered. Was it forbidden by my religion? Another sticky question. Before, on other islands, when I clumsily tried to explain I did not eat meat out of compassion for animals, or a way to cleanse myself spiritually, I was considered to belong to a special class of lunatic. So again, I gave them an answer they could understand, that indeed my religion did forbid it. What I didn't say was that my religion was the study and love of nature, that my church had neither bible nor other members, and was a philosophy that evolved as I evolved.

While we spoke, the men continuously chewed betel nut. All over Oceania, tree-grown bunches of betel nuts are peeled of their husk and the soft inner nut chewed together with lime powder extracted from burnt seashells and a certain green plant leaf that neutralizes its bitter taste. A chemical reaction turns teeth and lips bright red and makes the mouth water with scarlet juice. The men here chew it endlessly, without sign of it affecting them. Tofua handed me a nut and some lime wrapped in a small leaf. I plunked the whole nut into my mouth, followed by the leaf, and began to chew. Within half a minute I was in a cold sweat, my heart pounding and head spinning, and a mouth filled with saliva that could not be swallowed. I stood up on rubber legs and staggered outside the hut to spit the nut and red juice into the sand, then took several deep breaths and came back inside to find my hosts greatly amused. Ha – some chief I turned out to be! Eventually, I, too, developed a tolerance to the betel nut, but though I chewed it many times to be sociable, I never acquired the islanders' insatiable taste for it.

Their questions turned to navigation techniques, which the elders knew were based on a knowledge of the position of certain stars that could point the way to those who could read them.

"Which star will you follow from here?" asked a man old enough to remember the long since abandoned two-day canoe trips to trade with relatives on Anuta Island, seventy-five miles away. I simplified my explanation of modern celestial navigation and said, "There is a star that rises over the big island of New Guinea and that is the way I will go." They knew of the island of New Guinea, though they did not know which stars could guide them there.

Until the islands of the Pacific were conquered and pacified by Westerners, the double-hulled sailing canoes ranged across this part of Oceania carrying native settlers and soldiers between Tonga, Samoa, Fiji and other island groups. Tongan chiefs even ruled outlying islands like Tikopia at times, demanding tribute from the local chiefs. Those great voyages are now only distant memories. Oddly, the modern native craft are frail, hollowed out logs with a bamboo outrigger attached, barely suitable for short trips across the harbor, let alone inter-island voyages. Somehow the Pacific peoples lost their boat-building and voyaging skills and became land-bound. But why? I could only think that it was Western civilization, with its dependable cargo boats and restrictions on inter-island raids and a thousand other discouragements. It simply wasn't worth the trouble any longer.

Between pauses for betel nut, one of the elders told of the islanders' encounter with the outside world during World War II. Many of the other islands in the Solomons, such as Guadalcanal, had suffered terrible destruction. The only soldiers to come to Tikopia were survivors of an American plane that ditched in the sea nearby. "The great bird fell out of the sky over there," the old man said while pointing past the reefs. Despite the shock of seeing their first airplane, the islanders had quickly launched their canoes and saved three of the flyers. Sadly, another four drowned. "We all cried for the dead men," he said as sincerely as if they had been his own relatives. The islanders cared for the survivors until a passing Navy ship took them away.

Another man said that soon after that incident, an American named John flew his "great bird" over the island, passing so low that he shook some of the palm fronds loose. "How could you possibly know his name was John?" I asked. "Because he dropped us a carton of cigarettes with his name 'John Player' printed on the boxes." I couldn't ruin the legend by telling him that John Player was a brand of English cigarettes. Fortunately, that was as close as the madness of war came to this happy island.

The light of a single kerosene lamp cast a dim yellow glow on our faces as we sat around talking late into the night. Thinking I knew the way back to the anchorage, I foolishly refused the offer of a boy to guide me. I crawled outside the hut into the complete blackness of a moonless night. Even the starlight was blocked by the tree canopy and overcast skies. On an island without electricity, night fully eclipses the day. I took a few steps until I walked into a tree. Should the would-be circumnavigator descended from chiefs crawl back and ask for help from a boy to find his way home? That thought was discarded as soon as it appeared. Oh, what pride I had!

With hands outstretched, I groped my way from tree to tree, guided loosely by my memory of the path and keeping the sound of surf from the reef on my left until I reached the beach in front of the anchorage and, literally, stumbled over my dinghy. There was no visible sign of *Atom* in the darkness, though I knew it must be anchored nearby. Rowing the dinghy back to my boat, I heard the soft voices of young courting couples on the beach at the other end of the bay. I rested at my oars and drifted as the girls' hauntingly beautiful song pierced the darkness of the calm, starless night. It faded into the laughter of young lovers and I wished I were one of them.

On the day of the big ceremony, people from all over the island met at Bot sa Taumako, carrying every imaginable food from garden and sea. Even large packets of fermented masi were dug up for the occasion. The four chiefs took their seats on mats outside Taumako's house. Tucked under their belts were branches of a perfume-scented bush that appeared to sprout from their backs. A few men with clubs beat out a monotonous rhythm against the bottom of an upturned canoe. A group of village elders wailed discordantly, making eerie, inhuman sounds. The chiefs hung their heads till their chins touched their bare chests and they wept real tears in a show of respect for Taumako's father.

I had been invited to sit next to the chiefs and take pictures of the entire event. The sudden outpouring of emotion caught me by surprise and I felt I was intruding on a private affair and lowered my camera. Then, as suddenly as they'd started, the tears stopped and the chiefs got up and began dancing slowly around the upturned canoe, stamping their feet hard in the sand as they circled around and around. Tofua came over to me smiling and asked if I got some good photos. Was their ability to turn emotions on and off, at will, a sign of insincerity? Or was it that, unlike myself, these people did not have to search for happiness, or run from sadness, but carried both within themselves and always in reach?

Later, baskets of food were brought out and the chiefs ate in silence while bare-breasted girls clad in tapa cloth skirts hovered around them like fairies and fanned away the flies. Other women sang songs in loud bursts of harmony as the rest of us ate our feast. The celebration turned into an all-day fiesta of singing, dancing, feasting and story-telling that the ancient Romans would have applauded.

Children guide me around Tikopia's crater lake

Being confined to the boat for weeks at a time while on passages between the islands made me appreciate the chance to take long walks on the beaches and along the bush trails through the mountains whenever I could, but on Tikopia, it is impossible for a visitor to walk alone. A group of laughing children were always at my side, each trying to clutch a finger and guide me along. I enjoyed having them around, chattering like monkeys, singing and running off in all directions when something caught their eye. They were the best and most patient teachers as they taught me to speak Tikopian in the simple, direct words that children use. As I parroted back their words and sentences, it brought looks of amazement, or more often, unsuppressed laughter when I made a mistake. Now I was the mimicking, chattering monkey providing their amusement.

Accompanied by a dozen of these excited children, I set off to walk the fifteen-mile circumference of the island. Our troop followed the beach for a few miles until overhanging cliffs blocked the shoreline and we were forced to detour inland, always conscious to avoid the forbidden valley. What could be in that valley, I wondered – a temple for human sacrifice? Perhaps they sequestered their loveliest virgins there whenever a palangi sailor was loose on the island?

A light, warm rain fell as we made our way through gardens of cassava and bananas and then into uncultivated forest. As we walked, I stopped often to wait for children who scampered off into the forest to gather wild fruits and nuts. There was nothing that grew or lived in the forest that the islanders had not taught their children how to identify and utilize. A particular bird song caught the boys' attention. A naked boy about eight years old scrambled up a tall coconut tree and deftly snatched the mother bird sitting to defend her eggs. As the bird protested loudly, the boy returned to the ground, tied the ends of the wingtip feathers together so it couldn't escape, and offered it to me. When I asked him to let it go free, he looked at me as if I had asked him to toss away a gold coin, then proceeded to carry his squawking prisoner home as a tiny contribution to the family dinner.

The boys also chased after the dark-brown fruit-eating bats known as "flying foxes" that hung upside down from the branches of *casurina* trees. Fortunately, the bats eluded the boys' grasp and we took no more captives.

On the island's windward side the walking became difficult on steep slopes of mud and loose rock. This uninhabited shore is a maze of cliffs, balanced boulders wrapped in creeping vegetation, and deep caves beckoning to be explored. The sure-footed children never slipped, while I was off my feet many times. My harmless falls in the mud brought cries of alarm and eager hands pulled me back to my feet.

Protruding incongruously from the reef on this uninhabited northeast coast was the battered wreck of a Taiwanese fishing boat that landed here during a storm in 1980. In their canoes, the Tikopians rescued the entire 20-man crew. The islanders sympathized with the shipwrecked fishermen and took them into their homes until another Taiwanese fishing boat picked them up a month later. Before they were rescued, a government boat arrived from Guadalcanal with the intent of arresting the fishermen for poaching in the Solomon's territorial waters. However, the island chiefs, being happily ignorant of the concept that the deep sea could be owned as if it were a parcel of land, refused to hand them over. Unable to overrule the chiefs' authority, the officials had no choice but to leave empty-handed. I could only hope the chiefs would protect me as well if a government boat came and found me on the island without "official permission."

The broken northern shoreline gradually gave way to the smooth beaches of Faea on the island's leeward side. When the tide runs out, it reveals an expanse of shallow tidal flats. Generations ago, low walls of stone were built to form pens on the flats in front of each village. Each day, as the tide drops, fish are still trapped in these ancient pens and groups of women wade into the water to scoop the fish up with handmade nets that resemble loosely strung tennis rackets. This daily ritual usually ends up looking like a game of water polo as the women chase the fish into corners and frantically slash at the water with their nets. Farther out in the lagoon, men drift about in canoes fishing with hand lines under a languorous midday sun.

Here at Potikorokoro Village, the weekly soccer game attracts hundreds of spectators, perhaps half the island's population. The tournament is held at low tide when the tidal flat, being the only level playing field on the island, is clear of water. After a few hours playing on the moist sand, the players yield the field to the incoming tide.

Having finished my walk around the island, my friend, Joseph Roto, invited me to join him one moonless night in his canoe for a flying fish hunt. "When we can see the first seven stars of evening, we go," Joseph told me.

A kerosene pressure lamp was tied to a post in the center of his canoe. The flying fish are attracted to the light and are swatted out of the air with a net attached to a long bamboo pole. The kerosene lamp, acquired by bartering their copra in Guadalcanal, has mostly replaced the ancient method of coconut sheath torches.

We paddled out of the bay until we were about two miles offshore, where we stowed our paddles and the bombardment started. Flying fish shot back and forth just above our heads, the humming sound of their wing-like fins giving only a fraction of a second warning of their approach. Joseph leapt into action with his net and pole. In three hours, swinging his net from side to side, he filled the canoe nearly to the gunwales with stunned, gasping fish. There was now only a couple inches of freeboard and each small wave threatened to sink us as we paddled through the black night towards the faintly visible island. With our feet safely planted on the beach, and the women unloading the fish into baskets, Joseph mentioned the sudden storm that came up two years ago when several canoes were out fishing. Three of the fishermen were lost in what the Tikopian still refer to as a "sweet burial."

On another day, I visited the single room wooden schoolhouse at Potikorokoro Village, where the teacher, a village elder who spoke some English, asked me to give a talk about my travels to the children. I tacked a world map to the wall and outlined my trip thus far and the projected route ahead as nearly a hundred wide-eyed children listened to the teacher interpreting. Then I took their questions – ranging from navigation techniques, to sail-handling, to what foods I ate. Their level of awareness impressed me.

One boy asked, "Aren't you afraid to be alone on the sea in a big storm?" I had yet to be in a "big" storm or faced the kind of incapacitating fear that could strike in any number of crises. If the interpreter was more skilled, I would have been tempted to try to explain my quest for adventure alone at sea. I had as many fears as most folks but my choice was to move forward to meet these demons, to have it out with them, rather than be pursued by fear of this or that thing, to the end of my days.

In return for my talk, the entire class entertained me by singing a number of Tikopian songs. I can never forget the natural charm and spontaneity of the children of Tikopia.

For more than two weeks, my visits to Taumako's house had been a near-daily affair. In Taumako, I sensed a man of rare sensitivity. His preliterate mind contained a library of information passed down by previous generations. His wise council was sought and heeded by the villagers on all manner of disputes or community projects. He aspired always to preserve their traditions and values, while keeping himself free of the age-old vices of ambition and greed. Occasional travelers who respected their customs were welcome – demanding, insensitive tourists were not.

A chief had very few more possessions than anyone else on the island. What they had, they shared. What they wanted, they took. If it was unavailable, they realized the desire created the need and rather than turn the world on its head to find it, they ceased their wanting. Things would change here as they do everywhere and I wondered how long the Tikopians could withstand the coming whirlwind of change brought by the onslaught of our all-consuming civilization. Even then, I knew these would be the freest, happiest days of my life. I walked the island with empty pockets, as rich a man there, as ever I would be.

One reason remote, placid Tikopia is spared the corrupting influence of too many visitors is due to its poor anchorage, exposed to all westerly winds. The anchorage is generally safe during the southern hemisphere's winter of May to October when southeast winds predominate. Now it was late October and the Northwest Monsoon and its threat of squalls and cyclones was not far away.

On the morning of October 19, I sat in Taumako's hut and listened absent-mindedly to the pattering of raindrops as a shower passed over. I had grown as complacent as a Tikopian in a few weeks and had not kept a close eye on the weather. A boy ran into the house telling us the wind had shifted to the west. I stepped outside, saw the trees bending to the west wind, and ran for the anchorage with half of Taumako's clan on my heels. *Atom* was plunging her bow in the short choppy waves and had already started to drag her light anchors. Waves broke over the bow of the small dinghy as I slowly made progress towards the boat. Climbing aboard I saw one of the anchor's lines had chafed through and *Atom's* stern was within feet of hitting the hard sharp fingers of the reef. I was perilously closer to my dream of staying permanently on the island than I really wanted.

My fickle old engine started this time on the first touch of the ignition button. I motored forward, then ran to the bow, brought up the remaining anchor and raced back to steer out of the bay. When clear of the reef, I hoisted a storm jib and reefed main and hove-to for a couple minutes while I hauled the dinghy on deck. Then I made short tacks to hold my position while I considered what to do. I knew I couldn't stay, yet I hesitated, for I had not said my goodbyes to my friends.

Seeing I must leave, Taumako ordered two canoes launched. With great difficulty the four paddlers forced their frail craft into the waves. One of the men dove over and retrieved my lost anchor, some 40 feet below. Then they made their way offshore into the breaking waves, stopping often to bail out their boats with empty coconut shells. I sailed in as close as I dared and met them. They handed me my anchor and two baskets of fruit and vegetables and wished me a good journey. I gave them a bag of quickly gathered gifts. My thanks could not be enough for people who risked their lives to take care of their friends, but these were people who well understood unspoken feelings. After I saw they had made it safely back to the beach, I took a long, final tack offshore.

On December 28, 2002, Tikopia was directly hit and devastated by tropical cyclone Zoe. This was the strongest cyclone to hit the island in living memory, with winds estimated at well over 150 knots. Reports say that as the islanders took refuge in caves, their homes and crops were completely destroyed and trees were uprooted or stripped bare. Giant seas breached a narrow strip of land and contaminated the life-giving freshwater lagoon with saltwater. It wasn't the first storm to furiously beat the island and, as saddened as I am at the hardship they endured, I expect the islanders will recover as they always have.

9 Adventure Country

There is no sea innavigable, no land uninhabitable.

- R. Thorne, Merchant and geographer, 1527

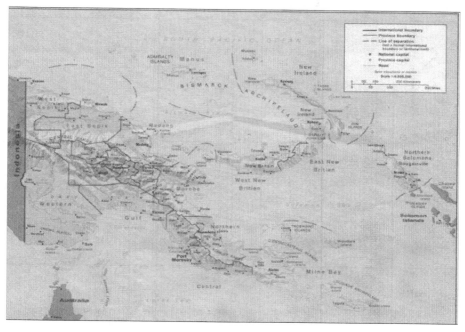

Papua New Guinea

I'd been sailing all day and there were still coconuts and papayas rolling around the anchors and tangled lines strewn about the cockpit. Sails needed mending, the wind vane was acting sluggish and needed its swollen nylon bearings filed down again, the bottom was beginning to foul with barnacles and grass that should have been scrubbed off, and loose gear inside the cabin wasn't properly stowed for sea. I hated to begin a trip without first putting things in order. Sloppiness of this degree was an invitation to a thousand possible problems. My only excuse was the hurried, forced departure and the fatigue I suffered from a flu virus that likely arrived on the island aboard last month's mail boat from Honiera. It had been circulating around the island from village to village, slipping into the huts like a Fijian war party out for blood.

Children of New Guinea see a ghost

With the boat moving slowly to the west-southwest under reefed sails, I crawled into my bunk, letting the rest go until later. It was a lousy way to begin what might be one of the toughest legs of my Pacific crossing – 1,400 miles across the Coral Sea to Port Moresby in Papua New Guinea. For three days, I was mostly in my bunk, unable and unwilling to give anything more than minimal attention to the boat's navigation and maintenance. I did get up to see the high peak of Vanikoro Island in the Santa Cruz Group as I passed a safe 30 miles to its south. Fortunately, the winds had returned to the southeast and steadied so I wasn't needed much on deck until I recovered a few days later.

After I passed the dangerous Indispensable Reefs (Who ever thought of naming hull-rending reefs after the high-sounding names of the ships that first reported them?), the feeble trade winds exhaled their last dying gasp for the year. It was now the transition time between the southeast and northwest monsoons, a time of calms and light airs from all points of the compass. For hours at a time, the sails hung exhausted and limp, panting for air as the swell rolled them with the boat. With constant attention to sail trim, we recorded two days of 40-mile runs; a big change from the easy progress I'd become accustomed to in the trade wind zone.

For two days, I sailed through what must have been the scattered remnants of the same fields of floating pumice I'd encountered 2,000 miles and four weeks earlier between Tonga and Fiji. In a kind of tortoise and hare race across the Pacific, the pumice, pushed by current and wind, passed by while I laid over in Tikopia. Now I moved ahead of it again. After a rare windy night, I walked around the deck in the morning and brushed off the gravelly bits of stone the waves had tossed aboard. Some of the stones had a colony of small creatures clinging to them. In the past month since they were created, the stones had become floating islands for tiny clams, crabs, grasses and a kind of jelly fish that gripped with suction cups. The apparently empty waters around me were full of opportunistic life in search of a home.

Even the fish and birds became scarce some days. Twice I saw a ship on the horizon and once heard a jet high overhead. Otherwise, I lived alone. Slowly, *Atom* and I ticked off the miles westward while the days fbwed one to another from sunrise to sunset, moonrise to moonset. Across the Pacific, I had been amazed and enchanted by the ever-changing moods of the sea, the glorious landfalls and the friendly people who helped me on my way. Remembering it now is like being drawn into a strangely familiar and vivid dream.

The spinnaker was my best ally to harness the light winds; its billowing spread of light nylon allowing me to gain a knot or two above what the jib provided. It meant the ability to sail even at one knot – an extra 24 miles a day – instead of sitting dead in the water under a breeze that barely flickered a candle. It was something of a handful to manage alone. It had the nasty habit every now and then of wrapping itself around the forestay during wind shifts. Somewhere on the Coral Sea, it played this trick and wound itself so tight around the forestay I had to climb hand over hand halfway up the stay to unravel it. Then, I dashed back to correct the helm before it could wrap up again.

A few hours later, the spinnaker halyard broke and the whole sail went overboard, pinned against the hull as we moved over it. By the time I got the mainsail down, the spinnaker had wrapped around the rudder and propeller and would not pull free. I dreaded the thought of leaving the boat in mid-ocean, even on a calm day, and hung my head over both sides of the deck to make sure there was no shark hiding under the hull. Then, I lowered the rope ladder and attached a floating safety line to my harness, in case the boat should drift away faster than I could swim. After a few dives, I had the sail untangled and hoisted it back on deck. I was relieved there was only one small tear in the sail that I patched in a few minutes. Not to be beaten so easily, I hoisted the wet and salty sail on a spare halyard and had no further troubles with it that day. For five hours I hand-steered under a fierce sun before the wind freshened enough for the self-steering to take over.

At sunset on my fifteenth day at sea, I sighted the mountains of New Guinea off the starboard bow. For the last fifty miles to Port Moresby, I sailed cautiously along the reefs that extended five to ten miles off the coast. A few miles from the harbor lay the hulk of an old freighter stranded on the reef, within sight of the calm harbor I wanted to enter. I might have taken the wreck as a warning and kept my distance. Unfortunately, I noticed that my traced copy of the chart of this coast lacked detail and I had unwittingly strayed too close to shore. In a moment, I found myself in a sea of foaming breakers and could see the brown coral heads a few feet under the keel. I swung around to an offshore tack, any minute expecting to feel coral crunching into fiberglass. Somehow, I managed to avoid contact with the bottom and gained deeper water.

A mile farther down the coast, I found the buoy that marked the true inlet to the harbor. I steered through the shallows of the harbor, probably appearing to be a ghost to passing fishermen in canoes, as I was draped in a white sheet against the scorching sun, which had badly burnt me during yesterday's long stint of hand-steering.

From seaward, the capital city of Port Moresby lies hidden behind a hill until it suddenly exposes itself with a few modern multi-story office buildings and a hotel. Around the next headland, The Royal Papua Yacht Club docks and clubhouse contrasts sharply with the dilapidated shacks of discarded tin and lumber that comprise the squatter settlements on the city's perimeter. With all the anchorages within the bay being exposed to the variable winds of this time of year, I went straight into the security of the yacht club's inner basin. Leaning over the bow I picked up a line to a guest mooring. As with my neighboring boats, a second line tied the stern to the shore so that more boats could squeeze into the small basin.

Aha, New Guinea at last! A name in my mind that was synonymous with adventure. The name still quickens my pulse when I envision its rain forests and impenetrable swamps, snow-capped equatorial mountains, a recent history of brave missionaries facing headhunting stone-age tribes. Here, I planned to cease my sea wanderings for a few months of jungle trekking.

There was little hint I was in adventure country when I walked in to register with the Yacht Club secretary. Its formal atmosphere (no t-shirts or sandals at the bar, please) and white-washed tidiness conjured up images of a British colonial outpost from the past where tea is served promptly to club members by silent, white-uniformed, dark-skinned natives. For a small monthly fee, I had a guest membership giving me indefinite use of the mooring and club facilities. Even if it hadn't been so agreeable, this was the only safe place on the south coast to leave the boat to explore the interior. As I exchanged my last $100 bill for some similar amount of local *kina* dollars, I was reminded that I also needed to find temporary employment here.

More than 30,000 years ago, New Guinea was a bridge for man's migration from Asia to Australia. Among islands, its size is only surpassed by Greenland. The Portuguese explorers called it Ilhas dos Papuas (Island of the Fuzzy Hairs). With no visible wealth to exploit and some very inhospitable natives, the island was ignored for a few hundred years by the colonial powers as they sought out more valuable "ungoverned" lands to occupy.

Such a sizable island ultimately could not go unclaimed. First, the Dutch included the western half of the island in their Dutch East Indies Archipelago and named it after the African country of Guinea. In 1884, Britain annexed the southeast section of the island and Germany claimed the northeast corner. After World War I, the Australians controlled the former British and German sectors. In 1962, Indonesia pushed the Dutch out of western New Guinea, later changing its name from the awful sounding Irian Barat (West Hotland) to the less descriptive but more appealing Irian Jaya (New West). By 1975, Australian New Guinea became fully independent Papua New Guinea, although Australia still supports its former colony by subsidizing a sizable chunk of its national budget.

New Guineans, or "nationals," as they are called by Australians living in the country, range from the jet-black-skinned Buka tribe, to the short, bearded people of the highland interior, to those resembling brown-skinned Polynesians along the island's south coast and off-lying islands.

Among the massive mountain ranges that fragment the island are peaks standing over 15,000 feet above the sea. Great rivers, some whose headwaters are yet unexplored, cut through the island's rocky backbone in rushing rapids, then slow and widen in a meandering search for the sea through hundreds of miles of lowland swamps teeming with crocodiles, snakes and malaria. This rugged and uninviting topography isolates the tribes as much as any man-made border, resulting in an island where some 700 dialects are spoken and tribalism runs as deep as the valleys separating each tribe. I had at least six months ahead of me, until the end of the Northwest Monsoon in May when the southeast trades would resume, to explore this enormous and diverse island.

While researching travel routes and copying maps at the University of PNG, I met John Stevens, a resident Australian accountant and weekend explorer. The following weekend I joined him and some other members of the PNG Bushwalkers Association for a day-long hike, or bush-walk, as the Aussies call it, to Mount Diamond, a nearby wilderness area fifteen miles outside the capital of Port Moresby. Six of us climbed out of our van at the end of the road and followed a trail called the Aerial Ropeway. Here a cable car system had carried ore out from a copper mine in the early 1900s and now lay abandoned. Sections of steel cable still drooped low over the valley, suspended from rusting hilltop towers. We ascended some steep pitches on our hands and knees. Then we sprinted down into valleys of tangled bush, bamboo clumps and rock-lined creeks. It was a good day of tough training for future treks. By the end of the day one of our group was laid out with heat exhaustion and I was not far from it myself.

The PNG Bushwalkers Association was largely a social group of 260 members, mostly "expats," or resident expatriate Australians, living here on temporary work contracts. They gathered mainly for drinking parties and occasional day hikes on the weekends. A core group of the more active members organized occasional expeditions where they would fly into some of the island's remotest corners. John Stevens had just heard about a recently completed mountaintop airstrip in the Goilala Valley, in Papua New Guinea's Central Province. Previously, the people of the valley were cut off from the outside world by an arduous five-day trek through vertiginous mountains and across bridgeless white-water rivers to the nearest road. The several thousand natives in the Goilala area had barely begun the transition from the stone-age to the 20th century. John and I and two other Bushwalkers immediately began planning a trip that would make us the first hikers to fly into the valley.

The airstrip was constructed next to a Catholic mission station in the village of Inonge. Years before, Father Gerrard had walked into the lower Goilala Valley to work single-handedly among the natives to save lives, if not souls. For the past ten years, he had toiled alongside the natives with picks and shovels to carve a short airstrip into one of the mountain peaks. There is no level terrain in the Goilala, and even the finished airstrip runs at a crazy angle with a cliff-hanging dog-leg in its center and sheer drop-offs at both ends. The national airline of PNG described it as the world's scariest white-knuckle airstrip. We found one of the very few Australian bush pilots willing to run supplies, and the occasional passenger, into the valley in his single engine plane.

At daybreak, on a Saturday morning in November, our small group met at Port Moresby Jackson Airport. We had arranged to charter the plane to take us to Inonge and return to pick us up on Monday. There was no way I'd miss a trip like this, even though it cost me most of my last remaining $100 bill.

Our pilot, who introduced himself as Rusty, arrived late, complaining of a hangover. He led us onto the already hot tarmac and opened the tiny baggage door of his single engine six-seater for us to load our backpacks. To our eyes, the plane was a disappointment – no, it actually scared the hell out of me. A window was cracked and taped, the seats and headliner were shredded, and a suspicious puddle of oil lay on the tarmac directly under the engine. When John pointed out the growing oil slick to the pilot, he rubbed his scraggly gray beard, slapped the wing and said, "No worries, mate. This bird's got plenty of hours in her yet. Yer bags aren't too heavy, I hope?"

John echoed my feelings when he whispered in my ear, "I guess it's too late to turn back now."

After our bags were in, Rusty somehow managed to cram in two 50-pound bags of rice for the mission, stowing them under my feet and forcing my knees up nearly to my chest. The plane rattled and shuddered as we labored down the runway, seemingly unable to gain the air. "No worries," Rusty shouted over his shoulder, "she'll be much lighter on the return trip." It wasn't the return trip that concerned me at that moment. Finally, the wings found their lift in the humid morning air and we rose and banked to the northwest where a mantle of green below replaced the squatter shacks and outlying settlements of the capital. Below us, the serpentine twists of the Brown River ran like chocolate milk as it doubled and tripled back on itself in a final attempt to postpone its appointment with the sea.

Moments later, we were within the mountains, not entirely over them, but skimming through gaps in the peaks in an attempt to stay below the mist and clouds that built above us on either side. While weaving our way between purple and black storm clouds being buffeted by mountain thermals, Rusty felt moved to announce, "A little rough today. Should have got an earlier start." He went on to thrill us with the popular bush pilot's truism: "When you see a cloud over New Guinea, you can bet there's a mountain inside, mate."

Staying below the clouds, we shot through tangled mountains and gorges until a small earth-colored scar appeared in the endless green canopy. We tightened our grip on the seats as we dropped onto the low end of an impossibly short patch of dirt. "Amazing how that 15 degree incline slows you right down," Rusty said after he braked to a halt a few feet from the cliff edge marking the end of the runway.

Father Gerrard, some porters and a small group of children had walked out along the dirt track from the mission to meet the plane. Rusty shook the priest's hand as he gave him a packet of letters. Then he hustled us to quickly unload the plane as if he were expecting incoming mortar rounds. We helped spin the plane's tail around so Rusty could get out before the lowering cloud deck boxed him in.

"Man's got nerves of steel," John said as we watched him drop off the low end of the runway and then reappear, a few long moments later, rising up and out of the valley before finally disappearing in those mountain-filled clouds.

"Yes, nerves of steel no doubt fortified by that bottle of booze I saw stashed under his seat," another in our group added.

Tall and black-bearded Father Gerrard had received our letter on the previous flight and was obviously pleased to have visitors. We had many miles to travel that day, so after the priest pointed out the path for us to follow for a circular trek of the lower valley, we agreed to return to stay at the mission the following evening.

Compared to the sweltering coastal heat we'd just left, here at 6,500 feet above the sea, the air was refreshingly cool. We followed the footpath as it clung to the mountainside, running parallel to, and just below, the encircling ridges. This track, we were told, circled the entire 20-mile-wide valley with one dip down to cross a bridge over a major river. Like walking around the inside edge of a giant bowl, we had the impression the whole world begins and ends in this valley. For the people of the Goilala, that is their reality. The Goilala doesn't just feel remote from the world, it truly is its own world. Below us, the powerful Vanapa River, now in flood from days of rain, brawled and beat its way between great black boulders and over fallen trees.

Our path took us through a village of huts with sides of woven strips of split bamboo and roofs covered in grass thatch. As we approached, we startled a group of women who shrieked in surprise when they saw us and then vanished into their homes. Little naked children ran terrified and crying after their mothers. "I don't think they care much for the looks of your mug, John," someone called out to John, who was walking ahead of us. Most people here had never been out of their valley or seen any white men aside from the priest. Before Father Gerrard had taught them otherwise, people here believed that all white men were the re-embodied spirits of their dead kinsmen. From the astonished looks we received, it seemed they believed it still.

Alerted by the cries of the women and children, a few men stepped out to meet us. Soon every man in that village had lined up to shake our hands. Emboldened by the men, many of the women and children reappeared to stare at the invaders in wide-eyed amazement. From then on, the same scene of initial shock turned to inquisitiveness was replayed at each village we passed. The natives clustered around us like pigeons around a few seeds as they reached out to touch our skin or clothing.

Many people in this province speak three languages. The first language they learn is Ples Tok, literally "Place Talk," which is usually confined to one or two adjacent valleys. Hiri Motu is an ancient language spoken along the southern coast and by those mountain natives who have trading contact with the coastal areas. Melanesian Pidgin is a corruption of English taught in mission and government schools throughout the country. This Pidgin, or Tok Pisin as it's called, is used as the *lingua franca* throughout the linguistically divided islands of Melanesia. Two members of our group spoke Pidgin, I had a basic and growing vocabulary of Pidgin that I had first heard in Tikopia, and John Stevens spoke some Hiri Motu. Between us, we communicated in a mishmash of Pidgin, Motu and hand signals.

At this first village a gray-haired old man, wearing a bark cloth laplap and wide grin of black stumps of teeth, took hold of my arm as I passed. He kept repeating "Yangpela!" (Young one) with a look on his face like he just discovered a missing son. My 26-year-old pale baby face was the youngest of its kind he had seen. In the mountains of New Guinea, the hard life aged people prematurely. Living with untreated tropical diseases and malnourishment takes its toll.

Later in the highlands, I was to see people existing on little food besides *kau-kau* (sweet potatoes) and sleeping through cold nights on the bare dirt in their huts with no blankets. The average life expectancy in PNG was around 40 years – although no one counts the passing years or could tell you their age. It was enough for them to know which still-living generation they belonged to in their family. After we were well past the village, the old man released my arm and indicated he would catch up with us later after returning to his village. Someone joked that he wanted to take me home as his adopted son, which was probably true.

We walked past neat garden plots where kau-kau and corn clung to the steep hillsides surrounded by fences of vine-lashed logs. Outside the fences, pigs heavier than men freely roamed the bush. At Visi Village the population consisted of some 30 people and at least 100 pigs kept in pens. Along the trails we encountered pigs of all dispositions. The bravest ones held their ground as we approached only to crash into the bush at the last moment. Pigs are an important source of wealth throughout New Guinea. They are far too valuable as symbols of wealth and as trade goods to be eaten except on special occasions. Pigs were then used, as they most likely still are, for purchasing brides; the number of pigs paid to the girl's father depending on their social position and her reputation at working hard in the gardens. Even after marriage the women usually live, not with their husbands, but in separate huts they share with the young children and the family's pigs to ensure the pigs are well cared for. In those days, it was not uncommon to see a woman breastfeeding a piglet whose own mother had died or run off.

Often when coming around the corner on a trail, we met people traveling to or from their gardens. Upon seeing us they inevitably started walking backwards, tripping over each other as if Martians had materialized in front of them. Usually, they regained their senses within a few moments and we'd exchange greetings and handshakes all around.

The natives used to live in fear of meeting strangers on the paths between gardens and village. The cannibal Kukukuku tribe (pronounced "cooker-cooker") inspired such dread they were referred to in whispers as "the terrible ones in bark cloaks who come down from the mountains to kill us." Such was the ferocity of the Kukukuku, and the universal horror of them by the other natives, that they were recruited by security companies in Port Moresby and often guard the homes of expat Australian families. Knowledge of one diminutive Kukukuku, armed with a spear and bush knife, protecting a compound, was enough to dissuade any modern street gang.

Native tracks crossed these valleys for thousands of years but this road, as they call it, was not typical of native paths that mostly run helter-skelter up and down the hills. This track, begun by Father Gerrard, was laid out at an average incline of within five degrees from level, was clearly designed for easy traveling.

As we made our way along the valley perimeter, we passed under icy waterfalls cascading over the road before they plunged headlong into the river that rushed along the valley floor. At each turn in the trail we had another view to the east of vegetation-soaked gullies rising to cloud-splattered peaks. From one vantage point, looking across the valley, I counted ten small clearings where clusters of bush houses stood among fenced gardens. We stopped for lunch in a shady spot next to one of those convenient waterfalls, filling our water bottles from its cool mineral-laden waters. Soon enough we were moving again to the music of crunching boots on the trail, the hypnotic rush and rumble of the river over rocks, and the squeal of pigs fleeing our approach.

In a late afternoon mist, we entered Oro Village, the halfway point of our walk around the valley. At this point we planned to descend to the river, cross its log bridge, and return to Inonge along the valley's eastern ridge the following day. At the village we met the local headman, or chief, of the fifty village inhabitants. The chief warned us that the Vanapa River bridge had been washed away again by flood waters a few days before. We walked down to look at the missing bridge and saw that it was quite impossible to get across. The rain-swollen river still ran fast and deep as it rushed over its boulder-lined bed. The height of the flood was such that now there was little sign that there had ever been a bridge here. To reach the next village, which lay clearly in view on the river's opposite shore, would require a two-day detour to the very end of the valley and back up again.

Since we could go no further, we accepted the chief's invitation to stay the night in the village schoolhouse. The villagers built the schoolhouse a year earlier in hope a volunteer teacher from the Peace Corps would come to stay with them – they were still waiting. The two-room building built of local timber and a corrugated tin roof sat on sturdy posts that raised it high enough off the ground to allow a family of pigs to make their home underneath.

The entire village followed us up the stairs and into the building. Those unable to fit inside crowded on the porch looking in at us from the windows. In the dim light I looked up at a mass of dark faces with white teeth and eyes that glowed with delight as we unpacked our gear on the floor. The crowd, who were dressed in an assortment of native fabrics and donated western clothing, discussed among themselves with great detail every strange new item that emerged from our packs, the ones in back pushing forward to see. The novelty of strangers in town began to wear off with the wet chill of evening and most people returned to sit around the smoldering earth fireplaces in their windowless huts.

From what I later came to know from living with similar tribes, here the villagers would undoubtedly talk late into the night, debating what important mission had brought us here, unable to believe we had come all this way only to meet them and look around at the scenery as we had claimed. No, it was inconceivable that we would walk away tomorrow, never to be seen here again. Surely, now their prayers to the new white God would be answered, and at least one of the white men would remain or come back to be their teacher, assistant to the missionary, or perhaps open a health care center, as Father Gerrard had promised would happen one day.

In the last light of the gray afternoon, clouds formed around and below us to drift along with the mist hanging in the air. On the near opposite ridge, inaccessible to us, smoke rose like puffs of cotton from the cooking fires of a village. These low, wet skies brought a dank, brooding atmosphere of wilderness, despite our location at the edge of a village.

In Papua New Guinea

As we settled in to our quarters, I heard the familiar cry "Yangpela" from my gray-haired old friend, coming up the schoolhouse steps. He said only "kai-kai" (food) as he proudly presented us with a basket full of steaming ears of corn, roasted over a fire only minutes earlier. With some difficulty, I persuaded the old fellow to accept a few of our PNG dollars, called kina, named after the island's traditional shell money. To anyone who might doubt the paper's value, there was a picture of a kina shell printed on it. We chomped on the roasted corn and listened, without quite understanding, to the old man's monologue, given in a mixture of Pidgin and Ples Tok.

After a long day of straining muscles too long underemployed, sleep came easily, in spite of the hardness of the uneven wood floor and the noises of the pigs rooting around on the ground beneath us. Up before dawn to get an early start, we found the sky had cleared, exposing stars shimmering in the chill air. We shared a breakfast of cracked wheat cereal cooked over our kerosene camp stove, then packed up and were gone with the gathering light. Because of the washed-out bridge, we retraced our course of the previous day back to Inonge. We walked under clear skies typical of the mountain mornings while below us puffy clouds decorated the sides of the gorge. In several directions, columns of rising smoke revealed the morning cooking fires.

All morning, the hills were ringing out with the haunting hoots and yodeling cries from villages near and far. These strong-lunged criers passed information from one village to another, akin to relay stations on a telegraph line. We were clearly the main feature in that day's news bulletin because we were surprising fewer people along the trail and some were even expecting us with hands outstretched to grip ours as we passed. Then those eerie yodeling cries began anew as we moved on towards the next village.

Unlike our sociable trek, the first Australian patrol officers, called *kiaps*, to arrive in the mountains of New Guinea were regularly under siege from hostile natives. The grandfathers of these same hilltop criers that called out the news of our movements had alerted the warriors to prepare an attack. If the friendly intentions of the natives were not known to us, we would have been filled with fear at the haunting sound of the criers.

As we passed under a slope of tobacco plants, we met a group of women carrying string bags, called *bilums*, bulging with vegetables on the way home from their gardens. Since the telegraph had announced our presence throughout the valley, there were no more scenes of hysteria such as we caused the day before. The women laid out some of the corn, kau-kau and cabbages from the bilums onto the trail for us to take, then shyly stepped back for us to pass. We thanked them for the offering, stepped over the piles of vegetables and moved on out of their way.

Afternoon brought the inevitable rainy-season torrential downpour of cold rain teeming down from low curtains of clouds. We found shelter under an open sided lumber mill powered by a paddle wheel in a creek running noisily under its floor. Constructed by the priest and his helpers, the mill wheel was engaged only when a local building project was underway. Without roads to transport it out of the valley, the lumber cannot be exported, thus saving the forests from man's greed. Their practice is to fell only enough trees to complete the project at hand, thus balancing the people's needs with the regenerative powers of nature – then the mill blade falls silent again. Sharing the shelter were two families that came in from the muddy trail shortly after us. The men sat patiently puffing harsh local tobacco stuffed into a long bamboo pipe they passed between them.

The rain eased slightly so we shouldered our packs and walked on to the mission. We arrived, wet and cold, during another heavy cloudburst, to a warm welcome by Father Gerrard. He led us to a new guesthouse next to the church where we rinsed off the mud from the trail under a cold shower fed by gravity from an overhead tank. When the spirited French priest met with us that evening, we learned more about the many development projects he was involved with in the Goilala. Besides building the church, lumber mill, visitors' guesthouse and airstrip, he ran the mission school and worked to introduce new crops to the valley. He hoped the mission could earn a small income if more visitors like us come to stay in the guesthouse while sightseeing in the valley. This was a man who could not be idle. He had accomplished much here and intended to do much more.

In his parish, I noticed that the people were not coerced to abandon their traditional culture and the women were not forced to cover their breasts in Western civilization-induced shame. Unlike many zealous missionaries who flocked to New Guinea over the past century in a race to transform the societies they encountered to fit their ethnocentric view, Father Gerrard's way was to convert souls through the quiet persuasion of example and tolerance. The natives responded to his example by working alongside him on his many projects. We had to admire his resourcefulness. I was sure that a man of his drive and compassion would have come to help these people even without a church's sanction.

The pragmatic style of some early missionaries in PNG is illustrated by the story of Father Ross, an American missionary working in the New Guinea highlands in the 1930s. By then, a few missionaries had been killed by natives anxious to get their steel tools and other equipment. Once, a visiting priest from Port Moresby accompanied Father Ross on his weekly rounds between villages. Several times, when they passed natives on the trail, the visiting priest held out a crucifix at them as if fending off vampires. He told father Ross, "Over by Port Moresby, when we go out and meet natives, we show them the crucifix, so they know who we are."

"You do, eh?" Father Ross said, and pulled a .38 revolver out of his holster. "Over here, we show them this."

Another time, a village chief approached him and said, "Let us go to Ginde Village – they are our enemies – and clean them up. We'll take all their pigs and young women and burn their houses and run them right out of the area."

"Oh no, we don't do things like that," Father Ross said.

"But you've got the guns and the dogs! Why don't you do it? It doesn't make sense that you've got the power to take what you want, and you let the Ginde people come down here and haggle with you over the price of a pig!"

Gradually, the missionary's ideal of living in peace with their neighboring tribes took a tenuous root. Yet even today, tribalism and clan enmities frequently erupt into feuds. Despite the best efforts of the colonizers to vaccinate the natives of New Guinea with Christianity, the ancient beliefs, and the practice of sorcery, run deeper in their soul than Western teachings can yet reach.

Father Gerrard told us that the heavy traffic we passed on the trails the past couple days was from people busy preparing for a sing-sing ceremony to be held next week. The event would involve several villages in a ritualized system of gift exchange, mostly of pigs and the valuable kina shells acquired through trading runs to the coast over many generations. This was a carefully crafted compensation settlement to appease the clan of a young woman who was "stolen" from her parents by a man from a neighboring clan. After the ceremonial payoff, they would feast on pork and kau-kau. As the feasting went on, warriors would face each other in a dance of mock battle carrying spears, bows and arrows, and wearing bird-of-paradise plumes in their towering headdresses. The government and the churches encourage the sing-sings as an alternative to the inveterate and bloody tribal wars sometimes involving hundreds of warriors and lasting several months.

At dawn the next morning, Father Gerrard invited us to breakfast in the main house adjacent to the church. In his simple and solid colonial style home, the five of us sat around a finely-crafted circular hardwood table with rotating centerpiece. On it, his native servant and cook placed bowls of scrambled eggs, loaves of hot homemade bread with jams, and a pot of locally grown coffee to wash it all down. The priest sent the loaded centerpiece slowly spinning with a turn of his hand and we served ourselves as items rotated within reach. This medieval scene, with us like knights out of King Arthur's Court, was in stark contrast to the dirt-floored thatch huts of the natives. The church's view, Father Gerrard told us, was that the natives were favorably impressed by their spiritual leaders living in relative grandeur, and that they were uplifted and learned more by this example than if the priest lived in a more humble abode. As they learned, they too would improve their living conditions.

Our plane was overdue. We watched the clouds rolling in and wondered if Rusty was sober and more importantly, if he would be able to find us. If he could not locate this little mountain pad in the overcast conditions, he would be forced to return to Moresby and try again another day. My fellow hikers were watching the sky anxiously as they were expected back at their various jobs in the city that morning.

While waiting at the edge of the airstrip Father Gerrard approached me and asked if I would consider staying at the mission for a while and help him with his various construction projects. I could tell he was a man used to getting what he wanted. As much as I would have liked to stay and help, I knew I had to return to the city and find a paying job right away since my empty pockets made me nearly as poor as his parishioners. I told him he could write me in a few months if he still needed someone and I would try to come back then. He never wrote, so I assumed he found other volunteers. In the years since my life has led me in many directions, yet I often feel the urge to return to the Goilala to engage in the honest, hard work of charity.

We heard the distant hum of the plane as it searched for an opening in the clouds. Rusty made several passes overhead, unseen by us, until he found a clear spot of sky to drop through. He lined up and literally dived onto the airstrip. No chance to go around for another shot here. Moments later, we were loading our gear. Having settled our bill earlier with a donation to the church, we said goodbye to Father Gerrard and hastily got underway before the clouds rolled back in. We raced downhill at full throttle using every bit of the bumpy dirt strip, and then ran off the end while still dropping into the thousand foot deep gorge. The engine strained as we dropped into the abyss, every soul on board praying in his own fashion and willing the plane upward. Once we gained enough air speed, we made a slow ascent out of the valley.

Our one-hour flight back was a twisting course around mountain peaks and dark rain clouds. As an empty beer can rolled back from under the pilot's seat, I made the same oath here that I took on the way in – that I would never for any reason fly again. Though cursing "this bloody New Guinea weather," Rusty expertly interpreted the scrambled jigsaw puzzle of terrain and cloud and brought us safely home. Hazardous flights like these make for hard-drinking pilots and short careers.

Back among the concrete high-rise buildings of the capital, I marveled at the contrast of our one-hour leap back to the 20th Century. One mighty mountain range was all that separated the Goilala from the logging roads that would perhaps, one day, destroy its rugged beauty. The double-edged sword of an airstrip or a road brings the people what they want – we can't deny them that. But we can also hope some of these last wild places will be left as they are. It should be enough to know they are out there and they do exist. Now can we let them be?

10 On the Kokoda Trail

Time and rain will obliterate
this little native pad —
but for evermore will live the memory
of weary men that have gone,
gone far beyond the Kokoda Trail.

- Major General F. Kingsley Norris

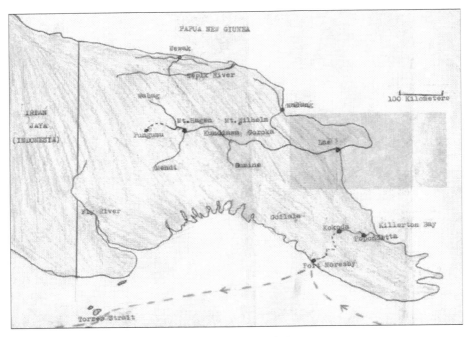

Our trek into New Guinea

The Northwest Monsoon now kicked in and the dry, dusty Port Moresby I entered a month earlier was swimming under the deluge of the rainy season. When the sun came out, the city steamed like a pressure cooker. Laundry I hung out to dry, clipped on the lifelines in the humid morning air, was brought in wet after a day hanging limp in the sun. I slept naked with a plaited fan in my hand, fanning myself to sleep, waking up drenched in sweat an hour later, then fanning myself to sleep again. It remained breathlessly hot, even as the rains came down. Sometimes, it seemed to rain for a week straight, day and night, with few breaks. On those days, the city streets turned to ankle-deep rivers and the electric power failed almost daily.

With the rains came strong gales of wind out of the northwest, gales that later became cyclones raging across the Coral Sea. Like it or not, this island would be my home for another seven months. Then, when the southeast trades returned, I could cross the Indian Ocean to Africa without fear of headwinds or getting clobbered by a cyclone.

I was halfway around the world, without money, in a strange land. But I did have some prospects – I had my boat, my freedom, two hands fit for work and, despite some discomforts, I was where I wanted to be. Most of the other trans-Pacific cruising yachts had sailed to Australia or New Zealand to wait out the cyclone season. Australia was a safer bet for someone seeking comfort and employment. But I had not sailed halfway around the world to sit in a comfortable country much like the one I had fled, especially when a wild land of opportunity like New Guinea lay more directly on my route.

At any rate, I believed in making my own luck on this voyage and was fortunate to have been offered a job through my new friends at the yacht club. In a land of mostly agricultural labor, my modest shipwright skills meant I was qualified to take over the final fitting out of a 40-foot wooden sailboat that had been under construction off and on for the past three years at the shipyard next to the yacht club. The builder of the boat became fed up with the difficult and primitive working conditions and sold the unfinished boat to a couple of Australians who ran a building supplies import company. They hired me to work alongside and supervise the unskilled laborers and be a general problem-solver in order to get the boat finished and ready for sailing. The job paid US$500 per week, tax-free, which I considered fair. I certainly earned it though. For over three months, I worked up to 65 hours a week, finishing the deck, fitting out the entire interior, the plumbing and electrics, installing a diesel motor, rigging the boat as a ketch and painting the entire boat.

During that time I went through six workers from four different tribes. None of them spoke English, so I learned to communicate in

Pidgin. At times our progress was painfully slow. I'd start at sunrise and continue for ten or twelve hours, often without the electricity working. The heat was terrific and sapped all my strength by the end of the day. If we were not working in the scorching sun, we were working in the rain. The minute my back was turned, all work came to a halt. If I had to leave for a few hours to get supplies, it was inevitable when I returned I would have to awaken my crew, who were sound asleep on the ground beneath the keel, or curled up in one or another corner of the hull. My crew was just marking time, doing the absolute minimum they felt they'd get away with. Sometimes they left after a few weeks on their own, but I refused to fire them. The Melanesians do not all believe in the European work ethic, much to the consternation of those who see themselves as their masters.

I couldn't blame these men for their apathy because they were only paid the going rate of the equivalent of US$8 a day in a city where the cost of living was nearly as high as in most U.S. cities. Since I was earning ten times their wages, I felt obliged to do ten times the work. In their situation, I would also have little enthusiasm for this kind of work, and would probably go back to a life of subsistence farming in the bush country, a life that these men had left for the lure of the good life in the city. It is the same throughout much of the undeveloped world, where desperate people leave their small farms for a life of squalor and crime in cities where they cannot support themselves.

Typical of this situation was a young man named Kerowa, who approached me for a job soon after I began work at the shipyard. This big, strong fellow, about 20 years old with a beaming grin, told me in Pidgin that he had just left his village in the Western Highlands Province for the first time in his life. If he got this job, he planned to send money back to his family and the village chief who had paid his travel expenses. He had begun his journey by foot, then by truck, and because the fragmented road system doesn't connect the capital city to the rest of the country, took a plane from the north coast to Port Moresby.

Many of Kerowa's countrymen were doing the same thing. Most would be sadly disappointed. They are usually faced with returning to their village in shame, and in debt, without finding a job. Some resort to crime by joining gangs called "rascals." That is a cute name for organized gangs of up to thirty men and boys who roam the streets at night committing mass rapes, robbery and murder. Even the police turn and flee from rascals armed with guns, knives and clubs. While I was there, the attacks had become so frequent and vicious the Prime Minister declared a state of emergency, imposing a curfew at night and ordering the military to patrol the streets of the capital.

Meanwhile, many of the Australian expats earned a fair wage and had their house servants and swimming pools and locked themselves behind roof-high electrified fences. Some hired house guards, preferably from the short-statured and short-tempered Kukukuku tribe, so feared by all other tribes. Even a gang of murderous rascals avoided messing with one five-foot-tall Kukukuku carrying a long bush knife.

I tried to live as a bridge between these groups of nationals and expats. I doubled our workers wages as an incentive to get them to take their work seriously. It was unpopular with the other expat foreman in the yard, but it seemed the right thing to do. As for myself, I had no official work permit and paid no income taxes, but through my travels around the island, I would be putting much of what I earned here back into the local economy before I left.

During the next few months, despite our boss/employee relationship, Kerowa and I became good friends. Because he had no close relatives here and he wanted to save money on rent, I invited him to stay aboard *Atom* and bunk in the forward cabin v-berth. Kerowa was so unsophisticated and lost and homesick in the city that I became like an older brother to him. He in turn, told me stories of tribal wars and sing-sings and chasing small game through the forest with wooden bows and bamboo arrows. He also taught me some of his village Tok Ples, which is spoken by only a few thousand people in one highland valley. Learning one of the 700 Tok Ples languages of New Guinea might seem the ultimate exercise in futility, but it proved a great asset later when I went back into the mountains.

Kerowa did have some annoying habits. He insisted on calling me, and all white people, "Masta," meaning "Master," one of those old colonial terms that was introduced into Pidgin and now proved difficult to be rid of. He also stuck closer to me than a noontime shadow wherever I went, partly out of loneliness and partly for mutual protection. A few times he grabbed hold of my hand as we walked together to go to work or the market. In PNG, men and women from small villages frequently held hands with clan members of the same sex. It has nothing to do with sexual preference, since it was often said there were no admitted homosexuals in PNG. It was simply an unselfconscious sign of friendship that gave them a feeling of security, especially when walking among strangers. It felt mean to pull my hand away, but his innocent, child-like gesture was frowned on by white sophisticates in the city, and well, it did look odd.

Every week Kerowa gave me half of his pay to hold for him, and in this way saved a few hundred kina towards his return to the village of Pungumu. He knew if he didn't give it to me to hold, his friends would have him spend it on them. Saying no to sharing your last dollar was unthinkable in Melanesia.

In the city, Kerowa felt alienated. In his village, he knew where he fit in. By returning with useful gifts ("cargo" in Pidgin) for his clan, he could gain prestige and fulfill his obligations. Besides, his parents had picked out a local girl for him to marry and soon he hoped he could afford the bride price of several fat pigs.

Kerowa invited me to return with him to his village once our work was finished. He promised to guide me on treks through the mountains to hidden valleys where white men had rarely been seen. Although visited yearly by a priest from another valley, his Pungumu clan never had a Westerner stay with them before. Here was a chance to live with a people who were as distant from my culture as it was possible to be. I was eager to go.

During the time I worked in Port Moresby, I made several more friends among the "nationals" and received invitations to visit families in other parts of the island. An idea began to form that I could walk across this island as I had done on every other island on this voyage. Before I had these friends and their invitations, I had not thought it possible; it was said a traveler could not just enter strange villages in New Guinea unannounced without risking attack. All land is claimed and frequently fought over by one tribe or another. Even the remotest mountains and most fetid swamps are jealously guarded. Yet, if you can give the name of even one local person as a friend, you are guaranteed a welcome.

Thus far on my voyage, by walking across the islands and climbing their highest mountains, I experienced the places and their peoples on a level a casual tourist could never imagine. Why, I wondered, could I not continue to walk across each island throughout the voyage ahead? New Guinea would be my greatest challenge, and if successful here, I could surely walk across the smaller and less deadly islands that lay ahead. I was so determined to explore the mysteries of these places that I both burdened and motivated myself with this additional challenge.

Kerowa agreed to join me on this trans-island trek that would eventually take us to his highland village. It was obvious he thought I was slightly mad to even consider it. It was not so much the physical hardship of the trek that bothered him; the jungle was his element. What terrified Kerowa was the thought of being unprotected by his clan when moving through "hostile" tribal regions. Nevertheless, he was willing, and probably felt obligated, to see me safely through.

The only way to cross PNG, other than by plane, is by walking. From Port Moresby, a wandering road runs northeast for 40 miles where it ends at the beginning of the Kokoda Trail, a twisting narrow 60-mile jungle footpath leading to Kokoda Village. From there a rough road leads to the town of Popondetta, and then on to Killerton Bay on the north coast. The island of New Guinea is shaped something like a crouching dragon and this route only cuts across the dragon's tail. It's over 100 miles across by plane, but by land it is far longer and a formidable trek no matter how you measure it. At Killerton Bay we hoped to find a boat to carry us up the coast to the city of Lae, which is connected by road to Kerowa's village in the Western Highlands.

The rainy season was winding down when we left the Yacht Club on foot one morning in March. Kerowa wondered why we couldn't take a bus to the end of the road, then easily accepted my explanation that I had to walk across the island from seashore to seashore. He couldn't quite understand it, but he accepted it just because his friend wanted it that way. An hour before morning twilight, the city streets were deserted as we walked at a fast clip, burdened with some 40 pounds of gear in each of our backpacks. By dawn, the hilly paved roads of the city were behind us and the mountains loomed ahead. The morning sun was hot in our faces and hotter still at noon as we slowed our step along the shadeless road. We trudged along as fast as we could, knowing that on the mountain trail ahead of us the forest canopy would partly shield us from the tormenting sun of the coast.

That night, we stepped off the road to make an inconspicuous camp behind a hill. I pitched my low-profile, one-man tent, and nearby, Kerowa tucked himself into my Gore-tex bivy bag, which he placed on a cushion of grass he tore up and piled under the bag. I slept fitfully, as I usually do my first night on the trail, and noticed that Kerowa was up most of the night peering into the darkness, worried that traveling through the rough outlying neighborhoods of Moresby, with a white man at his side, was an invitation to attack by rascals.

At dawn we continued down the winding, dusty road, passing small villages and banana plantations. The houses here, a full day's walk from Moresby, were ugly boxes of discarded timber and rust-streaked, corrugated tin sheets. Yet the people in these villages always greeted us warmly. One wrinkled old farmer had been waiting all morning under the sun at roadside for a bus to take him, and four sacks of his garden produce, to the city market. As we approached, he lifted his weary head, smiled and handed us each a pineapple.

From the road head at Ower's Corner, we turned onto a trail where a wooden sign marked the beginning of the Kokoda Trail. Over the crest of this ridge, the land unfolded ahead of us in its green-mantled, savage splendor. Natives have used this primitive shifting track across the island for centuries, yet the rugged terrain has defied all attempts at building a road through this section of the Owen Stanley Mountain Range.

The trail led us down a steep, nearly vertical path to the Goldie River far below. To slow our descent we clutched handfuls of grass as we slid by. There was no bridge spanning the river and it was too high and swift to cross at this point. Around a bend downstream we made a dry crossing by leaping from one giant egg-shaped boulder to another until we gained the opposite bank. My topographical map showed little but jagged lines and elevations without roads or towns. I could more or less follow our course by these lines of elevation and a compass, which taken together, indicated we faced a steep climb of 1,600 feet over a portion of the trail known as the "Golden Stairs."

During World War II, the Australian Engineer Corps cut over two thousand steps on this spur to aid foot soldiers on their way to halt the advance of Japanese soldiers intent on capturing Port Moresby. Erosion and jungle growth had reduced it to a narrow serpentine track of orange clay, crisscrossed with exposed tree roots.

Although this was the beginning of the dry season, a downpour of rain caught us by late afternoon as we made our way along a knife-edged spur of slippery clay. In New Guinea, "dry season" only means that it might rain two hours a day and half the night, compared to most of the day and all night. As darkness fell, we made a hasty camp along the narrow ridge. I spent the next nine hours wrapped in my cocoon-like tent. Kerowa crawled under a thick bush and pulled the bivy bag over his head. Neither of us moved until dawn. Kerowa had the native smarts to travel light and I never once heard him complain about the discomforts of the trail.

After the first night, Kerowa never again used my pen light, saying it ruined his night vision. Even faint starlight couldn't penetrate the forest canopy, leaving me, lacking the eyes of a jungle cat, totally blind without my flashlight.

At dawn we were ready to go. The mornings were cooler for travel with less rainfall than in the afternoons. Our diet on the trail was basic but sustaining: cooked cracked wheat cereal with raisins and tea for breakfast, and a choice of rice, pasta or potato flakes with dried vegetables for dinner. This was supplemented regularly by fruits and vegetables offered to us at villages we passed through. Fortunately, Kerowa was used to a mostly vegetarian diet, even though it was by necessity rather than choice.

The next morning we dropped to lower elevations and moved in perpetual twilight under a heavy forest canopy that swished and gently heaved like an ocean swell to the wind above. Yet, no breeze entered below to disturb the dank humid air. The green tunnel we walked through swallowed the sounds of our voices and footsteps.

Once you find your rhythm with the mountain, like sailing a boat on the sea, your movement becomes hypnotic, almost effortless. You feel you can go on and on as the miles fall away behind you. We walked on a carpet of soft green moss, now and then lifting our heads to follow the strange trumpeting songs of Birds of Paradise. From the core of rotting stumps sprung new growth reaching for the canopy, lifting groundwater from roots to the sunlight. The giant trees of the forest link their branches with their neighbors, secured so well with intertwining vines that a tree with a severed base remains standing indefinitely. Occasionally, a laser-like shaft of sunlight cuts through the murkiness to illuminate a single point on the ground. We panted for breath in steamy air, thick with the scent of rotting vegetation.

We took our lunch of fruit and nuts beside Ua Ule Creek, still close to sea level, though dozens of miles inland. For momentary relief from the heat, we pulled off our boots and lay down in the cool rushing waters. On the trail, to avoid blisters, I changed to dry socks whenever possible, while the wet pair hung to dry on my backpack. An infected blister here can lead to nasty tropical ulcers that take months to heal. Kerowa noticed the new boots I'd bought him were starting to blister the backs of his heel, so he hung them from his pack and went barefoot across the mountains, as most of the natives here do. The only time he stopped to put the boots on his enormous feet was before entering a village. Once away from the impressionable villagers, the boots came off again.

We moved along the Ua Ule, crossing the river at each obstacle by leaping from boulder to boulder. Here, where several creeks met in a labyrinth of water and jungle, the trail was invisible. We followed several false leads that led us blindly into the green maze. I recalled recent reports on local news about a Canadian woman who attempted to cross this trail with a friend, became separated in this area, and was never seen again. People lost in the forest become desperate and keep moving in a panic, always thinking they will find their way to a familiar trail or village just over the next hill. Often, they blindly wander deeper and deeper into the jungle, becoming exhausted, injured, tormented by hunger and biting insects, to die in madness.

A creeping sense of desperation welled up in my gut while I oriented the compass to the map in a futile attempt to find my way forward. It was Kerowa who found our way out by studying the ground for native footprints in the mud, the faint clues of bent grass and twigs snapped in three pieces as if stepped on, and noting hatchet marks on the trees. Like a bloodhound, he had no use for maps and couldn't read one in any case. The more I realized my life depended on reading these unwritten signs, the faster I picked up the native path-finding techniques.

Crossing rivers on the Kokoda Trail

In the rainy season, even the smallest creeks grew into mad torrents of racing brown water. One fast and deep river almost took me for a ride as I stepped from an overhanging boulder onto a bridge of vine-lashed bamboo. After a few steps out, I felt them giving way. I leapt back to land spread-eagle on the side of the rock just as the bridge dropped into the swirling waters below. We crossed this river by detouring downstream, clinging to trees and rocks along the eroded riverbank until we found a felled tree that reached over to the other bank. It was a test of balance and nerve to step across that slick, moss-covered log with wet boots and a heavy pack. "Perils," explorer Alexander Humboldt once said, "elevate the poetry of life." Kerowa and I both knew the feeling.

We passed a barely recognizable village once known as Ioribaiwa and now abandoned. Everywhere he goes, man beats back the fast-growing jungle with bush knives and fire until he tires and moves on. When the population is small and the island big, as in New Guinea, what humans leave behind is soon engulfed by the jungle as if we were never there.

Most of the Kokoda Trail was easily distinguishable, even to me, as a narrow, tunnel-like channel through the bush, but there were numerous places where any of two or three paths looked equally appropriate. Here we became sidetracked in fields of head-high kunai grass, Kerowa leading unseen and unheard just a few steps ahead. One step off the trail is like stepping into a green wall. The mind sees it as a place beyond our control – impenetrable, forbidding and frightening. In tricky areas, as a backup to Kerowa's bush sense, I made sketches with compass bearings clearly indicating the way back to the last known point.

There were more similar-looking ridges and creek-lined valleys to cross. Once past the wide and shallow Ofi Creek, we started up the interminably long ascent marked on my map as the Maguli Range. We struggled up the slippery clay trail, always thinking the peak was at hand, only to find the trail make a short dip and then soar upwards again. Though the topography of the map indicated nine false peaks, I stopped counting at twenty. Then, at last, we were moving down – slipping and sliding over tangled roots and rocks on a steep two-hour descent to Naoro Village.

In the village, women tended gardens of corn and taro, and supervised children as they pulled up clumps of peanuts from the cleared ground. A village elder came by and invited us to stay in the broken down shack once used as a traveler's rest house. We paid two kina for the shelter, but the uneven boards of the floor convinced Kerowa to sleep on the soft grass beside the steps. Even though we remained in the bosom of the jungle, protected only by a shell of bamboo and grass, being next to a village overnight eased my child-like anxiousness to get out of the jungle after dark. I awoke at dawn, surprised at how good I felt after my first full night of sleep since hitting this trail. The aches in my legs and back were gone. I had even forgotten the incessant itching of the burrowing mites that attached themselves to us when we brushed against the grass. Either I'd outlived them or was too tired to let them keep me awake.

On the way out of the village, we passed a stout bamboo pen holding a nervously pacing cassowary bird. The world's largest forest bird, this Melanesian version of the ostrich defends itself with a powerful kick from its clawed legs that can easily knock a man down and shred his flesh. At the next village sing-sing, the cassowary would become part of the feast and its feathers part of the ceremonial costumes.

As we climbed out of the valley, the rising sun bathed the east-facing flanks of the range in an orange glow. Patches of misty clouds clung to the mountains above and below us. The sweet fragrance of coffee blossoms hung in the air around bushes with plump red coffee beans ripe for picking.

Just as I had been wondering if anyone else ever used this path, a man appeared before us who introduced himself in Pidgin as Masta Giumi. He had just set out on a days-long trip to fetch medicine for his baby daughter suffering from malaria. When I gave him half my supply of anti-malarial, he hurried back ahead of us, promising to see us again when we reached Menari Village.

Entering Menari, the entire village turned out to greet us. Because Masta Giumi had told them we were coming, even the women and children lost their natural shyness, gathering round us, all laughing and talking at once. The women loaded us down with mandarin oranges, pineapples, bananas and roasted corn. We accepted as little as was polite, stuffing the food into our mouths and backpacks. It seemed we could have stayed here for a good, long rest, but I could tell Kerowa was uncomfortable among this foreign tribe because he did not take his pack off and join me as I entered Masta Giumi's hut. While I had a short visit inside, Kerowa stood outside the door, smiling and nervously rolling his eyes side-to-side. The baby would probably survive now that she had some anti-malarials, at least for now.

Within minutes of arriving, we set out in company with a local family on their way to the market in Kokoda; a two-day walk, they claimed, and led the way up the next hill at a frantic pace. The woman in the lead carried a bundle of fruit and vegetables in her string bilum bag suspended over her back. It was perhaps twice the weight of our backpacks, most of the load being transferred to her neck by the carrying strap across her forehead. Behind her, the eldest daughter carried another loaded bilum on her back as well as her younger sister on her shoulders. The son carried only a small handbag. The father carried just his walking stick. I was half-running and still falling behind. Seeing me struggle, the father halted and asked for my bag. Handing it to his wife to carry, the old man proudly said, "Meri bilong me em strongpela tumas" (My wife is very strong).

I took back the bag and motioned them to go on ahead. The traditional role for PNG men is hunter and defender of the family. A short generation ago, the men made war on their neighboring tribes or stood guard while women did all the work in the gardens. The women still do most of the work and the men watch approvingly, often doing nothing productive all day. Besides, as Kerowa reminded me, when a man pays several fat pigs as bride price to a girl's father, he expects in return that she will work hard to repay his investment.

We stopped at the summit where the women dropped their packs and I gasped for breath. The old man told us about his life here and recounted being a child caught in the war zone in the early 1940s. Japanese soldiers arrived at his village, gave his family the equivalent of $50 in useless war currency, and took over the family farm. Forced to flee into the bush, they lived as hunter-gatherers until the end of the war. When they returned to the destroyed village, they found every single root crop had been pulled up by starving Japanese soldiers, who were expected to live off the plunder of the lands they conquered.

Since our pace was slowing down our friends, I asked them to go ahead of us. Not surprisingly, we never saw them again. Kerowa and I descended to the edge of a vast swamp where we crossed another multitude of creeks. Over the deeper waters, we balanced precariously on bundles of slimy, semi-submerged logs – the waters swirling around our feet as we crept uneasily forward.

Our camp that night was under a lean-to, which Kerowa threw together from branches and broad leaves as a light rain fell. I had come down with a fever and chills that day, sapping my remaining energy in the afternoon heat, until each step felt like my last. That night was miserable, made worse by a too-curious wallaby – a type of small kangaroo – that kept dragging our camp gear away. I got up twice during the night to chase him away, only to have him return minutes later.

In the morning, we gathered our gear strewn out around the camp and discovered the beast had chewed through two of our four water bottles.

That day we moved along muddy slopes infested with leeches, reminding me that in the jungle, humans were not always at the top of the food chain. As numerous as ants on an anthill, the ground was blanketed with black, worm-like bodies flipping from end to end, waiting for some warm-blooded mammal to latch onto. Kerowa stopped each minute to flick them off his bare feet and legs. I had better protection with long pants tucked inside boots laced up tight. Still, a few managed to inch their way up to my waist for a meal. Several times that day we took turns inspecting each other and held a lit match with trembling fingers close to the heads of the blood-engorged leeches until they dropped off. All I could think of was to keep moving, hoping to lose them on higher ground.

By the end of another day of hard climbing, we crested the high point of the trail at the 6,700-foot elevation of Kokoda Gap. In this area at least, we were above the altitude of the malarial mosquitoes that make life in the lower bush areas so miserable. From here to the coast, I was cheered by the knowledge that the ups and downs ahead were mostly down. From the ridge, finally above the forest canopy, I could see across the cloud-speckled valley to the next ridge and the one beyond; an unending ocean of waves of green. I took a photograph that – no surprise – captures little of the grandeur of that non-transferable vision.

As we immersed ourselves in the green of the next valley, we took a detour to Myola Village, a several hour walk beyond another ridge, along the edge of a dry lake bed. Observed from the western ridge, the lake bed was tucked between the mountains like an alpine meadow. We treaded on its spongy surface among blankets of yellow buttercups and wild forget-me-nots, flushing up quail as we went. Near the top of the eastern ridge, a cascade tumbled from a creek that was the source of the mighty Iora River we had crossed so many miles ago.

We took this side trip to Myola Village in order to visit a British VSO (Volunteer Service Overseas) station, the equivalent of the U.S. Peace Corps. At the edge of the village, we met a young Englishman who introduced himself as Gary Thomas. Here he was demonstrating to villagers how to care for the sheep he had recently imported. The little settlement of Myola was scrupulously clean, as if it had been swept end to end each morning. We followed Gary around to trout-rearing ponds he had stocked with thousands of New Zealand Rainbows that he hopes to introduce to nearby rivers. That evening we dried ourselves around the cooking fire in Gary's house of timber and split bamboo set on stilts.

"Did you know bamboo is the world's fasting growing living thing?" Gary said. "As you can see, it provides much of the framework, siding, floors and mats for these houses." As he spoke, behind him a well-fed rat walked at ease through the open door and up the corner post to the roof rafter where he sat as if he were another regular guest here. To avoid direct contact with rats and insects, and for Gary's amusement, I slept that evening in my tent erected within the hut.

Heavy rains that night saturated the lakebed, flooding sections of it. A man from the village offered to guide us back to the main route of the Kokoda Trail. Gary sent us off with a warning: "Stay to the high ground and don't try any shortcuts. If you step into the bog, fall face-down into it and swim or crawl out. If you remain standing you will be sucked under." I had read the same in an Army survival manual, but was not eager to test the theory.

We followed our guide in a zigzag course, always seeking the high ground until we found the trail. Along the way, I picked up several brass shell casings stamped MG VII 1941. Gary had told us this lake bed had been an ideal drop point for supplies during the war, and showed us the remains of a crashed American fighter plane, its aluminum frame still recognizable more than forty years later.

Far from Myola, we stopped to boil our rice and vegetable lunch on our compact stove, placed on a large flat rock midstream in the Iora River. At this point the river was widening, a sure sign we were losing altitude and getting closer to the north coast. It felt good to lay back on the stone island for a brief rest away from the biting ants of the trail. The waters swished and danced over the stones, even more eager than I to be somewhere else.

That day we progressed as far as the ridge above the next valley. Fading light, and the closeness of the bush, forced us to camp directly on our narrow footpath. All night the darkness rang with the now familiar jungle songs. The chirps and buzz of insects provided an incessant background to the barks and grunts of small animals, mostly unknown to me but familiar to Kerowa. On some nights, I'd awaken suddenly to a crack and groan, followed by tearing noise as a dead tree finally broke free of its entangling vines and crashed to the ground. And always there were aggravating bush rats that tore into our gear in the middle of the night. The size of small dogs, these fearless creatures would climb right over your sleeping body in their search for food.

An uphill walk the next day brought us into the abandoned village of Isurava. A few of the thatch and timber buildings still stood upright and taro flourished in the gardens. It was hard to picture this village as the scene of some of the fiercest fighting of WWII's Kokoda campaign, where hundreds of men died in a grim back-and-forth struggle of guns and bayonets, desperate to possess this patch of jungle. The knowledge of this bitter history made me uncomfortable. Sometimes it's better not to know too much. As for the jungle, it has a short memory of man's passing, even his wars. The pits where soldiers dug in and died are now filled and healed. In a few more years, the remaining buildings would drop and disappear into the soil, feeble symbols of our own mortality. But the spirits of the dead still roam in the minds of the living who walk the trail.

A few hours later, we entered Alolo Village where there were shrieks and cries from a group of women and children as they left their laundry in the river and disappeared into the bush. Either Kerowa and I looked as rough as we felt, or it was another standard response to strangers when the men of the village are away. We moved on, feeling hidden eyes upon us.

Near Kokoda Village, we walked through an expansive plantation of rubber trees – row upon row of trees, each with a gash near its base that oozed white latex into cups waiting to be gathered.

In the village, we met the dirt road that began here and ran some forty miles to the north coast. For the past several days, Kerowa had been suffering from what we later found out was a relapse of dysentery that had him holding an aching gut and making hourly sprints into the bush for bouts of bloody diarrhea. We decided he should go on ahead by bus to more quickly reach a doctor. He could then proceed by boat and a series of buses back to his highland village. As he climbed into the back of an open truck, I assured him I would meet him in his village a month later. He looked at me with a long face that seemed to doubt ever seeing me again. I stayed in a village guesthouse that night and continued on my way to the coast the next morning by foot.

11 In the Shadow of Sumburipa

Two roads diverged in a wood – and I,
I took the one less traveled by,
And that has made all the difference.

- Robert Frost

Paharija and her sister at the farm

The brooding peak of Mt. Lamington loomed over me as I walked alone through a now-peaceful valley, towards the north coast of PNG. In January of 1951, the long-smoldering volcano had erupted with cataclysmic force, sending a cloud of burning hot gas roaring down the slope into the fertile valley where I now walked, wiping out Oro Province's district headquarters of Higatura. The entire population of some four thousand natives and 35 Europeans died instantly. Now, hiking through the lower valley, there was no sign of the previous destruction.

The long, pleasant, two-day walk from Kokoda brought me to the new district headquarters of Popondetta, established at a safer distance from the volcano. The road held a fusion of scenes: wooden bridges spanning small rivers, villages with their gardens and palm groves and friendly people waving as I marched past. Several times a day, an open truck filled with passengers standing in the back raced by on the narrow track, leaving me momentarily engulfed in its trailing dust cloud.

Months earlier, in the library at the university in Port Moresby, I met a girl named Paharija, whose family lived in a village near here. When she finished that year's course, she returned to her village and wrote a letter inviting me to visit her family's farm. We shared a love of mountains so she finished her letter with: "Come and we can climb Sumburipa." Mt. Lamington, called Sumburipa by locals, is quiet now except for steam vents and a hot crater. The natives who have returned in recent years to the mountain slopes know of places where they can bake vegetables simply by putting them in a shallow hole in the ground. Sumburipa is far from dead — just sleeping for now.

By chance, I met Paharija and her mother at the Popondetta Post Office. They were surprised to see me, particularly after hearing I walked all the way from Moresby. At the general store, we loaded bags of rice, sugar, two tins of tea and powdered milk for Paharija's sister's baby. Carrying their supplies, we walked the two miles back to their farm. After turning onto a footpath, we crossed over a stream on a log foot bridge and entered a clearing where their houses stood, concealed from the road by thick gardens and rows of palms.

In the compound, three simple huts stood close together, raised above the ground on posts. One hut was for the parents, one for Paharija and her sister, and one for her four brothers. Near them, under a thatched roof lean-to, was a cement oven and a wooden table for taking their meals. The houses were typical: bamboo walls and floor and hand-hewn timber frames with bundles of kunai grass for the roofs. The four sturdy posts that raised each dwelling off the ground helped keep them free of some of the jungle pests and allowed a cooling breeze to circulate freely. Alongside the huts sat an open-sided guest house where I set down my backpack.

Beside a stream, staggered rows of coconut palms bordered the gardens of pumpkin, cassava, bananas, pineapple and taro root. Hidden behind the rest was a grove of cocoa trees, then a string of wire fence stretched between wooden posts enclosing several acres where the pigs run. The climate and soil are so favorable that young trees cut down and trimmed into fence posts and pounded into the earth take root, sprouting green tops and budding branches within weeks. Another rivulet, used for washing clothes and bathing, ran opposite the gardens. Upstream from there, the clear, cool creek provided pure drinking water.

During the night, I listened to the dull thumps from falling ripe coconuts as they hit the ground. In the mornings, Paharija and I gathered all we could find and carried them to the pigs. Since pigs cannot open the hard nuts by themselves, my job was to split them open with an axe, while taking care not to strike any pigs as they pushed and shoved to get a feeding place. I would inevitably be knocked off my feet and splattered in mud and coconut water during the pigs' excitement to get at the rich, oily coconut meat. Some of these baconers weighed over 300 pounds so they simply pushed me aside with gluttonous indifference. At least it provided great amusement to Paharija, who shouted warnings and instructions from the safety of the other side of the fence. To enhance their coconut diet, a few times each week the pigs received a wheelbarrow full of cooked green bananas and cassava root and steamed leaves from the papaya tree – a tropical hog's banquet.

Later, while planting pumpkin seeds in the cleared garden soil, Paharija grabbed my hand and told me to use a stick instead of my thumb to press the holes in the soil for the seeds. She explained that a year earlier, her sister had pushed a seed into the garden earth and been stung by a spider that injected a poison egg under her skin. Her thumb had swollen to three times its normal size. The doctor in town said he could do nothing; the egg must hatch and then the spider would eat its way out of her thumb. If he tried to cut it out, it would release its poison and she'd lose her hand or it could possibly kill her. It took months of tormenting pain for the flesh-eating spider to come out and her thumb to heal. Even innocent-looking soil held terrifying dangers.

In the cocoa tree grove, the ripening purple cocoa pods were soon to be harvested and separated from the inner nuts, which were baked and crushed to produce the aromatic cocoa powder. While the girls pruned the cocoa trees, my job was to clear back the bush with the machete. The tangled vegetation I was clearing around the gardens required clearing several times a year. So fast was the growth on this farm that one man with a machete could not keep more than a few acres clear. The rest of their land was left in its natural forested state, which was good to see because once an island habitat is clear-cut, it can permanently lose many of its original animals.

I stayed with the Hotota family for two weeks, helping where I could with the farm's daily work. Whenever I thought we had finished our work, there was more to be done. Once we caught up with tending gardens, we collected bamboo and thatch for a new house. These bush houses need replacing every two years as the grass roofs dry out and wood rots and becomes riddled with termites. Fortunately, all the housing materials grow nearby and constantly replenish themselves in a timeless cycle. Resting at night, I imagined I heard the jungle growing with buds bursting open and vines creeping out to willfully fill any sunlit void.

When the day's heat overwhelmed us, we retreated to the cool waters of the river. I remember wading knee-deep up that lovely stream bed of sand and smooth stones and swirling clear waters to lay in the shallows next to the bank. Vines reached down to touch the water. Brightly colored butterflies the size of two hands swirled around us as sparkling flakes of color dancing on air. Paharija's dark, wet skin was bathed by an emerald radiance of diffused sunlight filtering through the forest canopy.

In the evenings, Paharija's family of eight and I gathered around the table next to the cook house for dinner. Her father began dinner with a prayer. Afterwards he told long bible stories in Pidgin, as related to him from the resident white missionary from Ohio. The country seemed to hold more priests than tourists.

I started out my travels eager to criticize the motives and effects of missionaries attempting to convert souls and cultures to their version of God's own way. I had largely bought into Gauguin's version of Polynesia and the noble savage myth. However, it soon became clear to me that what the missionaries created, at least on this once dark island, was far better than what they had found. Though they did not perform miracles and there was much help these people still needed, I saw many instances of how missionaries across this island had assisted the natives in lifting themselves up from a short and miserable life filled with fear, violence, disease, ignorance and suffering. The whining and cruel-tongued anti-missionary crowd are as self-righteous as those they try to tear down. Yet, by comparison, what have they done to help the islanders? Few of them came to share the islanders' diseases and poverty and work alongside the natives to ease their sufferings.

The road to town was deserted at night and cool enough for pleasant walking. On an aimless evening stroll, we looked up from the road to see the silhouette of Sumburipa in the moonlight, its peak continually wreathed in steam-filled clouds. I felt drawn to it and wanted to see the people who bravely returned to live on its slopes. Because it was their land, and they had nowhere else to go, they defied the mountain to strike out at them again.

Early one morning, Paharija and I hoisted our packs and set out with hopes of climbing the mountain. She had relatives in most of the villages along the way so we could expect assistance if needed. Outside the vegetable market in Popondetta, we found a truck going in the right direction, so we stepped up into the back and found a place on one of the two wooden benches crammed with passengers. Between the benches were piles of string bilums, stretched to the limit with fruits and vegetables the people were taking home from the market. Other people followed and found seats on sacks of flour and rice. After we got moving, the truck made circles around town for an hour, picking up more people and packing them into places I thought already filled to capacity.

Once we thought we were finally underway, the truck pulled to a stop in front of the general store next to the market – the same spot we had boarded an hour earlier. One of the passengers had some last-

minute shopping to do. This was Melanesian time, where bus
schedules did not exist and waiting around was of no consequence.

While we waited, a couple of women came out of the store and
stared at me blankly. Our driver exchanged a few words with them
before they lowered their heads and crept away as the whole truck
burst into laughter. By this time I spoke Pidgin well enough.
Unfortunately, I knew nothing of the local languages, such as
Orokaiva, which was spoken in this province. When the uproar settled
down, Paharija explained to me there was an old custom here that
before a crop of taro was planted, the women needed to do something
auspicious, either procure magic from a sorcerer, visit a sacred place
or make an offering. So when the driver asked them what they
wanted, they replied that someone had told them there was a white
man in the back of the truck. This being somewhat rare, they came to
have a look. The native driver had then bellowed, "All right, you've
had a good look at our white man. Now go plant good taro."

Eventually, we got underway. By ones and twos, everyone was
unloaded at villages or farms along the route, slowly bringing us
nearer the mountain. The empty truck dropped us at the dead end of
the road. By my map, I calculated the half-day truck journey had
brought us less than twelve miles in a straight line. We might have
walked it instead.

Nearby we found the home of Paharija's aunt, where we asked
directions for the best route to the summit. She became nervous and
asked us to forget about the climb and go back. Apparently, a local
sorcerer was stirring a pot of trouble and claiming people should stay
off the mountain until he had pacified the spirits with certain
sacrifices. Paharija also became worried, but I assured them both we
would be alright. Reluctantly, the aunt called a young boy to guide us
to the village near the sorcerer's camp, where we could spend the
night and get further instructions.

Three of us now plunged into the bush, the boy leading us quickly
down dark, narrow footpaths that forked off into other paths every
few minutes. The boy must have had the route imprinted in his genes,
for he always knew which of two identical-looking paths to take, even
after I was hopelessly lost. We climbed to the ridges, descended to

cross shallow streams, then up other hills. The late afternoon sunlight was fading under the green roof of the forest. Vines hung down in massed loops from the treetop canopy to the ground, creating a surreal dream world around us. Our footsteps were muffled into silence as we stepped on a carpet of decaying plant life.

Suddenly, the boy stopped. We stood, staring up where the boy stared, and listened intently to a bird singing a song sounding oddly like flute music. Still hidden, it ended its song and we heard the faint fluttering noise as it flew away. The wide-eyed boy said he must get home before dark and vanished down the trail.

"We're almost there. Let's go ahead quietly now," Paharija whispered. Later, she explained the bird we heard was the *bisohi*, or messenger bird. An Orokaiva legend says it warns people of impending danger with its mysterious song. "The bisohi keeps singing until you interpret his message correctly. Then he moves away," she said. According to the boy's interpretation, the bird was warning me not to enter this place.

"With your education," I asked, "Do you really believe that story?"

She gave me a look of indulgent pity and replied, "You heard it yourself, didn't you?"

We moved on regardless, since there was not enough light left for us to safely find our way out of this maze of paths. When we approached a few huts in a clearing, she asked me to wait out of sight while she went ahead to see if we were in the right place. She found our sorcerer, Haugaturu, and afterward came back and told me that he'd been expecting us. Even though no one had time to tell him we were coming and before she could tell him herself, he had told her she had a white man with her and that we were on our way to the mountain. "Must have been that loud-mouthed bird that gave me away," I joked.

In the fading twilight, I walked up to the tall and thin Haugaturu standing on the step to his hut. With expressionless face and deep-set eyes that seemed to look right through me, he sized me up carefully before reaching out to shake my hand. He motioned for us to sit next to him. A decrepit woman gone senile sat nearby talking to herself while laying sweet potatoes and taro to roast on the glowing coals at the edge of a fire. He welcomed us to stay the night — where else could we go? — then warned us this place was *tambu*, under a bad spell. His father, he told us, had died the week before and we must take care not to offend his spirit. "The white man," he told Paharija, "must never raise his voice or walk around alone. He may shock my father's spirit." It seemed she had interpreted the bisohi bird correctly.

There was a stark loneliness about this little settlement, perhaps because there were no children around to lighten the mood. Smoke from the cooking fire hung in a dense low cloud as if held down by the heavy moist air. The four huts of the compound sat on a bare dirt courtyard bordered by tall *areaca* palms, the type that produce the ubiquitous betel nut that all the native men chew. Selling betel nuts at the town market was Haugaturu's main source of income. Meanwhile he worked his sorcery and watched the crops grow, as his father did before him.

The guest hut we occupied sat on the usual stilts a few steps above the ground and carried a thick roof of pandanus leaves. It was as simple as it could be: no furniture, no lantern, no walls. Near the foot of our steps, a mound of fresh earth marked the grave of Haugaturu's father. His presence was very near indeed.

Paharija crossed the courtyard where she spoke in low tones with the sorcerer. She returned saying our host did not think it wise for us to continue up the mountain just now. He reminded her that his father had died from black magic and that another man had recently died on the mountain of mysterious circumstances. Probably because of Paharija's irresistible way of pouting, he relented, saying if we were determined to go, he would stay up late that night to make magic for our safety. "Go if you must," he added, "but you will not reach the peak."

The slightly mad woman, hunched over from her many years, appeared suddenly out of a fusion of shadows with a basket of cooked vegetables for our dinner. She turned and was swallowed into the night. Later we unrolled our blankets on the bamboo floor and tried to sleep. Fireflies blinked on and off in random patterns above me. I pulled a sheet over my head as the drone of hungry mosquitoes, homing in on our breath, filled my ears.

The mosquitoes of New Guinea have evolved into efficient blood-sucking machines. Unlike the timid and harmless mozzies in Western countries, here they seem to dive head first and stab their rapier-like stinger into your skin and are drinking your blood before you know it. What they leave behind is the malarial parasite to inhabit your liver, periodically erupting to fill your blood with disease. I'd been taking anti-malarial medicine continually since I first stepped foot on the island. But there was still a risk of the deadly fever, for there were several strains of malaria here, some of them now drug-resistant. Despite having occasional access to medicine, the natives of these lowland areas are never free of malaria. Everyone in Paharija's family has suffered the fever numerous times without much complaint, because it's a fact of life. If a native lives past their second year without dying from the fever, they usually will not die from the malaria directly. Their survival through infancy means they are partially resistant. That is, unless the dead blood corpuscles of a relapse inexplicably gather to coagulate in the brain. In that case, death is swift. Another worse possibility, is the dread blackwater fever, in which the kidneys slowly dissolve, turning the urine black before a painful death. With these continual assaults on their health, it is no mystery why their bodies are worn out by the age of forty.

For hours, Haugaturu chanted spells from his porch, joined from time to time by the old woman. I could just make out her face, eerily illuminated by the fire she huddled over. The remainder of the night was broken only by the jungle's eternal nocturnal chattering.

I did not sleep at all that night and thought of the explorers who came to this area of New Guinea in the late nineteenth century. They reported the natives engaged in a particularly gruesome form of "living cannibalism." An unfortunate victim, captured by an enemy tribe, was staked out alive and strips of flesh were cut from his body, as needed, to fill out their mostly vegetarian diet. To prolong life, and so prolong the feast, the wounds were bound and covered with banana leaves. Meanwhile, the victim was subjected to the most sadistic torturing the women of the village could devise, which I won't go into here. The poor wretch lived in this agony, sometimes up to two weeks before succumbing. And we modern Westerners still blame the missionaries for destroying native "culture" in New Guinea.

This horrid practice ended before I got here, but the black magic continues. Poisoning is still a favorite method for the sorcerers to use to back up their magic. People have become so terrified when told a curse has been put on them, that they die within a few days, victims of the toxicity of suggestion. This confirms the sorcerer's powers, and the next victim's fears are reinforced. Although the missionaries have worked hard, the natives have been merely vaccinated with Christianity and still live in a spirit-filled world. None live free of the fear of sorcery and the witch doctors do a thriving business throughout the land.

The demons fled with morning's light and our world seemed less hostile. We received directions from Haugaturu to guide us through the maze of trails and villages that lead to Sumburipa. The old man acknowledged my ten kina banknote, and my wordy thanks for his hospitality, with a deep grunt. We shouldered our bags and moved back into the tangle of vines, creepers and trees. We passed the familiar banana, mango, sago palms, rubber trees and blooming orchids. As I pointed to an unfamiliar plant, Paharija named it for me and explained how it might be used for food or medicine: "This plant the women know how to make into a tea, that when drunk regularly, prevents pregnancy," she said with authority.

Our pack load was light and we easily scrambled up the mountain slopes, along ridges and across narrow ravines, slowly and steadily gaining altitude. We walked through or around several villages nearly buried under the weight of the jungle. One village of over fifty huts was sprawled out along a riverbank. There was no road in the area so we often met people commuting along the well-worn footpath.

We took lunch along the trail and soon were joined by a group of Ragiana Birds of Paradise gathered on a branch overhead. Three males, resplendent in red flank plumes, made trumpeting calls to a plain-feathered female on another branch of the same tree. They fanned wings and tails, calling out raucously as they hopped up and down in what was certainly a dance contest. If sufficiently impressed, the female offers herself to the most inspired dancer. Birds of Paradise live only in this corner of the world and even here are becoming rare, as the native population hunts them down to add their colorful plumes to ceremonial headdresses.

Birdwatchers have counted some 650 species of birds on this one island, almost as many as in all North America. Animals are comparatively few, the commonly seen ones being the wallaby, large bush rats, wild razor-backed hogs and a raccoon-like tree-dwelling marsupial called the couscous. Crocodiles infest some rivers, but snakes and insects are the more common threat. I brushed through countless silken webs of spiders whose outstretched legs sometimes were as big as my hand. Not knowing which varieties were poisonous made each encounter memorable.

Arriving in remote Kiorota Village we met more relatives of Paharija. They recognized her immediately, even though they hadn't seen her in years. An older man with an uncommon sparkle of youth in his eyes shook my hand vigorously, introducing himself as Sinclair, and insisting that we stay for tea. Sinclair moved his family back here thirty years ago to rebuild the village that had been destroyed by the eruption of Sumburipa. Every single thing that lived or grew between here and the summit began life less than thirty-four years ago. Already, a thin forest covered the slopes. As in most of the villages I had been to on the island, every bush and blade of grass had been removed around the huts, probably to reduce insect and snakebites, leaving the rich volcanic soil exposed.

With tea finished and the usual warnings given us to turn back unheeded, Sinclair grabbed his walking stick and led us down one of the many trails out of the village. In spite of thick bush, we caught a few hopeful glimpses of the summit drawing closer as we crested the succession of ridges. Sinclair led at a young man's pace, stabbing the ground with his walking stick and telling stories as he went.

At the edge of a cliff he halted, saying, "Me olpela tumas. Me go long haus bilong me. Yu mas wokabot long hap" (I'm too old for this part. I'll return home now and you can cross over there). He pointed below us to a chasm in the earth a hundred yards deep. It was clear why he was going no further. Below us lay a near vertical wall of wet clay, vines and rocks. He assured us it was the best crossing place available. We thanked him and dropped over the side, groping from vine to vine and sliding to the river below. Fortunately, the opposite bank was less steep. In a half hour we were up and entering Kenbata, the highest settlement on the mountain.

A group of noisy children surrounded us as we approached the village elder resting on the steps of his hut. No matter what we said, the chief remained adamant in his refusal to let us continue. "Sumburipa is tambu," he repeated over and over. "Come back in a fortnight when the spirits may be quiet again."

From here we had a clear view of the steaming forbidden peak, tantalizingly near. Because of superstition and fear, I could no more reach it than I could clutch a handful of its smoke. These people lived precariously on a mountain of fire that awed them with its mystical powers and could destroy them again at any time. Because this village owns the upper slopes we needed to pass through, and claims possession even of the smoldering crater itself, we had to respect their wishes. Reluctantly, we turned away and followed a young man that led us down to a road on the other side of the mountain. Eventually, we came full circle around the mountain by the time we reached Popondetta.

The final leg may have been the hardest of all as we walked several miles along the road, under a blistering sun, carrying the disappointment of the failed climb. The first empty truck that came by stopped to give us a ride. We climbed in the back and then found out it was used for hauling drums of oil. Every surface was covered in a thick black goo of oil and dirt. To increase our discomfort, the truck rode empty as if it had no springs and the driver managed to hit every available pothole and rock in the road. We suffered this for an hour or so before being dropped near Hotota's farm.

There was more work to do on the farm and I stayed for two more days to help out. My last day there, I helped cut and haul the posts for a new hut to be built along the river next to the pineapple patch. When she married, Paharija planned to raise her family here with the gardens and river at her doorstep. I planted a sprouting coconut next to the site and she smiled in approval as I carefully packed the soil around it and asked it to grow quick and tall to shade her home and provide fruit for her family. She and I lingered at the site of the new house that evening. With a rising moon, we sat protected by a mozzie net hung under a branch. Each passing breeze caught the green tops of giant bamboo, rubbing their tapering segmented stems together with creaks and groans. The soft, bubbling noises of the river and the ever-present insect chirps completed the gentle night orchestra.

Next morning Paharija joined me for the long walk down to the coast at Killerton Bay. This now peaceful road had been the scene of a bloody rear guard retreat during WWII as the Japanese were pushed out of the Kokoda Trail. Some 16,000 Japanese died between here and the beaches of Buna and Gona at the end of this road. Walking past these now empty settlements along the bay was a personal triumph. I had crossed a part, even a narrow part, of this untamed island in twelve days of walking, not counting the detours. Despite my fatigue and blistered feet, I was too happy for words.

At Killerton, we found the 90-foot inter-island trader of the Lutheran Shipping Company tied to the wharf. I had a couple hours to wait until it sailed for the town of Lae, so we walked down to the bay where a point of land juts out into the sea. We relaxed on a blanket on the sand under the welcome filtered shade of the palm fronds.

A solitary outrigger canoe approached the beach and the man began unloading baskets of produce from his gardens to be sold at a nearby market. Paharija grabbed some coins and went to see what he had. She returned with a couple of green drinking nuts and an armful of soft vegetables they call *pitpit*. These pitpit resembled a small ear of unhusked corn on the outside. Once roasted on our driftwood beach fire and peeled, they tasted like a soft sweet squash. We ate as many as we could, washing them down with the slightly sweet coconut water.

It was well after sunset when the gate to the wharf opened. Inside, it was as a refugee camp. Hundreds of people waited around with their belongings in bilums, cardboard boxes and crates seemingly scattered in chaos all over the yard.

By the time I got to the ticket booth, all the 14 kina (US$12) "below deck" tickets were sold, and I got one of the last 21 kina "above deck" tickets. The gang plank lowered and the rush was on with two hundred people and their cargo negotiating one narrow plank. As the others boarded quickly to seek out the choice spots for the overnight passage, Paharija handed me a note containing the address of her relatives in Lae. I thanked her as best I could and said my goodbye.

"Will you come back and stay with us after you return from the Highlands?" she asked. I said I would and started my way up the gangplank. "When you return we will climb Sumburipa to the very top," Paharija called out.

Yes we would, I thought, spirits willing.

12 Highlander

*I went to the woods because I wished to live deliberately,
to front only the essential facts of life, and see if I could
not learn what it had to teach, and not, when I came to
die, discover that I had not lived.*

- Henry David Thoreau

Meeting villagers in the Highlands

Once onboard the steamer, I was thankful to hold an "above deck" ticket, despite the extra cost. I'd looked below deck and saw standing room only. The heat from the engines was stifling below and its explosive pounding shook my bones as I climbed the stairway to the top deck.

I threw my pack onto the top of one of the empty double bunks covered by a tin roof. Up here we had room to move and fresh air to breath. Most of my fellow topside passengers were members of the Popondetta cricket team on their way to a test match in the town of Lae. They celebrated with cases of Hong Kong beer till late that night, as if they had already won the match instead of preparing for it. As I moved about the boat, I noticed I was the sole white person aboard, captain and crew included. I was always treated courteously, even if countless staring eyes followed my every move. For sixteen hours we steamed through a perfectly calm sea. Our frothy wake lay undisturbed by waves as it stretched for miles astern.

We docked in Lae under the hot afternoon sun. Sweat streamed down my face in the calm, heavy air as I fell in with the press of people ready to disembark. I wondered how the passengers below decks survived all night and day crammed next to that hot pounding engine on a ride through hell. Even before the ship was secured and the gangway attached, many people had already flung themselves over the rail and several feet down to the pier.

Lae is Papua New Guinea's second largest city in population, and its main industrial center. As I walked through the sprawling town on Sunday afternoon, I found it nearly deserted until I reached the residential section on the city's edge. The address Paharija had given me led to a small brick home where I introduced myself to her cousin Timothy and his family. Trying not to impose on strangers, I stopped only to ask where I could find information on the buses that travel to the Highlands. After a shower and dinner, Timothy and his wife insisted I stay over night, telling me we would find a bus in the morning. To my embarrassment, they also insisted I sleep on their bed under the mozzie net while they slept on the floor of the front room.

At sunrise we walked to the bus station where Timothy made sure I got on the right bus bound for leg one of the journey to the Highlands. The night before, Timothy had worried about my traveling alone through country he considered rife with dangers from outlaws, rascal gangs and tribal conflict. "Be very careful," Timothy had warned, "they're not civilized up there yet." As the bus pulled away, they looked as though they were sending their only son off to war. These were good people, typical of all those who had helped me thus far.

Our bus, in the form of a stretched van, had a capacity of about twenty people. It was half full when I boarded it at 7 AM. By the time we made a fuel stop and visited a few roadside markets we were full and the driver felt ready to get underway. Women with tattoo-covered faces sat with runny-nosed children on their laps. Bags of betel nut lay piled high in the aisle. Men worked at separating the green nuts from their unwieldy branches and flung the unwanted brush out the windows. The Highlanders are as addicted to betel nut as the lowlanders. Since the nut only grows in coastal zones, everyone traveling today brought as many bags of it as they could carry, either for personal use or to sell at a profit in the Highland markets.

We motored across the wide grasslands of Markham Valley, notable as the only significant area of flat land I ever saw on this convoluted island. A few solitary trees stood scattered around the grassy plain, each tree guarded by a single cow claiming its patch of shade in an otherwise shadeless valley. The country ahead looked more like Colorado than New Guinea; mountain ranges loomed in the distance on either side of the level savannah with a strip of blacktop running straight ahead to the horizon. What would have been out-of-place in Colorado was our vehicle, racing across the valley, with branches flying out the windows, our bearded driver lustily chanting out Highland songs to the accompaniment of our dark-skinned and colorfully dressed group of passengers.

Our long, straight road finally turned as it crossed a bridge over the Leonora River. Little water moved there now, but deep gulleys and erosion scars attested to its fury in the rainy season. At a tiny village that emerged suddenly from the steaming plains like a mirage, we found room for another passenger and his bags of betel nut. At this point, the driver asked me to move up to the front seat next to him. Often drivers offered this seat as a courtesy to foreign visitors who were not used to the competition for space in the rear, where your neighbor's luggage is under your feet and their children are crawling on top of you. All the drivers loved to "tok stori" and our driver provided a running commentary in colorful Pidgin phrases on everything from his family and village to the Apollo moon landing sixteen years earlier: still the favorite topic of discussion whenever they meet an American.

The road divided at the village of Waterais – one going north to the coastal area of Madang Province, and our road piercing the western interior. Our driver never failed to stop for a betel nut vendor and somehow room was found for a few more betel sacks and some local peanuts. Straining in low gear, we moved up the valley toward Markham Pass. We resembled a working plantation on wheels with people busily husking coconuts and pulling betel nuts from their vines, all the debris landing on the road behind us. From the cool heights of the pass we entered the Eastern Highlands Province, where neat villages of low round huts drifted past our windows.

Gold-seeking Westerners in the 1930s resulted in the first outside contact with over one million previously unknown inhabitants of these highland valleys. Before then, the interior of the island was thought to be an impenetrable tangle of uninhabited peaks. The Leahy brothers from Australia discovered the heavily populated, and well cultivated, highland valleys in 1930. When the natives first saw these strange white men they went crazy. Often the white explorers had to travel within a movable rope fence to keep the sometimes friendly, and sometimes angry, natives from carrying away their every possession. When the first small airplane landed here, natives brought baskets of food to the great metal bird and then crawled underneath to try to discover its sex. The white man was as strange to these isolated people as if he had just landed from Mars.

New Guinea – and particularly this part of the island – contains the densest array of tribal cultures in the world. Until these highlanders were discovered, anthropologists spoke of Homo Sapiens without fully knowing their subject. Though the white man's lust for gold opened the highlands, they were little explored until the 1950s. Even when I was there, some valleys in the far west were unknown to outsiders.

On the heels of the gold hunters and anthropologists, the missionaries quickly followed. When several managed to get themselves killed by the natives, the Australian government restricted the territory, not letting outsiders in without good reason. The Western Highlands, where my friend Kerowa lived, were not unrestricted until the early 1970s. In 1975, under pressure from the United Nations' fixation on eradicating colonialism at any cost, Australia granted full independence to their half of the Island. It was an unprecedented rapid transition from stone-age to democratic self-rule. Not surprisingly, the various tribes remain separated by clan quarrels, diverse languages and the geographic barriers of mountains.

We passed through Goroka, one of the main commercial centers of the highlands. The town lay clustered around the airstrip and surrounded by miles and miles of coffee plantations. Australians brought coffee trees to the highlands thirty years before and now most of the plantings have been returned to the natives. One cause of tribal conflicts has been the land shortage brought about by an increasing population where much of the fertile land is growing the cash crop of coffee instead of food.

Again, our road to the west took us creeping slowly up the next mountain range. As the straining engine pulled us up through Asoro Village, children ran alongside the slow-moving bus selling wreaths of flowers.

This road we all enjoyed the use of was a hard-won and heroic effort. Tribal wars and rivers rushing down the mountains that could take out a newly built bridge in a single day of floods, required a joint effort by the colonizers and the colonized. Each district's Australian Patrol Officer, called the *Kiap*, organized each village to build the road up to a certain point. The next village picked it up from there, and so on, until it reached hundreds of miles inland from the coast. Each man was ordered to work one day a week on the roads. Although some didn't like the compulsory work, the roads got built. Since independence, people are not forced to work, so not a single new road has been built.

Our road peaked out around 8,000 feet altitude at Daulo Pass. Ahead lay the deep valleys of Chimbu Province, bordered by ever-higher mountains on all sides. There is perhaps no more corrugated land on earth than this. Its ridges and plunging valleys run parallel, north to south, as though God's own giant plow had furrowed the land.

In a chilling late afternoon rain, I left the bus at Kundiawa, a town of a few thousand people. From here I planned to detour south to Gumine Village, where a letter of introduction to the family of Newli, a school friend of Paharija, assured me of a welcome. It was too late to get another bus so I walked around town looking for a cheap guest house to spend the night. The girls working at the general store informed me the only place in town was the overpriced tourist hotel that I couldn't afford. While the girls debated whether they could sneak me in with them at the "haus bilong yunpela meri tasol" (house for single girls only), a man who worked at the local bank came in and offered to put me up in his apartment next door. We retreated from the store while the girls carried on a heated discussion about whether they could have taken me home or not.

Early next morning, my host Peter, directed me to a corner at the edge of town where I waited for a truck heading south. Eventually, a small pickup truck arrived and I found a place in the back perched high on a pile of rough-cut wood alongside four other passengers.

We rattled on down an incredibly narrow ledge of dirt clinging to cliffs above the turbulent Wahgi River. It was hard to believe a road could exist on these precipitous cliffs, especially a road as poor as this one. The driver later confirmed my fears by telling me that sections of the road frequently disappeared due to landslides. Most of the road was single lane, requiring passing traffic to back up and park at some small indent against the cliffs. Our driver held firm to the accelerator, rounding the blind corners with horn blaring. A passenger pointed to the twisted wreck of a truck at the bottom of the gorge. I held on tightly to the shifting pile of wood as we bounced and slid along. Twice we stopped to shovel our way through fresh landslides partially blocking the road.

We ate dust for three hours until the truck coughed over the last rise, then stopped, for lack of fuel we guessed, next to the village of Dirima. A couple hundred people gathered around us near a white-painted church, looking straight out of a New England postcard, complete with tall pointed steeple and brass bell. It was Palm Sunday and people streamed out of the church after services ended, many of them wearing traditional dress. A teen-aged girl was escorted proudly through the group by her parents who asked me to take her photo. As a skirt she wore a short, coarse woven cloth hung in front from a bark belt. Her backside was covered only by a few beaded strings hanging from the belt. Radiant bird of paradise plumes fanned out from her headdress and armbands. Across her naked breasts hung necklaces of pig's tooth and seashells. Her body shined from a coating of pig's grease that enhanced her appeal in the eyes of the men in her tribe. What was most remarkable to me was to see her dressed this way as she stepped out of a Christian church.

Here I was met by the village headman who, when I questioned him, told me that the village I sought was only a couple miles down the road and that he would lead me there later. He sent a messenger boy running ahead to tell them I was coming. Before I could go, he insisted I meet everyone in this village. The headman introduced me with elaborate gestures and led me down long lines where I quickly shook everyone's hand. It was tedious and embarrassing to be treated as someone of such importance. Aside from the missionary, I was the only white man in the valley, which they considered special enough.

After meeting everybody, from the missionary himself to the littlest *pikinini* (child), the headman and I walked down the road towards Gumine. The chief was eager for me to stay in Dirima for a few days but I thought it wiser to first get to Gumine. It seemed there was some rivalry between the two villages that I did not want to get involved in. The headman insisted on carrying my heavy pack for me until handing it off to Kumulgo Sipa, the father of my friend Newli from Port Moresby, who had rushed up the road in his pickup truck to meet me. Newli, I learned, had sent a letter telling him I would visit so he was expecting me. From the way I was treated, like a prospective son-in-law, I later wondered if her letter had somewhat exaggerated our brief friendship.

We entered the small village of Gumine, literally at the end of the road, and Kumulgo beamed like a proud father as he introduced me to the gathering crowd. I stood as an old man, thin as a rake and nearly naked, fell to his knees and put his arms around my legs. For a moment I was stupefied until Kumulgo pulled me away and led me to one of the huts.

Inside the dark room sat three of his wives who began wailing and crying as soon as I stepped in. They continued their sobbing several minutes as the men sat in silence. Was I such an instant disappointment? Had someone died? I was confused and felt I should leave. Finally, Kumulgo waved them out of the hut and explained they were welcoming me according to their custom. This sorrow is how they show sympathy for a relative who has traveled a long and dangerous journey to visit them.

This man Kumulgo, I found out, was one of the village elders. Being a large landowner and of some wealth and importance, he had collected five wives who had produced fourteen children so far. Because of the expense of the bride price, an average man here has only one or perhaps two wives. Each wife purchased must also be furnished with her own home. The husband typically stays in his hut alone and visits his wives on a rotation basis.

Kumulgo's fourth wife was now visiting relatives in Mt. Hagen in the Western Highlands Province. His third wife, Newli's mother, was in Port Moresby visiting her daughter. As the story of the complicated family ties was explained to me, it seemed not all that unfamiliar. His first wife was nearly his own age of about fifty and each of his subsequent wives was progressively younger, the latest wife being about eighteen. In that way, while his wives aged, he retained the pleasures and strong back of a young wife. Meanwhile, the older wives worked in his gardens and tended the pigs to prove their continuing usefulness.

Then it hit me — this was like a version of the California lifestyle. The main difference being that our modern Western man pays his first wives to disappear. In this case, our noble savage indeed does have a higher morality. I now understood what Herman Melville meant when he wrote that rather than send more missionaries to the South Seas, we might be better served by having some native islanders come to bring us a more civilizing influence.

I was grateful there were only three wives present, because each one wanted to care for us at the same time, causing some confusion for me at mealtimes. Wife number five brought us dinner. Before we finished, wives number two and one each brought us another dinner. During my few days here, I ate from the pot of each wife in order not to offend, while wishing they had worked out a rotational cooking schedule as they did for Kumulgo's sleeping arrangement.

The ground level huts were spacious inside, there being not a single piece of furniture or decoration to clutter the soft floors of woven mats. I sat there all evening visiting with the male clan members. Women apparently were allowed inside only to bring food or tobacco and betel nut supplies. Here again, I learned that the Highlanders love their story-telling. They wanted to hear about my clansmen back home, and my journey here, but they really perked up when someone asked how the Americans got to the moon. If you want to captivate the Highlander, don't bore him with facts about the Cold War, Vietnam, fast cars, or good wine. Tell him how we put a man on the moon – that's how big his dreams are!

The Kumulgo clan expressed great relief I did not stay with those "bad people of Dirima Village" whom they had warred against just two years earlier. They had already forgotten how it started as being unimportant. Kumulgo thought someone had stolen a pig. A friend of his suggested a woman was taken from the village without paying enough bride price to her family. Off-and-on for six months, several hundred warriors from each village had fought, mostly with traditional weapons of spears, bows and arrows, and hatchets. Houses were burnt down and gardens destroyed, causing what they call "taim bilong hungry" (hungry times).

Tribal fights of today are supposed to be stylized wars, more like a sporting event. Loud taunting and name-calling start the games off. Then, from a safe distance, the spears and arrows fly, only to be swatted down or blocked by shields. When one side advances, the other dutifully retreats. With a thousand warriors clashing in this way, it results in only a handful of injuries. But the latest Kumulgo/Dirima fight had turned ugly and over thirty people were killed. The sacred rules for their fights, written and enforced in past years by their Australian colonial masters, such as not using guns or harming women and children, were forgotten. When Dirima captured an enemy, they dismembered him with hatchets, putting parts of the victim's body on the ends of arrows and spears and flinging them back to the Gumine side. Suitably enraged, the Gumine people engaged in similar outrages. When someone was killed, the family was not permitted to cry for him for fear it would bring bad luck and cause others to die. Instead, the family would provide a *mumu* (feast) for the village to entice them into a payback raid.

Eventually, the government did get involved. Police dressed in riot gear patrolled the roads causing the warriors to flee to the ridges. From there, helicopters chased them back down to the waiting police who arrested many. They were finally encouraged to settle their dispute with exchanges of pigs, beer and money that went to compensate the families of the victims.

Early one morning, I went with two of Kumulgo's sons to visit the next valley where an American missionary was working in an isolated outpost several hours walk from the nearest road. As we made our way up the high slopes, we greeted people at work in their gardens tending corn, cabbages and sweet potatoes. I was beginning to think of this valley as mostly two-dimensional – up and down. There was not a level patch of ground of any size, anywhere. Gardens were planted on forty-five degree slopes and anywhere the tilled earth could be coaxed into staying in place, it was cultivated. Some of the fields were so steep I could barely move without laying flat on the ground and pulling my way up by the bases of corn stalks.

One group of men and women slashed the brush with machetes to clear new fields. After the chopped vegetation dried, it was set afire. Then some of the ashes were removed and planting begun. Lacking fertilizer, every second year they had to abandon the tired plot of soil and start again somewhere else. After several years of letting the bush take over, they cleared it again in a timeless cycle. Across the hills I could see fields in every stage – faraway smoke rose from burning fields, while closer, women carried baskets of ash from yesterday's fire. Others were planting or mending wooden stake fences that keep foraging pigs out of their gardens.

From the highest ridge above Gumine, on this unusually clear day, we could see far down the Wahgi Valley past Kundiawa and forty miles beyond to the 14,800-foot peak of Papua New Guinea's highest mountain, Mt. Wilhelm. The mountain dominated all the surrounding peaks and as I looked at it, I knew I would climb it before I left the island.

We followed the trail down the next valley until we met a group of men halfway through their two-day trek to town. One of the men bent low under the heavy load of a manual coffee-grinding machine he was taking to town for repair.

We finally emerged from the wet bush into a clearing on a hill called Dimikul. From here, we saw the full extent of a new valley as large as the one we had left – a pristine valley, untouched by man's machines. We spiraled down the trail until a passerby told us the mission station ahead had been abandoned. After several years of lonely work, the priest had "gone finis" back home to America. He had left a couple months earlier and they did not know if he would return. We turned back, all of us eager to get home before dark, where we greedily tucked into another baked vegetable feast put on by the wives of Kumulgo.

At night in the village, the chilly mountain air was thankfully free of insects. We watched the stars shine bright above our dark valley. I explained to Kumulgo's children how the ancients had looked up to the skies and, trying to make sense of the chaos, had cataloged the constellations. My friends here saw other patterns and the folks in the next valley saw still others in the same sky – a reminder that there are few, if any, universal truths.

The next day, Kumulgo and I took two of his horses on a bareback riding tour of his property in the valley. We raced up and down the hills with me trying to steer my horse clear of the gardens. My headstrong horse often leapt off the trail, crashing into the thickest bush in an attempt to dislodge me. I had been taught to ride horses on my grandparent's farm in Minnesota so I knew his tricks and laid down flat, with my arms circling his neck, until he regained the trail. His next trick was to bump strongly into the sides of the huts we passed where he would scratch his hide against the rough woven walls and crush my leg in between. This sent the occupants tumbling out of their huts. Imagine their surprise seeing a crazed white man on horseback, apparently trying to knock down their home with his horse.

In the afternoons, we all took our bath by going for a swim in the icy waters of the Wahgi River. Boys gathered at one place and the girls discreetly stayed around the next bend in the river, their playful laughter barely audible above the rush of water against stones. In this spot, the river's color was green and ran deep and full. Further downhill the waters shoaled until they tumbled and leapt in a white foam.

From the moment I arrived, Kumulgo worried that a gang from Dirima might come at night on a raid to capture me, and so spark a new conflict. What they wanted me for, or what they might do with me, I couldn't imagine, and told him so. Nevertheless, Kumulgo insisted I sleep in his hut while he guarded the door. I awoke several times during the night to see him propped up on one elbow, staring at me through the light of a dim kerosene lantern. The next night I convinced him I would be alright and sent him off to visit one of his wives. Once he had gone, I noticed he had locked me in from the outside as he might an unruly child.

These people of the highlands have distrusted their neighbors for so long that people from two villages, only a few miles apart, speak totally different languages. Now that's one hell of a long feud! Often I was warned not to go to the next village because they were "robbers and killers." If I did go to that place of evil reputation, I'd invariably find the people there as kind as those I'd left. And this new village would be amazed that I survived a trip through the previous village. On some scale, these are the common fears all of us have towards neighbors seldom visited and breed such enmities as to prevent peace among nations.

Because Kerowa awaited me in Pungumu, and I knew he would be worrying about my delay, I left here after only three days. I exchanged some gifts with the family and a truck was arranged that would take me back to Kundiawa. As I left, Kumulgo's wives stood at the roadside and again shed tears for my journey. I was touched deeply and knew there was so much more to these people than their violent reputation.

As we rode back towards the highway, I recalled my first night in Gumine. It was Palm Sunday and each man, woman and child from villages on both sides of the valley climbed to the highest ridges and spread out along them in single file. Like an Olympic flame, each person held up a torch of long stalks of flaming dried pitpit, passing flame from one to another until the entire valley streamed with red streaks, as if hot lava were flowing from the mountaintops. With flares burning, the highlanders were heard miles across the valley singing out to their neighbors. After the last tribal fight, the priest had organized this event for each Palm Sunday as a showing of goodwill. I held my torch high and watched wordlessly until the last flame was extinguished.

13 A Mountain Too High

Those Himalayas of the mind
Are not so easily possessed
There's more than precipice and storm
Between you and your Everest.

- C. Day Lewis

At Kundiawa I boarded a bus for the town of Mt. Hagen, the transfer point for a bus towards Pungumu Village where my friend Kerowa awaited. The patchwork of gardens and tangled terrain of Chimbu Province gave way to the substantial, if less dramatic, hills of the Western Highlands Province.

We rolled into Mt. Hagen, a bustling frontier town and the largest settlement in the island's interior. Alongside the timber-planked trade stores were a few modern buildings, including a new bank where I changed traveler's checks into the local kina. I stood in line on the slick tile floor behind a barefoot man in the traditional attire of a wide belt, made from a hard but pliable tree bark, supporting a drape of woven string cloth in front and a pile of long leaves covering his backside. In polite Pidgin terms, these leaves are called arse-grass, from the Pidgin word arse, or "behind of." Unofficially, it's an Australian corruption of "ass-grass."

It looked bizarrely out of place: this man in stone-aged bush dress, depositing a stack of money into his bank account. His son waited outside in jeans and T-shirt in their new Japanese pickup truck, probably to return them to their coffee plantation. At least a few of these local landowners have enjoyed a new found wealth since the Australians were forced out. So many expats had left that, even in a big town like this, it was rare to see a white face these days.

As I walked through town seeking the bus terminal for points west, several ragged-looking tribesmen-turned-sidewalk-vendors followed me thrusting their wares in my face. I didn't particularly need a pig's tusk necklace but, thinking it would let me slip away without offending, I bought one. Instead, like the scent released after the sting

Magistrate Ragowa and his father in Western Highlands Province

of a killer bee, it had the effect of alerting every craftsman and panhandler in town that a cash-laden tourist had arrived for a good fleecing. They even followed me through the vegetable market and into stores, pressing around me so thickly with spears and stone axes thrust in my face that I could hardly move. I settled the matter by stepping into the post office and telling them to fill two large boxes of their wares, which I paid for and shipped on the spot back to my mother in Michigan. Months later, a postman struggled up to her door with bulging and ripped-open boxes containing enough artifacts to fit out several Highlanders in ceremonial dress and weaponry.

At the market I met a man named Ragowa and his son Kiap, who knew Kerowa and lived in the village near him. Ragowa was appointed by the government to be the magistrate of his village and empowered to settle local disputes. He named his son after the Australian Patrol Officers, who were highly respected by the natives for their tough fatherly image. The Australian Kiaps had been lords of the highlands, settling disputes, organizing labor to build roads, arresting lawbreakers and generally taming a savage land. I met their legacy in men named Kiap in every village I entered.

This particular Kiap owned a truck that he used for what the locals refer to as a PMV (Public Motor Vehicle). After loading with passengers and produce from the market, I joined them for the trip to Tambul, the stop nearest the roadless village of Pungumu. From the paved streets of Mt. Hagen, we bounced our way onto a rough track meandering up the mountains toward Tambul. As the altitude increased, the temperature decreased, until I was thankful to be riding in the warmth of the cab this trip. In the open back, the passengers huddled under blankets trying to find shelter from the chill wind and light rain. Some men walked along the road, nearly naked, as if impervious to the cold. Higher up, two men sat huddled over a tiny roadside fire they tended intently.

Our driver stopped for long discussions with every person he recognized along the road, which seemed to be just about everyone. Again and again we stopped while Ragowa and Kiap shared betel nut and stories with old friends. At one of these roadside meetings, Kiap became alarmed and ordered all the passenger's valuables hidden behind his seat in the locked cab. He had been warned of trouble ahead. "Plenti rascal come bombai" (rascals ahead), he said as he shoved the truck in gear and accelerated. Outlaws were raiding travelers ahead and we were heading straight into the fray since it was the only road going west.

We slowed down to pass around a late-model car recently abandoned on the edge of the road with its tires all flat and windows shattered. Around the next bend, sat a similar wreck. Just beyond it, some ten men stood in the center of the road with axes, machetes and clubs in hand. My pulse raced as we came to a stop. I looked behind and saw another group of men come out of the bush to surround us.

While Ragowa was conducting a long negotiation through his ever so slightly opened window, a few men boarded the back of the truck and shouted at some passengers. The hostility and undertone of violence in their voices shot back and forth like a gun fight. I understood nothing except that we could be hauled out of the truck and killed at any moment. At last, the men stepped back and let us through the barricade.

After catching my breath, I asked Ragowa why there were no police here to guard the road. He told me police could do nothing because the leader of that gang was, until yesterday, a member of the National Parliament. The other men were his constituents, or clansmen. Yesterday, he was ousted from his seat in parliament by a no-confidence vote instigated by a local opponent. Now he was taking revenge on anyone connected to the opposition's clan. Highland-style retribution, swift and severe. Fortunately for us, Ragowa convinced him no one in our truck was involved in their fight.

It was late in the day as we pulled up to Ragowa's village and unloaded the truck. I saw my name scratched on a wooden sign tacked onto a roadside tree. In barely legible Pidgin, it asked people to keep an eye out for me and direct me towards Kerowa's village. For me, it was as welcome as if I had stepped off a plane that had narrowly escaped hijacking to see a limo driver holding up a sign with my name on it. Good and dependable friend, that Kerowa.

We were met here by a lively group of children cheering and running in circles around us. Slightly annoyed, Ragowa picked up a spear and feigned throwing it at them, which scared the kids he took aim at, but only excited the others to more mischief. Some children wore pieces of grass tucked under little belts in imitation of their elders. Others wore nothing at all. Ragowa sent some of them running down the trail to alert Kerowa I was on my way. The rest of the group led me in the same direction at a slower pace. In fading daylight, Kerowa came running down a hill and greeted me with his firm handshake and huge smile. We were both delighted our long journeys had brought us together again.

Using my pen light, I followed Kerowa down a trail that he knew well enough to follow on the blackest of nights. I saw nothing beyond two steps in front of me. My muscles told me our trail wound up and down, always more up than down. We crossed and re-crossed a shallow river and stepped over rough wood fences and past dimly outlined huts.

We arrived at a hillside clearing where the village was partly illuminated by open hearth fires visible through the entryways of a circle of windowless thatched huts. On one side of the clearing stood a row of three huts, one for Kerowa's father, one his mother stayed in with the family piglets, and the newest hut I was to occupy with Kerowa and his brother. Like most other huts in this region, ours was no more than 12 feet across, dark, unventilated, and due to the lack of a chimney, stinking of smoke. The nightly fires in the open dirt hearth were the only way to ward off the cold mountain nights in a village without blankets. The smoke slowly fltered through the thatch, blackening walls, ceiling and lungs along the way. The best air was found by keeping your face as close as possible to the mat on the dirt floor. I thought of the contrast: someone this very minute is walking into a Holiday Inn somewhere and demanding a non-smoking room.

Some fifteen of Kerowa's *wantoks* ("one talk" means a clansman "of the same language") followed us inside where we sat around the central fire. Kerowa made introductions in the flickering firelight. I felt like I was living the pages of some previous century anthropologist's diary, reaching across time with every hand I clasped.

As usual at every stop in the Highlands, I was asked to recount the events of my travels between here and Port Moresby and, by their questioning, I saw they wanted me to leave nothing out, no matter how inconsequential. Judging by the prolonged, quizzical, wide-eyed stares and the background chatter of people crowded outside the doorway, it was almost too strange for them to believe. In the eyes of my audience, I might have been a messenger from the world of dreams; a white man staying in their village! Why is he here? What will he do? Where are his clansmen? Something important must be happening!

I handed out some of the rice, flour, tinned milk, sugar and tins of tea I had bought at the trade store in Mt. Hagen. Eventually, the fire burned down to a pile of coals and ashes and the group moved on to their homes. I fell into a deep sleep, wrapped against the cold in my down sleeping bag. The only other blanket in the entire village was the one I had given Kerowa; he and his brother now lay under it together in unaccustomed comfort.

Roosters loudly announced the dawn long before it arrived. At sunrise, I stepped outside to find about fifty of Kerowa's wantoks gathered for an official welcome. Kerowa's brother was village spokesman for the day and he gave a long and eloquent speech. He droned on and on to the delight of the audience while Kerowa haltingly translated the plestok to me in Pidgin. By the time I mentally retranslated it to English, it was barely comprehensible. Oratory is a respected art form among these people and is performed for any reason at all, perhaps mostly to satisfy the speaker's desire to hear himself addressing a crowd.

When he finished, it was my turn to reply. Compared to Kerowa's brother, I was a big disappointment. With Kerowa interpreting, I thanked them for the welcome, praised their village, their gardens, the fat hogs, the strong women, whatever came to mind.

By prearrangement, Kerowa announced I would purchase some of their handicrafts. Gift exchange up here was not optional and people give according to their means. I anticipated the problems arising if the entire valley thought I was buying unlimited amounts of bilums and spears. So I gave Kerowa four hundred dollars in kina and told him to purchase the items that best represented his people's crafts, and to buy at least one item from everyone. Mainly, I was trying to avoid offending anyone.

I didn't really need these things though I did value them. It was not my desire to outwit them and plunder their possessions. The problem is you can't just hand out money for nothing. Do that and you lose their respect and they will expect a handout from every white man they ever see, eventually losing their own self-respect. This was the only practical way I could think to put some money into the local economy. It was also a good way to encourage pride in their culture. Seeing that others placed a value on their traditional crafts could encourage them to produce more and help pass the skills to the next generation.

It's hard to know when charity or trade does more harm than good. Everything a visitor does has a potential impact on local culture and health. For example, if you innocently pass out blankets to people who have lived without them and who don't see the need for frequent washing, they risk developing skin problems from insects, fungus and bacteria they otherwise would not have known when curled up nearly naked around the fire. The difficulty is in knowing the lasting effects of your choices – before you make them.

Kerowa collected an assortment of intricately carved bamboo arrows, wooden bows, ceremonial stone axes, woven armbands, kina shell necklaces and some items I couldn't readily identify. We later carried out four bundles, delivered them by truck to Mt. Hagen Post Office, where they were fbwn to Port Moresby, then shipped to Michigan via Australia. It was a five-month journey and not everything arrived intact. A longer postal route is hard to conceive.

At least one day a week, Kerowa and I traveled to his family's gardens on the high slopes above the village. A constant escort of children accompanied us along trails cut through gardens left to fallow. The children formed a single-file safari line in front and behind us. The ones ahead swung bush knives to clear the way, their arse-grass bouncing around as they walked. We stopped to watch a long-tailed bird of paradise floating across the valley on slowly pulsing wings, dragging a black-trimmed white scarf of a tail, until it faded into the green misty hillside.

We crossed the next river on a series of rocks as the rushing water plunged over a precipice and landed thundering at the valley floor.

Kerowa, at right, and his brother display some highlander crafts

The children played a daring game of dancing on the slippery submerged rocks at the edge of the waterfall. I was anxious someone might be swept over the side but they were sure-footed and well-practiced. A woman crossed the river carrying a full bilum of sweet potatoes on her back. A string tied to her wrist ran down to the leg of a baby piglet struggling to keep its head above water as she pulled it along. She continued towards the village, the piglet now sliding along the muddy path at her heels.

We passed people in fields landscaping mounds of earth into sweet potato gardens. Once the potatoes were planted, the earthen mounds allowed for better drainage of rainwater. Kerowa stopped to admire one of the girls who had stopped work and was eyeing us shyly. "Em mari bilong me bombai" (she will be my wife later), he said. His parents had arranged for him to marry this girl. The bride price had not yet been settled and until it was, the couple was not allowed any contact with each other. Kerowa's tender expression towards her indicated he approved of his parents' decision, although the Western notion of love and the ridiculous notion of compatibility doesn't enter into the courtship at all.

Farther up the hills we harvested a bilum bag full of cabbages. Children brought us handfuls of red berries and sticks of a celery-like plant that we ate on the spot. A boy climbed a pandanus tree and chopped free a few coconut-sized *karuka* nuts. Another boy rapidly started a fire by using a vine to spin a stick on a block of wood. A friction-heated ember ignited a pile of dry grass and sticks and within minutes the karuka nuts were roasting on the fire. The baked nut tasted of a combination of coconut and sweet potato.

Walking through the forest above the gardens, I discovered a bird of paradise nest built on the ground. Constructed of tightly packed ferns and moss, the nest spanned the width of my arms. In its center, the birds erected a tower of interlocking twigs reaching above my head. I looked up as Kerowa let loose an arrow into the trees overhead. Seconds later a brightly colored bird fell in a slow pirouette to the ground. Stunned by the three-pronged arrow, it fell silently, but was now protesting loudly, as Kerowa held it up by its wingtips.

I recognized it as a King of Saxony Bird of Paradise, distinguished by two enormous feathers streaming back from the sides of its head to more than five times the length of its palm-size body. I wanted the bird released to add its colors to the sky but Kerowa preferred to see its colors in his headdress. To amuse me he did agree to keep the bird as a temporary pet and wove a bamboo cage for it. A few days later it died, either a result of physical trauma from the arrow or the loss of freedom that a wild creature needs. It was not a complete waste, for the two long checkered feathers ended up decorating Kerowa's headdress and his father made a bite-size meal of its tiny body.

In a section of dead forest above the village, a man axed down one of many lifeless trees. He carried the log over his shoulder back to the village. To cook their food and heat their hut at night, each family uses as much timber as one man can chop and carry in one trip up the hill each day. As I watched him at his work, my mind wandered back to the brisk autumn days I spent chopping firewood in the northern Michigan forests and bringing it home by the trailer full to heat our home through a long winter. It's a strange thing to dream of faraway places, only to find when I reach them, I am dreaming of home. The affliction of the dreamer, I suppose.

On the way back to the village, the boys sighted birds in the treetops high above us. With bow and arrows slung over their shoulders, four boys silently climbed four trees. They sat near the tops on branches and we quietly sat on the ground below. Even the birds went silent as they sensed danger. Most creatures of the forest sense your presence and quietly disappear before you see them. Others stand their ground, confidently defended by poison or with camouflage that mimics something inedible. To hunt successfully here, you must sit still in one place long enough that you become part of the forest.

On a silent signal four arrows let loose simultaneously. A blackbird dropped dead from the sky and another small meal was won by the hunters.

In the village, we unloaded our sacks of sweet potatoes, cabbages, karuka, miniature tomatoes and some guava-like fruit. When divided among so many people, aside from plenty of sweet potatoes, it was a meager supply. The gardens provide grudgingly here when they produce at all. The soil is tired in most places and the elevation too high for most crops. Bananas and other tropical fruits will not grow here at all. Neither does the continually cold climate allow for growing beans and their corn is pitifully stunted and sickly. In the lower valleys, tea and coffee are cash crops. The Pungumu sell nothing except for a sparse wildflower they collect and sell to an agent of a pharmaceutical company in Mt. Hagen for 50 cents a kilo. The total annual village income from this feather-light crop averages less than thirty dollars.

When crops fail during a year of too much or too little rain, the people survive on one meal per day of sweet potatoes and such wild plants as they can gather. The pigs are almost sacred to them and are only eaten at special ceremonies, resulting in hunger for much of the rest of the year. During the yearly sing-sing, about half of their pigs are killed and eaten in two days of frenzied feasting. By definition, a Highlander is either mentally and physically tough or he is quickly dying. Weak children don't survive to adulthood.

In the evenings, we visited in one or another crowded hut. Firelight stabbed at the darkness and flickered on the faces of storytellers. Kerowa's father was usually among us. He was typical of the men of the valley; medium height, thin and muscular with strong facial features. A curved pig's tusk pierced his nose. The only other clothing he possessed was a loin cloth and the arse-grass that covered his buttocks. As the rain drummed down outside he told stories of tribal wars, famines and cannibal feasts; a simple and severe life little-changed from his father's years when white men and the world outside were unimagined. Sometimes as he squatted on his heels he would play his bamboo flute, softly conjuring up a temporary tranquility. These are the typical sights and sounds I remember most when I think of the Pungumu living in their world primeval, where time passed over them with no more noticeable effect than the clouds passing overhead.

I was beginning to get comfortable here, feeling I was learning something valuable from my hosts and about myself, strengthening spirit and body, until....

Rambling down the trail one morning towards the river, a growing pain throbbed through my head, lodging behind my eyeballs and finally bringing me to my knees. Later that day, as the stabbing pain subsided, my limbs ached until I felt I had barely the energy to move. That night I sweated profusely while a quaking fever and chills racked me with uncontrollable spasms. Like an ocean tide, the fever swept over me in spells which started anew every six hours or so. Added to this, a raw throat and constant muscle aches kept me in a thoroughly miserable state. Was it malaria or something even worse? I had been above the malarial altitude for over two weeks and I was daily taking the recommended anti-malarial so I feared it must be something ominous.

The next day, I rested as best I could between hourly trips to the partially enclosed hole in the ground that served as our outhouse. Fluids were running out of my body from all directions. The daily dinner of a bowl filled high with sweet potatoes now revolted me. I could not eat but forced myself to drink two gallons of water each day to keep from dying quickly of dehydration. My kidneys were out of control and seemed to pour out twice as much water as I took in, no matter how much I drank. Then they started to shut down. The urine looked dark. I told myself it was not dark enough to indicate blackwater fever, which might give me only 24 hours to live. The fifty-odd steps from hut to outhouse became so much of a struggle that I made the trip on hands and knees when I thought no one was watching.

Another day and night of this hell passed and I wondered how long I could go on. An old, heavily tattooed man who served as shaman in the next village came to examine me. He looked long into my drawn face and yellowing eyes and announced I had malaria. I held up my medicine bottle and said, "Impossible." He ignored me and the little plastic bottle of white man's magic I shook in his face.

He told Kerowa and his brother they must immerse me in the cold river nearby to reduce my fever. I was already shivering under my coat and blanket as close to the fire as I could wrap myself without going up in flames. When Kerowa translated their plan, I swore at him and told them all to go away. They stepped out. Minutes later they returned, picked me up and carried me to the river with me too weak to do more than futilely flail my arms, threaten, and curse them all.

After surviving the initial shock of the cold water the fight went out of me. They picked me up and laid me out on the grass next to the river to live or die. My fever had temporarily reduced and my brain began to think clearly again. We talked and agreed I must get to the hospital in Mt. Hagen. The soonest we could leave was the next morning at first light.

The sickness returned that afternoon and I spent a hideous night with the nightmares of my fever-inflamed brain. The smoke from the fire hung just above the floor, causing my eyes to water and my chest to ache. I had the urge, but not the strength, to cough. I vaguely remember Kerowa crying over me as he repeated prayers in Pidgin to Jesus and the white God not to let me die.

Later I awoke, not sure of where I was or who I was. Kerowa and his brother shared my blanket as they lay close on each side of me to keep me warm. At my feet sat the shaman, his face furrowed with lines like a weathered cliff. He droned out haunting melodious chants to the spirit world. I recall the coals of a dying fire casting a subdued red glow to the close walls of woven bamboo. I studied their tight pattern and then looked above to the low roof of kunai grass that seemed to press down on me. What is this? A panic swept over me that I was inside a shrinking coffin. I groped for the doorway and crawled outside to be engulfed in a welcome tide of open sky and clear air.

In the morning, seeing I was unexpectedly still alive, Kerowa smiled, though it was doubtful to all of us how long I would remain so. We began our long journey to Mt. Hagen with me trudging on grimly with rubbery knees, blurred vision and pinwheels of light flashing before my eyes. I took ten steps, rested, took ten more steps and rested again. As I grew weaker, Kerowa and his brother supported me with my arms flung over their shoulders. They pulled, dragged and carried me up the steepest parts of the trail. Descending the final steep section above the river, I slipped and slid face first down to the river's edge, dragging my companions with me. My mouth and eyes caked with mud, my friends picked me up and carried me the last few steps into Ragowa's village, where they propped me up against the outside of a hut as they went to flag down a truck on the road.

A bony and bent old man crouched on his heels and put an arm around me as I sat there shivering. It was Ragowa's father, a man who had been a warrior and tribal chief in his day. Now his frail and aged body marked him as being near the end of a hard life. We sat there like that, old man comforting a sick traveler, as a mother would a baby, until Kerowa returned with Kiap and his truck.

An eternity of body-shocking bumps ensued until I was carried feet first into Mt. Hagen Haus Sic (the "sick house," or hospital). A blood test was quickly analyzed and a harried-looking Australian doctor came up to my gurney in the hall. "What is it doctor?" I asked.

"Another bloody bush adventurer, eh? You've got at least two strains of drug resistant malaria with a very low blood count and that fungal rash all over your lower body has gone into secondary infection," he said as he poked a gloved finger around my groin. He then directed the nurse to wheel me into the critical condition ward.

The rash! In my brush with death I was beyond that kind of pain and I'd forgotten about it, until my mud-caked boots and pants were peeled off me. It was shocking to see that the jock itch and athlete's foot fungus that had bothered me for weeks had spread unchecked due to my low blood count and was consuming my flesh from my toes to my waist.

The doctor told Kerowa to return in three days, by which time I might be well enough to leave, if I wasn't dead. Then he turned me over to a couple of nurses who spent the next hour unsuccessfully trying to insert IV needles into my shrunken veins. They then gave me the first of several near lethal doses of quinine sulfate tablets to kill the malaria. That night my ears rang and buzzed from the effects of quinine. Behind my eyes hung a dull weight, like a heavy stone was lodged there. The fever continued coursing through my veins with alternating floods of fierce heat and icy cold. The battle of parasite and immune system and medications raged on.

I should have headed for the hospital on the first day of the attack. At least I survived. Not so fortunate was the girl in the bed next to mine. Sometime during the night she died, they said of the dreaded blackwater fever. Her mother stood next to her bed wailing her sorrow long after the tearful nurses had carried the little girl's limp body away. This room is where her spirit departed and this is where she cried out her lament. Don't think because of their rough ways that these people don't feel sorrow as strong as any of us. As preoccupied as we were with our own troubles, no one in our room who was capable of consciousness could help but to grieve with her. The girl could have been saved with one dollar's worth of timely medicine − that was something to cry about. I saw clearly that I had always lived in a privileged and sheltered environment. In this other world, life is short and seldom kind.

The next day, I suddenly broke out of the fever and into a drenching sweat that saturated my sheets but somehow felt refreshing compared to what I had been going through. From that point on, the medicine took effect and I slowly recovered. Now the soreness and incessant itching of my infected rash became unbearable. The nurses offered some ointments that gave only slight relief. It drove me near madness with desperation for a month longer until I saw a specialist in Port Moresby who pumped me full of antibiotics and a three-month course of antifungal griseofulvin that came in liver-straining tablets the size of horse pills.

On Sunday, an underemployed native priest visited the critical ward. He roared at us in Pidgin to repent our sins before it was too late. Up and down the aisle between our beds he stomped, pounding his bible against an open palm for effect. Occasionally he stopped, pointing an accusing finger at one of us, and blared, "Em samting bilong yu tasol" (This means you, brother)! Imprisoned in our beds as we were, he had us at a disadvantage. This man was an artful master, hitting us with the message that we had only ourselves to blame for our predicaments. His God was rightly punishing us and we must repent now while there was still a chance or face the well-stoked furnace of Hell. No one responded. Disgusted, he left no room for doubt as to our fate, then left us to it, mumbling about the futility of his job on the way out. I pictured myself getting up and punching him in the nose, then imagined he would have enjoyed beating me to death with his bible.

After the priest left, another man in our room gave his last rasping breath and died. The news reached his family in minutes and about fifteen of them burst into the room screaming and wailing. They continued for hours, refusing to let the nurses remove the body. I hid under my sheet, hoping to go unnoticed, and wishing this world of nightmares would go away. When the body was finally moved, they continued their ceremony just outside my window until daylight. The men kept up a steady rhythm of chants, while women shrieked horribly and pounded the walls until they dropped in exhaustion, allowing other women to take up the ghastly wailing. Nobody slept that night.

When Kerowa returned to the hospital after three days, I was as weak as a baby but on my feet again and more than ready to leave. We returned to Pungumu where I convalesced and took short walks around the valley. Soon I must leave the highlands to continue my voyage, but I first wanted to climb PNG's highest mountain, Mt. Wilhelm. Kerowa agreed to join me and when I felt strong enough, we left the village. As we walked down the trail to the road with our heavy packs, we were followed by most of the clan with women crying in the familiar highland's farewell.

A series of trucks took us to Mt. Hagen and back east along the Highlands Highway to Kundiawa, where we turned north to Keglsugl, a village at the base of Mt. Wilhelm. At Kundiawa the road ascended the awesome Chimbu gorge. For two hours we clung to our seats watching the canyon recede below. Black clouds enveloped us and barricades loomed out of the mist to signal road shoulders fallen away. The broken track of a road rose through the cloud deck where the village of Keglsugl lay shrouded in a cold mist. From there we slogged on foot along a muddy trail and into the equatorial high-altitude cloud forest.

Exhausted from the day's travel, we dropped our packs and set up camp at an alpine lake named Aunde. At 11,500 feet above the sea, the air was noticeably thinner and I was surprised how the damp, cold air sapped my energy and will to keep climbing. The next day, as we set out for the summit, my lungs heaved for oxygen and a pain in the front of my head pounded relentlessly. Kerowa was not looking his usual, healthy self either, and our progress was measured in short, deliberate steps. At just over 13,000 feet, we were halted by near freezing rain and risked losing the poorly marked path in zero visibility. I had underestimated how penetrating the cold was here, even within a few degrees of the equator.

We spent an uncomfortable night perched in bivy bags among the jagged rocks in befogged isolation. We had no camp stove and it was too wet to start a fire. Rain continued to fall darkly and leak through to my soul. The wind moaned as it gusted over the rocks, matching our outward desolation with our mood within.

A gray dawn brought no reprieve. We grimly held on, unable to go forward, unwilling to retreat. There was nothing to do but watch the rain settle into puddles in the rocks that overflowed and trickled into rivulets and flowed eventually to the lake below. I could imagine the lake waters overflowing into a river that brought the waters back to the sea where they evaporated and condensed into new clouds driven by the winds back up the same mountain to release and begin the cycle anew.

We retreated back to Lake Aunde that afternoon where we stayed three more days trying to recover our strength while awaiting better weather. Kerowa pointed to a valley far to the west of an anonymous fold of mountains where "the land is so terrible that men cannot live on it or even step on it." I had heard of it before, a tortured mass of eroded limestone so sharp it was dubbed "broken bottle country." People wandered in there and did not always return.

On the third morning, the skies cleared and we briefly saw our objective, the peak of the mountain that the Chimbu people call Enduwa Kombugu. Optimistically, we set out for the summit and were driven back, yet again, by heavy rains and the fatigue of my malaria-weakened body. I was trying to surmount my own limitations, as well as the menacing peak. I had grasped its flanks and couldn't bear to let go. Before I could give up, I demanded at least for this mountain to teach me something.

We were now out of food, my body was exhausted, and my spirits depressed. Cold, wet, hungry – I couldn't justify punishing Kerowa, or myself, with this madness any longer. Yes, I was sick of this cursed mountain and finally admitted it had beaten me. I had reached deep to summon both my resolve and strength and yet it was not enough. After five long days of battling the mountain, we turned to go home in defeat. Courage, it is said, lies somewhere between recklessness and cowardice. My lesson here: humility.

14 Surviving New Guinea

When a man does not know what harbor he is heading for, no wind is the right one.

- Seneca, Roman Philosopher

It was now well into the season of the Southeast Trades in the Indian Ocean. I needed to get back to Moresby and prepare my boat for the next leg of the voyage in order to cross before cyclone season. When I passed through Mt. Hagen earlier on my way into the Highlands, I had reserved a plane ticket back to Port Moresby. With the delay on the mountain, there was now just one day left to make my flight.

After his taste of the outside world, Kerowa decided to remain in his village but offered to accompany me to the airport. It took a full day to reach Kundiawa where we were again invited to stay the night at Peter's apartment next to the bank. A cold shower, hot meal and eight hours sleep on a hard cot – such unaccustomed luxury. In the morning, after a late start, I phoned the airport to find the time of the last flight out and felt there was just enough time to catch it.

We arrived at Mt. Hagen by PMV early in the afternoon where we unloaded in the "Chinatown" section of the town, so named because three Chinese merchants ran general merchandise stores selling mostly identical items along that dusty street. My flight was leaving in one hour and I was still ten miles from the airport. Ten miles in New Guinea, I learned, can be impossibly far. We checked for buses at the PMV stop and found none going to the airport. Each empty bus that pulled up was set upon by a horde of people pushing and shoving to get a seat. It was clear I stood no chance of getting on any bus here, burdened as I was with two large packs.

I wasted precious time looking around in vain for a taxi or a telephone. By now, a crowd of men pressed in around us and from the hostile looks on some of the faces, I felt an increasing urgency to get out of there. Some looked to be scrutinizing us to see if they could get away with mugging us and stealing our bags. Feeling like a rabbi at the

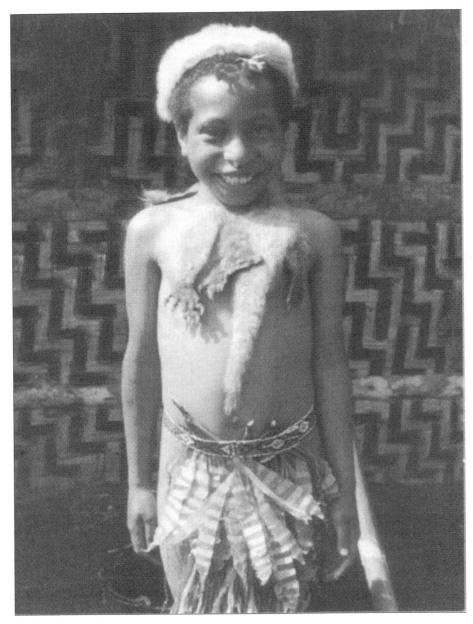

Child of the Highlands

hadj, I stood out as the lone white man in a crowd of hundreds of ill-tempered PNG tribesmen. To make things worse, Kerowa was from a different tribe. He knew a confrontation of some kind was imminent. Though we each carried a long knife on our belts and tried to look unafraid, I noticed Kerowa's hands trembling.

A man in the front of the crowd, who looked like the headman for at least part of the group, reached down to grab my pack while watching my face for a reaction. On impulse, I grabbed his arm and he froze in a moment of indecision. With my other hand, I thrust a five kina bill in his hand and told him in Pidgin I was hiring him to help Kerowa watch my bags while I went to find a taxi, and that he would get more money when I returned. This move took him by surprise. He seemed to agree and, at any rate, I had no choice but to trust him.

Perspectives of reality change when you're terrified. What I saw in the gathering throng looked to me as threatening as a thousand Zulu warriors rattling spears and bows and hissing at me. In reality, they may have been as indifferent to me as a crowd of New Yorkers. How could I know? There was no time for these thoughts as I pushed my way through the agitated crowd.

At the police station two blocks away, a man inside shut and locked the front door when I approached. I went next door to the fire station and pulled in vain on another locked door. Around back, I peered through a window and saw the fire chief asleep on a couch and woke him up by tapping on the window. He unlocked the fire station to let me use the phone. His five-page phone book listed no cab company. The local phone operator said yes, there was one taxi in town, but his number was unlisted. No, she could not give me the number unless I could tell her the owner's name. Apparently, I was stuck in the Twilight Zone. Hanging up the phone, I explained my predicament to the native fireman, telling him my flight leaves in fifteen minutes, I had no money left with me to stay at a hotel, and a riot was about to break out in the street where I left my bags if he didn't help me.

He listened calmly, then dressed in his uniform and fireman's hat and told me he'd take care of it – as if mine was a common request. He stepped into the street with outstretched arms and stopped the first empty bus that came down the road. When the surprised driver halted, he pushed me into the bus and ordered the driver to take me to pick up my bags and go straight to the airport – no stops. Still amazed that the fireman had done this for me, I directed the driver down the street to where Kerowa waved at me from the middle of the crowd. As the people parted to allow the bus in, I could see Kerowa's expression change from fright to a relieved grin. The crowd pressed back in around the bus but I held them back at the door until Kerowa got inside with my bags. I handed another five kina note out the window to outstretched hands as the bus pulled away.

We jumped out at the airport with no time to spare. At the check-in counter I flashed my minister credentials bought from Universal Life Church, Inc. for ten dollars when I was a teenager. Originally bought as a ruse to keep me out of any possible military draft, the official-looking card had finally paid for itself on the edge of the priest-ridden jungles of New Guinea. The agent at the counter had seen every type of missionary come through there, and with a sideways glance at my rough attire, credited me a twenty-five percent clergy discount. Playing the part, I stupidly said, "Bless you," and ran for the departure gate.

Kerowa and I had done and seen so much together it was a shock to find we had only seconds to say goodbye, never to see each other again. I had put him through hardships, testing his friendship to the limit. His every waking moment seemed devoted to my welfare and he was as true a friend, in his way, as I've ever had. Kerowa had little concept of where my home lay and the extent of the oceans I must cross to get there, but he imagined many dangers ahead of me. "I hope you live to reach your village again," he told me, "and will tell our story to your clan." I promised I would. Through our unlikely friendship, we discovered something of the wider worlds within each of us. He returned to his mountain village and I to the sea. The stories of our shared adventures would be told and retold around the night fires in Pungumu Village and in my own house one day.

The twin prop-driven plane to Moresby held about fifty passengers, none of them, I was sure, as relieved as I to return to sea level. After take-off one of the pilots came down the aisle and I recognized him as a friend from the Bushwalkers Association. I rode the rest of the way to Moresby in the cockpit in the navigator's jump seat. Below us lay an exceptional darkness with occasional pinprick dots of light marking the outposts of towns spread thinly across the jungle. The lights marked the relentless spread of civilization, eventually reaching people like the Pungumu who will have to adapt. A navigation instrument in the cockpit flickered as it counted down the miles remaining to Port Moresby. The pilots saw Distance to Go. To me it was a countdown for our time machine back to the modern world.

The population in Port Moresby was probably about one percent European, yet I was still startled to see so many white faces. My first impulse was a desire to hug each and every one of them. Not that I thought less of my Highland friends, for better friends could not be found. It was the way I was scrutinized like an alien life form that had worn me down. Day and night, wherever I went, I was on public display and could feel the unending spoken and unspoken comments of the villagers: "Look, the white man puts his boots on, he stands up, he's walking, where is he going now..." and so on. I was not paranoid and don't like complaining, I was simply exhausted from the months of intense scrutiny.

Before departing New Guinea, some friends at the Bushwalker's Club invited me to join them for a day trip hike from Mt. Diamond to a waterfall just outside Port Moresby. The same pilot who flew us back from the highlands picked me up at dawn on Sunday in his jeep and we drove to a plantation outside town where we met several other hikers. About ten of us walked from there to the abandoned copper mine at Mt. Diamond. I had hiked this area before but had wisely not entered the old mines.

This time several of us decided to explore the mine's tunnels and I followed behind someone who held a flashlight. The close sides and low roof of the tunnel were tarnished green from water seeping onto the copper ore. Bats flying out startled us as we continued in, skidding on the accumulated guano underfoot. A flashlight beam froze a rat staring back at us. Once we lost sight of the entrance, we decided to turn back since we were ill-equipped for cave exploration. As my friends moved ahead, I noticed a smaller shaft off to the right side and stepped into it to see where it led. I clearly remember the absolute blackness ahead of me. I sensed danger in the dark but, inexplicably, decided on one more step before turning back.

Whoosh…with nothing under my feet I dropped down a vertical shaft like a trapeze artist on a final fatal leap. As I fell, I grabbed at the face of the rocky shaft to slow down and succeeded only in burning the skin off my fingertips and elbows. In the midst of a terrified adrenalin rush, the mind works at incredible speed. My first thought was that the shaft must not be very deep and soon I would feel ground under my feet. Two seconds later, I was in full free-fall and imagined breaking bones when I hit bottom, if there was a bottom. A half second later, I thought I was dead and got angry at myself for dying in this mineshaft over a stupid misstep after I had come so far, and had so far yet to go.

The next thing I knew I was under water struggling to find a way up with no reference as to where up was. Long moments later I broke the surface and sucked in a lungful of dank air and spat out a mouthful of muddy water. The relief of a soft landing in deep water was soon displaced by the knowledge that this was a deep pit and no one in our group had a rope to pull me out. Drowning was now a possibility as the weight of clothing, boots and backpack pulled me down. I called up for help and wondered if they'd forgotten me and already left the mine. My thoughts raced; how long could I stay afloat, how far had I fallen? My shocked mind guessed it was hundreds of feet. I wiggled out of my small backpack, dumped its contents, and raised it to trap air for flotation. Within a minute it was empty and I repeated the process. The knowledge that I could do this for hours calmed me somewhat.

Finally someone noticed I was missing and a dim light from above illuminated my prison walls. In answer to my call for help, the man holding the flashlight calmly asked, "What are you doing down there?" as if maybe I had plunged into the shaft for a bath.

Now I could see it was only about fifty feet up the smooth-sided circular shaft that was just wide enough for me to touch each side with outstretched feet and hands. I remembered hearing a story about two men stuck down a shaft like this who escaped on their own by pressing their backs against each other and walking up the sides of the shaft. I didn't expect anyone was willing to join me to try that trick. Instead, they sent a runner to the nearest village to fetch a rope.

About an hour later, a thin rope was lowered into my hole and I secured it around my chest. Several men hoisted me until about halfway up when the rope broke and sent me plunging back to the water. Not only was the rope rotted, it was now too short. They found a solution by tying together their belts and trousers and doubling what was left of the rope.

Once I emerged into the daylight, I saw I was covered in bloody scrapes, clay and bat shit. We walked to the nearby waterfall where I soaked and cleaned my wounds on a pool of clear shallow water. Before leaving, I borrowed a flashlight and forced myself to return for one last look at that watery tomb in the hope of quelling my new-found terror of dark caves. From malaria to this mineshaft, I didn't just visit New Guinea – I survived it.

While I healed from the scrapes from my spelunking adventure, my grandmother, an aunt and a cousin visited me on their way to Hawaii, after a tour of Australia. With no room aboard *Atom* for four people, they stayed a few days at the only good hotel in town, which was a short walk from the yacht club. One day I borrowed a friend's car and drove them along the coast and into the nearby mountains for sightseeing. Along the road to the interior we stopped and met a transplanted highlander decked out in his ceremonial finery. He turned out to be a shrewd businessman when he waved us over to take his photo. In Pidgin he told us it would cost "one kina for the little camera and two kina for the bigger camera." Before they left for Hawaii, I took my relatives aboard *Atom* for a sail under a blistering hot sun around Port Moresby's spacious harbor.

New Guinea was full of strange characters, especially those from the white "expat" tribe. Someone had labeled the majority of them "missionaries, mercenaries, or misfits." Old plantation managers and assorted white bosses could still be found in the yacht club bar, bitterly complaining over the loss of their prosperity to the post-independence nationalists and criminal gangs.

Among the new generation of expats I met at the yacht club was Marek, a Russian dentist who fled the Soviet Union when it was not entirely legal or safe to do so. He needed temporary work while his application at the local hospital was processed, so I helped find him a job rebuilding the deck and cabin top of a plywood catamaran owned by an Australian businessman at the club.

"How hard can it be, this carpenter work?" Marek shrugged as he began ripping the deck apart with hammer and saw. Over the next couple weeks, while the owner of the boat was in Australia, Marek moved aboard. I wondered what plans he worked to as the cabin sides grew high and square above the deck. One hot afternoon, I saw a local girl stumble disheveled out of the boat pushed along by Marek, who then stood on the dock and shoved a water hose down the front of his shorts. "In this country, I suggest you wear two condoms for protection," he said with a twisted smile.

The next time I saw him in the bar and asked how the project was going, he said, "Terrible. That damn Australian fired me and he won't pay me. Claims I ruined his boat, that it looks like bloody Russian cathedral, not sailboat!" To the relief of the yacht club members, Marek gave up his new shipwright trade and went back to drilling, hammering and chiseling the teeth of the locals.

I was fortunate to make friends with a German couple and their young son on a 32-foot steel sailboat who were upgrading the boat at the yacht club. They gave me their old, but still serviceable cockpit dodger, manual anchor windlass and slightly rusty anchor chain. They installed new equipment as I attached the old hand-me-down gear on *Atom*. I also took the opportunity to careen *Atom* at the yacht club dock and applied fresh bottom paint while standing ankle-deep in mud between tides.

Also hanging around the yacht club was Peter, an Australian with his local fiancé who were looking for passage on a yacht to Australia. The month before they had left Moresby in a hurried departure to sail to Australia in his small sailboat. Two stormy days later they had wrecked on a reef and were luckily rescued by a passing boat that returned them to Moresby. Problem was, Peter could not afford the bride price of two thousand kina her parents demanded, so in their view she was stolen property and they were hunting him down. I was sorry to explain to them I was on a solo voyage and could not make the detour. Eventually, I heard they found a boat to crew on before the angry parents could catch up to them.

While I was there, the Prime Minister of PNG repeatedly announced on radio and newspaper that they would soon bring television to the island. He did not say why they needed it, other than to say it was part of his "modernization program." At the same time, he declared a curfew and martial law to clamp down on the lawlessness in the cities. My impression was that European-style civilization was utterly failing here in the capital city. In total contrast to the purposeful, disciplined family life in the rural areas, native men in the city had a penchant for drinking the white man's alcohol until they were either out of their minds or unconscious – a symptom of their broken spirits in a competitive city full of strangers. And still the Australian business community and PNG government were calling for more foreign investment and industrialization. To what end? To turn a proud tribal people into hopeless city dwellers? The biggest improvement, I thought unkindly, would come by sending people back to their villages and burning this city to the ground.

But that is not how I choose to remember New Guinea, this land that took so much out of me and gave back so much in return. There has always been the human impulse to seek the unknown, to test oneself in the wild places. New Guinea is where this "Ulysses factor" – the exploring instinct of man – can be pursued until fantasy comes face-to-face with reality.

I will remember the people of the timeless Goilala Valley and everywhere those that took me into their villages and families. There was Paharija and her clan who helped me explore the haunted slopes of Sumburipa, the strong-minded people of Chimbu Province who put down their spears to line the mountaintops with flaming torches of friendship on Palm Sunday night, and my friend Kerowa, who saved my life when malaria struck and who clung alongside me for days on the frozen crags of Mt. Wilhelm. He did not feel a need to go, but went because his guest and friend needed to reach another elusive summit. In return, I failed to conquer my highest mountain, but learned the experience of a journey is more important than its destination. If you ever go to New Guinea and live with the people as I did, it will both transform and haunt you for the rest of your life.

15 The Sheltering Atoll

Here we will moor our lonely ship
Murmuring how far away are the unquiet lands.

- W. Yeats

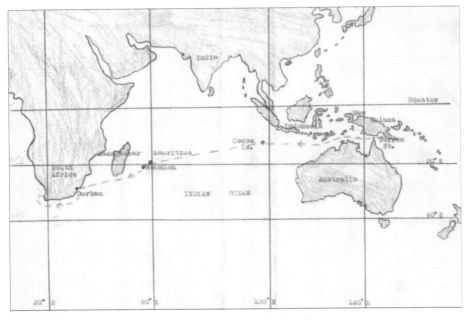

Atom's course across the Indian Ocean

The Coral Sea heaved and rolled to a fresh trade wind as *Atom* sledded downwind from Port Moresby towards the mass of disconnected reefs, low islets and rushing currents of the Torres Strait. Before the age of GPS satellite navigation, the seas separating New Guinea from Australia were as dangerous to seafarers as any in the world. When Cook sailed these waters he nearly lost his ship and noted, "incessant and prodigious dangers." One of Bligh's officers wrote, "Perhaps no space of three and a half degrees in length presents more danger." The salt-stained photocopy of the chart I plotted my estimated position on gave menacing warnings of the hornet's nest ahead: "strong currents, numerous shoals, coral patches."

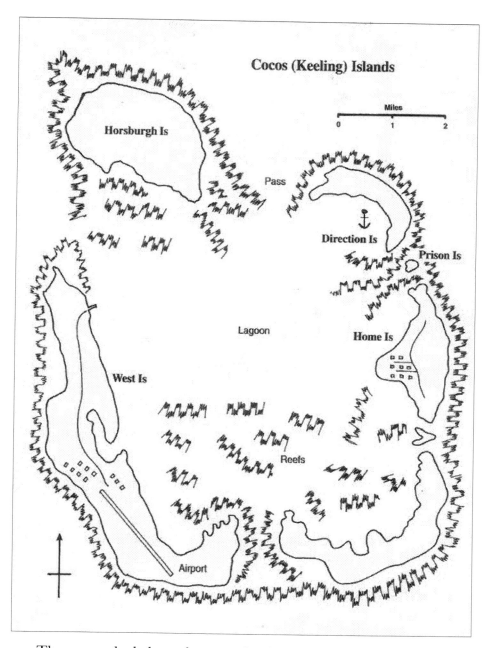

Cocos (Keeling) Islands

The sun poked through a gap in the gray, overcast sky just long enough for me to get a measurement with my sextant. The resulting line of position I drew on the chart ran close to a reef that I expected to lay far to the south of my position. These are the times when you really need faith in your calculations. I confirmed my sextant sight soon after when I spotted a shipwreck through the binoculars, sitting on the reef a mere two miles away. To counter the south-running current that had carried me off course, I drew a new course line a few miles north of Bramble Cay where the chart indicated a flashing light warned mariners of the surrounding reefs. French solo sailor Jean Gau missed sighting this light and soon was tossed up on Warrior Reef where he made a narrow escape. His heavily built wooden ketch pounded on the reef for half a day before floating off at high tide. My fiberglass hull might not take such abuse. As I recalled Gau's book chapter titled, "Incident on Warrior Reef," my hair stood on end. Either the light would appear soon or I'd feel the keel-splitting reef when I landed on it. Tortured with indecision, I prepared to turn away and heave-to for the night and carry on in the morning.

That night the sky remained black overcast, the only light coming from luminescent organisms sparkling on the breaking wave crests. With tired eyes I stood in the cockpit straining to see Bramble Cay Light, which guards Bligh Entrance to the Torres Strait. Presumably, this is where Captain Bligh entered the strait in Bounty's overloaded lifeboat after mutineers set him adrift near Tonga. On a final look into the blackness ahead, with great relief, I spotted the faint white beacon. Throughout the night I kept an eye on that life-saving light as I tacked back and forth, holding my position upwind of the reefs.

At dawn I entered the strait and altered course to southwest. As if trying to prevent my passage through this devil's necklace of islets and reefs, the winds veered to south and blew forcefully for the next two days. I pressed on under reefed sails sheeted in tight, heeled over hard on the wind, checking off the sandy islets as they passed. On the lee side of Rennel Island, I saw a local fishing boat anchored off the beach. I could not safely carry on among the reefs here at night so I tacked over and anchored in the slight shelter the island provided from the seas and currents. The uninhabited palm-covered isle looked like a perfect South Seas setting for a native village. A pair of barely visible coral block buildings marked an abandoned settlement where pearl gatherers had lived until the pearls became scarce and they moved on to another island.

My alarm clock announced the sunrise but I was so fatigued and drunk with sleep I slept on until the morning sun struck my eyes through the open companionway. I thought of waiting another day to get an early start, but decided to make a dash for the next anchorage some forty-five miles away before darkness fell.

The current was running at an angle across the wind, forcing waves to pile up steeply and close together. *Atom* lurched in a quick, jerky motion, burying her bow then lifting it up to fling back the seas pressing her down. If I slowed down to ease the motion, the current would gain the upper hand and drag me off course, so I held her nose hard into the wind.

Fortunately, in Port Moresby, I had installed the used cockpit dodger over the companionway. Now I huddled behind its vinyl-covered aluminum tubing frame, staying partly dry as sheets of spray flew past overhead. Every five to ten miles another island drifted past, sometimes a mere stone's throw away, providing a welcome few moments of calm water on their lee side.

As the tide fell it revealed extensive tidal flats encompassing each island that increased their minuscule land area up to five times. On one of these dry reefs lay a mighty freighter on its side, high and dry, hundreds of feet in from the sea. Fascinated, I sailed by the rust-streaked hull as close as I could, wondering how a full-size ship with 20-foot draft could have landed on a reef covered by only a few feet of water at high tide – my guess is storm surge from a passing cyclone lifted the ship and carried her inland.

By late afternoon I came upon the sister islands of Bet, Sue and Poll. The only anchorage here was a tiny scrap of sandy ledge close to Sue where I dropped *Atom's* anchor precariously close to the reef edge. To the east of the island, tidal flats lay exposed for two miles. Through binoculars I watched two women carrying baskets on their backs, bending over to pick mussels at the sea's edge. As they roamed over the newly exposed flats, clouds of spray rose like smoke signals where waves hit the wall of dry reef. With full baskets the women retreated home before the rising tide engulfed their watery island garden.

The settlement contained two fishing boats pulled up on the beach next to three whitewashed houses and a matching church. If I had been tempted to go ashore, I was dissuaded by an Australian Navy plane labeled "COASTWATCH" that buzzed low overhead and circled back a second time. I had heard from other sailors that trespassers were not welcome ashore, and the official port of entry for the region lay miles away from my course line.

That night the southerly swell that hooked around the island at high tide sent *Atom* rolling so wildly I was pitched out of my bunk onto the cabin sole. Since I could fall no farther, I spent the remainder of the night there, not sleeping, just listening to the wind howl through the rigging, as I waited in hopes that the dawn would come before my anchor dragged. At first light I hoisted anchor and got underway. My immediate goal was to gain ten miles to windward without letting the five knot cross-current pull me onto the reef.

With my #3 jib and a triple reefed mainsail, *Atom* lay over and dove into the slab-sided waves. Coming on deck to check my position with compass bearings, I looked up to see a vertical wall of water rise above me and momentarily hang there blocking out the sun before collapsing and submerging the deck. The force of the wave threw me to the opposite side of the cockpit where I came up tight on my safety harness. *Atom* came to a halt, then popped up like a cork and carried on as if nothing had happened. Bending low to see under the sails, I was alarmed to see jagged spires off the leeward starboard bow. Labeled Harvey Rocks, the surf beat furiously against the stone pinnacles, sending my heart racing as I calculated my chances of clearing or being crushed against the rocks. It seemed I could skirt it, but just barely. Several soul-wrenching minutes later, we cleared, with a scant few yards to spare. I cheered the victory against the rocky executioner and gratefully turned downwind to less restricted waters.

Later that day, I breathed a final sigh of relief as I passed Thursday Island and exited Torres Strait. Perhaps the most dangerous part of the world voyage was behind me. Once again I had traipsed through the lion's lair and escaped unscathed. As wind and current flushed me at ten knots out the straits and into the Arafura Sea, I watched Cape York, Australia's northernmost point, drift by ten miles to the south.

Hours later I passed solitary Booby Island, previously used as a refuge for shipwrecked sailors. Passing ships left food supplies in a cave there and retrieved letters to forward home. Here I closed the log on the Pacific and Coral Sea and opened a page to a new ocean.

The trade winds moderated and hung steadily in the southeast as I crawled along just out of sight of Australia's interminable northern coast. During my five days on the Arafura, I seldom touched the sails. In these calm waters, far from the steaming heat, insects and fevers of New Guinea, I felt freed of nature's savagery and happily fell back into a familiar and comfortable sea routine. I wasn't bothered at all when I saw brightly colored poisonous sea snakes tumbling on the wave crests in the Arafura – until that night I dreamt a snake washed aboard on a wave and fell into my bunk. My only real visitors were the familiar thump of those evolutionary-half-stepping flying fish and the lighter plunk from ink-filled squid falling on deck.

Atom entered the Timor Sea at a point midway between the Australian port of Darwin and the islands of Indonesia. I had attempted to gain an Indonesian visa at their embassy in Port Moresby, but the functionaries there fled my application under "security risk," took my twenty dollar application fee, and never replied. Though Indonesia was out, I might have stopped in Australia. I'm sure the people of Darwin are friendly enough, but their harbor was not convenient with its high tidal range and mud flats. Besides, the image it represented to me was not unlike small-town America with a different accent. I kept *Atom's* bow pointed towards Africa.

Fifteen days out of Port Moresby I left the green, shallow waters of the Timor Sea and sailed over the abyssal Java Trench. During the night I passed south of the ex-Portuguese colony of East Timor and its ongoing guerilla war and slipped unnoticed into the wide embrace of the Indian Ocean. Ahead lay some 5,600 miles to South Africa with only a handful of islands between. I laid my course now for Cocos (Keeling) Islands, which I expected to reach in another two weeks.

A comfortable southeast wind brought the clear, almost cool weather of the Southern Hemisphere winter. *Atom's* tiny deck was my observation platform to the vast vistas of sea and sky. By night I checked our constant westward course, keeping Acrux, the pointer star of the Southern Cross, on the port beam. Each morning and evening twilight, when clouds permitted, I shot a three star position fix – Achenar to the northeast, Antares to the southeast and Acrux to the south. The daily x-marks on the chart crept their way westward.

Here I sailed into an utterly barren stretch of water. I saw none of the familiar fishes. Even the birds were absent. Sailing past the longitude of Bali marked the halfway point of the circumnavigation – some thirteen thousand miles out and thirteen thousand to go. This little milestone had seemed impossibly distant on those early days sailing on Lake St. Clair; days when I sailed alone, going nowhere just for the joy of sailing and dreaming of faraway seas. Now I was as far away from that little lake as I could be. Oddly enough, I took comfort in the thought that each mile sailed carried me closer to home as I scrawled in large print in the logbook: HOMEWARD BOUND.

My string of fine weather was disrupted by a high swell rolling in from the east that collided with the regular southeast wave pattern. This was fair warning of dirty weather headed my way. A day later the swell was higher yet; now and again a breaking wave crest tumbling into the cockpit with much foam and hissing drama but little punch. Low clouds scudded overhead as the wind backed to east and rose to gale force. As the barometer dropped, I tapped it hourly with my finger in some vain hope to reverse its fall. But sailors know a gale of wind from behind, and plenty of sea room ahead, is not such a bad thing. It speeds you on your way and punctuates an otherwise too-easy life.

The wind continued to build, lifting the seas and flogging their breaking crests into streaming spray. Under storm jib alone, *Atom's* rigging hummed and moaned as the wind brushed its heavy hand over every wire. Over and over we rose stern first, gaining height until a breaking crest foamed all around us, then plunged down the face into the trough, sometimes digging the bow into the wave ahead. When I had to go forward to adjust a line, I crawled along the deck on hands and knees. Growing weary of the roller coaster, whenever I wasn't needed on deck, I retreated to the cabin sole where I wedged myself in with cushions and sailbags between the bunks.

Down below in the closed cabin the sound of the wind was muted, but the vibrations of mast and rigging seemed to penetrate through my bones. With only the false serenity of the cabin's interior visible to my eyes, my ears concentrated on the mad symphony of flapping canvas, drumming lines and rig, and groaning and creaking within the hull. Unable to relax to a deep sleep, with eyes closed I mentally worked as an orchestra conductor, counting over twenty individual sounds before losing my point of concentration. The noises I could do nothing about – the breaking waves, the wind whining in the rig, the whirling of the speed indicator propeller – didn't bother me much since they were unavoidable. But the dozen or so noises originating inside the boat aggravated me to the point I repeatedly set out to silence them. Some were easy to find and eliminate, like the rhythmic clank of a pot in its locker or a book sliding on the bookshelf. One by one I tracked them down until only a few mysterious creaks and taps remained. Satisfied with my efforts, I finally fell into a light and uneasy sleep.

After a week of heavy weather and twenty-eight days alone, the idea of a respite from the sea was a welcome thought. Approaching Cocos Atoll, I seriously doubted I could find its low line of palm trees hiding between the high running seas and low clouds. Getting an accurate position fix each day was doubtful as I popped my head through the hatch to measure a star or sun against a rolling indistinct horizon. If I missed this atoll, the next island lay two thousand miles beyond.

Just before another gray dawn, I was relieved to sight the flashing beacon of Pulo Panjang, or West Island, and took a compass bearing on it before the next curtain of rain erased it from view. Later, the green tops of palm trees appeared on the crest of a wave and disappeared again as we dropped into a trough. As I rounded the north coast to enter a gap in the reef leading to Port Refuge, the sky went black, as a violent squall forced me back out to sea. The horizontal rain stung my skin like a thousand shots from a BB gun as I reefed down, hove-to and retreated to the cabin. Outside was zero visibility in rain and spray thick as smoke. I had the anxious feeling I was being drawn towards the reef, but there was nothing to do but wait it out. As soon as the squall let up, I tacked again towards the inlet. Minutes later I was anchored in two fathoms of clear, calm water close under the lee of horseshoe-shaped Direction Island. I waved at the crews of two other yachts already anchored nearby. Then another squall arrived and it rained so hard and long I wondered if the sugary sand island would melt into the sea.

I slept deep through the night, oblivious to the weather and awoke the next morning to clear skies and a clear head. A custom's launch from West Island motored across the lagoon and into the anchorage. The officer handed me a line to tie the launch alongside, heaved himself aboard, gave me a back slap that knocked the air from my lungs and bellowed, "Names Harry, welcome to bloody paradise, mate."

He pulled a can of Australian beer from his bag, saying, "How 'bout a tinnie of blue – my shout, mate?"

When I said I hadn't drank any alcohol in over two years he looked at me with pity and disbelief. As he stamped my passport he said, "You're the first God-damned Yank to pass through this year. Not carrying any of that funny stuff, are ya?"

Assuming he meant marijuana, I assured him I carried nothing as funny as that and he said, "Good on ya, mate. There's bugger all to do here, but stay as long as you like – no worries," then added something about enjoying this job "way out to buggery on Cocos." The next day the two Australian yachts departed and I was the sole inhabitant of Harry's so-called paradise of buggery.

Cocos is rare – the world's remotest atoll and only recently inhabited by man. If the ancient Polynesian canoes did stop here, they left no trace. This privately owned island group that voted to join Australia the year before I arrived is a seven-mile wide lagoon encircled by a dozen sandy islets, called *motus*. Of the two presently inhabited, West Island is the administrative center where about 400 Australians live, mostly on temporary work contracts, with "bugger all to do," as Harry put it.

Home Island, at the opposite end of the lagoon, is home to an equal number of Malays, brought here generations ago to work the coconut plantations. There was a rigid apartheid-like separation here: all the white Christians keep to West Island and the Muslim Malays live on Home Island. As the Malay population increases, some are sent off to live in Australia, apparently so the government is never in the awkward position of being a white minority in charge of a Muslim majority. Actually, the Australians main purpose in buying and governing the island is to keep it out of the hands of their unwelcome neighbor, Indonesia. So cleverly progressive – and so bizarre.

The atoll itself is easier to understand than the people that live on its fragile foothold in the sea. One part land to many parts water, it's simply the eroded remnants of a larger volcanic island in the final days of its existence. The central lagoon mirrors a big sky where clouds, stars and wind pass by unobstructed. The motus are just a few feet above sea level now and are destined to drown under rising sea levels and eventually disappear. For now, the motus lay like a necklace of pearls on an azure sea, providing a sanctuary in a vast, watery desert for fish, birds, plants and people.

Long before humans arrived, a single coconut carried on ocean currents from far away settled into the sand to take root. A thousand years later and all the motus in the group are lined with "that giraffe of vegetables," as Robert Louis Stevenson so aptly described the life-giving coconut palm.

There is an anchorage in front of Home Island as well but, of course, special permission from the Malay council is required to use it. Remember, this is South Seas apartheid: Westerners to the west island, Easterners to the east island, and those troublesome visitors on yachts, well, they can have the northern island. To reach Home Island I rowed my plastic dinghy, little more than a toy when exposed to wind and wave, for a mile along the inside edge of the reef, ever mindful of the nearby sea battering the reef with thunderous fury. Landing on Home Island, I dragged the dinghy up a long sloping beach and secured it to a bush above the high tide mark.

As I had learned firsthand, gales and violent squalls of wind are common in this part of the Indian Ocean, not to mention occasional cyclones. Along the windward shore of Home Island was the sobering sight of a small sailing yacht dashed to pieces on the reef, probably within the past year or two, judging from the bits of unrotted wooden cabinetry strewn about. Back on the lagoon side, I found two rusted iron rails of an old slipway and wondered if this was the spot where Joshua Slocum hauled the *Spray* when he visited here during the first-ever solo circumnavigation. His historic book, *Sailing Alone Around the World*, was always at hand on my bookshelf and I was thrilled whenever I called at one of Joshua's ports.

I walked through coconut groves where five plump and elderly Malay women in colorful dresses and straw hats gossiped as they worked separating the coconut meat from the husks. Next to them a flatbed car loaded with copra sat in the sun to dry. Steel rails allowed it to be pushed under an open-sided shed at night or on rainy days. Since the sale of the islands to Australia, this aging group of women were all that remained of the plantation's workforce, all of the others preferring welfare checks from their new landlords to the hard physical labor of harvesting copra.

Pausing at a nearby graveyard under the palms as a distant loudspeaker called the faithful to perform one of five daily prayers, I stepped over a low wood fence for a closer look at the Malay graves. Many of the sites were adorned with offerings to the dead. Cans of peaches were a favorite offering. One grave was topped with a broken electric fan and a child's grave was marked by jars of candy and peanuts, a broken doll, a wooden spoon and a mirror.

Not far away, but predictably separate, was the abandoned Christian cemetery. One of the marble headstones read: "In memory of Maria, relict of Capt. James Clunies-Ross, 1899." For over 150 years these islands were the private territory of the Clunies-Ross family who imported the Malays to run their sole industry of exporting copra.

As I walked through the Malay village of new, government-supplied, prefabricated homes with indoor plumbing, I couldn't help but notice the contrast to the friendly people of Polynesia and New Guinea. The few people I saw here pretended to take no notice of me at all. With less than a mile of road that leads to nowhere, the Malays rush about on motorized bicycles as if on some urgent business. At the south end of the island, a low wall of coral stones fenced off a corner of the lagoon into a large, and now empty, turtle pond. Today the Malays prefer their turtle soup in cans flown in on the weekly flight from Australia.

Through their long years of isolation, the shy and handsome Cocos Malays had been mostly self-sufficient. Besides the hard work of producing copra, the men were skilled woodcarvers and built their *jukong* sailing canoes for fishing. They even operated a blacksmith forge to produce any needed brass and iron fittings. Government handouts brought rapid change, afflicting the Malays with malaise. The formerly sail-powered jukongs I saw on the beach were now powered by large outboard motors. The few Malay men that work at all, do so by commuting daily to West Island on the high-powered ferry to perform such indispensable labor as watering the governor's imported lawn. The VCR in every house has largely replaced neighborly socializing, just as hot metal roofs have replaced the traditional cool thatch. The government policy for transforming and pacifying the

Malays has worked so well that I wouldn't be surprised if one day they all packed up and moved to a slum outside Sydney.

I passed several carefree days on Direction Island, jogging barefoot along the beach, harvesting ripe coconuts with a machete and snorkeling over the reefs among shimmering schools of fish. One day I sailed *Atom* across the lagoon to West Island for provisions. Such a joy it was to ride *Atom* as she heeled to the fresh wind and skipped over the shallow waters. Widely scattered coral heads stood out as yellow-brown clumps among the pale green waters and were easily avoided with a sharp lookout ahead. My silent approach startled several sea turtles basking on the surface, who upon seeing me almost on their backs, took a gulp of air and dove underwater. The southern half of the lagoon was not navigable, being mostly shallow coral studded with deep pools, but its silent remoteness looked worth exploring by sailing dinghy. Unfortunately, the winds picked up by the time I neared the West Island pier where the anchorage was exposed to six miles of fetch across the lagoon. Too choppy to safely anchor, or land the dinghy, I turned around and tacked my way back to Direction Island.

Still needing to resupply with fresh fruit and vegetables, the next day I rode with Harry in the custom's launch back to West Island. Disembarking at the jetty at the island's north end, I walked four miles through scented pine forests and along the empty ocean-side beaches. Next to the mile-long airstrip I visited the weather station to read the long-range forecast. More of the same settled trade winds was basically all it said. At the island's sole settlement, I bought a small bag of produce, imported by plane, and got taxed 150% on it because I was "from a yacht." I then walked back north and boarded the launch just as Harry was casting off for Home Island and he kindly detoured to drop me off at Direction Island.

In these few days, I had almost come to think of this secluded island as mine alone, a little piece of Eden inaccessible to the thundering hordes of the outer world. Later, in the cool evening breeze, I rowed the dinghy over to Prison Island, which is no more than a lump of sand sprouting a dozen palms and scrubby bushes. I walked from one end of the islet to the other in less than one hundred steps. It was difficult to imagine the drama that was played out here in the early 1800s.

Prison Island

Back then, Alexander Hare, a wealthy ex-governor of the colony of Borneo, landed on uninhabited Home Island with a private harem of forty Malay women, planning to retire. Two years later, a ship landed Capt. James Clunies-Ross, his wife and family, and eight sailors to settle the same island. There was understandable animosity and disputes between the two camps and the lusty sailors could not keep their hands off Hare's harem. Eventually, Hare and his few remaining women retreated to what became known as Prison Island, where he lived a short time before finally retiring to the Dutch colony of Batavia.

Standing in the center of Prison Island, I could not imagine Hare's group living on such a tiny scrap of land. Later, when I compared an up-to-date chart to an earlier survey, it was apparent the island had eroded considerably over the years and may one day disappear, adding its sand to one of its neighboring motus.

I camped overnight on Prison Island, setting up my one-man tent on the beach. On this windy night the rustle of palm fronds and incessant drone of surf seemed mixed with voices from the past: "Ahoy, you there, on Prison Island!" I looked to Home Island and saw no one there. A coconut fell to the ground and I cracked it open for a drink and a taste of its oily flesh. I thought how *Atom* so resembled this isolated islet, seemingly pushing its way as a ship into the steady trade winds. They both held the same serenity and shelter and promise of deliverance. At sunrise I packed my dinghy to leave. The rising tide soon erased my footprints from the beach, and like Alexander Hare, gone was all physical record of my having passed this way.

Atom and I were refreshed and ready for the next sea passage, yet I took one more night here to sleep on deck and soak up the atmosphere of the tropic isle. Under a magnificent southern sky, a cascade of stars spilled to the horizon. After moonrise, the transparent waters took on a luminous glow, the boat seemingly floating on air, casting a moon shadow on the rippled sand below. Ashore, the palms gently bowed before the wind, mixing the rustling of fronds with the murmur of surf in a captivating voice of mid-ocean solitude. With fully restored mind and body, I sailed away the next morning on a light wind, headed for a distant island of a million people.

16 Solitary Sailor

I must go down to the seas again,
to the lonely sea and sky.

- J. Masefield

We were bound for Mauritius Island 2400 miles to the west. I'd expected a passage of steady trades at this time of year in these latitudes. Then, barely one hundred miles past the Cocos Islands, the wind fell away to nothing. For two days *Atom* drifted within a void of blue sky and water, sails snapping from side to side as we rolled on the leftover heaving sea.

A ship appeared on the horizon and I watched him make a deliberate course change to approach us. She slipped by close enough for me to see the faces of the crewmen who stepped out of the pilothouse to gaze down on our boat adrift. When later that day two other ships passed within a mile of us, I judged by their course that *Atom* was crossing an Indonesia to South Africa shipping lane and I kept a more attentive watch.

Within a period of several hours the calm gave way to a gale from the southeast. The finest hour of a voyage is when a new wind arrives and the boat slips quickly through calm water. Again I observed the magic of cat's paws wavelets born of the opposing forces of wind friction and water surface tension. I watch with infinite patience as they grow into majestic, mature waves, now propelled by even greater wind friction coupled to the restoring force of gravity. Science explains wave theory but knowing the formula does little to explain the magic.

As the seas built, their frothy tops tumbled aboard as they swept past. For five days we eagerly rushed before the blow. A few times each day a high swell from a distant southern ocean storm synchronized with the southeast wind-driven waves to produce an episodic wave with shocking impact against *Atom's* beam, skidding us sideways under a cascade of falling water. As always, *Atom* and I shrugged it off and resumed our course.

Mauritius Island

A wave's signature is as individual as a snowflakes and because of
their relatively large scale, waves are endlessly fascinating to watch.
This one building as it approaches at some fifteen to twenty miles an

hour – will it break before or after it reaches us? When not staring at this blizzard of awesome seas, I mended chafed sails, read books and pumped water from the bilge that accumulated from leaking deck fittings and hatches, all the while struggling to hold myself against the boat's forceful lurching. Eventually, the rain and spray and deck leaks dampened, if not soaked, virtually everything inside the boat.

Little miseries and minor emergencies become bigger when they take place on a stormy night. On one of these nights, a steering line on the wind vane chafed through and *Atom* spun around in an uncontrolled gybe: a stalling out with sails pushed aback. Within a minute of being snug in my bunk, I hung upside down from the stern rail, threading a new line as my head dunked under each sea. Two nights later the drama repeated when the other line broke. The next thrilling moment came when the shackle on the jib halyard broke letting the halyard run irretrievably to the top of the mast. The jib then dropped overboard and tore a seam before I could haul it aboard. After a half day with palm, needle and waxed thread, I hoisted the repaired jib on the spare spinnaker halyard, leaving the jib halyard to be retrieved when I could safely climb the mast in port.

The next notable event was hearing the speed instrument propeller ripped from the hull, possibly by some floating debris or the jaws of a shark attracted by its spin. This speedometer was installed before electronic speed logs were common and its mechanical cable, between prop and meter, had rarely gone more than a thousand miles at a time without snapping in two from fatigue. I had spent hours repairing it, over and over again. From here on out, I could only guess at my speed, which at first frustrated the navigator. By day I judged the rate of water as it moved alongside. At night the movement of the boat and sound of the water as it gurgled past the hull were clues that eventually became as accurate as, and more dependable than, the old speed log. Even laying half asleep in my bunk I knew the boat's approximate course and speed within a half knot by the way she rode over the waves. Like a blind person developing an extreme ability to sense their surroundings through hearing what the sighted cannot, the sailor's natural senses can only fully develop when he sails without instruments.

The night's moaning gale gradually, almost imperceptibly, reduced to a strong constant trade wind that sang a less-threatening sonorous note through the rigging. As my latitude dropped to almost 20 degrees South, my daily bucket showers in the cockpit had the cool signature of the southern hemisphere winter. Another 15 degrees of longitude, or about 900 miles, passed under the keel and I reset my local time back one hour to match the new time zone. With these strong winds behind me, I crossed into the next time zone seven days later. At this point I had set my clock back fifteen times since departing Florida with only nine more hours to bring it full circle.

While traversing over the waves, I was fascinated by a contour map of the floor of the Indian Ocean. Like other oceans I crossed, beyond the continental shelves the land below me was rarely flat. Its convoluted floor held mysterious abyssal trenches between its unclimbed mountain ranges, only the highest peaks of which broke the surface, like the Cocos Islands behind me and Mauritius ahead. Those lower mountains lay flooded and unborn to us, unknown except as irregular soundings under passing ships' sonar. Again I was reminded the nearest land was only a couple miles away – directly below me, yet a world away.

The unmistakable sound of a whale spouting nearby brought me on deck in time to see him cross my track two waves behind me. It was probably a humpback or sperm whale, judging by its size: nearly double *Atom's* length. Its colossal beauty was partly lost on me since whales are known to sink yachts, either accidentally, or otherwise. Thankfully, I never saw a whale that large again, but the next day a group of pilot whales, half the length of *Atom,* encircled us, behaving like overgrown porpoises playing with a big brother. Either boredom or fatigue, at pacing us at 130 miles a day, sent them veering off in unison a few hours later.

The shifting, fickle gallery of radio stations heard on my portable short-wave receiver, which only picked up the strongest signals, was evidence of our progress across the Indian Ocean. Short-wave broadcasts from Australia and the singsong voices of Indonesia faded into the static. I briefly heard Sri Lanka discussing their Tamil troubles as I passed a thousand miles to the south. The powerful transmitters of Radio Moscow, Voice of America and the BBC were often in range and gave me what I needed for accurate navigational time with a distinctive beep tone at the top of each hour. The news that followed; the Holy Wars between communists, capitalists and Islamists, was less welcome within the serene cocoon of *Atom's* cabin and I listened sparingly to reports from that other world.

In a rising wind, I went forward to change down to a smaller jib. Rigged as usual for downwind, the whisker/spinnaker pole held the sail out to one side to prevent flogging as the boat rolled. When I released the pole's end latch from the sail, the pole broke free of my grasp and swung from its topping lift line above my head. Before I could catch it, the tip punched a hole in the mainsail. I hurried to patch the sail and just as I finished, looked over my shoulder and sighted Rodriquez Island off the starboard bow. I did not plan to stop at the island, which at the time had a poor harbor, though its cloud-capped peak proved useful as a waypoint to confirm my position. Shifting winds and rain squalls now compelled me to set a course passing south of the island.

Once committed to that course, the wind increased and shifted ahead, forcing me closer to land than felt safe. My relatively new number two jib was oversized for this wind strength, but there was no time now for changing sails. Fearful of hitting the reefs that extend five miles off the coast, I sheeted the sails in tight and beat into the wind and waves. A compass bearing on the island at dusk showed I was gaining distance to windward. Then the jib exploded under the force of the wind. We slowed to a crawl, drifting back down on the island as the pieces of sail flogged in the wind. What had been my best sail, I now retrieved in three pieces. Working frantically and mindful of having my back against the wall of reefs, I replaced the shredded sail with the smaller sail I had just repaired. The breakers on the reef were hidden by darkness as I regained my course. By dawn, the island was safely astern and out of view.

The excitement continued as a second gale arrived unexpectedly. One moment, I was putting together a sandwich of cornbread and mung bean sprouts topped with mustard and pepper, and the next, I was thrown with pots and dishes against the cabin side, as a blast of wind laid us over sharply. A minute later, wearing nothing but my harness and an anguished expression, I crouched knee-deep in waves submerging the bow as I fought to lower the flailing jib. Step by methodical step, I wrestled the jib into its bag and dragged it back to the cockpit locker, pulled the storm jib bag forward, then hoisted and sheeted it in to maintain steerage while I moved on to triple-reef the main. Even in my weariness and anxiety, I was thrilled to ride the breast of a violent sea displaying its raw power. The sea, especially in its moments of fury, demands first your attention, then your endurance, and finally your patience and acceptance. If you lack this capacity, the sea will soon find you out and make it known to you that the shore is where you should make your home.

Each day the barometer needle jumped upwards a bit more as the anti-cyclone passed over us. Between low, scudding clouds I caught the sun at least twice a day for a shaky and approximate position. Each sight tested my balance as wind vibrated and spray soaked the instrument in my hands while I worked to bring the sun tangent to a chaotic horizon only briefly seen from the crest of the highest waves. In these conditions, the delicate maneuver of twilight star sights was as out of the question as building a house of cards on a roller coaster.

On the night of my nineteenth day at sea, a dim glow from city lights on the east coast of Mauritius appeared in the distance ahead. The gale still hammered at the sea the next day as the island grew from a smudge on the horizon. Squalls raced by every twenty minutes like commuter trains on a tight schedule. If I hadn't seen the island, I could still have felt its presence as the upward sloping seabed heaped up the swells and the bold coast bounced them back to mix with trade wind-driven waves rolling unimpeded for thousands of miles across the Indian Ocean.

By evening I was on the western, or leeward, side of the island. Protected from the weather by intervening mountain ranges, wind and seas dropped to give me a calm, peaceful sail up the coast to the island's capital and port of entry at Port Louis. By reefing sails, I slowed our progress to arrive off the port at dawn.

When I pushed the starter button to motor up the port's narrow channel, the engine coughed once, blew out a puff of gray smoke, and quit. Again I knelt in front of the engine, not in prayer as might have been more effective, but with arms wrapped around that inscrutable contraption of grease, iron and rust, vainly adjusting the carburetor. As I disassembled and cleaned the rusty monstrosity, a crucial, tiny part rolled out of reach into the bilge. Turning my back on this truculent iron mule, I went on deck and noticed we had drifted in the current some ten miles back out to sea. The next several hours I spent in a more fruitful task of tacking into the unsteady breezes drifting down the semi-circle of mountains forming the backdrop to Port Louis.

Ahead lay a visual assault, from rolling green slopes and jagged peaks visible miles away, to the closer-in spectacle of a busy shipping port. Men labored to unload ships' cargos while others loaded sugar from quayside storage sheds. A dredger worked at deepening the harbor. An overtaking tugboat sounded its horn as I zigzagged my way into the small boat harbor on the city waterfront pier and tied alongside two other yachts on a cement quay.

I had barely finished securing my lines when an Indian man stepped aboard uninvited and thrust his business card at my face. Perhaps because it was his only card, he did not hand it to me, but allowed me to read it from the end of my nose. "Mauritian Laundry Service – Recommended by Her Majesty's Royal Navy," it proclaimed in bold type.

"I sail naked," I apologized, while holding up a nearly empty laundry bag, which sent him scurrying down the pier. There went my first contact with humanity after twenty days alone at sea.

Atom's yellow quarantine flag flying from the starboard spreader drew the attention of two French-speaking Indian customs and immigration agents wearing British-style uniforms. They climbed aboard with that air of mild suspicion and annoyance common to the breed, their briefcases stuffed with important documents. I scribbled the appropriate information in their forms as one of them poked about down below until satisfied I carried nothing illegal, or more importantly, nothing of dutiable value.

After a brief hello to my neighbors on two Australian yachts, I prepared a dish of rice garnished with my last onion. Only half-finished with dinner, the shot of landfall adrenalin wore off and I fell instantly asleep as I slumped into my bunk. It's amazing how a steady bunk drugs your sleep after a long strenuous voyage, particularly as it often culminates in long hours on constant alert during the coastal navigation of final approach. Finally at rest in safe harbor, your subconscious tells you the dangers are past and nothing else is of any significance. I did finally awake early the next morning to a metallic voice chanting the Muslim call to prayer from a loudspeaker located on the roof of a nearby building. Its volume was set at air-raid siren level lest any Muslims, Hindus, Christians, or heathen sailors in the harbor try to sleep through prayer time.

Stepping refreshed onto the pier, I moved past the Indians and Africans who work and loiter along the waterfront. Back then, before Mauritius grew a moderately prosperous textile manufacturing and tourist economy, strolling down the back streets and alleys of Port Louis loosed visions of old Bombay – Hindus, Muslims, Africans, Chinese and all shades of Creole crowded the streets where curbside vendors sold every kind of cooked and uncooked foods from roasted peanuts to fiery curries wrapped in tortilla-like flatbreads. As in India, labor is cheap, people plentiful, and small businessmen hawk their wares with a sense of urgency. Shopkeepers leaned out of windows and doorways imploring me to come in and inspect their goods as if our mutual survival depended on it.

Buses, bicycles and pedestrians jockeyed for right-of-way on the streets, and motorbikes considered the sidewalks their territory. Mauritians behind the wheel of cars, trucks and taxis express themselves with the same impatient jostling as the pedestrians in the crowded markets. I happily immersed myself in this revolving chaos and, with no particular place to go, allowed myself to be swept along by the human tide. Having spent most of the last sixty-five days alone at sea since leaving New Guinea, I felt as foreign as a visitor from another planet.

When I asked a local policeman on the street corner where to change dollars to local money, he openly told me the black market rate was better than the bank and directed me to the back room of a Chinese jewelry shop. With a bulging pocket of Mauritian rupee notes, I entered the chaotic Indian market where vendors shouted at me from all sides in a demanding way they knew was hard to ignore. Here I bought two bags of fruits and vegetables, some croissants and a crispy French baguette three feet long, and lunched on curry-filled pancakes known as *dhal puri* washed down with a glass of fresh yogurt. At the end of the day, I calculated my indulgent shopping spree cost me only eight US dollars.

Unlike the Pacific, where nearly every scrap of land was inhabited by the ancient peoples of Southeast Asia before discovery by Westerners, this 29 by 38 mile-wide island knew no men of any race when discovered by the Dutch some 400 years ago. For a long time, French settlers ran sugar cane plantations with slave labor from Africa and later with indentured labor from India and China. Even though Britain ruled the island from the time of the Napoleonic Wars until independence in 1968, the local hybrid population of over a million people from Africa, Asia and Europe have retained French and Creole as their daily language.

The noisy, colorful circus of life in Port Louis is squeezed between the sea and the surrounding mountains, each with a distinct name and shape, all beckoning to be climbed. Giant boulders balance on sharp peaks and saw-tooth cliff edges pierce the sky. The thumb-shaped "Le Pouce" stands prominently among the three-thousand-foot mountain range backing up against the city.

Two and a half hours after lacing up my boots aboard *Atom*, I gazed down on Port Louis from the narrow sky-piercing tip of Le Pouce. Opposite the city, to the east, small villages punctuated the checkerboard pattern of sugar cane fields, some tall and green, others harvested and brown, others burnt black. Shadows raced across the fields as puffs of trade wind-driven clouds blew past, bathing me in their fine mist as they went.

In succeeding days I climbed to the tops of Le Pouce's neighboring peaks, often inching my way along finger and toeholds ascending the vertically crevassed rock faces. As I carefully made my way up a tricky route, a group of cane cutters paused to watch me, then waved as I emerged looking almost straight down on them from an overhanging ledge.

Between rejuvenating sorties to the mountains, I tended to necessary maintenance and repairs on *Atom*. I climbed the mast to retrieve the lost jib halyard. In those days, instead of having a helper hoist me aloft in a bosun's chair, I preferred the body-strengthening task of free climbing by gripping the rigging with my hands and clamping my thighs against the mast to inch-worm my way up and down. Halfway up, I could sit on the spreaders for a rest and further up, I could stand on the upper spreaders to work at the masthead.

With hacksaw and hammer and chisel I worked to cut an inspection port into *Atom's* dirt-clogged fuel tank. The tough monel steel of the tank resisted attempts to cut it with dull hand tools. My noisy struggle with the tank attracted the attention of a tall, rail-thin Creole man about 20 years old who leapt off the quay into *Atom's* cockpit. "Permettez-moi," he said as he grabbed the hammer and chisel from my hand and struck the tank top with vigor.

How can you not be impressed when someone fishing for a job sees a task and begins work without negotiation? I hired Anthony for a few days at the local labor rate of about a dollar an hour to help finish the two-man job of removing and recaulking leaking deck fittings – a never ending task when the core of the deck is waterlogged. Instead of making a long walk home each night, Anthony chose to sleep stretched out on *Atom's* cockpit bench.

My conversations with Anthony were all in French, or I should say, he spoke to me in a French Creole and I blathered like an unselfconscious idiot in phrase book French. I guess Anthony had known other sailors before me since he asked if I wanted him to find me a five dollar girl for the night. I acknowledged the price was fair but Anthony smiled knowingly when I said I preferred a woman with a less mercenary approach.

Once our work was done, Anthony took me to his family house in the Port Louis suburb of Roche Bois for dinner. "Tonight I will introduce you to my cousin Dolores. She's single and almost eighteen," Anthony said as we walked the dirt road past decaying houses, little more than shacks of timber and tin. His numerous relatives lived on the same street in adjoining shipwrecks of houses.

Inside their house I met the generations from grandparents to grandchildren, including Dolores, her Indian mother and Tanzanian father. Dolores was tall and slender with gorgeous dark almond eyes that shyly met mine as I frequently looked her way that evening. To her family she spoke Creole in musical tones. To me she used her schoolbook French to be more easily understood. She would have been in her final year of high school but was forced to drop out when the family could not afford the tuition. Now she borrowed friend's books and studied on her own at home. While Anthony's mother served dinner of rice and spicy curry that brought tears to my eyes, Dolores moved around fussing over her grandparents and younger brothers and sisters. I could see why they seemed to love her so much.

With dinner finished, the table was pulled away and the guitar came out. We sang and danced in the small room as Dolores and her sister laughed while teaching me the hip-swaying steps to a Mauritian Creole dance. As I left the house, the grandmother handed me a bag of leftover desserts and Dolores kissed me innocently on both cheeks, the memory of which distracted my sleep that night. There is a richness and joy within these people that remains undamaged by the poverty surrounding them.

"Be careful you don't fall in love," Anthony warned me the next day with another knowing smile.

"Your warning may be too late, mon ami," I replied. "I'm invited to Dolores' house for dinner tonight." When I asked her that night to come visit me at the boat, I quickly learned that in this family there would be no loose American-style romance. I saw Dolores nearly every day after that, at her house, my boat, picnics at the beach or mountain, the botanical gardens, and for the first few weeks, always with at least her mother, grandmother, or sister as chaperon.

My frustrated passions found a useful diversion when I got underway on my long walk across the island's tilted terrain. I planned an unhurried, foot-paced tour of the southern half the island, some forty miles or more of twisting roads from one side of the island to the other, including a detour to the island's highest mountain, Piton de la Petite Riviere Noire.

Dolores and Anthony joined me for the first day of the trek, starting with a bus ride to our starting point at the coastal village of Grand Case Noyale. Along the way we crossed the central plateau where Corps de Guard, an impressive flat-sided mountain rose over flat fields of sugar cane. At Tamarind Bay we passed rubber-booted workers sweeping up piles of salt from terraced clay and stone-floored tidal ponds where a strong sun continuously evaporated seawater.

Mauritius Island

From Grand Case Noyale we set out on foot for the next village of Chamarel, three miles to the east. The road bent mostly upwards with occasional welcome, breath-catching dips. Higher up we rounded a bend and Dolores pointed out the seacoast in the distance. There on the southwest corner of the island stood Le Morn Brabant, a massive square-shaped mountain thrusting out like an island-size nose sniffing the salt air. Because its cliffs are nearly unclimbable, it had once been a refuge for runaway slaves. When the British abolished slavery on the island, they sent a detachment of police to climb the mountain and tell the slaves of their freedom. Seeing police coming, the slaves assumed they would be caught and hung so instead they threw themselves from the cliffs. The sad ironies of ancient history seemed of little consequence to my companions who, unburdened by a heavy backpack, teased me for my slow progress uphill.

From Chamarel, Anthony and Dolores returned home by bus and I walked alone up out of the valley, stopping here and there to pick a ripe guava from roadside bushes. The road brought me to a clearing at Seven Coloured Earths, a field of heaped bare volcanic residue where I caught view of my target, the low-sounding summit of Little Black River Peak. A few miles on I turned onto a trail and could tell I was moving up along a narrow ridge, but thick bush prevented measuring my progress until I came out in a last steep scramble where I pulled myself up onto the island's most skyward point. Below me the Black River gorge cut deep through the central plateau, the river cliffs punctuated with waterfalls in a verdant miniature of America's Grand Canyon. My route behind and ahead of me was clearly visible as were the jagged peaks surrounding Port Louis standing as distant castle spires to the north. I sat on this perch a few minutes chewing on a baguette while listening to a family of monkeys chattering in the bushes below.

With precious few hours of daylight remaining, I descended the mountain and walked east through a pine forest planted years ago in orderly rows from seedlings imported from France. In a ft of homesickness, the early colonizers named several towns on the island after corresponding French cities. With a sense of humor a mapmaker named a nondescript hill Cocotte, meaning "Prostitute." Another was named Montaine Duex Mamelles (Two Breast Mountain), and more remarkably, Tres Mamelles.

As daylight faded I picked up the pace to reach my planned campsite at the crater lake of Grand Basin. The fresh soreness in my muscles reminded me how far I had traveled in just one day. A chill rain began as I unrolled my tent next to an ornate dome-roofed Hindu shrine. Across the pond stood another temporarily-deserted temple. During February, at the Festival of Maha Shivaratree, Hindu devotees carry flower-covered wooden arches on a pilgrimage to the lake. Here, the largest percentage population of Indians outside India comes by the thousands to collect holy water in a scene reminiscent of the rituals on the banks of the Ganges.

Because in my quest to travel light I had not brought a blanket, I was kept awake by the cold night air of the high plateau. Rain pattered lightly on my tent as I lay under my raincoat until dawn when I packed my backpack in the gloomy fog and scampered off for other places. The road descended into finer weather as I entered emerald fields of tea plants. The pickers bobbed as they moved among the low bushes, pulling select leaves from the top and tossing them into cane baskets tied to their backs. The closely spaced bushes, as even in height as the pile of a carpet, only just allowed the pickers enough room to push their way through.

Beyond the tea fields, the road led past a string of dreamy sounding villages: Bois Cheri, Grand Bois, La Flora and Beau Climat. At each settlement I received friendly greetings from the people I met and they, correctly assuming I was not stopping at their particular bend in the road, offered unsolicited directions to the next village. It was perhaps the people's incongruous speech that fascinated me most, especially French-speaking Indo-Mauritians that predominated the interior. As I stood in a little country store drinking chilled soda water, a woman in a multi-colored sari dress came in for baguettes. The red dot on her forehead indicated more boldly than a ring that she was married. She wore her wealth as a solid gold ring through the side of her nose. Her correct French speech indicated she might have been to school in France. Next to enter was an African boy who called out his request in the rhythmic Creole patois to the old Chinese shopkeeper who conversed with us all in Mandarin-accented French.

Back on the road, sun-darkened men slashed at stalks of sugar cane with long-bladed knives and filled truck beds and mule carts with the raw ingredient of the island's main export of sugar. Since cane planting began some two hundred seasons ago, these fields have been cleared of large and small boulders that now stand in pyramid-like piles in the center of most every field. All roads in this region converged at the stone arch gateway of the sugar cane processing plant where mechanical crane claws plucked the towering piles of harvested cane from trucks and creaking over-burdened oxcarts.

Hot, sun-baked cane fields rutted by oxcart wheels stretched to the horizon as I walked through the dusty village of Rose Belle. Past Duex Bras, a village so small and nondescript it barely broke the horizon, I marched out of the cane fields and crossed a river on a bridge of hand laid stone arches. Walking down a steep one-lane street in Ville Noire, I confronted a cane truck moving up from the bottom. It was loaded so heavily that its overhanging cane scraped the stone walls on either side of the road. He could not stop on his uphill run and I could not back up in time. At the last moment, I dropped to lay flat in the shallow gutter. I turned my head to see if the driver noticed me near his front wheels. The unconcerned look on his face seemed to say he often saw pedestrians lying in the ditch when he passed.

Another mile and another elegant old stone bridge passed under my boots and I was suddenly at the coastal town of Mahebourg. The briskness had gone out of my step. My leg muscles now ached continuously and my pack grew heavier with each step. I sat next to a fruit seller's stand and bit into a sun-ripened mango while my eyes feasted on the rich scenery of people moving through the outdoor markets and fishing pirogues drifting inside the reef line. A bus brought me back to *Atom* in Port Louis before nightfall where my three-inch-thick bunk cushions had never felt so luxurious.

I had walked the island and stood on its highest point, but there remained one other peak that captured my attention. Visible from Port Louis, this slender peak was capped by a massive rock looking like a man's head set on the shoulders of the mountain. It seems too delicately balanced and artful to be a natural formation. At first I attempted this climb alone and found myself hanging from my fingernails on the wrong approach and unable to move up the vertical rock wall. On my second attempt, I took a bus to the village of Creve Coeur (Broken Hearted) and wandered around looking for a local guide. I checked first at the general store, where idle old men passed the time conversing in Hindi while sari-wrapped women came in for daily household supplies.

I found my guide when 23-year-old Pareep Singh attached himself to me as I walked past his family's stone house directly under the mountain. Pareep said he had guided tourists up the mountain "many times" and we agreed on a price of 50 rupees, or about three US dollars.

I followed Pareep down a path along a maze of old volcanic stone walls erected around family-sized plots of land. Above the cane fields the path forked in several directions. Here my guide proved indispensable as we made long strides, quickly working our way through the labyrinth of interlocking trails and up the wooded ravine. We continued up a steepening dry stream bed that showed eroded signs of turning into a waterfall on days of hard rain. The valley opened up below us, but my attention stayed focused on the narrow ledge we crept along. As slight insurance against the unsure footing, we gripped handfuls of grass sprouting from cracks in the rocks.

Pieter Both Mountain, Mauritius

Once we emerged just below the peak on the shoulder of Pieter Both, we paused to sort out our climbing rope and eat our lunch of oranges and bread. As we gazed down on his neighbor's gardens, Pareep told me the legend of this man-shaped mountain: "An Indian milkman came upon an angel one day while making his deliveries. They made love after he promised the angel he would never speak of it to anyone. Of course, the next day, he boasted of his conquest to his friends and soon the whole town knew about it. In her embarrassed anger, the angel turned the milkman into this mountain. We are standing on his shoulders here and you can plainly see his neck and head above us." Pareep pointed straight up to the head and then added, "Our Creve Coeur (Heartbreak Village) is named after their misfortune."

The overhanging head of Pieter Both, frozen in a geologic moment, is poised to tumble down one day on the houses in the valley below. They used to say here that when the head fell it would portend the end of British rule over the island. Independence has come and still it teeters, buffeted by storms and rumors.

We tied ourselves together with my fifty-foot safety line and crawled up the neck for a final ascent. Pareep pointed out a bronze plaque placed on the rock as a memorial to an English family of four who were killed here in a lightning strike several years earlier.

The final pitch up the face was only possible because the Royal Navy had years ago cemented iron rungs into the overhanging rock. These essential handholds had since rusted dangerously thin. When I mentioned my concern to Pareep, he calmly said, "Never mind." I wondered if by that he meant, "It's okay," or maybe less convincingly, "Don't think about it." With me below him at the end of a taut line, Pareep surprised me by looking down and saying: "I think 50 rupees is not enough. Maybe you could pay a little more?"

With feet dangling in air at times, I pulled my way up the rungs of this very rusty ladder hanging over a nasty drop, and finally stood on the head of Pieter Both. "You're right Pareep, 50 rupees is not enough." The view was worth the small terror of the final pitch and the last-minute price negotiations. Below us to the east lay a quilt pattern of cane fields and puffs of smoke from factories processing the cane into sugar or rum. To the south were the buildings and horse racetrack of Port Louis and beyond it, in the distance, stood the island's highest peak at Riviere Noire. Off the northern coast, I picked out four islets lying like a fleet of ships anchored on the blue sea.

After our descent from the mountain, Pareep invited me to his home where we drank the cool water pulled from his well by a bucket on a rope. Together we filled my pack with cabbages, carrots and ginger root from the family garden.

The remainder of my days on Mauritius were spent with Dolores either at my side or in my thoughts. In the cool of the morning just after sunrise, she awakened me with a tap on the cabin trunk window and a soft call of my name: "Je-mees." We returned again to the shady and sprawling Royal Botanical Gardens at the town of Pamplemousses. Hidden among the leafy Raffia and stubby Bottle Palms, we picnicked on the grass at the edge of a water-lily pond. We spent hours here, sometimes leaning back on the scrambling roots of the Bo Tree of Ceylon with Dolores coaching me in French and the Creole patois. Here I came to view English as the masculine language; descriptive, precise, exact as science. French is the feminine; mellifluous tones of romance and sensuality, especially as spoken by an island girl. To compensate for our lack of fluency in a common language, I also grew to learn the unspoken language expressed in the emotion of the eyes, the knowing smile between friends, the unconscious gestures of her body and the rhythm of her breathing.

Once we had the long-awaited permission of her parents, Dolores joined me for a day of sailing around those islets off the north coast and then to anchor in Grand Bay. Her first day on a sailboat proved her natural abilities as she learned to hoist and trim sails and steer a compass course without a tinge of seasickness. Away from the dirt and noise and prying eyes of Port Louis, we swam and played off a powder-soft beach fringed with coconut palms and *casuarinas* until the sun set behind mother-of-pearl clouds. Then we hurried to a taxi stop in Grand Bay village and negotiated with a driver to return her to Roche Bois before her parents began to worry.

The next day Dolores, her relatives and friends, arrived in Grand Bay by bus carrying cooked food in baskets, blankets and guitars. I joined them for an all-day, all-night party on the beach. The older folks ate and napped while the younger ones swam and collected driftwood for a fire. After dark, two sets of leather-faced wood drums appeared and guitars were tuned up and the Sega dance began.

Originating from slave-era Africans, this pulsating folk dance is a combination of fast-paced shuffling and hip swaying, while the extremely flexible dancers lean back on their feet to rest the top of their head in the sand and thrust their hips suggestively. The provocative and yearning Creole lyrics and uninhibited, erotic movements are like a voodoo party without the dark side. I was pulled in and clumsily followed Dolores' lead while the party-goers circled around clapping hands to the music and shouting encouragement. Sure, I looked the fool, but a happy fool at least.

Later I walked the beach with Dolores under the faint light of the Milky Way. A warm wind brushed the bay, sending wavelets to lap at our feet in gentle strokes. We sat in the sand in a secluded spot leaning against a large rock. The moon began to rise as I listened to Dolores sing in Creole to the beat of the distant music. Then she asked me why I had sailed so far alone. "I came to find you," I said. And at that moment, it was as simple and true as that. There was nothing else I felt I had to do.

She threw her head back and smiled at my silliness. Then she looked at me and asked, "Do you know of the Chagos Islands? I've heard they are not so far away and nobody lives there now. But the gardens are still there and fish are in the lagoon. Maybe you and I and *Atom* could sail there one day, yes?" She smiled again and I instinctively reached out and pulled her dark body on top of me.

From other sailors I heard of the charms of those palm-lined atolls in the Chagos Group, offering wide lagoon anchorages and seagirt tranquility. The idea of us going there together was powerful. It was no small thing for Dolores to leave her family to maroon herself with me on a distant island. No woman had offered themselves so completely and unconditionally to me before. But if we went, I would be here through the next cyclone season and it would be a year later before I could leave for Africa. Regardless how I interpreted their Sega dance, I knew her family expected us to get married before we spent one night alone together. I didn't ask her yet but felt maybe I should marry this girl and give up the role of solitary sailor.

I was many miles and moods from America when I wrote and told my parents of these thoughts. I was an independent adult and could make my own choice, but I was unsure of the right path. Perhaps I said too much, too soon, because the reply I received from home came as a shock. "How can you even think of marriage to a girl you've known less than two months who doesn't speak a word of English?" and adding, "You don't have the money or job prospects to support a wife and she would feel out of place in this country so far from her family. Don't be so foolish and selfish."

Their message was clear — it's all right to have your romance over there, just don't bring it home with you. I was shocked back to reality and sad to realize they were at least partially right. It was true, Dolores would not be happy where I had to go. Taking her away from her family would be selfish of me. I now wondered if I even wanted to return to America. Would I ever be content there again? I certainly could not run with the same close-minded group I had known and even imitated. A storm of emotions brewed inside me. This was not the time and place to settle down. I knew it — but could not bring myself to speak to Dolores about my inner turmoil. In Mauritius, tomorrow is a lifetime away, and we contented ourselves with the moments that rushed past.

Bill Tehoko, known also as Tonga Bill, was my age and my best friend among the yachts in the anchorage here. He had little advice to give about my predicament other than to lend a sympathetic ear and advise me not to worry and "do what you feel and it'll work out just fine."

Bill and his new French bride Nicole, that he found on the neighboring island of Reunion, lived aboard *Mata Moana*, a little 18-foot plywood and fiberglass sailboat he built himself on his home island in Tonga. The year before, he sailed it alone across the Pacific and Indian Ocean. He was the only modern Tongan voyager I ever heard of but I wasn't surprised he was here on his tiny boat, since his Polynesian ancestors were the greatest seafaring people in the world a thousand years ago. The truly surprising thing is that there are not more Polynesians sailing the seas. Bill supported himself working as an artist, doing carvings and sculpture and making jewelry from whatever was at hand. Nicole and Bill often came aboard *Atom* for dinner with me and Dolores, where there was more room to stretch out than on their little boat.

One of the many humorous stories Bill told was about a Swedish Navy boat that invited him aboard for dinner in some remote Pacific port. The captain was impressed by Bill's voyages alone in his small craft and asked him to speak of his experiences to his officers. At dinner, the curly-haired, dark-skinned Tongan said in a straight face, "Did you know, captain, that I am part Swedish?" With that he had everyone's attention. After noting the raised eyebrows, he continued, "Yes, my grandfather ate the first Swedish sailor to land in Tonga." Bill said the Swedes didn't know whether to laugh or throw him overboard.

Bill's four-horsepower outboard motor was even less reliable than *Atom's* inboard motor, so we decided to build a sculling oar for each of our boats. This way we could at least maneuver our boats in and out of calm harbors if the engine was not working. Bill picked out two planks of African hardwood at the lumber shop that we shaped with handsaw and plane into 14-foot oars. For a finishing touch, Bill carved an auspicious Tongan motif along the blade of my oar. After practicing the twisting figure-eight sculling motion with an oarlock on *Atom's* transom, I was able to propel the boat across the harbor at about one knot; not fast, but dependable when the wind went too calm to sail.

Bill and Nicole were preparing to depart in *Mata Moana* for a voyage up the Red Sea to France, a hard trip even in a much larger boat and I worried to myself about their fate. On the morning of their departure, Dolores and I escorted them out of the harbor with *Atom*. With blustery trade winds astern we sailed side-by-side several miles out to sea, gliding over the waves like two wandering albatross. The twin jibs set out from *Mata Moana's* tiny mast contrasted starkly with the empty sea ahead. The contrast grew even sharper as we waved farewell and turned *Atom* back to Grand Bay. The next time I looked back they were a spot on the horizon and then they were gone.

Ten years later, when I met them on Reunion Island during my second circumnavigation, I found out that they had encountered a storm off Madagascar, had taken some damage to their boat and diverted to the Seychelles where they lived for several happy years before returning to live on Reunion Island.

Tonga Bill departs Mauritius

With Bill and Nicole gone, I fell into an unlikely friendship with a local Indian named Sunil who anchored his wooden sailboat next to *Atom*. Sunil had two French tourist girls living on his boat that he claimed were both his "girlfriends," and when not occupied with them, he spent most of his time trying to swindle everyone he met. Somehow he had traded a few hundred dollars to a down-on-his-luck visiting sailor for this old and leaky engineless boat that he now used to take tourists out for a sunset harbor sail. The first day we met he left with my spare mainsail and broken VHF radio under his arm, saying, "Not to worry, I'll trade you something very valuable."

The next day we went to Port Louis to his friend's antiques shop to get my valuable mystery gift. I gave Sunil 50 rupees for our taxi after he insisted we shouldn't take the cheaper bus. "You're a tourist but don't worry, I know how to bargain for the Mauritian taxi rate," he said. Like in much of south Asia, everything is priced in two tiers, local and tourist.

As I got out of the taxi in the busy downtown street, Sunil began arguing loudly with our Indian driver. "But he is a tourist, so it is 100 rupees," the driver pleaded.

"Oh no, you filthy thieving son of a whore, he is with me and I am no tourist you can rip off," Sunil shouted in English for my benefit. I shrank onto the sidewalk as Sunil sucker-punched the driver in the face and ran away after saying, "You tried to rob me and now you get nothing." I noticed Sunil kept my 50 rupees for himself.

At the friend's shop, I was presented with a ninety-year-old reconditioned gramophone, a couple of old records, some spare parts, and a repair bill for 300 rupees. I decided I'd pay the bill and keep the gramophone rather than risk a punch in the nose for being ungrateful. That night the anchorage was entertained with the scratchy, tinny sounds of Perry Como drifting over the water from the gramophone's enormous brass horn sitting on *Atom's* cabin top. Hearing it actually play and thinking it might have some value after all, I boxed it up in the forepeak with my other hoarder's collectibles picked up throughout my voyage. The gramophone still sits as an ornament in my mother's apartment and as a testament to my own bloody-minded stubbornness at not leaving it in the shop where I found it.

The day was fast approaching when I had to depart Mauritius in order to make it to South Africa before the cyclone season. A few days before I left, Dolores and I made one more climb together of Le Pouce Mountain. We moved easily upward, each step putting the crowds of Port Louis farther below. Soon the forested upper slopes dropped below us in a feathery blanket of green. We sat on the grassy ridge a few steps below the peak and let the wind rush over us. It was warm on the mountain and I noted the nearly indiscernible change from tropic winter to tropic spring.

I wanted to tell Dolores I would send for her to join me when I reached home or that I would try to sail back to her the following year. But these options were more like trying to squeeze and stretch a rainbow than real possibilities. I was as Captain Bligh to my inner Fletcher Christian in Tahiti. Finally, I spoke and told her I would soon sail alone for Africa, that I would write her, but did not know if we would see each other again. When I looked at Dolores I realized my words had been carried away on the wind for I had been speaking in English. Still, she understood I was leaving alone. With a smile capable of melting mountain ice she leaned on my shoulder and whispered in French, "You'll come back to Ile Maurice and I will be waiting for you."

It seemed it was not paradise I was looking for. Maybe it was just the search for paradise that feeds this wanderlust to explore. Returning to sea, I hoped, would untangle the knots in my mind. With *Atom* back in Port Louis and ready for sea, I said my goodbyes to Dolores and her family the night before my early departure. Dolores wished me a safe voyage and promised to write, then turned away with a tear on her cheek.

At the first sign of morning twilight I sculled *Atom* out of the calm harbor. As the morning breeze wafted down the mountain I hoisted sails and gained the sea. Looking back at the seaward end of the breakwater I thought I could see through misty eyes the dark silhouette of a girl waving goodbye.

17 To the Peaks of Reunion

Solitude is the home of the strong; silence, their prayer.
- Ravignon

Aerial view of St. Pierre

The early morning land breeze dropping off the mountains of Mauritius carried me ten miles out to sea before shutting down completely. Without moving forward, *Atom* lurched drunkenly in the swell. Following a scent of gasoline fumes I lifted a bilge board and discovered a fuel leak from the engine had dumped a gallon of gas into the bilge. I stopped the leak, pumped the bilge out as much as I could, and then escaped the nauseating fumes by staying on deck the remainder of the day.

As the current carried me slowly away to the west, my eyes kept drawing back to the island. Memories, desires and tidal flows of contrary emotions left me numb for the first time to the excitement of beginning a sea passage. Part of this voyage was about seeking the solitude of the sea. True loneliness, at least as I've known it, is more keenly felt when you are among people but remain detached from

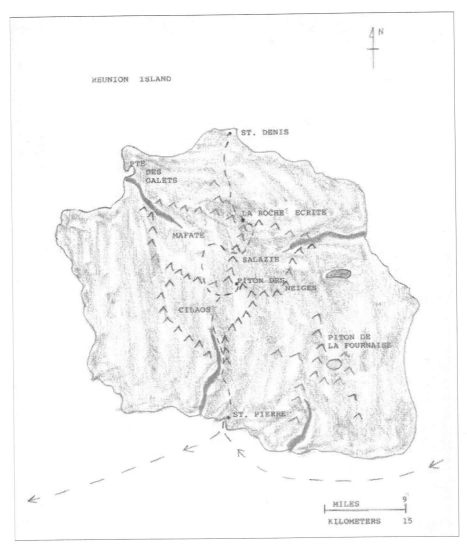

Reunion Island map

them. The loneliness of the sea had not much entered my mind before. Out here I did not expect human companionship and it was little missed. It had always been enough that on each return to land I smothered myself in new friends and new cultures as well as a full embrace of mountain and forest. But on this day I deeply felt that stab of despair I had not known before. The pact I made with myself to stay alone on this voyage now had me looking out the bars of a self-made prison and I didn't much care for the windless, hopeless void around me. Action was needed to break the spell but what action can be taken on a boat adrift in the calm?

Finally, the caress of a freshening wind on my face gave me something more than self-pity to contemplate. Instinctively, I trimmed the sails and set course for Reunion Island just 130 miles away. Still trying to avoid the gas fumes below deck, I lay on the cockpit bench, drifting in and out of semi-conscious sleep.

Just before sunset, as *Atom* crested a wave, I chanced to open my eyes halfway and spotted an orange canopy life raft drifting past our beam. I sat up and stared in stunned disbelief, then sheeted in the sails and tacked back into the wind, expecting to end my heroic misery with a heroic rescue. As I sailed past, I saw the canopy entrance flap was closed and so shouted to alert anyone inside the raft. No response. On the second pass I brushed up against the side of the raft, backed the sails to stall mode by pulling their sheets to windward, reached over and lashed a line tightly to the raft.

Floating tethered alongside the raft was a radio locator beacon that seemed not to be functioning. I felt compelled to enter the raft to see if perhaps there was anybody dead or unconscious aboard. First I dropped the sails to ensure *Atom* would not break free and sail away, leaving the rescuer adrift in need of rescue. I cautiously reached over and pulled back the canopy entrance flap. The raft was empty except for several canvas bags lying on the floor. Trying to resolve the mystery, I released the safety harness line that forever bound me to *Atom* and slid down into the raft. Inside I saw the bags were filled with sand, I presumed as ballast to prevent the raft turning upside down in the seas. There was nothing to identify where it came from or how it got here, just the words "32 person capacity" printed on its side. Yes, it was huge, about 15 feet in diameter – over half the length and almost double the width of *Atom*.

I didn't know enough about ship-sized life rafts to know that bags of sand ballast are not standard issue. I thought perhaps it had been lost overboard accidentally from a ship. A smarter man would have left it there or put a knife in the side to sink it and sailed away. Lacking that degree of common sense, and having long had the poor man's tendency to collect all valuable things abandoned, I felt an unreasonable pride of discovery, even of ownership. I even imagined maritime law might permit me a nice reward from the raft's owner if I could salvage it.

But how does one man on a 28-foot boat pick up a heavily ballasted 32-person life raft? I rehearsed a plan in my mind and then set to work. The first task was to remove the ballast and dump it over the side. It's remarkable how awkward it is to lift bags of wet sand while standing on a bouncing fabric floor. While the raft rose and fell in the waves, it was like bouncing on a trampoline while lifting and throwing hundred pound barbells. Second thoughts about the whole scheme kept recurring as I looked up at *Atom* with an uneasy feeling of separation as she lifted to each sea. Each sharp snub of her line jerked the raft under my feet as if she was reminding me I was now on the wrong end of a dog's leash.

Once the bags were out, I rushed to unscrew the four deflation plugs and re-boarded *Atom* as the raft deflated. Heaving aboard the half sinking, half inflated raft onto *Atom's* foredeck took all my remaining strength. Finally, as darkness fell, I had it lashed down in a great untidy pile that sprawled waist-high clear across the deck. I then hoisted a small jib above the pile and a reefed main, set up the self-steering, and collapsed in the cockpit. Still unable to inhabit the cabin or light the stove because of the gasoline fumes, I spent a miserable eternity of a night on deck, watching compass course and sail trim and getting doused by a shower of spray from the occasional wave slapping the side of the boat.

At dawn the cloud-capped mountains of Reunion lay a few points off the starboard bow. With a slight course correction I approached the southern coast, carried in the arms of a wind strengthening as it accelerated around the windward-side mountains. For twenty miles I flew down a rocky shore backed by summits floating above the cloud rack. All at once the miniature man-made harbor of St. Pierre appeared in front of me. A lather of breakers foamed against the stone jetty. I made two ninety-degree turns to enter the narrow harbor, packed wall-to-wall with a dozen local sailboats and assorted fishing craft. From shore a Frenchman called out, directing me with waving arms to lie alongside one of the sailboats on a mooring.

St. Pierre, at the time, was not well known to foreign cruising yachts, most of whom layover at the west coast commercial harbor of Port Des Galets. A local French sailor in Mauritius had recommended this little port to me as being more convenient, which turned out to be true. The neat and modern little town was built right up to the waterfront where local boat club members welcomed me ashore. One of the yachtsmen escorted me up the steeply inclined main street to check in with officials at the police station.

Reunion is a French possession, or "department," and every bit as much of France as Hawaii is of the United States. At the gendarmerie a police officer issued my entry papers without delay and listened intently to my story of the daring and daft raft rescue. Another policeman then drove me over to the office of Affaires Maritimes where I retold my story to Francois Gangnant, who in turn called the French Navy headquarters, who sent an officer over to question me all over again. Francois escorted me back to *Atom* where we waited until a navy launch pulled alongside. In a flash, the three sailors off-loaded the raft and sped out to a French Navy ship waiting offshore.

As they left I asked Francois whom to contact for my salvage award. Looking surprised and embarrassed, he said, "Sorry, there is no reward but the good thing is they have agreed not to arrest you for interfering with a naval operation and theft of government property." Francois went on to explain the Mauritian Navy set out the raft a day before I found it, as a joint rescue exercise with Air Mauritius and the French Navy, who were supposed to locate it. To their great embarrassment they were unable to find the enormous bright orange raft, at first because the radio beacon was not operating and later because I had plucked it from the sea. To save face, navy officials blamed me for the operation's total failure. I was just glad no one was actually in the raft expecting rescue from the French Navy.

My raft struggle was not completely unrewarding since Francois felt moved to befriend me and brought me to his parents' home for dinner. The Gangnant family told me their ancestors arrived on Reunion with a wave of other immigrants from France in the late

1700s. Like Mauritius, the economy was then, and still is, primarily based on sugar cane, worked by its kaleidoscope population of Indians, Africans, Europeans and Chinese.

The following day I joined Francois as he toured the southern coast fishing villages checking registrations and condition of the local outboard powered fishing boats. I watched as sea-hardened fishermen launched their wooden dory-like craft by sliding them down ramps on the harborless, surf-pounded rocky windward shore.

Reunion Island's volcano

Near the village of St. Philippe, we walked on a shore of congealed rivers of lava: raw and recent rock, pocked by craters and crevasses. The twisting lava bled down the slopes of a nearby volcano where it was instantly petrified by the sea. Its latest eruption of just a few weeks previously, left the cauldron still smoldering. On our drive back to St. Pierre we detoured inland, upland you could say, to where a creek cascaded over an escarpment into a pool flanked by perfectly vertical vine-laced cliffs. In the distance rose the shimmering peak of Piton des Neiges, over 10,000 feet above sea level, and higher than any other in the Indian Ocean. I promised myself then I would stand on its summit before leaving the island.

With a map of Reunion in hand, I once again shouldered my backpack, leaving *Atom* secure on a mooring in the care of friends at the boat club. Francois drove me to my starting point at St. Denis at the north end of the island, along the way passing towns and villages, each named after a greater or lesser Saint. Beyond Port des Galets the narrow strip of pavement built from the rubble of dynamited cliffs crouched low between mountain and sea. The crumbling mountainside is held in place by gigantic wire mesh and a stone barrier wall protecting motorists from rockfalls during torrential rains of tropical cyclones.

Francois dropped me in front of a bakery in St. Denis. I was soon walking up a steep road looking like a bread peddler with two baguettes sticking out the top of my weighty pack. My planned route was to go up and over the highest peaks, down the lowest valleys, searching out footpaths instead of roads whenever possible and ending up back home at *Atom* on the opposite side of the island.

Several hours of nonstop footslogging along the ridges brought me thousands of feet up among the cool moist white clouds and scented tropical pine forest. At Plaine des Chicots I passed the first of the island's many "gites" – the log cabin rest houses constructed by the parks department for weary travelers to spend a night. Here along the footpath I approached a man of African and Chinese features, leaning on his rake, perhaps pondering the fallen leaves littering the park grounds. I stopped in front of him and asked directions to the next peak, more as a traveler's reflexive greeting than a real need for information, since the frequent signposts and white paint marks on stones and trees obviously pointed the way. Perhaps he was a mute or found my accent disagreeable, because in reply he merely pulled up the corner of his straw hat to look me over and silently pointed down the solitary trail I traveled.

With miles yet to cover and still-fresh memories of my ordeal at the bottom of a New Guinea mineshaft, I resisted the urge to explore the numerous caves my map indicated lay nearby. Approaching the rocky outcrop of La Roche Ecrite, I climbed above the forest onto an inclined surface of smooth stone slabs separated from one another by cracks hiding trickling streams of clear water. I walked into a cloud and found myself at the rampart's edge overhanging empty space. Straining to see through the enveloping cloud, slowly, as if awakening from a drugged sleep, the cloud thinned until I could just make out a village in the valley far below, trimmed with a ring of haze around the edges of my view. Then the dream-like haze of cloud cleared, bringing the entire valley and surrounding mountains into focus. Drifting by me was a rainbow, one of many that so often arch across the rain-washed blue skies of Reunion.

Perched on Reunion's La Roche Ecrite

I stood here at the entrance above three valleys, called "cirques," located on three sides of the craggy heights of Piton des Neiges. Sometime after the island was thrust up from the depths of the ocean floor some three million years ago, the central volcano cooled and these three cirques collapsed into these now lush funnel-shaped canyons. From La Roche Ecrite, the way into Cirque de Salazie led down a seventy-degree inclined slope. Gravity tugged me downward as I cautiously placed each footstep and clung with both hands to rocks and bushes.

At the bottom of the valley, I made camp at an empty park. Daylight was nearly gone as I unrolled my sleeping bag under a picnic table beside a river. Nestled deep within this narrow valley, the sun is eclipsed early behind high horizons. The twilight was long and the night passed slowly. The cadent utterance of church bells woke me early. I took a single cup of tea prepared over a fire built from two handfuls of twigs, packed my kit, and set out across the valley.

I entered St. Martin, a little village out of a Dutch storybook. But these tiny storybook house porches and gardens were bursting with an exuberance of flowers of every tropical shape and hue. Perfect amounts of temperature, sunshine, rainfall and rich volcanic earth produce geranium, vetiver and ylang-ylang, which are gathered and their essences distilled into the perfumes of France. Also, begonias, asters, gladiola and other gaudy plants splashed their colors against the green canvas. The dried pods of vanilla orchids are the only other visible export of the valley.

People trickled out of a country store and bakery, each one carrying those delicious long loaves of French bread. Unable to resist, I had the shopkeeper cut two crusty loaves in half and I tied the four sticks to the top of my pack. As I walked I reached back and broke off chunks of bread to snack on. Later I calculated that I was getting a mileage of five miles to the baguette.

The people of the cirques are a handsome and mostly unidentifiable mixture of races; an island melting pot where French is spoken by all and signs of racial or cultural enmities absent. Perhaps nowhere else on earth with a history of slavery have so many races and religions merged to live side-by-side with such ease and tolerance. In much of today's world, the fad is to encourage cultural diversity for its own sake, despite the prejudice and suspicion it breeds. Once again in my travels, I saw this hybridization of cultures is the outstanding difference between so many of the French and the British or American territories. This impression of Gallic culture on the people of France's overseas possessions is made richer by the penchant for intermarriage between colonizers and subjects.

I followed the road up out of the valley towards Cirque de Mafate. On this trek across the island I was always moving up or down and I was always in view of another ridge of mountains to cross. The road bent back on itself until it dead-ended near the pass of Col de Forche, as if knowing it had nowhere to go but back. Ahead, the verdant amphitheater of the valley of Mafate bore few man-made scars, chiefly because no roads penetrated its mountain barriers.

To call Mafate a valley is misleading. It resembles a valley only from the heights of the surrounding cordillera. As I dropped into Mafate, I entered a world tipped on its edge: a roadless, buckled terrain where hamlets of a few houses are scattered like islets on plateaus between river gullies. A grazing cow and a farmer mending a wooden fence took little notice as I passed along the trail. Along the moist banks of a stream bloomed the whitest Lilly of the Valley orchids. Footpaths and wagon tracks laced back and forth among the hilly pastures and vividly colored farmhouses. The sun bathed the circular wall of cliffs that guard and emphasize the valley's air of impenetrability. Reveling in the quiet rhythm of solitary walking among stands of tropical pine and tamarind forest, I wound down my pace to match a more slowly ticking internal clock.

By mid-afternoon, when I entered the village of Marla, the sun had begun its hours-long twilight behind Piton Maido. The population of about fifty people and a dozen cattle had several hours walk separating them from the next village in the next valley. Marla huddled here under the crater wall with its back to the cliffs – the embodiment of seclusion. And yet the local inhabitants were used to passing hikers whom they referred to as "moun dehors" (strangers). No one going about their business looked twice as I prepared a dinner of rice and onions over a small fire started for me in the center of the village by some local boys.

Later, a barefoot brown-skinned farmer came over to me. In the low rolling tones of Creole patois he invited me to spread my bedroll on the covered church porch. He sat there pointing with outstretched arm the route out of the valley, six hours on foot to the nearest bus stop, a trip he had made many times over the years. His face seemed hewn from the same rocks I clamored over to reach this place. Like the land that holds them, these mountain people do not change in a few generations. When they die, they are replaced by children almost exactly like them: children secure in the knowledge that life is hard, but predictable, and would always be the same. Well, not exactly the same anymore. A weekly helicopter now brings a few tourists and the more welcome visits from the doctor and postman. As a misty darkness settled in, the shy villagers drifted away to sit around hearth fires. I sat there in chilled silence contemplating my solitude.

I was up at first twilight, eager for the warmth of an uphill march. The rising sun crept over the mountain to meet me as I approached the pass into the next valley, Cirque de Cilaos. From here, the town of Cilaos stood out clearly six miles ahead. A path through banyan trees and red cabbage palms led me to a narrow paved road, then over a bridge spanning a gorge where the river Bras Rouge boiled below. Frequent flooding of the river shifts the rocks that scour it deeper every year. This very spot holds the world record for seriously rapid rainfall, an almost unfathomable 74 inches in twenty-four hours during a 1952 cyclone. Even with the forces of erosion working overtime on Reunion, everywhere the choking grip of vines and creepers is tenaciously stabilizing the crumbling cliffs.

The town of Cilaos, which in Malagasy means "place of no return," since it was once a hideaway for runaway slaves, is now a place of easy return with a well-traveled road connecting it to the coast. Even with the vices and virtues of development and easy access, the white-washed town remains pretty, buried under its frangipani, hibiscus and all the colors of the flower garden bouquet and family-sized vineyards. Beyond the flowered streets of Cilaos, I followed a path through the acacia forest and then up through the clouds and dripping wet vegetation. A signpost pointed to Hell-Bourg, eighteen kilometers to the right and Piton des Neiges, two kilometers to the left.

Here I met another solo climber, I guessed to be in his forties, who was resting seated on a flat rock. I stopped to share his seat and Philippe told me he was a Catholic priest from France now on his way down the mountain after spending the previous night at the peak. Over his wool sweater hung a curly black beard under which protruded a heavy silver crucifix on a chain. Philippe told me he was on his pilgrimage, one that he made each year, always to a different, far, and inspiring place. He summed me up in a glance it seemed. "And you too are looking for something here; something more than the mountain," he stated, rather than asked.

"Does it show? Well I guess I am on my own pilgrimage of sorts," I said and then unselfconsciously spilled my story – that I was sailing the world alone, walking across each island that crossed my bow, and climbing every penitentially steep mountain within reach. As if we were close friends I told him of my defeat at Mt. Wilhelm in New Guinea and the girl I'd left in Mauritius. The unspoken message was that on this mountain I looked for more than a hike and a view; I expected some solace to the soul, if not redemption.

No doubt the priest wondered what manner of sins I had committed to require this manner of ultimate penance, though with the knowledge gained of witnessing a thousand confessions, he wisely knew the futility of pressing the point. It was an unlikely meeting of two unlikely men seeking out their own paths to purify the soul. Knowing we would probably never meet again, Philippe touched my shoulder as he rose to walk away and gave me a blessing as he said: "A man who sails alone and walks alone is a seeker. It's a good thing to be."

A chilling rain ran off my jacket and soaked my pants and boots as I continued up the trail into the clouds. The landscape became more menacing, almost moon-like with boulders of every size perched on furrowed slopes of bare gravel, all colored in grays and blacks. I was surprised then to step around a rock and see a single yellow flower. Such a display of strength and tenacity of life, sprouting here in a tiny foothold of sand and stone, was not lost on me.

At ten thousand feet elevation, my pack seemed to double in weight and I paused often to catch my breath in the thinning air. At the summit I stood on a sprawling cone of dead volcanic cinders in pale sunlight. Ahead, the crater wall dropped with frightening suddenness into an abyss of cloud tops. As the high clouds retreated, remote summits stippled the horizon like separate islands floating above the cloud rack. The peak of Grand Bernard, four miles to the west, lay as crisply outlined to my eyes as my own boots in the sand, a distance-minimizing clarity pulling together the vastness of the scene.

As I watched the afternoon clouds recede to the lowest depths of the valleys, surreal shapes of towering peaks, misty waterfalls and wooded green valleys emerged from all points of the compass. The rocky ridges falling away from all sides of me looked like the exposed ribs of the earth's skeleton. The serrated mountains plunged seaward in a fantastic geologic overstatement of crag and precipice. The island of Mauritius, where I had left a part of myself, was just visible as a spot on the horizon, one hundred miles away to the northeast. Despite the loneliness tugging at my heart, I was standing on top of my world, feeling a fierce joy in the freedom above the clouds, even a kind of salvation. There is something about the hard physical effort to gain a summit that restores the spirit of a man – and being alone, no one can dilute the experience. An absurd possessiveness overcame me as I laid claim to everything in view on an island of over half a million people.

Through the rarified air, I watched the sun set in an orgy of colors and with its departure the temperature plunged. Without a single twig to start a fire, I put on the least-wet clothes in my pack and slipped into my lightweight and easily compressible tent, which is a nice way to say I shivered all night under a thin layer of soggy Gore-tex fabric. The high-sounding name of Piton des Neiges (Snow Mountain) warned it could get cold enough to snow when the cloud ceiling lifted. Lights from towns along the coast shimmered below. Overhead, frost-sharpened stars pulsed in their brilliance just out of reach. The trade winds that caress the sea can be notoriously shallow. I was above them in air so still I could hear my heart beat. The unearthly silence settled over me: no sound of man or machine. As Philippe well knew, such is the place where priests can talk to the heavens. Restless from the cold, I got up and walked in circles. Only the crunch of my boots broke the dead silence, bringing me back to the reality of my austere and lifeless mountaintop world.

From a half-sleep the next morning, I awoke to a tarnished gray dawn inside a cloud of howling wind and rain. The temperature felt barely above freezing as I laced my boots with stiff, aching fingers. With the cold wind knifing through me, I wondered that within an

Waterfall in the cirque of Reunion Island

hour, people would be lying about on the sun-warmed beaches, perhaps chancing to look up at my cloud-capped mountain above them.

Here I was thankful for the marks of white paint on rocks that guided me down the slopes. Without these scars on nature's flesh I could not have found my way down until the fog cleared. With their help, I descended quickly into the warmer climate to be clear of the storm.

Rain persisted most of the way back to the village of Cilaos. But what of that? I was warmed by my labors and felt a renewed confidence in meeting the challenges of the voyage ahead. Aches and pains aside, I had to admit that summiting that peak was literally the high point of my travels. On the mountain and on the sea, I learned that loneliness in itself is neither good nor bad. It is what you do with the feeling that counts. For me, loneliness was a hunger that urged me on to new experience and I embraced it.

What yesterday had taken me most of the day to climb, today I descended in just a few hours. A well of cool spring water refreshed me at the bottom of the trail. Strolling through the flower-scented village of Cilaos, I was lured into a pastry shop by the smells of warm croissants and herbal tea – such inexpressible luxury after a long, cold night on the mountain.

All that day I followed the hairpin road exiting the cirque alongside the river Bras de Cilaos. Because of the high vertical riverbank, it took eight years to construct this one road. Single lane in too many places, it clings to the cliff sides, spans gorges, and tunnels through mountains of rock. Today, the Bras de Cilaos river and I both were headed for the sea. We both moved serenely but the high, eroded banks testified to the potential fury during cyclones where river water carried boulders into bridges, dragging the stony debris out to sea.

I shared the road high above the river mostly with small passenger buses that sped around blind bends, horns blaring a futile warning to oncoming traffic. One bridge was so narrow the approaching bus had to stop, back up, and realign itself so as not to tear off its mirrors on the guardrails. I ran through the tunnels hoping not to be caught by oncoming traffic but still had some close encounters. In the riverbed I spotted the corpses of vehicles that had plunged over the side. I liked my chances better on foot. By late evening I was back aboard *Atom*, having gone from summit to sea level in one excruciatingly beautiful day.

As I prepared to depart for the passage toward Africa, Francois Gangnant insisted on taking me to the market where he bought four bagfuls of expensive provisions for my trip. His kindness embarrassed me and he dismissed my profuse thanks with a wave of his hand. Francois claimed that when a Frenchman is diagnosed with terminal illness he will try to come to Reunion for a peaceful place to die. Once here, he finds life so pleasantly invigorating that he recovers and lives to a ripe old age. Anyone who has been here could hardly doubt the possibility.

18 Trek Into Zululand

We need the tonic of wildness, we need to witness our own limits transgressed, and some life pasturing freely where we never wander.

- Henry David Thoreau

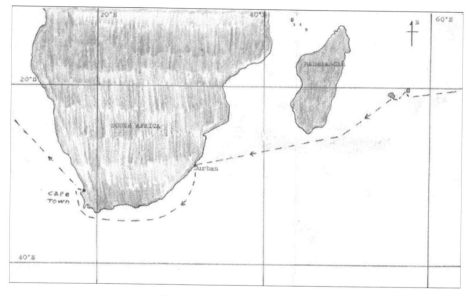

Reunion Island to South Africa

On November first, a French gendarme in his office one block uphill from the port issued me a clearance certificate. Within the hour I was back aboard *Atom*, slipping out of St. Pierre's small-boat harbor. My planned course lay to the south of Madagascar where the steady warm breezes of the tropics give way to variable and strong winds born along the tight isobars that encircle passing anti-cyclones. The pilot books and weather charts indicated that once I got closer to South Africa, the southwesterly gales would follow one-after-the-other in menacing processions. I expected to face a storm-ridden passage, and from the stories of other sailors, it looked like few yachts make the passage without a good bit of punishment.

As intimidating as it sounds, the alternative route to the Atlantic, via the Red Sea and Mediterranean, is far more challenging for the solo sailor. The choice for me was easy. I would sooner face ten storms on the open sea than contend with the contrary winds and currents, the reefs and pirates, the hostile Arab ports and the bureaucracy of a Red Sea passage.

For four days my sails did their work quietly under the last breaths of the Southeast Trades. The motion was easy and the progress steady. On our fifth day out, I began to feel the swells of a distant storm mixing it up with the familiar wave patterns. A boat as small and light as *Atom* cannot hide from the effects of changing wave patterns as she lifts and rolls to the slightest touch. After a few of these cross-swells tumbled on deck, I took the warning and tucked a reef in my mainsail.

All day I had felt unusually weary and could not find the strength to finish my habitual two hours of exercise. That night a terrific pain grew behind my eyeballs, followed hours later by fever, chills and an agitated stomach. I recognized the malignant stowaway of malaria come back to haunt me.

My thoughts went back to New Guinea where I lay close to death in a mountain village during my first encounter with the fever. What would it bring this time? Incapacitated and unable to navigate, would I drift uncontrolled into a storm or be pulled down on the lee shore of Madagascar? The Australian doctor I saw in Port Moresby had prescribed anti-malarials to kill the parasites hiding in my liver, but explained that the other second strain of malaria I carried was drug-resistant and had a lifespan of five years. As it turned out, I had yearly relapses for exactly five years, and nothing since. That night before retreating to my bunk I swallowed a heavy ear-ringing dose of quinine from *Atom's* medicine cabinet.

My journal for the next few days is mostly blank. But I have snatches of recollections, beginning with *Atom* hard-pressed for another reef in the sails, as I lay lethargic and deaf to her plea, drifting through fragmented dreams. Flashback to a wild-eyed shaman chanting to the spirit world in cadent monotones as he drifts above me where I lay in a smoke-filled mountain hut. With the next sideways slam in the trough of the sea, my mind flew forward to Mauritius where Dolores ran across a pink sand beach, the wind blowing her dress into a cluster of dancing flowers. Dawn overtook the night, as lonely hours turned into lonely days.

Sledding down the building waves, *Atom* repeatedly broached under too much badly balanced sail, burying the side deck under the sea and sending me sprawling across the cabin with a cascade of loose gear. At some point I pulled myself on deck and put a sloppy third reef in the mainsail and changed down to the storm jib. My worries were not so easily reefed-in as I lay face down on the cabin sole, dripping with salt spray and perspiration and shaking with fever.

A loud bang and my world turned on its side. The steering line from wind vane to tiller snapped and the tiller began pounding itself against the side of the cockpit seat. I listened and waited. I tried to care. Storing up my energy, I told myself, "Action is needed. Get up. Do it now." I don't remember getting up but do recall hanging over the transom trying to get a new line routed through the aluminum tubes of the steering gear. The sea repeatedly lashed out with a wet fist to my head and, more than once, I felt a hot jolt of pain as the steering gear rudder pinched my fingers against its metal frame as it swung from side to side.

Eventually, the quinine took effect and, to my great relief, the fever disappeared almost as quickly as it came, leaving me in a weakened state as my blood rebuilt its exploded cells. I was able to bring out the sextant for the first time in days and found myself some 80 miles south of Madagascar. Somehow *Atom* had run wildly along, without my control, and was still, more or less, on course.

Here I turned more directly west to compensate for the south-setting current. As the weather and my health improved, the seas calmed. We drifted all night without a breath of air to stir the limp sails and I welcomed the rest it provided. The following day was less restful as I worked to trim the sails and adjust the helm to light puffs of wind, mainly from the north.

The lazy, care-free days and familiar puffy white cumulus clouds of the tropics lay behind me. Cirrus, and other high-altitude clouds, suggested a shift in weather patterns. Sunsets here were no less brilliant, as the pink-tinged sky reflected off the aquamarine sea, but while sunrise the world over is a universal symbol of hope and renewal, a setting sun evokes something different. Even the most scenic sunset, for the solo sailor entering high latitudes, is a harbinger of a long night filled with the slight unease of the unknown.

The jumpy barometer, recording a series of frontal passages and shifting winds, kept me jumping to the sails at all hours. Tack, reef, adjust course and count each mile as its own success. The days passed in this anxious way until one night I stood on deck sniffing for the next breeze in the calm and noted a flashing light sequence identifying a lighthouse ahead. I was approaching the African coast some eighty miles northeast of my destination at the port of Durban. This was no accident of navigation, it was exactly where I wanted to be. With the current moving at seventy to eighty miles a day to the southwest, wind or no wind, I could be certain I'd be carried to Durban the next day.

Lightning flashed in the distant north as I spent a peaceful night drifting along the coast. As if by command of the sun, a fair wind rose at sunrise and bore me over the waves with a combined speed over ground of eight knots. A thick haze hung over the low hills and empty coastline in the rising heat. The local radio station reported the noon temperature ashore at 35 C (100 degrees F). When the concrete towers of Durban's skyline pierced the horizon, it lifted my spirits to think that *Atom* and I had coaxed and cared for each other across yet another ocean.

I passed a group of anchored ships lying exposed in the open roadstead outside the harbor inlet, then hoisted the yellow quarantine flag to announce my arrival. Before I even entered the breakwaters, a police launch met me with a line and towed me towards the yacht club. As I glided through the harbor they shortened the towline and a customs officer reached over with a clipboard full of papers attached to a long pole. There I sat, filling out forms before even touching shore. It was a fair taste of the stiflingly eager bureaucracy permeating South African society.

The launch brought me along a pier where I moored alongside the other international yachts facing Durban's main waterfront street. Four officers in brightly trimmed uniforms, from three different offices, checked my documents and poked around my boat before handing me over to the secretary of the Point Yacht Club next door. I was pleased to hear I could stay at the pier and use the yacht club facilities for no charge.

Back among the cruising community, I recognized several friends and boats from earlier ports of call sharing a similar route around Africa. Canadian Alan Butler, whom I had gotten to know in Mauritius, was moored nearby with his 26-foot Heavenly Twins catamaran. He was attempting to make the smallest catamaran solo-circumnavigation (which he eventually completed). By coincidence, we had each departed different harbors on Reunion Island on the same day and both arrived in Durban within an hour of each other.

Other boats here were new to me, including the 25-foot wooden sloop I was moored alongside. This thirty-some-year-old boat named *Tarmin*, belonged to John Sowden, who was twice the age of his venerable little boat and had already been around the world, solo, two times, since the mid 1960s. As you might imagine, this senior singlehanded sailor was, by now, highly opinionated. He was also a touch eccentric and borderline anti-social as viewed by the younger and more gregarious sailors around the club and international jetty. Few of the other sailors here could tolerate John's dismissive attitude and he seemed indifferent to their companionship, or their approval. I looked at him as a godfather and took his advice whenever it was offered. Perhaps John and I saw something of ourselves in each other and we became friends in the way of men pursuing similar paths: myself at the beginning of my adventures and John nearing the end of life's voyages.

Early each morning John emerged from *Tarmin's* ill-kept cabin wearing the same old pair of torn and stained shorts, clutching a mug so encrusted with dried sediments that it remained half full even after he finished his drink. I almost asked John about that mug but when he offered me a similarly silted cup, I drank without comment. When not busy repairing and preparing our boats for the upcoming passage around the African cape, I spent hours listening to John recount his adventures in the South Seas. He had been to places where the islanders had never seen a Westerner on a sailboat. John witnessed the world as it was being discovered by yachts and tourists during the past twenty years, and he made a point of telling me that his experiences then were not repeatable. I thought I knew something of the sea by this time, yet when John spoke of those magical times, and related the techniques that kept him and *Tarmin* from misadventure, I listened like a wide-eyed child on his grandfather's knee.

There was little privacy for the yachts moored along this waterfront esplanade of Durban. Throughout the day and into the evening people wandered along the pier twisting their necks to peer inside the homes of this floating gypsy tribe. I imagine the foreign-flagged yachts coming and going from the pier made some of the locals uneasy – especially those who longed to travel but had put down roots too deep to pull up.

Working on deck under *Atom's* American flag, I was barraged by increasingly tiresome questions and comments from passersby. "Did you sail all the way from America? Don't you get lonesome, frightened, seasick?" At least once a day someone was so keen to see the boat that I invited them aboard. Most were the English or Dutch Afrikaners who ruled the segregated country in those days before black rule began in the 1990s. I also hosted Indians, blacks and the multi-racial Coloureds, each of whom came aboard in strictly segregated groups, as was their custom.

A block away from the yacht jetty was a secretarial school for Coloured girls and each lunch hour they came to ogle *Atom* and her skipper. Groups of four to five girls found their way aboard where I told them about the strange world of sailing and they told me about their stranger world ashore. The girls were mainly of African/Indian mixture, often with a trace of European ancestry as well. In America they would call themselves blacks, or for those identifying themselves as being of a tribe of hyphenated-Americans: African-Americans. Here in the stratified system of apartheid, they are considered one step above pure Africans on the social ladder to whiteness. If they could not decide this for themselves, there was a government tribunal to choose their racial classification.

For some people the fate of their entire life rests on a few percentage points of black ancestry. Families had been broken up because one member was too light or too dark. Once they are classified, they know which township to live in, where they can go to school, who they can marry, even which bus to ride or toilet to use. Ironically, a population of several million Coloureds in South Africa proves that white and black racial separation was not always popular in less "civilized" times.

One weekend the girls asked me to come with them to Durban's beach. As we walked the two miles through town to the beach, I felt the disapproving stares of the whites. More than one Afrikaner crossed the street to tell me I should not be walking with "Coloured girls." Someone called out "kaffir-boetie" (nigger lover) to embarrass us. I felt badly to be attracting this unwanted attention to the girls but they had heard it all before and pretending not to notice, told me to ignore it. I was glad I had not brought Dolores to this country because I could not bear to see her hurt in this way.

At the beachfront we passed a fence and sign declaring "Whites Only." We stepped on past the "Indian Beach" and "African Beach" and turned through the gate to the "Coloured Beach." If the sign was not there I could tell where I was by the exclusively brown bodies lying on the sand and playing in the surf. If this was a beach to be avoided by whites, I could not understand why. I was far more welcome here than I had been minutes before among the whites on the street. Stepping down a rung on the social ladder, as I was perceived to have done, was merely frowned on; stepping above your position was absolutely forbidden.

One of the girls came back with a paper bag from the Indian grocery across the street and pulled out some "bunny-chow" – a hollowed out loaf of bread filled with spicy vegetable curry, topped with grated carrots. We sat in a circle in the sand with our bunny-chow in the center. Many hands in turn broke off pieces of bread and scooped up the curry. The other popular food along the beach was a fast food version of the English potpie – South Africa's equivalent to the American hamburger – and even less appealing.

Back around the yacht club lingered a few black men seeking employment repairing and maintaining boats for the white owners. A man named Boi, from the Zulu tribe, approached me for a job, saying he had painted and repaired boats for several years and charged 10 Rand (US$4) a day. Boi worked alongside me for two weeks, varnishing *Atom's* weathered teak and mahogany trim, repairing leaks and repainting the deck.

We then moved *Atom* to a nearby beach where I careened the boat at high tide with lines to posts holding her along the shore. At low tide *Atom* lay over on her side exposing her fouled bottom to our scraping blades and paintbrushes. Every six hours, for three days and three nights, *Atom* went from upright to forty-five degrees as we painted one side, then turned her to paint the other side. Despite the discomfort of sleeping at various extreme angles it was an affordable alternative to the marine yard.

For lunch, Boi took over galley duty and invariably prepared cooked vegetables with red-hot chilies and *pap*, a lumpy porridge of cooked corn meal that is the staple of the African diet. If I had not employed Boi, I would not likely have a chance to get to know a South African black because friendship between black and white outside of work was considered not only incomprehensible, but dangerous as well. If I had tried to visit his home in the black township outside Durban, I would have been turned back at the police roadblock. If I managed to evade this obstacle, Boi told me he would be marked as a police informer by his neighbors. Anyone suspected of collaborating with the police risked receiving a "necklace," which is an innocuous-sounding name for being bound hand and foot with a gasoline-soaked tire lit afire around your neck. As if this weren't sufficient to keep tourists from wanting to visit the townships, Zulu and Pondo tribes had clashed recently in Boi's township using knives, firebombs and homemade guns, killing over a hundred people in a few days. As in New Guinea, the river of tribalism in South Africa runs deep and wide.

A peculiarly South African incident took place when Boi guided me to the outdoor vegetable market in Durban. At the market entrance, he stopped to use the public toilet while I waited with a crowd of blacks milling around outside. A minute later Boi came out chuckling quietly to himself and hurried me away from the staring eyes. Boi told me a young black man claiming to be a soldier for the

ANC (African National Congress) had followed him into the toilet and said, "Quick, change your clothes for mine and jump out the rear window and run away." The man assumed I was undercover police and bringing Boi to jail. Why else would I be walking with a black man in this part of town?

On another day, when I offered to buy Boi lunch I learned apartheid cuts both ways. We went to his usual place, a restaurant/bar called the Regent. At the door I sensed something wasn't quite right when the Zulu security guard asked what we wanted. "Just food," I replied and we were reluctantly waved in. At our table the waiter took Boi's order and then walked away as if I didn't exist. I called him back to take my order and he stood in silence looking at the floor. Eventually, the Indian manager noticed us and came over and told me he could not serve a white person because he might lose his license. "If you must eat here, perhaps we can serve your meal in the closet off the kitchen," he said with a bow and a smile. I felt deeply insulted — and then remembered that this was merely a harmless little taste of the injustices and humiliations millions of non-whites go through every day.

The passbook for blacks that Boi carried permitted him to enter the city only while working during daylight. The city at night belonged to the whites. I could see a deep resentment in his eyes as he showed me his passbook, though Boi guarded his tongue until he knew me better. Some days later he admitted his sympathy was with the ANC and believed in their goal of violent overthrow of white rule to be replaced with their version of a communist system. "I'm sure in my lifetime we will break apartheid and regain our dignity and the wealth that now is in white hands."

Since most blacks living around Durban were not permitted to enter the city at night, the side streets and alleys became deserted after sunset. As I walked by the park near the yacht club one evening, an unmarked van squealed to a halt next to me and five white police in plain clothes leapt out the back doors. I froze as they brushed past me with drawn nightsticks and pulled a black vagrant out of the shadows. Seconds later he was tossed in the van and sped away.

In complete contrast to how they treated their countrymen, the locals treated us sailors at the international jetty like heroes, inviting us to their homes for the weekends and on sightseeing tours of the countryside. Typical of the kind folks I met here was Colin and Mary Rose, English South Africans who, months earlier, had called out to me on *Atom* from the beach back in Mauritius where they were on vacation. They asked if I was stopping later in Durban and promised to look out for me when I arrived. I never expected to see them again and was surprised when they located me here three months later. I spent several restful days at their home in Margate, about an hours drive south along the coastal highway from Durban. Like many middle-class, white South Africans, they lived comfortably in a spacious home complete with built-in swimming pool, a black maid and gardener.

On my travels around the suburbs and small coastal towns of South Africa, I noticed there was something extraordinarily tidy about each place. It took some time to put my finger on it and then I realized there were no telephone poles or electric cables to mar the skyline. These lifelines of civilization were all buried underground where they belong. Colin said one of the first things they noticed on a vacation to America was that virtually every road was accompanied by a sky-cluttering array of poles and cables. It's funny the things we learn not to see.

Colin and Mary Rose acted as tireless tour guides, taking me to the scenic park of Oribi Gorge where waterfalls plunge over orange sandstone cliffs to land in the Valley of Mzimkulu (Great Home of All Rivers). In their effort to give me a more balanced view of apartheid, they drove me through the Coloured and Indian townships, pointing out how the people lived in subdivisions of brick and wood houses that on the surface looked not unlike some American neighborhoods.

The Indians are now the shopkeepers of the country after having been brought over by the British to work the sugar-cane plantations of Natal. Many now live in relative mansions with a staff of African servants and twin Mercedes-Benz parked in the garage. In most cases, whites have buffered themselves from the blacks by placing an Indian or Coloured township between them. This flaunted wealth at the edge of black townships is partly why blacks dislike the Indians as much as they dislike whites, and vent this anger when they burn and loot the Indian settlements.

We also drove through a newly built black township of neat brick homes constructed, and mostly paid for, by the government. The new school had already been burnt down and the whites pointed to this as proof the blacks could not yet be safely integrated and that they preferred to destroy that which could help them. The blacks, I suspect, would counter that it signified their refusal to accept the gifts of apartheid.

I twice visited with Colin's neighbors at their frequent *braais*, or backyard barbecue dinners. As a vegetarian I couldn't help notice the South Africans are ravenous meat-eaters, even out-consuming Australians in thick steaks, spare ribs and hamburger, all washed down with generous amounts of beer. At these gatherings their conversation always turned to emigration. Due to recent disinvestments and international banking policies, the South African currency had plummeted in value. This, along with the upsurge in ANC bombings and general violence, left South African whites feeling there was no future for their families in this country. The majority of the white people I spoke with were on an emigrant waiting list for Australia, Canada, or the United States, or had friends who had already left.

I returned from Margate to Durban by train to catch another view of the coastal countryside. At the station I dutifully took my seat in an empty passenger car marked with the sign Blankes (Afrikaans for Whites). I settled into a plush leather seat surrounded by varnished hardwoods, polished brass hardware and a porcelain washing sink as the diesel-powered engine pulled our ten-passenger cars forward.

The first thing we passed was an antique steam-powered locomotive moving the opposite direction on the narrow gauge tracks, spewing black soot as it trundled past. Our track followed the rocky coast, at times within sight of the crashing surf. We rarely got up to speed before slowing down to stop at the next station. There were about thirty stops on this three-and-a-half hour run, each stop part of a blur of children begging pennies beneath the windows and signposts marking the stations: Mercury Halt, Umzumbe, Scottburgh, Mtwalume, Amanzimtoti.

Our Afrikaans conductor herded the blacks on and off the train with his stick, then waved it to the engineer to set us rolling north again. Gangs of a hundred shirtless black men sweating under a midday sun worked repairing the track with their white overseer standing nearby.

Leaning out the window, I noticed a steady stream of mango and banana peels tossed out the windows of the cars ahead. Bored in my empty luxury car and curious, I made my way forward through two more empty first-class cars and flung open the door to third class. The rough car benches were filled to near-capacity and the aisles crammed with luggage and children. The air was filled with the lively clicking and musical sounds of the Zulu language. Young girls sold fruit from boxes as they moved up and down the crowded aisle. I bought a bagful of mangos, passed some out to my neighbors, and wedged myself into a hard wooden bench between a dozing, wrinkled, old man and a heavy Zulu woman with a baby on her knee. I looked up to see the conductor glaring down at me with a tired look of "here's another trouble-making kaffir-boetie." Instead of bashing me with his stick, he pointed with it back towards the first class cars and said, "No whites allowed in third class."

Back in Durban I accepted an invitation to travel inland to a strawberry farm in the Valley of a Thousand Hills by the manager who was a member of the yacht club. An entire village of Zulus worked the farm. Women harvested the crops with babies riding strapped to their backs or wrapped in a blanket and set under the shade of a banana tree. Some young women wore light brown clay smeared thinly on their face, claiming it kept them cool in the sun, though one admitted to me that the men said it made them more attractive. At dusk I heard them singing as they walked up the hill to their village. The men drove tractors, repaired fences and buildings, and drove the produce to town. These people work for a dollar a day and rarely go shopping in the city because the bus fare alone cost two days wages.

In the Valley of a Thousand Hills

I stayed in a guest room in an elegant house with the manager and his wife. One of the house servant girls spoke some English and told me her name was "Queen Victoria." When I asked for her real name she showed me her passbook and I saw she was telling the truth. Many Zulu children proudly own royal names of England I was told. Giving a powerful name to your child was a way of directing a portion of that power to them. Victoria's sister's name was, not surprisingly, Queen Elizabeth.

Despite the often-smiling faces, I felt tenseness in the atmosphere here. My host, I noticed, was never far from the pistol he usually carried in an ankle holster. At night the holster hung from his bedpost. Putting on a gun was just a part of getting dressed. There had been no confrontations yet on this farm, although closer to the Mozambique border, white farmers were being bombed, shot at, or burnt out by ANC terrorists, and sometimes by their own hired help. It was only a matter of time before the killing reached this valley as well. The thought of being murdered in our beds made for uneasy sleep.

Before I could make these excursions outside Durban's port area, I was required to obtain a special travel permit. Around the time I applied for the permit, I noticed visitors to *Atom* were becoming fewer by the day. Even the lovely secretaries were gone. Our novelty has finally worn off, I told myself. At the end of Boi's last day of work he said, "Did you know that policeman has been watching you for two days," and nodded towards a man in dark sunglasses and plain clothes sitting on a bench on the jetty.

"Don't be silly. Why would they be watching me?"

The following day the yacht club commodore visited *Atom*. "James, the police are watching you," he said.

"Are they? I can't imagine why."

"Perhaps it's because of...all those...those non-whites you've been associating with. Better watch your step," he warned.

As the commodore left I walked up to the man sitting behind the newspaper ten steps down the jetty and asked, "Are you here for me?" He looked at me expressionless for many seconds then got up and walked away. If my friends were wrong and he wasn't police, he certainly would have thought my question odd enough to send him on his way.

The next day at my immigration office appointment I was told to sit in the corner where I waited several hours like a punished child before being gruffly told to leave and come back tomorrow. This charade was repeated for the next three days until they grew tired of trying to wait me out. Compared to them I was powerless, but I had patience. At last, a huge, stern-looking Afrikaner in a uniform barely containing his bulk, presented me with the pass I had so long awaited. As he handed me the well-stamped paper, he glared at me with a look that said he would gladly crush me with his bare hands if only he could find an excuse for it in his color-coded law book.

These officials were descendants of the same people whose laws caused a young lawyer named Mahatma Gandhi to begin formulating his non-violent resistance-strategy when he lived in South Africa. Perhaps Gandhi sensed the futility of his struggle for men to be treated as men, regardless their color, at that time in this land. Later, he moved to India and worked tirelessly and successfully to drive the British out.

Rather than follow tourists on the obligatory bus tour of the African game parks, with my coveted travel document in hand, I accepted an invitation to join the Durban Ramblers Club for a three-day weekend, trekking through the Drakensberg Mountains of Natal Province. Our plan was to follow the Miambonja River to its source in the high plateau country of Lesotho and to climb nearby Rhino Peak. We would sleep in caves previously inhabited by a people known simply as the Bushman. Our group of ten, including Afrikaners, English South Africans and an ex-Rhodesian, drove in three cars to the Himeville Nature Reserve where we pitched our tents along the river as darkness fell. The mountain air was refreshingly cool during a night of light rain showers.

By dawn we were packed and moving up the river, crisscrossing in shallow places and making steady progress up the gorge – a watery avenue among giant wind-scoured peaks. From rolling grasslands we moved up into the narrow gorge, surrounded on both sides by fantastic rock formations jutting out over our heads from the red-orange walls. Below, the green grasses of the veld were littered with gray boulders as if tossed by Hercules from the high pillars. In the distance, rocky spires rose like islands across a sea of grass. Hawks and eagles soared on thermals up the faces of the cliffs. Dwarfing them all, with his ten foot wingspan, was a lone bearded vulture called a lammergeyer.

Our unspoken group leader was Tom de Waal, an Afrikaner in his early fifties who had traveled extensively in the "Berg." Being an amateur naturalist, he, best among us, understood the plants, animals and geology of this region. From Tom, I learned that millions of years ago in this area a volcanic upheaval lifted the basaltic lava miles above the surrounding plains to form this "roof of Southern Africa," which today is the independent black nation of Lesotho. For millions of years, wind and rain have eroded this eastern edge of the plateau, leaving a multitude of strange formations – sharp pinnacles, overhanging cliffs and caves, river-cut gorges among crumbly basalt and sandstone. Early European settlers named these the Drakensberg

(Dragon) Mountains for their jagged dragon-like spine as seen from the east. Zulus living below the mountains say the edge of the escarpment resembles a row of spears they call Ukhahlamba.

As we walked through a light rain, a troupe of baboons on the cliff above screamed and threw rocks at us before disappearing into the fog. Of all the dangers of the wild, until now I had never considered an animal might one day strike me down with a thrown rock. Footing became treacherous on steep, sliding gravel. The less-fit members of our group retreated to meet us at a lower elevation later in the day.

Hours later, four of us gained the ridge of the escarpment and were amazed to stand in patches of snow on the highland plain. Summer snow is uncommon, even at this high altitude, so we made use of the novelty with a brief exchange of snowballs. A Sotho herdsman on horseback, wrapped in a colorful blanket against the cold wind, passed us to round up a stray cow grazing on the sparse grass. He seemed as out of place in this sterile land as white men throwing snowballs. To survive here, the Sotho bring their cattle and pack mules down into Natal to trade wool, mohair and hides for cornmeal and other goods.

We took a compass bearing on Rhino Peak just as it disappeared behind a veil of rain from blue-black clouds. My companions stopped somewhere short of the peak and told me we must turn back or risk being caught in a flash flood in the gully on the way down. A group of climbers died this way the year before when a fast-moving storm overtook them and they were washed away in a flood of rocks and water. I didn't feel ten minutes more would change our fate and so ran off alone to bag the peak.

When I returned, my brooding friends asked what was the point of reaching the top when there was no view to be seen in the cloud and rain. What could I say? If one climbs mountains solely for the view he will often be disappointed. Inexplicably, I needed to reach every peak I set out for, regardless of the mountain's tempestuous moods. Fortunately, the rain remained light as we bounded down the loose rocks of the riverbed. Across the rocky slopes a group of deer-like rhebok outpaced us in sure-footed leaps and bounds.

We met up with the rest of our party and carried on to our night's campsite at Nutcracker Cave, so named because of its skull-cracking five-foot ceiling, as more than one of our group discovered the hard way. The cave was actually shallow, more of a recess in an overhanging cliff, with a trickling waterfall over the entrance and a sweeping vista over the river and valley below. Leaning back in our sleeping bags that night, Tom told us some stories by candlelight about the recently-vanished bushmen that inhabited these caves until driven out by Zulus and white settlers.

The Bushman was a little man, about five feet tall with brown skin and Mongolian facial features. He was superbly adapted to the feast or famine lifestyle of the African hunter, soaking up water and food like a camel before running across a barren desert. Actually, he preferred to run everywhere and was hardly seen to walk at all. A true stone-age man, he was a hunter-gatherer with few possessions and no agriculture whatsoever. His language was a complicated set of clicks and smacking of lips. He was so sensitive of his size that it could be fatal to mention his smallness in his presence, which was reflected in his standard greeting to fellow bushmen: "Tshjamm" (I saw you looming up from afar and I am dying of hunger). As an expert botanist, bushmen knew how to use the plants and roots for food, medicine or poison. While the women gathered roots and berries, he hunted Africa's largest game with his poison-tipped arrows, tracking a wounded animal for days if need be, until it dropped of exhaustion.

The bushmen's rock paintings of wildlife, hunting parties and dancing ceremonies scattered about these caves eventually came to record the bloodshed and tragedy of Zulus and Dutch settlers encroaching on their ancestral territory. His little poison arrows found the Voertrekker's cattle an easy target, but a poor defense against farmer's guns. By the 1890s he was exterminated from the Drakensberg. Other groups of bushmen retreated to the howling deserts of the Kalahari where they lived as close to perpetual anguish and deprivation as any human settlement on earth. Up until a few years ago, small bands of bushmen still roamed the trackless wastes in search of game and the life-giving rains that come briefly once a year.

As the evening rain fell, the streaming waterfall blocked our cave entrance and we tucked ourselves closer to the back wall to stay dry. The conversation eventually turned to the current strife in this country. The ex-Rhodesian in our group remarked with some bitterness, "We white Africans are like the bushmen of today, surrounded by hostile blacks and economic sanctions from the rest of the world. We surrendered to the blacks in Rhodesia and they are turning a prosperous country into another failed African state. The blacks don't care about our European standard of civilization. My family has been in Africa 300 years, developing and civilizing this land. I cannot, and will not, live as a black man and we will fight to keep South Africa under white rule. In any case, I have nowhere else to go."

He was right to see the irony of our group sheltering in the same caves where the Bushman sheltered when they ruled the land. The waterfall thundered outside like the beating of Zulu war drums. The Bushman had been a passing shadow over the land and the shadow of white rule was also destined to pass. Maybe whites and blacks would learn to live together, or maybe not.

I noticed the English South Africans in our group were less certain that their privileged white rule was sustainable or even desirable. By the time I returned to South Africa nine years later, the whites had handed the country over to the blacks, virtually without a shot being fired in its defense, despite the promises I heard from some Afrikaners that they would fight to retain control. Even though the "whites only" signs would soon come down, how long will the apartheid of our hearts linger?

We got up to meet the sun as it poured down the valley, turning the sky from pink to the flame blue of the African summer. Tom led us across the lower valley and up to the cliffs on the opposite side where he wanted to show us a gallery of Bushman rock painting on the overhanging ledges. While most of us walk blindly through life, Tom missed nothing, whether watching the bearded vulture soaring on air currents a half mile away or bending down to identify a specie of grass, calling out its botanical name as if Latin where his second language. Even if unaware of the classification, we could not fail to observe the masses of blossoms painting the high veld in waves of color: red bottlebrush, white, yellow and red proteas, and scattered terrestrial orchids.

Tom was fluent in Zulu, which sounded odd bubbling from the lips of a white man. With each peak that hove into view Tom delighted in shouting its name: "Indumeni" (Place of Thunder) then the jagged peaks of "Ndedema" (Place of Reverberations). With a tilt of his head he indicated "Intabayikonjwa" (Mountain at Which One Must Not Point) – if pointed at, you risk being punished by storms. One hardly need point at all, since almost daily, wreaths of black clouds and thunder spilled down the highest peaks.

During a lunch break I climbed a rock overhang for a better view with Michelle, an airline employee from Durban. Thousands of feet below, the Polela River lay out its serpentine course towards the sea. Michelle pointed out a herd of black wildebeest grazing on the sweet grasses along the river. Before the weekend ended, we also saw the elk-like eland and red hartebeest. Leopards and other rare creatures lived here but stayed well hidden.

Again we split into groups of those who wanted to rest and those ready for several more hours of strenuous climbing. To be back to our campsite before dark, we set out at a fast pace, moving through the sea of grass under a high and hot sun washed by the summer wind. "Safari" (we march), I repeated to myself as I kept pace with the others. And march we certainly did. The mountain's seemingly absolute shape morphed into an infinite array of profiles as viewed from the differing angles around its base. The heat intensified along the cliff side. We sucked our water bottles dry as we moved along rocks radiating the afternoon sun like spitting yellow cobras. All-too-real were the poisonous snakes watching us from under shaded rock ledges. An eagle climbed into the sun and disappeared.

Suddenly, we were in the merciful shade of a rock shelf and staring at a smooth light-brown rock surface adorned with the crude and eloquent stick-like figures painted by Bushman artists hundreds, or perhaps thousands, of years ago. What amazed me most was how the ancient paint of mineral oxides, blood, urine and tree sap applied with

animal hair and feathers, barely shielded from the elements, looked as
fresh as if applied yesterday.

Rock paintings by the Bushman

The Paleolithic graffiti began at one end with a group of hunters
pursuing antelope. Further along the rock face the figures danced.
Then a battle scene of bushmen being attacked by a black tribe. To
ease the artist's fears he painted himself as a giant among other giants.
At the far end of the wall he painted his last scene – white men on
horseback. The Bushman called themselves the "harmless people."
He lived simply off the land until he died and the land absorbed him.
He could not be tamed and so became one of the ghosts of Africa.
Only an aura remains, a state of mind, and a legacy of painted figures
on rock. To read the story requires only open eyes, an open heart and
an open mind. I'm reminded of "The Song of the Rain" from *The
Lost World of the Kalahari*, by Laurens Van Der Post. As they wait for the
life-giving rains, a woman sings:

> *Under the sun*
> *The earth is dry,*

By the fire
Alone I cry.
All day long
The earth cries
For the rain to come.
All night my heart cries
For my hunter to come
And take me away.

A man hears her song and tenderly sings back:

Oh! Listen to the wind,
You woman there;
The time is coming
The rain is near.
Listen to your heart,
Your hunter is here.

Returning to my boat in Durban, I felt as alien to the people of the city as a Bushman, and was eager to get under sail. Somewhere along the way I began to understand that my views, my values, my morality, had been largely dictated by society. This country of the cruel and the kind held no more absolute truths than any other. The world over, an angry person sees corruption wherever he looks, while the thoughtful person sees beauty. And it is a beautiful country.

19 Cape of Storms

*To face the elements is, to be sure, no light matter when
the sea is in its grandest mood. You must then know the
sea, and know that you know it, and not forget that it
was made to be sailed over.*

- Capt. Joshua Slocum

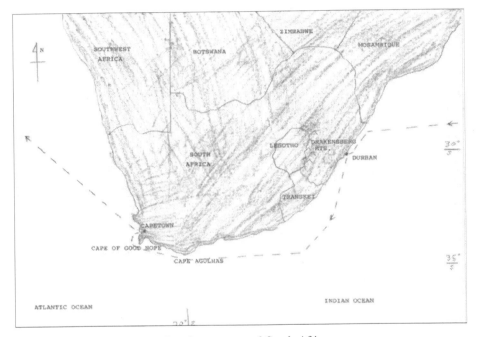

Atom's route around South Africa

My ten-week layover in Natal allowed the southern hemisphere
summer to settle in before I set sail for Africa's Cape of Good Hope.
The weather, which in this region finds fertile waters for storm
formation, was also the main concern of every sailor moored at the
international jetty next to the yacht club. As the frequent spring
storms gave way to milder summer gales, the dock became busy with
crews preparing their boats for the passage around the cape to the
Atlantic.

One evening the local yachtsmen invited us visiting sailors to meet at the Point Yacht Club to share strategy on making the passage to Cape Town. Here we heard stories of shipwrecks, sinkings and near disasters recounted by survivors who challenged these waters in the wrong season, with the wrong boat, had bad judgment, or just plain bad luck. John Sowden told us of his first rounding of the cape years earlier when he was caught in a storm offshore. His hands moved up and down like pistons as he described how the sea pumped itself up with storm winds blowing into the opposing current. Yet here he was, back to test the waters again in his little wooden boat.

An experienced local yachtsman informed, and frightened, us further, explaining how the weather pattern here is dominated by a succession of southwesterly gales sweeping up the coast in opposition to the swift-flowing Agulhas Current. Between the southwesters were brief periods of fair northeast winds. Winter storms here brought hurricane force winds creating some of the largest waves in the world, even threatening large, well-found ships. Now, during the two-month height of summer, was our best weather window to make the passage.

The usual strategy for yachts rounding the cape, as laid out by the resident experts, is to sail from one port to the next, ducking inside when each gale is forecast and departing with the next fair wind. The first leg is the longest, 350 miles from Durban to East London along the shelterless "Wild Coast" of Transkei. On the remaining 500 miles to Cape Town, there are five harbors offering refuge, provided you can safely approach shore in possible gale conditions.

The commodore told us about two yachts that sank in a storm during an offshore race the year before. A third yacht was heading inshore to escape the worst seas when it ran out of sea room up against the Wild Coast. Running blindly through the black night, a great wave picked the boat up and deposited it on the top edge of a cliff. The crew then stepped from the deck to shore, barely getting wet. The skipper, who had been asleep in his bunk at the time, was dumped, bruised but largely uninjured, onto the ground when the side of the boat cracked open, or so the story went. They walked to the nearest village to arrange their rescue and later a crane picked up the broken boat, set it on a trailer and returned it to Durban for repairs.

Despite the horror stories of their mishaps along the coast, all the local experts agreed on one thing: the port-hopping coastal route was the least dangerous and most logical choice.

Once they had their say, to the bewilderment and disbelief of most of the sailors present, John Sowden pointed out that the coastal route was actually the most dangerous and that he would make his third rounding of the cape as he had his previous passages – nonstop and well offshore. The commodore and his crew countered that shelter must be sought during storms because the seas were unmanageable by small craft. John responded that a well-found small boat, handled with good seamanship and a cool head, could survive most any storm at sea. What it could not survive, he stressed, was being driven ashore by overpowering winds while the skipper is searching for a port of refuge. Leaving us with that last bit of advice, he walked out.

By their nature sailors are an opinionated group, none more so than the solo sailor who is used to getting his way with no dissenting voices. John probably felt there was not one man among us he would trust to advise him on a course across the harbor, let alone around the cape. I was left with the dilemma of whether to follow the advice of an eccentric old salt who survived many solo passages, or to listen to the voices of self-proclaimed expert authority with that all-important "local knowledge." The lemming effect is powerful to those of uncertain mind. What it comes down to is that certain boats and certain crews are better suited to different tactics.

Cash on hand was getting low as I prepared for departure. I had waited in vain three weeks for my American bank to transfer $500 to a Barclays Bank in Durban. It was supposed to take two days. After numerous queries went unanswered, the Durban bank officer suggested that a third party bank in New York was stalling in order to make a few dollars off the rapidly dropping exchange rate. I couldn't wait any longer and just hoped the $300 I had would be enough to get me back home. That meant foregoing my planned stop in Brazil and staying longer at sea where money is not an issue. At any rate, a lengthy stop in Brazil would put me into the Caribbean during hurricane season, which was an unneeded risk.

The commodore of the yacht club was more worried than I about my vanishing funds and insisted on taking me to the local mega-market where he paid for a trolley filled with exceptionally low-priced food goods for my trip. Perhaps this was in repayment for the week before when he had taken me to see my first cricket test match, an excruciatingly slow game played over several days whose rules and purpose I never quite grasped.

This was the same commodore who some fifteen years earlier had a glass of beer hurled in his face at the bar by Robin Lee Graham, the 18-year-old solo-circumnavigator aboard *Dove*, who felt the commodore was behind the rumors and comments going around questioning the morals of his visiting live-aboard girlfriend. That was a time and a place when behavior of that sort was unwelcome at this conservative yacht club. According to the commodore, after tossing the beer in his face, Robin ran down the stairs with a gang of angry club members on his heels. They all rolled together into the club's lobby in a tangle of fists, arms and legs. I was surprised that the commodore was still so friendly and accommodating to solo sailors after that experience.

I was now as ready as I ever would be to set sail for the Atlantic. A rising barometer indicated a retreating atmospheric depression, confirmed by a weather bureau forecast for at least twenty-four hours of settled weather, which was the extent of reliable forecasts in this unsettled area. The port authorities proved as serious about documenting my departure as they were my arrival. After traveling to four different offices for various port clearance papers and a final visit aboard by immigration officers, on January 30, my South African friends cast off *Atom's* mooring lines.

I tacked offshore in light winds threading a course through several ships anchored and waiting to unload their cargo. Once I cleared the dangers near shore the wind settled in the northeast and I took some sleep while I had the chance. I stretched out on the leeward main salon bunk, and with what had become an automatic reflex, reached up and turned on the radar alarm.

This stretch of the African coast is notorious for congested shipping. But as long as a ship was using its radar, I was confident my alarm would detect its pulse and awake me if it approached too closely, in much the same way as motorists use radar detectors to alert them to a speed trap. This time, however, instead of awakening to the alarm's familiar beep tone, I awoke to the deep drone of a ship's engine. Barely a full second later I was on deck watching the black wall of a hull sliding by a few boat lengths away. I could clearly see his radar unit above the bridge was not rotating and told myself from here on I must sleep more lightly and keep a more vigilant watch.

A gradually increasing wind warned of more changes to come. By two o'clock the next morning, I was tying a third reef in the mainsail and hoisting the storm jib from a plunging deck. The disturbed sea whipped up whitecaps that glowed ghost-like in the beam of my flashlight. I knew immediately when we entered the Agulhas Current because the waves stretched out in length and doubled in height. The remainder of the night we set a fast stroke swimming down the coast, making a combined eight knots over bottom with the current's help.

At dawn a round of morning star sights indicated I was well off the Wild Coast somewhere along the Republic of Transkei. From late morning an overcast sky lingered and made the next day's positions all guesswork. In a compromise between John Sowden's advice to stay further offshore and the local experts who said to stay close to shore and run port to port, I steered a compromise route of about twenty to thirty miles offshore. Here I could catch a ride on the axis of the current and safely rest without risk of running ashore in my sleep, yet be close enough, in theory, to get into harbor within a half day if I felt the need.

By afternoon I was becalmed with the barometer pointing ominously to an approaching low. Rows of sullen black clouds swept towards me in wind-torn shreds from the southwest that seemed to scrape the masthead as they passed. The gale arrived all at once in a furious blast of wind and spray. We were deep-reefed and at first I was able to keep *Atom* mostly on her feet but she began to complain as we fell off the increasingly slab-sided waves. As conditions worsened I turned and ran downwind under storm jib alone. The chaotic waves flung their breaking tops aboard from all sides.

It was painful to think that a mere thirty feet below the water's surface was perfectly calm, and I found myself wishing I were commanding a submarine rather than a small sailboat. My periscope-like view out through the plastic dodger windows showed decks nearly awash, being swept stem to stern with foaming water. Each wire and line of the rigging moaned in the howling wind as I climbed onto the cabin top to secure the mainsail tighter to the boom. Bent over the boom, I looked up to see waves breaking above as we dropped into the troughs, giving me the feeling I was standing on the surface of the sea itself.

Our speed was too great for the sea conditions and I considered dropping the jib to run under bare poles. Too late! While dropping headlong down one flat-sided wave, the wind vane jerked so hard on the tiller that it snapped in two. The boat broached in a sideways slide to the seas. At the same moment, the lee spreader dipped into the sea and a sharp snap signaled a shroud had broken at its lower swaged fitting. *Atom* rolled with beam broadside to the pounding seas. The tiller stub slammed back and forth as I worked quickly with wrenches to bolt on an emergency tiller.

Since I had added extra masthead rigging in Florida, the mast thankfully stayed intact while I attached bulldog clamps and lashings to hold the broken wire in place. I also felt reassured that I had prepared for heavy weather by strengthening bulkheads and locker seals and reduced the volume of the cockpit footwell by installing storm shutters.

At midnight the faint glow of a lighthouse confirmed my estimated position and I hove-to on the offshore tack for the remainder of the night. The motion was better with the boat drifting slowly and had the added benefit that I was not losing as many precious miles to windward. I even managed a few moments of near sleep that night as the gale died out.

By morning a gray mountain range revealed itself some five miles away. All day I worked at coaxing and urging *Atom* to gain sea room against a current pulling me towards the uninhabited shore. Under full sail in light wind we struggled against the different leftover wave trains that intermingled and engulfed each other in a confused pattern, causing *Atom* to pitch, yaw and roll at the same moment. Again and again, waves broke over the bow and stern at the same time, slowing our slight forward motion until steerage way was lost. Then she rolled, dragging her boom in the sea, slowly building up speed to the next double wave set. As the feeble breeze strengthened it shifted around the compass. The same sea-building power of the wind also lessened the waves as it shifted against them. Vigilant sail trimming eventually allowed me to make progress to a safer distance offshore.

Just after midnight, as I close-reached at three knots, I set the alarm clock for one hour and let the accumulated fatigue and sense of security lull me into deep sleep. I awoke five hours later at dawn feeling refreshed and surprised at my carelessness. It was hard to shake that shore-side habit of sleeping through the night. If an ill wind shift and change of current had caught me during those hours asleep, I'd have become bones for the jackals of the Wild Coast. As luck had it, I was instead carried far offshore during the night. My next two sun sights put me an unexpected fifty miles from land.

The barometer jumped up and a strong easterly wind sent me scurrying on my way southwest. The strengthening winds and fair current combined to push us 180 miles during the next twenty-four hours. The lively roll and flying spray were uncomfortable to be sure. But this was, as they say, a fair-weather gale, with following wind under fair skies and high barometer. Back under storm jib alone, I climbed to the cabin top as the only partly dry spot on deck and enjoyed the view of the sea's friendly fury. Heading in the opposite direction would not be so friendly. I braced myself, standing at the mast, watching the sea puff up its chest and blow us ahead and downward with foaming and hissing water engulfing the stern.

A wandering albatross glided past in the high winds. These denizens of the Southern Ocean are habitual ship-followers and have long been a sign of good omen for mariners plying the empty temperate southern latitudes. The stronger the gale, the more effortless their flight. This albatross viewed me with unconcern as he displayed his superior power and grace, swooping low over the tumbling waters, yet never wetting a wing.

A ship passed less than a mile away. Plowing directly into wind and current, its progress was laboriously slow as it hammered into the seas, sending solid sheets of water high above the bow. We glimpsed each other only when, by chance, we both crested a larger wave simultaneously. Most of the time there was nothing to be seen between us but great walls of water.

Using the sextant was a challenge despite my being as familiar with it as if it were an extension of my own fingers. I needed half my concentration and strength just to keep myself securely on board, with one hand holding and protecting the delicate instrument. If I banged it against something hard it would be out of adjustment, perhaps permanently. As I lifted it to my eye the pressure of the wind gusts caused the instrument to vibrate producing an unclear and bouncing image. To compound the predicament, wind and spray made my eyes water so that after a few seconds I couldn't see clearly. When by intuition I felt I had two reliable sights, the resulting running fix put me well offshore at thirty-five degrees south latitude. We continued running hard for the cape, 180 miles to the west.

With the port of East London lying well behind me I realized that even if I wanted to, it would be too risky to head for any port in these conditions and so proceeded nonstop for Cape Town regardless of vagaries of the weather. Old John Sowden was right, if you sail far enough offshore to be safe, you are too far out to come cowering in at every bit of threatening weather before that weather is already upon you. One of the reasons today's sailors choose ever larger and faster boats is to beat bad weather into port. This tactic is part truth and part illusion. You cannot outrun all storms, nor all your fears.

My hopes of rounding the cape the following day were dashed when the wind dropped and then shifted against me. Again I patiently sat hove-to for a full day drifting about, this way and that, as the wind made its cloying dance around the compass. Winds in these latitudes were particularly vexing after the relatively settled trade wind passages I had become accustomed to on the last two oceans. Yet even these tiresome days provided their distractions. I spent a good portion of each day studying not only the ceaseless flight of the albatross but also swift storm petrels, sooty shearwater, cape gannet and other birds appearing too fragile for this harsh environment. Each day one or another of these inquisitive or exhausted birds perched on *Atom's* stern rail for a few hours rest.

Another short-lived wind blew in from astern and I resumed my westerly course. The waters turned cold as I entered a region where the icy Benguela Current from the Antarctic regions meets the warm Agulhas Current. The air also turned cold and I dressed in extra layers, reveling in the crisp salt air after over a year of monotonous tropic heat. At night the cold waters put on a spectacular phosphorescent light show. On each breaking wave crest burned a sheet of cold fire. *Atom's* wake contained uncountable sparkling lights tracing a path to the horizon. The knowledge that this marine version of the firefly was caused by billions of tiny bioluminescent shrimp called meganyctiphanes, rising to the surface to feed at night, did not diminish the endless wonder of the spectacle.

When we were again becalmed, the weather pattern of this region became clearer. A falling barometer precedes a gale from the southwest that backs to south a day or two later. Then the barometer rises as the wind backs further to the east. A few days of variable winds follow until the pattern is repeated with another southwester. If the northeaster blows strong it foretells an equally strong southwester.

For another day I waited in a calm off Africa's southernmost point at Cape Agulhas. Here the two oceans met in a shoving match with me in the middle. In these turbulent waters on the edge of the Benguela Current, a curious seal swam alongside, cocking his whiskered face at me before wandering off to other games.

The fickle breeze scratched cat's paw ripples across the otherwise satin cover of the rolling water and gave a call to action for trimming sails. A small, light, easily driven hull like *Atom* is just what the solo sailor needs in conditions like this. A big and heavy boat that offers more comfort in a storm is mulishly stubborn in fluky airs and the sailor ends up relying on his engine more than he might want.

By early afternoon I was tacking into a light westerly with a full mainsail and genoa sail that gathered the lightest of winds and drove us forward. Creeping along from one cat's paw to another, *Atom* lay suspended motionless for minutes at a time until a new puff of air filled the sails and worked its magic. On what I considered the favorable tack, we sailed parallel to a shore of empty sand dunes and scrub brush. Plain as it was, my eyes feasted on the slowly changing scenery of the beach and behind it where a mountain rose into the clouds. Sailing less than a mile offshore, I risked grounding, but the coast seemed to beckon me. I crept in closer yet, until I saw the waters boiling on the reef only a few boat lengths away.

Along this indent in the coast between Quoin Point and Danger Point, I sailed up to the half-submerged wreck of a fishing trawler. It held an alluring fascination for me as I watched the sea heave and pound its fist against the rusted hull, seeming to punish it further for the crime of closing in on a forbidden coast. Beyond the wreck, a Jeep kept pace with me by stopping and starting along the otherwise deserted beach. Finally, the siren's spell was broken when the low sandy paw of Danger Point threatened me with its embrace and I tacked seaward.

As the day's light faded, a fishing boat hosting a cloud of scavenger birds pulled close alongside. Three fishermen leaned over the rail and shouted a hearty greeting to me then changed course and pulled away.

Throughout the night on the Agulhas Bank, *Atom* tacked into a stiff wind in company with a steady procession of ships running blindly into the night. In the mix as well were clusters of fishing boats out from Hout Bay and Cape Town. The bright lights of the fishing fleet lit up patches of the night near and far like floating Christmas trees reflecting splashes of colored lights on the water. Eventually, in the background, I picked out the flashing light from the long-sought Cape of Good Hope lighthouse.

The morning of my ninth day at sea I sailed within sight of the cape's cliffs where the winds deserted me again. With limp sails under a sunny, cloud-flecked sky, a gentle current pulled me past the rock buttress of the cape. Staring enraptured at the southwest extremity of Africa, thrusting its dark cliffs into the sea, I completely agreed with the old pirate Francis Drake who wrote, "This Cape is the most stately thing and the fairest Cape that we saw in all the circumference of the earth." And even more fair for the struggle to reach it. For me, passing this cape marked more than a point between oceans. Having put the more dangerous passages behind me, I now had the confidence of knowing I was within reach of my goal, that my voyage could, and would, be completed.

While drifting past the purple-toned mountain range named The Twelve Apostles, I counted off their dozen weathered peaks. Beyond these saintly columns, flat-topped Table Mountain cut a horizontal slice across the sky. As I waited for the wind I knew would return, I used the day to organize gear and prepare for landfall.

During the night I coaxed *Atom* close to shore and found a light, cool, wind dropping off the mountains to fill our sails. Then, at sunrise, I sailed past a long stone jetty to enter Cape Town's Table Bay, behind which a sprawling city of high-rise buildings and Victorian-style homes stood between mountain and seascape.

At the Royal Cape Yacht Club I was given a guest membership and a spot on the dock to moor *Atom* for a small fee. At the club I met up with old cruising friends and sailors I'd met in Durban. An atmosphere of relief and satisfaction prevailed among the cruising community at the yacht club. The feared cape passage was behind us and we acted like climbers back at base camp after summiting our Everest. Ahead lay the South Atlantic with its kindly reputation for year-round trade winds. Unlike any other ocean, the tropical zone of the South Atlantic is generally regarded as having never hosted a storm of hurricane strength: a suitable reward for those having had the stuffing knocked out of them along the South African coast.

Within hours of settling *Atom* into her dock I discovered stowaways. The boat's interior and lockers were crawling with cockroaches regaining their appetite after their miserably rough passage. I had picked up a crew of roaches in New Guinea and though I had never quite succeeded in eradicating them with poisons and cleaning, we had developed a wary détente where they remained mostly hidden during the day. Apparently, another tribe of roaches came aboard in Durban and mated with their New Guinea cousins to produce a super race of roaches. These bold little vermin now began to roam the boat at will, day and night, laying claim to anything in their path. Again I offloaded every item from the boat and scrupulously cleaned out the lockers. Finally, I defeated them with a liberal sprinkling of boric acid powder, which kills them over time, apparently through dehydration and constipation.

During my Cape Town layover, I joined up with the Mountain Club of South Africa for some local mountain climbing. The next Sunday morning about twenty members met at the base of the Twelve Apostles where we prepared to climb to the summit and cross the tabletop of Table Mountain. I had done strenuous climbs on my own before, but had never tried a technical climb where I put my life in the hands of my fellow climbers, their ropes, harnesses and climbing gadgetry. We divided into five smaller teams, each group tackling a different route of more or less difficulty. I joined the beginner's group led by Mike, a rock-hanging veteran, who volunteered to introduce us to basic climbing techniques.

At the base of Kasteels Buttress, we strapped on our borrowed harnesses and began the first pitch. Mike positioned a man as anchor, or belay, who payed out a line attached to Mike's harness. Mike pulled himself hand-over-hand up the near vertical face, expertly using each crack and dent in the rocks as a finger or toe hold. At strategic

Our climb up Table Mountain

locations he stopped to attach a clamp into a crack in the rock through which he threaded his safety line. On his belt he carried five-sided aluminum blocks with wire leaders, called nuts, in several sizes, fitting the appropriate one into cracks in the rock and turning it until it jammed, more or less, securely. He also carried an ingenious gadget of four ratcheting aluminum half-wheels that rolled and locked into the rock cracks. Swinging himself over a narrow ledge far above us, Mike secured himself as top belay, calling down, "Off belay," to the man on the lower end of the rope.

One by one, we nervously followed him up, trying to remember Mike's exact route and use the same handholds. Firmly anchored to a rock, Mike took up the slack on our lines as we climbed. For me, on my first climb, the thrill is unequaled – heart racing as I cling to a crevice by my fingertips, the toe of my boot jammed into a small crack, while my other hand searches for the next handhold out of sight above me. Even with the safety line, the higher I climb, the more slug-like my progress as I attempt to press myself ever closer to the rock. Once attaining the ledge, I'm rewarded with a rush of relieved satisfaction.

We ascended four of these pitches, resting on ledges at each interval as the other climbers caught up, until we were far up the mountainside and nearly to the summit. A cloud, locally called the "tablecloth" that hung over the edge of Table Mountain all morning, was now dispersing in the afternoon sun. Here the winds blow vertically up or down the mountain. As the wind blew down on us, we paused to observe the progress of the other groups. Across the ravine of Kasteelspoort, I watched five climbers ascend the broken face of Vaulken Buttress. They were on a tricky pitch with an overhanging ledge that looked impassable. "They're on a difficult F rated climb," Mike told us. "The same one I did last week. It took us nearly an hour to get past that same ledge. A dangerous spot." Beyond the Vaulken was another group of climbers moving slowly and steadily up Barrier Buttress, looking like a team of assassins scaling a castle wall.

On our final pitch I had trouble locating a grip. The wind tore at me as I hung precariously from a tiny dent in the rock. The cliff face overhung here slightly, making it a constant effort just to hold against gravity. I could see no other hand-hold available. Mike called out there was a slight ledge about three feet above me. To reach it, I would have to let go of my only hold, and with blind faith, quickly stand up from my crouching position and make a desperate grab while falling away from the cliff. If not quick and accurate with my grasp, I'd end up swinging from the rope with feet kicking in the air.

For a moment I hesitated. Looking up I saw Mike silently watching me. He would not coax me further, it was up to me to trust him and make the move. Like a human magnet, I pressed myself against the rock and reached up, catching the promised ledge to stop my backward fall. With this firm handhold I was able to pull myself to the top alongside the others. The man behind me misjudged his grip on the overhang and when he dropped off the wall, he called out, "Coming off!" We pulled up his dead weight on the belaying rope until he was on our ledge.

From atop Kestreels Buttress we sighted along the Twelve Apostles ridge line all the way to the distant cliffs of Cape Point. After rendezvousing with the other climbing groups we split up again and most of the others descended back to the base using a series of rapid rappels on ropes with hand brakes. With two other members of the club, I headed on foot across the top of Table Mountain and descended the other side.

Overlooking Cape Town from Table Mountain

Up close, we found the apparently flat tabletop was not entirely level and held within it a depression named the Valley of the Red Gods. In counterpoint to the bare dirt and rock around its edges, the small valley is bordered by a green pine forest. I was surprised to find this hidden valley crisscrossed by marked footpaths, a stone rest house and a ranger's station. There was even an ancient series of water pools and dams, cut by hand from the stone, to provide water to the city below.

At one edge of the mountain we passed a restaurant and cable car station which brings the mountaintop within reach of anyone who has the fare. Beyond the pine forest, the tabletop held fields of brown scrub brush and rocks punctuated by the striking bright blossoms of the King Protea, South Africa's national flower. By descending the winding Platteklip Gorge, we returned directly into the heart of Cape Town's business district.

Several days later back at the yacht club, I met Eric Clapham, a retired English South African, living with his family in Wynberg, a suburb under the shadow of Table Mountain. We struck up a conversation and within minutes we were in Eric's car on the way to the Cape of Good Hope Nature Reserve where a grass fire had recently wiped out all visible life over a third of the park. We drove through extensive fields of scorched earth covered in gray and black ash, charred stumps of bushes and blackened rocks. The park had seen these fires before and the local naturalists expected the veld to recover within ten years. Meanwhile, a troop of baboons ran out onto the road in front of us screaming and grabbing at each other's tails. We parked and waited until the dispute was settled and then motored on. Near the lighthouse at the end of the road, another group of three baboons sat guarding a trash can as if it were their own.

At Cape Point I climbed the stairs to the lighthouse that, only a week before, had dutifully flashed its greeting to me as I drifted past in a calm. On this day a moderate gale blew in from the west, increasing in force as it funneled up the cliffs to the lighthouse. I gripped the circular steel railing and leaned into the fierce wind, thankful that I was not at sea that day. I looked down on the cape's long, rocky point where the sea smashed the coast, sending spray high into the air for the wind to blow back and I could taste the salt on my lips. Gulls tacked in winds alive with the sound of gale-driven surf.

Beyond the shoals offshore a ship rounded the cape, rolling heavily to the sea. Here, where no offshore islands give protection, the cape stands exultant in the embrace of restless surge from two oceans. Between the cape and the Antarctic Continent lie the roiling waters and ice of the Southern Ocean. Away to the northwest, beyond the Cape of Storms, lay the welcoming route home.

20 Emperors and Astronomers

No journey carries one far unless,
as it extends into the world around us,
it goes an equal distance into the world within.

-Lillian Smith

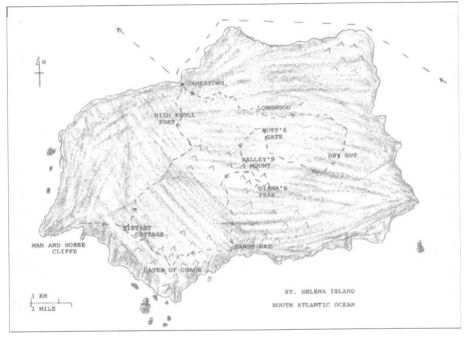

St. Helena map

On our way back to Cape Town from the Cape Point lighthouse the engine in Eric's car suddenly coughed and quit. By chance, we were close enough to coast into a repair garage along the roadway. Abandoning the car for the moment to the care of the mechanic, we walked on to the local train station.

Our passenger train rolled past a school field where a uniformed band stood in formation and we briefly caught a snatch of the anthem Die Stem Van Suid-Afrika, "The Call of South Africa," before it was drowned out by the rumble of steel wheels on rails. Under a "Whites Only" sign across the aisle from us, sat a Coloured man as comfortable in his expression as if he owned the train. There were several blacks also sharing this first-class car with no apparent hostilities among the mixed group. The Afrikaner conductor took the tickets without remark to anyone.

I recalled then my experiences on the other side of the same country, where conductors enforced the segregation laws with sticks and shouts. Eric told me that in recent years, many blacks in Cape Town challenged or ignored the dogma of apartheid. Cape Town is in many ways the most progressive city in South Africa. On the other side of the country, interracial friendship was scandalous. Here I saw mixed couples walking the streets without drawing a second look from passersby. White and Coloured families even shared one of the town's residential sections. Bit by bit, sanity and tolerance were seeping into the culture.

Another part of town is reserved for Muslim Malays, whose mosque stands incongruously close to the spires of the conservative Dutch Reformed Church. Unfortunately, "reformed" did not mean they held trendy notions of equality of the races or evolution but they had at least dropped the flat earth cosmology held by previous generations. Even so, it would be hard to find two more mutually exclusive organizations standing side by side than the Dutch Reformed and the Muslim Malay.

In this era the signs of apartheid were gradually coming down around Cape Town. It was as if the entire country had changed during my nine days at sea. Actually, it was more like I had sailed from 1960's Alabama to 1960's San Francisco. Besides trains, the beaches were now integrated with a secluded spot reserved for nude sunbathers. The changes did not come with unanimous support. On a radio talk show I heard a woman caller announce her disgust at seeing a black woman breast-feeding her baby on the public beach. She expected the government to protect her from the terrifying black usurpers threatening her modesty.

And what of the others, the so-called Coloureds, the people without a voice or homeland? No one I spoke to in South Africa expected the Coloured population to play a significant role in the future of the country. Accepted by neither black nor white, they are caught in the middle with nowhere to turn. In the looming conflict of white against black they were being ignored – just when the millions-strong multi-racial peoples of South Africa were most needed as a bridge between cultures. At least the progressive attitudes in Cape Town offered the hope of some chance at future peace in this troubled land.

Later that week Eric retrieved his car from the mechanic and generously drove me around town to gather the provisions I needed for crossing the South Atlantic. For another two days, I sat like a coiled spring ready to jump but found myself pinned down by a northwest gale. When Friday morning dawned clear and cool, I prepared to depart.

"You can't leave today," said the club secretary as I paid my dockage bill.

"Why not? I'm paid up and the weather forecast is fair."

"Because it's Friday," she explained. "Nobody leaves on a Friday!"

The customs agent, two sailors roaming the docks, and even the club security guard reminded me it was daft to depart on a Friday. To some ancient mariners, a Friday departure may have been inauspicious. My superstitious advisers knew nothing of the origins of their belief, yet they believed in it whole-heartedly and turned away with grim faces when I explained that Friday represents one of seven possible weather windows every week, and I was not inclined to throw away a good opportunity to appease the Bad Friday cult. So, despite the ill omen, I departed Cape Town Friday afternoon into a light west wind.

With all sail set I slipped into the open sea at a two knot pace – that of a leisurely stroll. On day two, Cape Town dropped from view, leaving the top of Table Mountain displaying its shrinking crown over the sea. A larger ketch on a similar course gradually outpaced me a few miles to starboard. As the wind settled in the south, I held course for St. Helena Island, 1,700 miles away and one of only two islands in the mid South Atlantic basin.

My return to tropic latitudes brought relief from the clammy cold nights and the threats of gales popping up from all directions. Regrettably, the albatrosses and seals preferred the colder waters to the south. In their place I gained the companionship of a school of fourteen tuna that paced *Atom* for two days, darting in unison from the shadow of the keel to snatch up small fish we encountered along the way. *Atom* was now part of a wolf pack. The hunted flying fish took to the air as we passed through, the lucky ones making good their winged escape.

For the duration of this passage, the wind caressed the sea as gently and steadily as only a South Atlantic trade wind can. Day after day, the sails hung wing-on-wing. I dressed *Atom* down for this light air passage by hoisting her oldest threadbare suit of sails in order to preserve her least damaged sails for later use. As the tranquil days unrolled my work was little more than to once daily oil the wind vane bearings and ease the sail's sheets in or out a few inches to prevent chafe on blocks and cleats. Aside from these minute adjustments, I did little to earn my passage, which became a dreamy, sleepwalking event, almost as if I went to sleep outside Cape Town and awoke in St. Helena.

I had been given a bagful of books, mostly novels, by friends in Cape Town. Now I fell into languorous hours of reading as I reclined in the cockpit. The books were so biodegradably forgettable that I took a perverse pleasure in tearing out each page read and dropping it over the side until I held an empty cover and it, too, went overboard. Depending on our boat speed at the time, each mile was marked by two or three pages floating in our wake.

Among the new books that came aboard was the Koran, which a Muslim devotee in Durban had thrust at me "for spiritual guidance." I read it through in a day and a night before it also went over the side somewhere in mid-ocean alongside the other fiction. If only all medieval zealots could so easily be cast out of the world. "There is no conqueror, but Allah," it said. Perhaps, but could not Allah's disciples put more emphasis on conquering ignorance, intolerance, hate and cruelty, than stoning women and putting infidels to the sword?

At sea I was spoiled to nature's regular performances, the unique perspectives of rainbows and sunsets that no one else would ever see. On this passage I had an entirely new night visitor. For the past month, Halley's comet was faintly visible from southern Africa. Populist astronomers had overstated its expected brightness and stirred up a frenzy of interest in the returning comet. For city dwellers, Halley's less than stellar brightness was a disappointment. Out here, a thousand miles from the desert lands of Namibia, as far from the star-eclipsing lights of civilization as a man could get, the comet's tail brightened and flowered.

The comet reappeared each night as a frosty-white streak over several degrees of arc across the southeastern sky. I lay in my bunk gazing at the comet for hours through the open hatchway. If *Atom* deviated from her northwest alignment, I knew as well as any telltale compass could show that I was off course by the comet's tail disappearing from my picture-framed view. My comet served as a guiding apparition as real as the star that led the three wise men to Bethlehem.

On a Sunday morning I put down the remaining pages of my tenth book since leaving Cape Town and lifted my eyes to the hazy outline of land below a cluster of low clouds. My eyes remained locked on the horizon for another hour until I was certain it was land and not a mirage born of the overwhelming emptiness all around it. The island lay anchored in mid-ocean isolation, rising above a range of dormant volcanoes resting just below the surface of the South Atlantic. From a distance, St. Helena, which is a mere six miles across, appears almost as tall as it is wide. In my imagination I follow its slopes down to the sea floor and picture its violent birth millions of years ago.

Hours later, we glided past a towering stone buttress marked on my chart as The Barn and its 2,000 foot-high peak named The Haystack. Here on the island's uninhabited north coast, the mountains display all their altitude in a single vertical wall. Five miles along this desolate, sunburnt coast, the small harbor of James Bay hove into view. A traditional three-masted sailing ship rested at anchor close under the scarred mountain. I lowered two anchors in forty-five feet of water in company with several other visiting yachts and moored local fishing boats.

James Bay is more of an open roadstead than proper bay. This slight indent in the rocky coast at the base of a valley is also the only permitted anchorage among the handful of bays on this coast of barren basaltic outcroppings. At least the island's wind shadow afforded some protection from the prevailing southeast trade winds, if not from the perpetual sea swell hooking around the circular island. Besides causing the anchored boats to roll their guts out, the swell makes landing a dinghy wet and hazardous.

Jamestown, St. Helena Island

St. Helena was long a favored stopover for ships returning to Europe along the East Indies spice trade route. Its sometimes tragic history of human occupation began in the early sixteenth century when a Portuguese ship exiled a horribly mutilated prisoner on the uninhabited island. In India, the unfortunate wretch had had his nose, ears, an arm and the thumb of the opposite hand removed for the crime of insurrection in the Portuguese colony of Goa, before being marooned on this empty island. He existed for ten lonely years on the island, surviving off the pity of sailors on passing ships who provided him goats and essential supplies, before he returned to Portugal and eventually had an audience with the Pope in Rome. There he was granted a wish – thus he returned to St. Helena, by choice this time, to live out the rest of his life in solitude.

Eventually, the British wrested control of the island from the contesting powers of Portugal, the Netherlands and France. St. Helena is best known as the home of a more famous exile, when the British brought the defeated French emperor, Napoleon Bonaparte, here to live in enforced isolation until his death in 1821.

Today, St. Helena is one of Britain's few remaining colonies. The population of six thousand people are mostly a coffee-colored mixture of European, African, Malay and Chinese. Someone aptly described the population as "twenty percent black, twenty percent white, and sixty percent not quite sure and don't much care." The Saints, as the islanders are known, are so interracially mixed that bigotry is an unknown concept. Saintly mothers were known in times past to encourage their daughters to fraternize with visiting sailors to expand the bloodline. The friendly atmosphere here was a refreshing change from the racial tensions of South Africa and it reminded me of Mauritius and Reunion Islands, an ocean away.

St. Helena is doubly blessed with having no airstrip and lacking good port facilities, thereby retaining its remote colonial charm. The harbor of James Bay lacks a pier or even a beach to land a small boat. The shore is fronted with a fortified stone wall, looking as much to repel visitors as the stones and pebbles tossed against it with each surge of the sea. The whole waterfront resonates with the clattering and deep-toned hissing of ocean meeting rock.

Before some improvements were made to the facilities in the years after I left, dinghies and lighters from the supply boat landed alongside steps leading down from the concrete quay into the sea. Local boats would approach the steps stern-to, with an expert oarsman timing his approach to match the rise of the swells. As the boat lifts to the sea, he would call out for passengers and cargo to come aboard quickly before the boat fell away on the retreating wave. Visiting royalty and common sailors alike swung themselves ashore from the deck of their small landing boats by grasping for a rope hanging from an overhead rail. The last person to step ashore would quickly pass the dinghy's line to others who helped pull the boat clear of the smashing waves. Lacking television, viewing the landing struggles was an amusing pastime for local villagers and fishermen who whiled away the hours watching visitors try vainly to make a dry landing. Often they missed their step and went for an unexpected swim.

As I approached the quay for the first time, the high surf deposited me at the top of the steps in one lifting surge. The waters receded under me as I stood up perfectly dry and pulled my dinghy up to avoid the next rush of water. To the audience watching from the pier, I hoped my lucky landing looked like I planned it that way.

At the quayside I checked in with customs and paid my $25 harbor dues, then entered Jamestown through the gates of the "Castle" which houses the government offices and bank. At the post office I purchased a finely detailed cartographic map of the island. Laying the map across a table at the town pub, local Saints gave me advice on the best routes to walk across the island, "if one were queer enough to want to do it." I picked out a circular route around the island that I guessed would take three days on foot. The high point on my planned trek was a pilgrimage to Halley's Mount, a peak named after astronomer Edmund Halley. It seemed fitting to pay my respects here to the history of the comet that helped guide me to this speck of land in a wide sea.

Before starting my hike I made sure *Atom* lay well secured with an added third anchor buried in the mud of James Bay, and friends on neighboring boats promised to look after her if the weather threatened while I was gone. I managed to land myself and my backpack on the quay, wet this time, but without injury.

I set out through Jamestown, whose whitewashed buildings spill down the narrow rift of Chapel Valley following a stream bed whose course is marked by a splash of green in the otherwise barren gorge. Thousands of hand-laid stones formed a continuous retaining wall for the road as it clung to the landslide-prone cliffs. The road forked and doubled back on its winding way up Munden's Hill, where it began to fall apart. Long in disuse, falling boulders had carried sections of the road crashing down to the sea below. I looked down through one of these gaping holes in the retaining wall to see the square-rigged training ship moored directly below.

On the hilltop, amid scrub brush and cactus stunted and shriveled by the dry heat, laid the ruins of an old gun battery. Cannon from iron foundries of 17th century England still overlook the harbor. Standing atop the ruins, I imagined the thunder of the cannons from siege and counter-siege by opposing colonial forces. Lying far below on the wave-swept rocks were remains of larger, WWII era cannons that in a display of war-weariness, had been pushed off the cliffs after the war ended. Weighing over three tons each, from this height they appeared as so many discarded toys.

Rejoining the main road on the upper slopes of Jamestown, I passed the sprawling colonial building of the cable and wireless station. Quiet and abandoned today, it was the busiest place on the island back in pre-satellite days when teams of men relayed messages in Morse code along the undersea cables linking the island from South America to Africa.

Continuing uphill, the road made a sharp turn at Button Up Corner and switched back again at Captain Wright's Turning. Jamestown may be the only town on St. Helena, but my map showed settlements as small as a single home scattered all over the island. This was not merely a map; it was an entertaining story documenting the lives and history of the inhabitants. Reading this map I got the impression that the British would name every bush and rock and label them on a map if given enough paper. Should he ever feel the need, even the poorest inland shepherd could fix himself in two dimensions relative to the rest of his known world. Here I overindulged my old weakness for a well-drawn map. I studied its features so often, at times losing myself in its intricate detailed contours, that I neglected to fully observe the land I was crossing.

On the high slopes past a house named Alarm Cottage the vegetation grew more varied and extensive. St. Helena has a remarkable flora that is unperceived from the harbor. The terrain near sea level is a desert of sand, rocks and cactus, washed by infrequent rains and baked by a daily sun. Higher up, the central slopes contain grasslands and forests. The changeover can be abrupt and startling. Suddenly, I was walking at an altitude where rain-moistened fertile volcanic soil supported flowery gardens and forests. Most of the flora I saw here was not indigenous but had been imported after early settlers and their goats had stripped the original forests and grasses.

A sign pointing down a footpath to Napoleon's Tomb lured me off the main road. I moved quietly alone through pine forest until I came upon a young man leaning against a wooden gate. He was caretaker of the tomb and guide for the rare visitor. As we walked together, he recounted exploits of Napoleon that he had clearly memorized from an encyclopedia. When we arrived at the tomb I discovered it was simply an empty concrete slab surrounded by an iron fence, a one-man graveyard seemingly abandoned to the creeping forest. Napoleon had been here once, in his triple lead-lined coffin, until the French rescued his remains and returned them to the motherland in 1840. Even the tomb's inhabitant had fled.

Continuing my hike, pushing through the brush to the ridge atop The Devil's Punch Bowl, I dropped into Deadwood Plain, where once was sited a Boer War prison camp.

Nearby, at Longwood Plantation, a French flag fluttered. Here, at the plantation house, behind a long, low stone wall, Napoleon lived in exile after his defeat at Waterloo. Inside the house, the groundskeeper of the restored building took me through the rooms, describing every piece of memorabilia..

Each room of Longwood House brought the past to life. The copper bathtub where the emperor took three baths each day still functioned. Two large world globes stood in the billiard room on which the brooding Napoleon traced his former conquests. Accompanied by a squabbling entourage of his generals, Napoleon lived in constant fear of poisoning and kept a food taster in residence. An autopsy performed in the billiard room found that he died of stomach cancer or, possibly, a slow poisoning. The groundskeeper confided to me that he sometimes hears Napoleon's ghost when here alone at night. On windy and misty evenings it's easy to imagine the horse-drawn carriage that used to race back and forth at a reckless speed, giving the emperor a temporary escape from a monotonous existence. Napoleon wrote here, "Death is nothing, but to live defeated and inglorious is to die daily."

At the end of the tour, the groundskeeper proceeded to question me at length about my travels around the world. He had worked here thirty-five years, immersed daily in a long past era, while occasionally dreaming of present day lands far away.

Leaving Longwood I turned down a dusty track next to the island's power station. From there I could see the backside of the Barn, which is the opposite side of the same mountain I viewed from the deck of *Atom* as I approached the island a week earlier. In view to the east was Prosperous Bay, a landing place in the late 1600s for an English invasion force tasked to march across the island and retake Jamestown from the Dutch defenders who themselves recently had taken it from the British. Above the high cliffs at Prosperous Bay (I thought better named Preposterous Bay since it held no possibility of shelter) the map indicated a spot called Holdfast Tom, where a young soldier named Tom climbed the rock face, fixing ropes for other soldiers to hoist their equipment of war up to the plateau.

I descended next into the dust bowl named Dry Gut, where the earth lay open in multicolored scars of mineral-laden sand dunes and washed-out, sun-hardened gulleys. The mineral-rich basaltic lava ran from brick-red to yellow to iridescent blue. Bristling cactus added the only touch of life to this desiccated landscape. With each rise and dip of the trail the vistas turn harsh or lovely. The beauty of eroded mountains and highland meadows and dizzying cliffs set against the dark sea was nearly heartbreaking. Walking over a wind-piled sand dune, each step had me sinking ankle deep into the fine powder as if struggling through a giant hourglass. And like an upturned hourglass, the wind-driven sand would erase my own passage upon the land. When I gained more altitude, I suddenly stepped into a green pasture. From a woody ridge, two farmhouses overlooked the veld.

Inside the dark, stone building of Hutt's Gate General Store I eyed wooden shelves sparsely stocked with a dozen or so cans of meat, soup and hard English biscuits. An old woman stooped over polishing an ancient brass scale, the same scales used in the same store by her mother's grandmother, she told me proudly when I admired them, as if unaltered consistency were as important in life as in the scales themselves. I filled my water jugs from the rainwater barrel on the porch and found room in my backpack for a loaf of the good woman's bread. On the wall over the counter, a calendar took the place of a clock. It felt like I could have talked to her for five hours, instead of five minutes, and she would not have been put out in the least.

Back at the intersection, I chose a road leading towards Halley's Mount. At the old brick church of St. Mathews, I left the road and moved through the church graveyard where, on the other side, I found the trail the shopkeeper had directed me to, "out thar beyond the graveyard." Through knee-high grass I scanned each scarred and flaking headstone. Nearly half the occupants here had died in the year 1936, I imagined by some epidemic brought by an unlucky ship. Two gravestones standing side-by-side caught my eye. One was barely readable, recording a man's death in the epidemic of '36. The other was his wife, who faithfully joined him forty years later. In the graveyards an island's history is laid out like an open book, but with every second page missing, leaving much to the reader's imagination.

Behind these last two headstones, I found my trail and followed it up the flank of Halley's Mount. Pressing in on all sides and growing above my head was an overgrown grove of broad-leafed New Zealand flax. Imported a century earlier as an export crop to produce ropes and linen, it is no longer harvested and proliferates across the island's highlands. Crouched over with my head nearly to my knees, I pushed through the dense growth until I emerged at a clearing on the peak of a long ridge.

Discarded stone blocks marked this spot as the observatory hastily built by astronomer Edmund Halley in 1676. Equipped with state-of-the-art clocks and telescopes, this observatory is where Halley studied and cataloged the stars of the Southern hemisphere. He paid for this first expedition out of his own pocket, but returned on the King's dime in 1699 as commander of *HMS Paramour*. Halley is, of course, best known for discovering the orbit of the comet that now bears his name by linking the one he observed in 1682 with similar great comets reported throughout prior centuries.

Near Halley's Mount

I camped here among the ruins and awaited nightfall. With darkness came a persistent, misty light rain that softened the sound of the wind. Each hour I awoke to poke my head out the tent's entry flap, looking for a trace of starry sky in the overcast. A few hours before dawn the sky cleared to reveal a white, powdery trail low in the southeastern sky. The harmony of the Newtonian universe is wonderfully highlighted by the 76 year cycle of this particular comet's approach to earth which approximates the human lifetime cycle. Few among us will see it twice.

As I peered skyward that early morning of March 13, watching the display from Halley's Mount, the European spacecraft *Giotto* approached the comet's head. Scientists found it was composed of nothing more than dirty ice older than life on earth. It was wonderful to think that at the same moment as I gazed through a window in time upon the long-haired star from my remote post, *Giotto* was rocketing through the comet's tail and sending its photos back for earth's astronomers to marvel at. As *Giotto* had steered for weeks towards the comet, I too had steered my ship by this celestial body, night after night, to bring me to this spot in time and a certain intimacy with the man who had cracked its mystery. It is said that Napoleon put St. Helena on the world map. But Napoleon was merely an emperor, while Edmund Halley holds the greater glory as a man of science.

With dawn's eclipse of the comet, I continued pushing along the ridge through walls of flax bushes. I found my way blindly by staying atop the sharp ridge as it tended slightly downward and then rose again until I emerged in the clearing atop Diana's Peak. From here the land fell away in a series of folded ridges. Neighboring Mt. Actaeon produced a lone pine tree standing as sentinel on its craggy top. According to Greek myth, Actaeon the hunter accidentally observed Artemis as she was bathing and in her anger she turned him into a stag who was then killed by Actaeon's own dogs.

A wooden box posted on Diana's Peak contained a visitor logbook and a letter from the island's governor proclaiming this 823-meter peak as the highest point on the island. After adding my name to the list, I looked across to Mt. Actaeon, which appeared equally high, but trusted the venerable governor's judgment that it was, in fact, three meters lower.

Down the southern flank of Diana's Peak I emerged from the bush onto a rough jeep track signposted as Cabbage Tree Road. Around a bend in the road I saw the way ahead resembled a tilted bowl pouring its contents into Sandy Bay on the island's southeast coast. Halfway down this giant bowl the vegetation thinned and the brown earth radiated the morning sun's heat.

Here stood a one-room Baptist chapel of hand-hewn stone blocks that looked as if it grew out of, and was as old as, the earth it rested on. In contrast to the barren hills, a leafy green slash of vegetation marked the course of a river so close to dry that I didn't bother to try filling my water bottle in it. A total of five inhabited homes dotted the valley, each standing as if painted into a portrait of a miniature Nile Valley.

At one house I stopped to ask for water and met Trevor Thomas, a lean, bronze-colored man who counted seventy-some years in this valley. His skin was as parched and brown-furrowed as the hills pressed around his brick home. From his well, Trevor filled my water bottle and then asked, "Are you that rock studying fella I heard about on the radio?"

Chapel on St. Helena

He was referring to a geologist visiting from England who was currently roaming these hills in search of specimens. I assured Trevor it was too hot to carry rocks around and that I was searching for much lighter souvenirs, no heavier than a few photos and memories. I briefly recounted my journey and told Trevor I wished to cross the next mountain range to the southwest corner of the island. My finger stabbed the map showing a grassy plateau above Man and Horse Cliffs. Trevor ignored the map as he sized me up from my wide-brimmed hat to my leather boots. Eventually, he said that no one had gone over that rough country in many years but that it was possible to do. He said there was a footpath to take me part way and then I'd be on my own among the crumbling mountains.

When I again held out my map for Trevor to point out the path he gently pushed it aside without a glance and said, "I'll join you, at least for the first mile or so." Trevor stuffed two handfuls of his homegrown finger-sized bananas into my pack and we each took long camel-like draughts of well water and set off down the road. As we passed ruins of old home-sites he spoke of his lost neighbors, "Most of us older folk have passed and the young ones mostly left this dry valley for the cooler, greener highlands. Some we hear went to England. They never come back." Drifting sand was now reclaiming the old homesteads.

I followed Trevor's surprisingly youthful stride down the valley to the black sand and rocks on the shore of Sandy Bay where a government-sponsored research garden bloomed alongside the river. With the efforts of the few remaining gardeners in the valley, the sparse and ungenerous gravel had been coaxed to yield a few annual basketfuls of bananas, corn and tomatoes. A row of flowering red hibiscus trees formed a natural windbreak to protect this last stand of life from the creeping desertification and provide the eye with a respite from the starkness of an otherwise lifeless land.

Here, at the end of the road, I listened intently as Trevor gave me directions. My eyes followed the course his bent finger traced against the background of basaltic domes. The thin line of a barely discernible trail snaked its way among the rocks up to a pass called the Gates of Chaos. How could a traveler not march directly toward anything with such an intriguing name?

The next range of mountains I needed to cross were not visible from here so I memorized every word of Trevor's convoluted instructions as if my life depended on it. Trevor had walked through those gates in his youth but did not know anyone who had crossed all the way to the opposite shore. I thanked my new friend and he wished me luck. Our goodbye was English style: brief and formal. I walked a while and looked back over my shoulder to see Trevor still rooted in his place, looking at me under cocked hat, or perhaps past me, as if to see the place where his youth had fled.

High up the desert path I stopped to lunch on a bag of bananas, bread and carrots. From my seat on a flat rock I looked over a coastline of rocky necks of land protruding into an ultramarine sea. The erosive forces of the southeast trade winds shape the raw and cracked character of this giant amphitheater. Blowing sand and rain have stripped the softer rock, leaving cores of harder basalt towers. Everywhere here the earth is laid open for inspection – truly a geologist's playground. The fluted pinnacles and ridges are all the result of free sculpture by wind and rain. The exposed strata hold streaks of porous scoria, dark basalt, rust-colored minerals, all bound together with cracked clay and gravel.

Beyond the tiny patch of green at Sandy Bay lay the scorched slopes of the Devil's Garden. Our mapmaker was a cartographic poet at heart who created a paper masterpiece. Looking at my position on the map, I noticed he had not named this particular hummock I sat on and so I named it Perseverance Peak.

Into the Badlands of St. Helena

When the indistinct trail I was following disappeared altogether I continued moving upwards until cresting a ridge where I saw the pass I sought. Though it was not far in distance, it looked difficult to reach. The mountaintops here form only edges without plateaus. As I moved along the sharp ridge on hands and knees the soft sandstone crumbled away at every touch, falling away in little landslides towards the valley floor. Wind gusts tugged at my pack, pulling me off balance. I began wishing I were somewhere, anywhere else. My next move, a leap across a downward arching gap in the ridge, meant I committed myself to going forward with no way back. There was exhilaration in willing myself on to new heights. In a few more precarious moves I stood within the Gates of Chaos, where I took in a vista of distinctly colored cliffs dropping at crazy angles into the seaward horizon.

The citadel of tormented stone at the Gates of Chaos deserved their name. The further I entered this land of hot wind and sun-baked rocks, the more I wanted out. Moving down a gully and lacking any familiar frame of reference or discernible patterns I lost all proportion of the dimensions of the land. The basalt monolith called Lot's Wife rose biblically above the surrounding ridges. How large it was or how far away I couldn't say. Corrugated layers of earth rose and fell leaving me light-headed and utterly alone in the strangely frightening and beautiful landscape.

Beyond the Gates of Chaos

At the bottom of a gorge I moved over the layered rocks of earlier ages, spanning perhaps a thousand generations in a single geologic stride. I drank from one of my two water bottles until it dripped empty. In these depressions there was no cooling wind to moderate the blazing sun as it baked the moisture from my body. My mapmaker was never here or he would have named it Land of Thirst. There was not a single tree to provide a spot of shade anywhere in sight. The land was so empty of life even my shadow had deserted me, or perhaps it was just the noon hour.

I kept moving until I reached the relative sanctuary of the next ridge where I halted to get my bearings. While orienting the map against the ground, I tried to recall Trevor's exact instructions: "Follow a long ravine towards the high rock of Lot's Wife. Stay on the north side of it and look to the west for a farmhouse on the far hillside."

Lot's Wife I could see, so I moved up the ravine Trevor had spoken of, or maybe near it. The weathered earth under my boots crumbled in a way that made me not trust my footing. Climbing this ravine was like walking on a tilted surface running with ball bearings. My boot prints in the sand lay like cat's paws on the sea awaiting erasure by the next wind.

Finally, I stood on the ridge next to Lot's Wife. I watched as dark clouds gathered over the peaks to the east and imagined a desperate situation if heavy rains came. Rocks and sand would slide down the saturated clay slopes carrying all things before them into the gorge. Previously dry riverbeds would swell into torrents, forcefully sweeping mud and boulders into the sea. There was little chance to survive here in a prolonged rainstorm.

To push these fears from my mind I returned to my reassuring habit of comparing the minutiae of my map against the landmarks around me. On the map were wild names for a wild country: the Devil's Cap, The Asses Ears, Castle Rock, even the single farmhouse I sought was marked as Distant Cottage. Then my target appeared across the valley where a fence delineated the desert from the pastured oasis of Distant Cottage.

The walking grew easier as I stayed on the ridge rolling away to the west. With one last ravine to cross, I dropped into the chasm at its narrowest point and began a slow crawling ascent up the final slope by climbing over the multi-hued clay dunes bulging from the inclined surface. Once again I felt the burden of a backpack that pulls at the shoulders, strains the back and teaches the legs the awful power of gravity.

At the fence line of Distant Cottage, the clay, sand and cactus magically turned to rolling pastures and lanes of shade-giving trees. This plateau of land mysteriously held the desert in check. I took it all in with a satisfying wide-eyed stare, as a blind man suddenly given eyes. This little house standing in its pastoral quietude, and lying apparently abandoned, held a magnified importance because of its position on the desert's edge. I called out, only to be answered by the rustle of wind and muffled sounds of a few cattle as they cropped the fragrant grass along the fence. I had already imagined a conversation with the cottage dweller: "Say, how did you find us way out here at Distant Cottage?" Proudly I'd reply, "I walked through the Gates of Hell to get here." Now, after my deliverance from the badlands, I stepped lightly, hardly noticing my previously heavy pack.

Along this plateau on the island's southwest corner, a trail led me past more neatly fenced pastures, roamed by a few cattle and sheep. A new lamb bounced limber-legged on the rolling hillside. A farmer led his loaded pack mule over a hill and another man mending a fence waved his hat at me as I passed. The sun hung low over the sea by the time I reached Man and Horse Cliffs. At my feet was a long straight drop to the bay of Shepherd's Hole. The name now seemed fitting, since that is where shepherds and sheep might find themselves after a careless step.

A man approached on a trail motorbike with a shotgun slung over one shoulder and a lifeless rabbit headed for the cooking pot hanging from his belt. This motorized cowboy was complete with blue jeans, Texas hat and high leather boots. I waved him over and asked permission to sleep on this spot for the night. He pointed to a lean-to where I could find shelter and then, without any questions as to my purpose here, rode off in a clatter of two-cycle motor noise and smoke. I was unsure if his indifference was due to the reserved English attitude, or because strangers crawling out of the desert asking to sleep in his field was commonplace.

I looked over the tin-roofed shelter the man offered and decided not to use it. I was content to sleep in the open pasture near the edge of the cliffs. For dinner I finished my bread with a can of cold English green peas, washed down with powdered milk as I listened to the shrieks of laughing gulls nesting in the cliff under me.

The sun vanished into the sea in a swirl of colors. I sat up well past twilight – silent and still as the night sky. It was not long ago you could count me among those men who live their lives in endless rehearsals for tomorrow. It was in remote places like these where my awakening to the present replaced the fears and desires of rethinking the past or planning the future, leaving only this infinite now.

Under a gray dawn the winds funneled up the face of the cliffs in rain-laden gusts. I packed my gear hastily, eager for the warmth in the exercise of walking. Swirling clouds hid much of the view this morning as I hiked the high plain northward. Faces belonging to cattle, framed by fences, momentarily studied me before vanishing into the mist. As the road straightened and continued along the high veld I might have been passing through the more temperate clime of an English countryside.

The clouds lifted as I turned down the paved lane leading to the governor's residence at Plantation House. I was lured down this path to see where Captain Joshua Slocum stayed for a few days as guest of a previous governor in 1898. Captain Slocum wrote of listening for Napoleon's ghost from under the blankets at night. The spacious white plantation house overlooked horse stables and a cricket field. The only people I saw here were two workers trimming and planting in the flower gardens.

Lacking an invitation from the governor, I continued along the road to a country store that served a cluster of houses given the collective name of Bishopsholme. I entered the store to beg some water and was soon surrounded by wide-eyed children. I bought and passed around a box of biscuits to the kids while I spoke to the elderly sisters who owned the shop. As soon as I opened my mouth they recognized me from an interview I had taped at the local radio station the day before my walk began.

A good way to get to know the Saints, I found, was to listen to their two-hour daily radio broadcast. It takes the place of an island newspaper by reporting anything and everything that happens locally. My interview was repeatedly broadcast between the two big news events of the week: one being that a car knocked over a road sign in town, the other from the local doctor describing as "nonsense" the rumor that people were catching venereal disease by swimming in the town's pool. "The only way to catch VD in the pool," the doctor explained over and over, "is if you are doing something other than swimming in it." It was evidently a persistent rumor because they rebroadcast the doctor's message every day during my stay on the island. I can imagine the unfaithful husband explaining to his wife that he must have caught some germs in the public pool. Most of the islanders, myself included, decided to stay clear of the pool just in case.

One of the boys from the store led me up to an old fort overlooking Jamestown. The path to High Knoll Fort was obvious even to me but I couldn't turn away an eager guide. Facing me while running backwards, the boy gave me a nonstop commentary on everything from his grandmother's house in the valley below, to stories of ghosts who lived in the fort. As with all the children of the Saints, each of the boy's sentences ended with "Sir," as if raised in a military school.

We entered the hundred-year-old stone fortress through a wooden drawbridge. The central courtyard, recently used as a quarantine yard for imported sheep and cattle, now stood empty. From the fort's walls heavy cannon pointed over the town and harbor. On the roof of what were once the soldier's quarters, there now stood satellite-tracking antennae.

Suddenly a heavy door on rusty iron hinges swung open and the startled boy ran backwards right into the stone wall. Our "ghost" was an American NASA technician who invited us into a room he had converted into a tracking station. On one side of the room stood an iron bed and oil lamp on a wood table. Across from it blinked a futuristic array of electronics. Information gathered here from satellites was relayed to the United States for the NASA space program. Our talkative boy now stood speechless as computers chattered and punched out data from a passing satellite onto a spool of paper. He had finally discovered his ghost of High Knoll Fort.

With Jamestown in sight, I resumed my trek alone. On a dry plateau I walked through the ridge top settlements of Halfway House, Cowpath and the assorted tin-covered shacks of Half Tree Hollow. Eventually, I stood at the top of a mountain of steps leading down Chapel Valley into Jamestown.

The town struck me as amazingly congested after coming from the quiet countryside. In reality, this capital city was a mere village of a couple thousand people. Before me, the 699 concrete steps called Jacob's Ladder were the last leg of my island circumnavigation. As I took in the scene, two boys brushed past me and launched themselves down the stairway by laying their shoulders across the steel pipe handrail with feet stretched over the opposite rail. In this way, they slid down the entire banister on their backs without ever touching a step. I timed their descent, which took some three minutes nonstop. A man standing next to me explained that long ago the servants from the hilltop kitchen delivered pots of stew to the garrison of soldiers below by balancing the pots on their stomachs as they slid down the banister in similar fashion.

I took the stairs of Jacob's Ladder one at a time and with each step relived a scene from the discoveries of the past three days of walking. The ladder deposited me in the center of town, a short walk from the small boat landing. I pulled boots off sore feet and rowed the dinghy slowly back to *Atom*, still safely anchored and rolling lazily in the swell.

I stayed on the island a few more days, long enough to witness the local phenomenon of Saturday night's town dance. Every Saturday evening, Jamestown swells to overflowing and there is even a traffic jam on the main street as people rendezvous from all corners of the island. In a dance hall on China Lane, hundreds of folks of all generations gathered to visit, party and dance to a variety of taped music. An outdoor bar and grill served the overflow crowd. Visiting sailors found plenty of friendly single girls on the dance floor. I was kept occupied by a lovely girl whose dark skin and flowery dress kept reminding me of nights on Mauritius. Like a scene from Cinderella, it all ended abruptly at midnight, for that is the beginning of Sunday, and in this regard at least, the Saints are ardently religious.

Boy slides down Jacob's Ladder into Jamestown

A light rain fell as I walked my date back to her home a few blocks away. As I turned alone towards the harbor the skies opened up with a downpour. Soon I could hear stones from the hillside above banging as they struck the tin-roofed buildings. As rain fell harder and rocks hit more frequently, I ran down the street with hands protecting my head. The run-off water from the cliffs above town was pulling down loosely held stones that struck with a resounding crash on the roofs, bounced off and landed with a thud on the streets around me. I recklessly ran down streets filling with rubble as if we were under cannon attack. I made it unscathed to the dinghy and laughed at the rain of stones as I rowed back to *Atom*.

Next morning, I filled my water jugs from the shore side tap, made last minute preparations for sea, and hoisted my anchors aboard. Busy getting the boat underway, setting up sails and wind vane and stowing my anchors, I hardly noticed the island retreating until I looked up and it was no longer there. I continued looking aft, feeling oddly like my stay there had all been a pleasant dream from which I was slowly awakening.

21 Martinique Revisited

Those who visit foreign nations, but who associate only with their own countrymen, change their climate, but not their customs; they see new meridians, but the same men; and with heads as empty as their pockets, return home with traveled bodies, but untraveled minds.

- Charles Caleb Colton

Atom's sails bent to the thrust of the trade wind, comfortably surging and rolling along her 3,800-mile course towards Martinique in the West Indies. Again, my Triton and I worked together as one. We stepped lightly over these gentle seas of the South Atlantic and I breathed deeply from the same fair wind she caught in her sails.

Life settled into that familiar sea routine that makes the days pass easily. Morning twilight found me scanning the skies for a round of sextant star sights. Soon after my position is plotted on the chart the flaming sun emerges and instantly another warm tropic day is born. I scan the horizon for some familiar sign of human life: wisps of smoke from a passing ship or airplane contrail overhead. Nothing appears. We are truly alone and I find it comforting. Usually for breakfast I have cold oatmeal with raisins, cinnamon and a few spoons of powdered milk all soaked in water. For a change of taste I fry up a cornmeal pancake instead and top it off with my last mashed overripe banana from St. Helena.

On these fine days of settled weather, hours drifted by as I sat leaning back against the shaded side of the mast, watching *Atom's* progress through the water, sometimes writing in my journal with notes from the islands in our wake. My midday meal these days, as on so many days before, was often a sandwich of sprouted mung beans and sliced onion smeared with a mustard and pepper sauce on cornbread.

Twice each day I rechecked the sails and rigging, which at this point in the voyage, were deteriorating rapidly. A few stitches added to a seam before it opened up further carried me through another day.

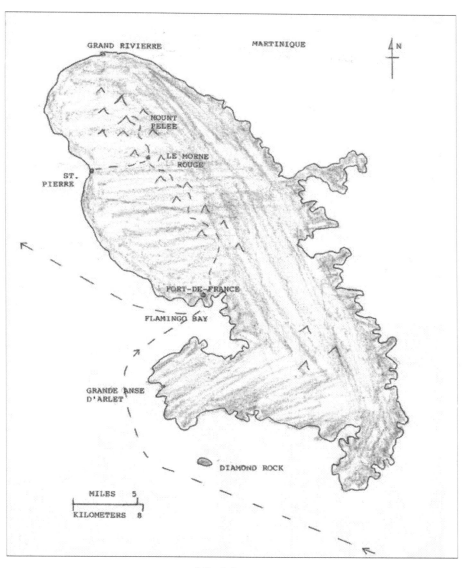

Martinique map

If clouds or sleep caused me to miss the morning's star sights, I'd shoot the sun twice in the afternoon. Across the South Atlantic, the noon-to-noon log invariably noted 100 to 120 miles of progress. In late afternoon's waning heat, a saltwater bucket shower followed a vigorous exercise session. Lately, while they lasted, my favored evening meal was a dish of rice and curried vegetables.

In the evening I read by oil lamp, then watched the swaying stars overhead until sleep came. Yes, I recklessly slept through most the night in these serene and empty waters. A few hours before dawn I'd look out the hatch to see my old companion, Halley's Comet. Its fifty million-mile-long trail continued to mark a parallel course to mine, though pointed in the opposite direction with its tail streaming out towards me and its head pointing to the lands I'd left, as if to lure me back.

At 10 degrees South latitude and 10 degrees West longitude, I sailed through an area unusually thick with shoals of flying fish bursting into the air attempting flights of record length. Several times a day I heard the thump of a flying fish stranded on deck and I moved quickly to throw them back to the sea. At night, when inside the cabin, I suspended lifeguard duty and left them to their fate. One morning I counted thirty-four fish had sacrificed themselves on the deck. *Atom* could have fed a crew of a dozen cats on this passage.

In this region, I was visited by flocks of birds that considered *Atom* a resting station on their migration route. Except for being of a brown and gray color, they resembled crows, especially in their bold, thuggish disposition. At night they perched everywhere in the rigging and all over the deck where they screeched and bickered with each other ceaselessly. On the second night of their occupation, one even flew in through the open hatch. In a scene nicely suited to an old horror movie, I struggled with the demented bird flapping about my head until I abandoned the cabin and he followed me out.

On deck the birds showed no fear of me, which they demonstrated by flying around my head, crossly shrieking their annoyance at my presence. I tried chasing them away by flailing my arms and shouting like a madman only to have them circle the boat once and land even more ill-tempered. Exasperated and a little frightened, I snapped a towel at one hovering in front of my face. It fell into the cockpit, flopping about with a broken wing. His shipmates eyed me now with more respect. I felt ashamed at my violence as I knocked the injured bird unconscious with an oar and dropped him into the sea. Now these innocent creatures knew humans were dangerous animals. By next morning they were gone and I was alone once more.

A light-air day in the Southeast Trades

Nearing the northern limit of the Southeast Trades I encountered squalls of rain and gray, overcast skies. One memorable but short-lived storm struck during the night, catching me asleep and laying *Atom* on her side. In a rush to reduce sail, I nearly stepped on deck without my harness, then thought again and clipped it on at the companionway. On the slanted foredeck a breaking wave slapped the side of the hull, showering the cobwebs from my mind. As I disconnected the whisker pole it came loose from my grip, knocking me into the lifelines with my feet dragging over the side in the warm sea. Some skin scrapped from my knee was the only damage as I pulled myself back to the deck and finished reefing down.

This brief storm marked the beginning of a long trial. My progress slowed from one hundred to ninety, then under eighty miles a day. Showers and shifty winds arrived hourly. I could have spent all my waking moments adjusting course and sails to best advantage and perhaps saved a day or two on this leg of the voyage. Instead, as long as I was moving in the right general direction, I tended to let things ride as they were. I'd learned many times that a course error frequently corrected itself with the next squall and wind shift saving me the trouble of resetting the sails and steering. In any case, I had no reason to brood much over a slow day; a day saved here likely would pay no greater dividends than one spent anywhere else.

In the logbook I recorded:

> *April 1 – DOLDRUMS! 2 degrees South, 31 degrees West. Drifted into the Doldrums today. Heavy rain and shifting winds. A ship passed heading towards Brazil – the first sighted on this passage. Today we are sailing past Arquipelago De Fernando De Noronha some one hundred miles to our southwest. It's a big name for a group of islets so small they are barely indicated on my chart. Got laid over by a sudden gust of wind this afternoon and my plate of carefully tended bean sprouts was tossed to the floor.*

> *April 2 – Last night again I awoke to a howling windstorm. I clearly had too much sail up, yet I stayed in my bunk hoping it would all settle down. It must have been several minutes before I made the decision to get up and reef sails and by that time both sails had ripped and the mast was shuddering under the load. Today I was hit by at least twenty rain squalls. But only one in four brought enough wind to require a reef. I find myself more and more waiting until the last minute to make a decision for action. I'm growing tired of this game and ready for some settled weather.*

> *April 4 – We drifted across the equator sometime last night, crossing into the North Atlantic at 33 degrees West longitude. I must be just barely across the line, having progressed only about ten miles in the past twenty-four hours.*

The oppressive heat was confirmed by my bulkhead-mounted hydrometer, which consistently measured humidity over 90 percent. The steady drizzle was only contrasted with heavy downpours. I stood naked in the rain to cool myself, moving as listlessly as the sails that caught the fickle zephyrs of wind. Sails and sailor hung slack in mutual lassitude. I longed to hear the sweet song of rising wind in the rigging instead of just the hiss of rain droplets hitting the sea. My old mainsail and jib flopped side to side with the boat's roll and seemed to say, "We've come so far. But give us a wind and we'll show you we have many miles left in us yet." Still we hung there, together in the sultry air beneath a glowering purple-tinged afternoon sky. On the close horizon a black cloud released a charge of lightning. I held my breath in anticipation of its thundering voice rolling over the sea.

A long time later the sea surface stirred. As slippery as a fish after the thorough bottom-scrubbing I'd given her in St. Helena, *Atom* cut a wrinkle across the glassy waters. The push of a single hand could send her moving as easily as this barely detectable wind. At first we moved silently and level as an iceboat sailing a frozen lake. I sat motionless so as not to break the spell. Though barely perceptible, after twelve hours I was confident I'd emerged from those interminable Doldrums into the realm of the Northeast Trades.

Within a few days *Atom* was again averaging her top speed running beam-on to the wind. The bumpy ride among the curling white horses on the wave crests was jarring after so many days of flat water, but the thrill of the unaccustomed speed made me press on with all the sail she could take. I looked at the straining sails and thought, "Now, show us what you're made of, my old friends."

On my chart I noted the coast of South America slowly slip by 300 miles away off the port beam. First Brazil, where the mouth of the Amazon flowed in a vast unending exhalation from the heart of the continent, carrying its earthy waters undiluted as far as a hundred miles offshore. Then French Guiana, Surinam and British Guyana fell astern as well. Even the rum-soaked island of Barbados, when its turn came, we passed unseen at a safe distance of fifty miles.

When the cloud-capped mountains of Martinique pierced the horizon, I felt the emotions of coming home after a long absence. I had last seen Martinique's green mantle of rain forest from this very deck some two and a half years earlier on the return leg of a voyage from Bermuda to Trinidad. Now in familiar waters with familiar land in sight, I longed for the smells and sights and sounds of the tropic island, from the spiced air and Creole chatter of the marketplace to the hidden creatures of the forest.

As the island jewel drew closer I recognized its features. It was a gorgeous day of puffy white cumulus, flying fish taking wing, and the air filled with the cries of tropic birds. Along the south coast we rounded Diamond Rock, a tiny but tall islet that at one time held an English fort that peppered cannon shots down on French shipping.

Atom sails across Fort-De-France Bay

On the sheltered west coast of Martinique, I was finally out of reach of the rolling Atlantic swell. As the ocean current carried me along, my eyes feasted on the greenness. I drew deep breaths of the aroma of growing forests mixed with the perfume of island spices. Around a point of land emerged a sandy bay where a fishing village centered itself around a white church steeple. Pulled up on the beach were several high-bowed *gommiers*, the outboard powered fishing boats hacked out of a single gum-tree log. One was visible on the west horizon. Soon he would be "A Miquelon" as the locals say when their boat is out of sight of land and they feel they have gone as far from home as Miquelon, a French island off Canada.

In mid-afternoon I released the anchor among a crowd of some fifty yachts in Fort-De-France Bay near the stone walls of Fort Louis. From on deck I watched the chaos of activity along the waterfront's main boulevard with detached interest. Happy to be here, yes, but not yet ready to join the bustle of society. Instead of rushing ashore, I prepared a meal and then fell into undisturbed sleep.

On Sunday I awoke to church bells and later rowed ashore to check in with the customs agent at their waterfront office. I then went for a long walk around town, reacquainting myself with its narrow streets and tropical Parisian atmosphere. The locals here are all French citizens and generally regard themselves more French than West Indian. If there were pro-independence feelings, they were not visible during my stay here. The Martinicans are too busy enjoying the prosperity of French rule to disrupt their lives with the radical ideas of self-rule the neighboring islands demanded of their standoffish British masters.

Sidewalk cafes are daily filled with people watching the passing scenery and sipping punch *vieux*. I read somewhere of an old sailor who claimed that any land looks good and every woman fair after a long sea journey. It is doubly true when the landfall is Martinique. The women are distractingly beautiful, dress in the latest fashions and carry themselves with proud elegance. It's enough to bring any sailor to heel, especially if he speaks French.

Walking through town I hoped it wasn't too obvious how I stared at the long, dark ladies parading by. In some way, I saw the island girl I had loved in every woman that passed me on the street and found myself imagining they were her. The reality was that I received no smile of recognition from these strangers. My romantic or erotic visions did not overcome my shyness, nor did any girl here express the slightest interest in me – just another tourist, or worse – a sailor with empty pockets.

Like most French territories, the prices here are out of this world and I found myself as poor as a Haitian refugee swimming ashore at Miami Beach. Fortunately, money and women were not my chief concern as I planned my exploration of the last island I wanted to visit before returning home. My earlier visit to Martinique had been brief and I had not gone far into the interior. Now was my chance to correct that mistake.

Before setting out to walk across the island, I strengthened my legs for several days by running along the waterfront at dawn and then again in the evenings. By studying a guidebook and detailed maps, I settled on a route along the mountain roads that lead north to the volcano peak of Mount Pelee and then back to the coastal town of St. Pierre.

I shouldered my pack, cinched up its straps, and began my walk through the daily traffic snarl in Fort-De-France, which on this day was compounded by a street protest march. This was no anti-colonialism protest but rather hundreds of striking government workers blocking the narrow streets carrying signs demanding higher wages and benefits. A man at the head of the mob whipped up enthusiasm by roaring his age-old complaints into a bullhorn. "Give us more money for less work," was the demand to a colonial government asking for just the opposite.

Along the River Madame, I passed the outdoor fish and vegetables markets where a Creole band of brass horns and bongo drums played a lively session. The hectic town apparently behind me, I walked Route De Balata as it steadily climbed towards the mountains. Unfortunately, it seemed everyone in Fort-De-France was leaving town on this route and there was just enough width to the road for two small cars to pass with precious little curb for a pedestrian to squeeze by. Cars even climbed the curb when trucks blasted by with blaring horns and noxious exhaust in their wake. I'd not want to walk this road again but there was no other road or path available heading north through the center of the island.

Along this tiresome route I met Bernard, a local unemployed electrician who had missed out on Martinique's prosperity. He was returning on foot to his village after a visit to the welfare office for his monthly check. We walked together, dodging traffic and getting acquainted, until we arrived at Balata Village. At his apartment we shared a bowl of salad, bread and cheese while Bernard looked over my map, pointing out the scenic areas, freshwater springs and campsites ahead of me.

Beyond Balata, traffic became scarce and less threatening and I enjoyed walking under shady trees adorned with mosses and vines. Fragrant flower and perfume plantations drifted by and reminded me that the island's original name was "Madinina" (Island of Flowers). All around me were heady scents and the colors of hibiscus, oleander, flame-red frangipani and bunches of anthuriums. Rows of papaya trees draped leafy branches over ripening fruit. Women carried armloads of flowers back to pastel-colored homes. Flowery, clinging vines decorated delicate fences. Like in Bora Bora on the other side of the world, long sticks of French bread hung out of mailboxes. Martinique fully awakened my memories of the other French islands I loved so much.

Under each bridge on the road was at least one family picnicking alongside a splashy stream. I stopped frequently to converse and always received the same warnings: "Be careful of thieves. Watch out for snakes." As for thieves, I carried little of value. The snakes I believed, could watch out for me, as they always had before.

The road tunneled through the mountain at Duex Choux and emerged at the entrance to a wide valley. A footpath led to the top of a hill where I made camp for the night at an open-sided shelter in a public park. Before me I enjoyed a view of forests of banana fields and in the distance, the lower slopes of Mount Pelee, whose peak lay hidden under the dark clouds. At day's end I unrolled my sleeping bag and lay myself out on the wooden picnic table. Lightning bugs decorated the darkness and the wind soughing through the trees combined its voice with distant waterfalls, or perhaps another fast, rock-bedded creek.

By dawn I was back on the road in a gray rain that persisted through the day. Banana fields spread across the valley. Along the muddy trails, tractors pulled wagons that workers loaded with bunches of the green fruit. I couldn't resist singing… "Come, Mr. Tally Mon, tally me banana (Daylight come and he wan' go home)."

In the country village of Morne Rouge, I stepped into a shop to buy bread and vegetables. Greeting the woman shopkeeper in French brought a continuous light-hearted rapid-fire Creole patois, the meaning of which was lost on me. To be sociable, I mutely nodded yes or no when it seemed appropriate until she turned to chat up a more conversant customer.

Outside town I turned onto a road snaking its way up the base of Mount Pelee. Eighty years earlier, this volcanic mountain abruptly blew its top. Within minutes, over thirty thousand people in the villages below perished under hot lava and poison gases. These days the mountain is again at rest, with its flanks only lightly repopulated.

Where the road ended, I followed a path, in a teeming rain, that by now had me soaked through. Progress was slow and none too steady on the wet, moss-covered rocks and muddy holes. Wood stakes and signposts marked the trail but they were not at all needed for I easily found my way by following the trail of litter. If I took more than ten steps without encountering a piece of trash, I knew I was off the path. How sad to see, throughout this otherwise beautiful island, the trash strewn every place people had passed.

The trail leveled off and from what little I could see through the fog, I determined that I had reached the summit and was walking the rim of the volcanic crater. Along this ridge I found a tin-roofed rest house with walls built of stone blocks. I entered the one-room shelter through an open door to wait out the rain. Inside were a wooden table and two hard bunks with room to take four steps in either direction – such unaccustomed mountaintop luxury.

A cold wind blew in through the swinging door and a broken window. I fortified myself with cups of tea heated over the meager flame of the solid fuel tablets I carried. Lacking a watch or the sun to look at, I guessed the time by the way the gloomy afternoon sky gave way to a dark and stormy night.

The blackness of night gave way to another chill gray morning. The corners of my roof wept from the endless light rain. As I lifted open the unhinged door a cloud rolled in to lay its damp hand on everything it touched. Strange to say but I was at home in this cloud-wrapped haven, despite the harsh environment and minor discomforts.

With long hours of little else to do, I worked, as I did at sea, to cultivate a freedom from anticipation – that urgent thief who steals the minute-to-minute awareness of life. I was content to stay another day in the good company of raw nature and a book by Thoreau. The philosophic adventures of *Walden* where Thoreau homesteaded in a forest cabin outside his New England village in the 1840s took on an entirely new dimension from the quietude of this dewy mountaintop stone house. I reconfirmed here a lesson I'm condemned to learn over and over again: our days are stolen by our constant grasping at the phantoms of future happiness as we think about living – rather than living itself – trapping us in our yesterdays and tomorrows. If children are not burdened by the knowledge that our pursuits may end in sorrow, that love may end in separation, that birth gives way to old age and death, then why should we dwell there if we are no less intelligent than a child?

For two days I strolled in mist and rain around the volcano's rim or just sat thoughtfully on my mountaintop porch, letting the world rush by unheard and unseen below me. I indulged my thoughts, as a disciple of Thoreau, somewhat out of step with the majority of society and feeling the better for it. Little by little, the silence of the mountain revealed it was not silent at all. On my first day alone here I perceived the silent spaces between the music of the wind and rain on the grassy slopes. By the second day my nerves and senses were restored to the point where every common thing becomes exceptional, as if the world was created anew with every sighing draft of wind. I thought of the native American concept of existence as a dream state, as expressed in the Aztec poem:

> *It is not true, it is not true*
> *that we come on this earth to live.*
> *We come only to sleep, only to dream.*

The clouds never lifted from my mountain perch, yet I was spiritually recharged as I jogged down to lower elevations on the road back towards Morne Rouge. There I joined another road toward the coastal town of St. Pierre. Down in the lower valley I emerged into sunlight and looked back at a mountain still enveloped in that cloud of secret gifts. This road to the west continued through banana fields, bordered by straight rows of coconut, royal palm and giant bamboo. I noted mango, orange, pineapple, avocado and custard apple fruits all flourishing alongside the houses and giving the valley the appearance of a life of perpetual fruit gathering and ease.

St. Pierre is a town facing the sea with its back up against a tempestuous volcano. I entered through the rear, walking down the narrow streets and alleys towards the waterfront. Once considered the center of civilization in the Caribbean, St. Pierre was devastated by Pelee's eruption in 1902. It now has the feeling of a town half resurrected. Much of the debris of former buildings still lay about in heaps and piles. The current buildings are built on top of the broken foundations of earlier buildings.

A story goes that the city's sole survivor of the volcano was found when rescuers pulled a man from an underground jail cell where he was protected from the tremendous blast of heat. Of the ships anchored in the bay, all were sunk at their moorings by the tidal wave that accompanied the eruption except for one ship that was getting underway. Her deck crew perished but the captain, choking for breath, managed to steer his ship away and bring news of the disaster to the outside world.

It was Saturday, which in St. Pierre means market day. The main street along the waterfront bustled with people crowded around the vendor's stands selling fruit, vegetables and fish. The gommier fishing boats were hauled out of the sea by volunteering hands and a bucket brigade that moved the day's catch from boats to vendors. On the beach I sat on the sand with my pack as a backrest, mentally retracing the steps of my last walk across my last island on this voyage.

My return to Fort-De-France was in a shared taxi – the preferred method of transport between towns. This was my first car ride in several months and if I thought the local drivers reckless as they passed me while I walked, the moment we took off I wished I were back taking my chances on foot. Our driver drove like he was in a life or death rally. Small towns passed us in a flash of buildings and narrowly missed chickens, dogs and pedestrians. The dark Frenchman next to me was surely a longtime veteran of this route, since he fell asleep minutes outside St. Pierre and was undisturbed by the sudden stops and starts and finally had to be shaken awake by the driver when we arrived an hour later at Fort-De-France.

Back aboard *Atom* in Flamingo Bay, I watched from deck as an island sloop, barely 25-feet long, skillfully tacked into the anchorage being sailed alone by a black West Indian. When close by, he lowered his patch-worked sails and stepped forward to release a homemade grapnel anchor. I called him over for dinner on *Atom* and that night I learned Joe Brown was a preacher and native of the nearby island of St. Lucia. He told me of his numerous passages between the islands in his old wooden sloop, carrying light cargos of island goods. Besides being a proselytizing Rastafarian – he brought his bible with him to dinner – he also brought over a thick, roughly finished clay bowl from which he ate my rice and vegetables. Shunning plasticware, he only took food from his earthy-tasting bowl.

On this trip to Martinique, Joe carried a cargo of vegetables and had contracted to deliver a motorcycle back to St. Lucia. The next day, after unloading his perishables at the dock, I assisted Preacher Joe in disassembling a 500 CC motorbike and loading the parts aboard his boat. When we finished the job the bike's frame, engine and wheels took up all the available space within the small cabin where it was partially protected from the ocean spray.

On May 4th I walked to the airport where I met my mother, Helen, who had flown out from Detroit to meet me for a one-week vacation. I was relieved to see she had brought some cash from my bank account, since I was down to my last ten dollars. It had been a long two years since our last meeting. After so long an absence, I convinced her to stay with me aboard *Atom* where we could see each other all day, instead of me on the boat and her miles away in an expensive tourist hotel. To accommodate her, and her hard luggage, I cleared away the accumulated sailing gear, Zulu war clubs, gramophone and other semi-precious cargo from the cramped forward cabin, which then became her suite.

We rented a Renault car to tour the northern part of the island, tracing the same route I walked the week before. This time we followed the road beyond Mount Pelee all the way to the last fishing village at the tip of the island. The road ended here between cliffs that wedged in the village of Grand Riviere so tightly it looked as if a good hard rain could wash the houses into the sea. We watched as fishermen returned to the half circle cove in their gommiers after a day at sea. Using long oars, they maneuvered the boats backwards through the surf. When close enough, a dozen lean men rushed waist-deep into the water, grasping the boat's gunwales and pulling it onto the stone-covered beach. Logs were laid under the keel and, by force of muscle, they rolled the boats stern-to above the high tide mark. A few paces above the landing they weighed their catch on scales and dropped the fish into their customer's bags.

A gommier comes ashore at a fishing village on the north coast of Martinique

One morning we sailed *Atom* out the harbor to explore along the island's south coast. That afternoon we approached the anchorage at Grande Anse d'Arlet. The wind was fickle as it came over the hills so we entered under power. The motor quickly overheated. Smoke from the engine room was already pouring out the cabin hatch as I let go the anchor among a tightly packed group of newer yachts. The smoke and the rattle of our anchor chain awoke our lounging neighbors who were mostly French charterers lying naked on deck to soak up the sun. A few stood up and glanced over at our intrusion with an air of mild annoyance and I was dutifully embarrassed at our less than peaceful entry. "Are those people naked?" my mother asked with wide eyes.

That night the wind shifted to onshore and a choppy swell rolled into the anchorage. By dawn we had been long awake from the extreme rolling and the snatching of the anchor chain against the bow roller. I now saw we had drifted dangerously close to the beach and most of the charter fleet had already fled under power. I hastily lifted the anchor aboard and tacked out to sea even before serving our morning tea.

I had gotten a bit careless here and my mother no doubt wondered how I managed to get nearly round the world unscathed. For several more hours we pounded into strong rain-laden headwinds. On each tack, *Atom* heeled sharply and the sea often crashed aboard, soaking us thoroughly. I hooked a harness around my mother's waist and she wedged herself into a corner of the cockpit where she remained without complaint until we gained the protection of Flamingo Bay. *Atom* took the day somewhat worse with seawater soaking into the lockers and a new rip in the mainsail.

To make up for the rough treatment she received under sail, I took my mother out to dinner at one of those high-priced, small-portion French restaurants. As we walked back to the harbor down a dark street she asked if this was a safe place to walk at night. "One of the main differences between the French islands and her neighbors," I explained authoritatively, "is the very low crime rate...." Before I could finish my lecture, a scooter raced up behind us carrying two teen-aged boys. At the last second they swerved towards us and the passenger reached out and nearly snatched my mother's purse away, but she was too quick for them.

It was perhaps not the vacation experience she had imagined, but the next day her visit was over all too soon. Although we did not speak much about it, my mother was obviously relieved that my long voyage was nearly finished, and equally relieved I had not make a hasty decision about marrying a girl from the islands. I wanted to tell her about the ways the voyage had changed me, to explain how, as the nautical miles remaining of the voyage decreased, the mind miles separating me from home increased. When faced with the inexpressible, nothing need be said.

22 The Blue Highway

Everything can be found at sea, according to the spirit of your quest.

- Conrad's "Mirror Of The Sea"

Along the west coast of Martinique, *Atom* moved quick and easy through the familiar waters, both of us aware we were homeward bound. I looked up again at the mainsail, so old and patched, but still pulling like a steady old plow horse. On my chart I plotted a nonstop passage of 1,400 miles through the islands of the Caribbean to Ft. Lauderdale. I knew most of these island coasts along my course almost pebble by pebble, and knew also that to avoid the frequent calms on the leeward sides of the high islands, I should give them a berth of at least fifteen miles.

I sailed there on a glorious beam reach — a point of sail where the boat balances well with steady heel and little rolling as she reaches out with long steady strides parallel to the lines of wave tops. The navigation chores, initially, were nothing more than counting off the passing island peaks as they appeared in succession off the starboard bow. Even from this distance the volcanic peaks stood out bold and dark against the blue sky. At night I identified the main coastal settlements by the clusters of lights shimmering on the horizon.

The long and high island of Dominica appeared first. Several years earlier I'd walked through the rugged interior jungles of that last stronghold of the Carib Indians. Here they held out against the white colonists for another century and a half after Columbus visited the island. Originally from coastal South America, the Caribs populated the islands from Trinidad to Puerto Rico with their frail-looking dugout canoes. Today, just a few of these remaining pure natives of the Caribbean reside on an Indian reservation on the harborless windward coast of Dominica.

My visit to Dominica three years earlier occurred during a time I call The Great Banana Glut of '83. When I approached the anchorage at Prince Rupert Bay at the town of Portsmouth, I was met two miles out by an outboard-powered skiff bearing two young men shouting at me to buy their bananas. Their impatient tone was something between a demand and a prayer as they lashed their boat alongside uninvited. I kept sailing, towing them along with me until they received a fair price for their box of ripe bananas. As I approached closer to the island, they cast off just as another boat boy arrived with more bananas at half the price of the first boat. So I bought more, thinking how clever I was not to have bought too many earlier. I'd heard of cheaper by the dozen but these were cheaper by the mile.

Once *Atom's* anchor was down more boat boys surrounded us, dropping banana crates on deck and begging a mere dollar per crate. Such a bargain I couldn't resist. In minutes I had ten crates of ripe bananas filling the cockpit and deck. Along the shore, boat boys were spreading the word, "That man out there loves bananas and can't get enough."

Finally, through binoculars, I saw the town docks piled high with ripe and rotting bananas. Later I found out the last two scheduled banana ships never arrived to pick up the entire island's crop. Despite my little contribution, this was a disaster for the local economy. Stupefied by my greed, I spent the next week eating almost nothing but bananas. I baked banana muffins, boiled them into preserves, and dried them in strips on deck in the sun until I couldn't look at another banana. Just as a sweet potato instantly reminds me of New Guinea, I still can't eat a banana without the fond memory of those days in Dominica coming back in perfect detail.

The French island of Guadeloupe hove into view the next morning even before Dominica fell out of sight. I well remembered exploring this high, lush island three years before, traveling its dusty roads through sugar cane plantations and into highlands of waterfalls, forests and small farms.

The following morning I greeted three more old friends: the triplet islands of Montserrat, St. Kitts and Nevis. St. Kitts' symmetrical cone-shaped Mount Misery wore a cloud halo over its peak. Behind the mountain's flanks, the glow of an orange-yellow sunrise gave to the island the appearance of a dark painting, cut out and pasted on the horizon. Due to the island's small size and the lack of proper harbors, this group was still so isolated in the 1980s that it was said the blacks spoke their distinct Creole laced with a trace of Irish brogue picked up from the early settlers.

The Dutch Island of Saba loomed up from ahead, rising sheer in one huge rock pyramid. As I passed close to its landing dock I exchanged waves with a fisherman casting a line from shore. High up and then down into the island's extinct volcano rests the main town, appropriately named The Bottom. On the top outside edge of the crater sits the village of Top. From my short distance offshore, I watched people walk along the road and disappear over the crater rim on their way into the pit of the verdant ex-cauldron.

At this point I turned downwind for the hundred-mile crossing of Anegada Passage. With current and wind in my favor, I crossed most of it during the night and by next morning lay a few miles off St. Thomas in the U.S. Virgin Islands. Lovely as the Virgins are, I had spent enough time in their over-developed, touristy, charter boat-filled waters to know they held little of interest on this particular voyage.

In the center of Virgin Island Passage, I sailed close to the bleached white cliffs of Sail Rock. It does resemble a sailing ship from afar, one with sails set but forever riding at anchor. Beyond Sail Rock I turned north into the open waters east of the Bahamas. For the remainder of the day, the silhouette of distant Puerto Rico bent the horizon. By night, a glow of diffused light pointed the way to the city of San Juan.

The darkness that night was further interrupted by curious rapid flashes of light over the straits between Puerto Rico and the Virgin Islands. When I tried to discern some natural or man-made pattern to the lights, the silence was broken by a shrill whine that instinctively made me duck and think of an incoming missile. Probably I was sailing past an area where the U.S. Navy was holding war games and the intense light flashes were the firing of a ship's cannon. Perhaps in the darkness, my stealthy vessel had sailed near a target. They could have incinerated me in a moment and who would know – just another luckless sailor lost in the Bermuda Triangle. The next afternoon a U.S. Navy ship passed close off my stern. As the gray hull thundered by, the crew lining the side deck shouted greetings while *Atom* footed across the sea in her butterfly stance of sails set wing on wing. In their wake floated an empty whiskey bottle.

Somewhere northeast of Turks and Caicos Islands I lifted a five-gallon water jug at an awkward angle while transferring it into the forward water tank. The sharp pain of a pinched nerve raced up my spine. I crawled carefully and slowly aft to my bunk where I lay tormented for two days enduring shots of paralyzing pain at each roll of the boat. As I lay there, I kept an eye on the telltale compass above my bunk. Fortunately, the weather remained fair and *Atom* mostly looked after herself until I recovered. Emerging slowly on deck, I sighted the long, and low, snake-like island of Eleuthera in the central Bahamas.

In the Northwest Providence Channel I navigated from island to island in company with several other ships taking this shortcut through the islands to Florida. At last, the reef-crowded Bahamas lay astern and I aimed *Atom's* bow across the Straits of Florida. The sun's great orange coin dropped for the last time into the sea off the bow. My seemingly endless days of riding the winds and chasing constellations across the sky as I furrowed my path across the seas, were nearing an end. The events of these two years branded my memory as a banquet spread before a starving man. Even now, these many years later, the sights and sounds come back with surprising clarity.

Cruising sailors wander the world's oceans, tucking into islands here and there, staying "as long as it's fun" as they like to say. I had pursued that kind of aimless travel before and would do so again, but this particular voyage carried with it a sense of purposefulness that focused my energies and brought me some of what I was looking for, and more that I hadn't expected. A sailor will go to sea again and again because the accumulated burdens and distractions of shore life seldom satisfy our genetic desire to roam through the world, experiencing nature one-on-one. At sea our expectations dwindle to the essentials and the immediate: are the sails trimmed and the boat on course, will we clear that reef off the bow, is the squall on the horizon heading our way?

From the afterdeck, I stood holding the backstay with one hand and looked beyond *Atom's* foamy wake as if I might see my way back to certain lands. Sunsets often remind me of a girl back there, a reminder as ethereal as the fragrance of flowers wafting in the open hatch above my bunk. I wondered, as time passed, did she also feel nostalgic about me? Did a sail on the horizon ever cause her a second wistful look?

Somewhere along the way, that nagging loneliness slinked away in the awareness of the difference between being lonely and being alone. Someone considering a solitary voyage, but afraid of being alone, should understand that they merely fear being face-to-face with themselves. If you have a reasonable grip on reality, it is a false fear. Besides learning to know yourself and your abilities, there are other benefits to voyaging alone. When truly alone on the wide ocean, your senses become acute, dreams more vivid, and the landfalls sweetly emotional. Even with the most personable companion, a group of two experiences a totally different world than the lone sojourner. Their impact on the environment, and each other, can be too overwhelming for them to observe the subtle, natural state of things. When ashore, the lone traveler cannot help but disturb the social order of the places he visits. Two travelers disturb it exponentially, without absorbing one half the experience.

I also had the added benefit of no one to say that my temperament at sea was disagreeable. Like Thoreau, I had yet to find a companion as companionable as solitude. Over that long road of 243 days alone on the ocean's blue highways, I learned to live within and beyond myself. In one of his books or articles, sailor guru Bernard Moitessier called it "sailing in a state of grace." You won't find it on your first day or week alone offshore. But with experience comes a competency and calm acceptance that brings peace to your world.

It is true the solo sailor has perhaps sometimes too much time on his hands. Through many days of solitary reflection, the soul alone on a broad horizon tends to imagine himself the center of the universe and proprietor of all that is wise. It's a compelling and foolish fantasy to indulge. At best, if his mind tended towards wisdom before he went to sea, he may cultivate it further out there to come home wise enough to live in the simple pleasures of the moment with a compassionate connectedness to everything around him.

The voyage nears its end

   Atom had also evolved. Ill-suited gadgets had gone over the side to be replaced by honest seamanship skills. Admittedly, my conservation in acquiring the latest comforts and electronic technology for my boat was a fortunate result of my poverty. If the money had been available, I'd surely have been tempted to buy more equipment, ending up slavishly devoted to things of doubtful value. Society's cult of spending large and living little, I turned on its head. I had long ago given up reliance on the boat's engine and got along well with only a sculling oar and a large dose of patience and forethought. My next projects on *Atom* were to remove her tired, old engine to make her the pure sailing craft that suited both our temperaments.

   With the graceful motion that only sail can give, *Atom* flew across the Gulf Stream, pushing up a curling bow wave that dipped as it ran along her sides. A sign of her designer's gifted hand revealed itself off the stern, where barely any evidence of her passing was visible in the bubbling waters of our wake. Taking a lesson from *Atom*, I strive to follow the minimalist creed, to make the most of the least. In my wake I leave little on this earth; in my passing, take even less.

When I sighted the Miami skyline, I had the curious feeling of not wanting the voyage to end. It had become a way of life that I wished could go on and on. Perhaps I feared it marked an end of youth and freedom when there were still so many places undiscovered. How we worry and make excuses for our inaction – we convince ourselves that someone needs us here. Shortly before I began this world voyage, my 93-year-old grandmother was moved to a nursing home after having lived with my parents in my unused bedroom for several years. On a trip to Michigan, I visited her where she lay ill with a "weak heart," the doctor told us. I sat on the side of her bed thinking of all the lives she had touched over the years. She was so weak she could barely sit up or speak more than a few words at a time. "How's your boat doing?" she asked. "Are you going on this trip you've been working toward?"

"The boat's ready, Grandma, but I can't leave now with you so ill," I said as I fought back the tears.

"Jimmy," she said softly, "I've lived a good, long life and I'm ready to meet God. I'm not afraid. Go on your sailing trip and don't worry about me. I won't be here when you get back but don't be afraid for me and don't be afraid for yourself. Go now and see the world." She was one of the few people to encourage me to begin this trip. At the end of her life she realized, if she had not before, that to worry over finances and perceived obligations was wasting precious life. I went, and though we never actually spoke again, we remain close in my thoughts. I always felt her courage and selflessness was her greatest gift to me.

In many ways I had come full circle. Curiously, when you consider the effect of following the sun across twenty-four time zones, I was now one solar day younger than if I had stayed at home. After a circumnavigation and two years absence, there is a sense that somehow things have changed upon your return, as if to mirror the distance traveled. Of course, nothing of consequence had changed in Ft. Lauderdale during those two years. It was slightly more crowded, the marine police a bit more diligent in enforcing city council ordinances against unwanted live-aboard sailors, and the cost of living ever higher. The sameness of the city brought within me an impression of closing a circle, of coming back, in more than a literal sense, to the same place it all began. To circumnavigate the world is not important. Many a solo-sailor have made perfect, and perfectly pointless, circumnavigations. It's how you live and sail that gives the journey any meaning.

Of course, solitary homecomings are bound to be anti-climatic. The voyage had been full of promise until the goal was realized. Strangely, the fulfillment was tinged with betrayal. My distant oceans had been crossed and my mountains climbed and still there remained the question; what does a man do after he has fulfilled his obsession? Then suddenly, I remembered what I already knew – to arrive is the end of a journey, not its purpose. I am here to make paths, not follow them. When the all-absorbing obsession is fulfilled, if one's heart remains open, another one looms up to take its place.

There would be another voyage, a return to those blue highways, I told myself. Soon after coming home I began working towards making it happen, and within months, I was underway again. At whatever age you begin your voyage, I hope you take with you that young person you remember yourself as throughout the voyage of the rest of your life.

As I let the anchor settle down into the mud of the yacht basin I thought of the old Tikopian navigator who asked me, "Which star will you follow from here?" In the many years since, I have rolled down countless seas, seeking something beyond the horizon. Note to self: go seek what you will, where you will, but be a seeker all of your life.

Table of Passages

The following table may be useful to others planning a similar route as it gives an idea which seasons and routes provide favorable winds. On most of these passages I sailed conservatively, reefing deeply and frequently to reduce gear failure and permit better control of the Aries wind vane self-steering. Use of the motor was mainly restricted to entering or departing ports. Your mileage may vary.

Date	Passage	Days	Miles
2-16 May 1984	Miami to Colon, Panama	15	1,539
2 Jun-16 Jul 1984	Toboga Is, Panama to Hiva Oa, Marquesas	45	4,182
2-8 Aug 1984	Hiva Oa to Bora Bora, French Polynesia	7	927
17-31 Aug 1984	Bora Bora to Vava'u Island, Tonga	13	1,534
20 Sep-1 Oct 1984	Vava'u to Tikopia, Solomon Islands	11	1,217
19 Oct-2 Nov 1984	Tikopia to Port Moresby, Papua New Guinea	15	1,432
24 Jun-21 Jul 1985	Port Moresby to Cocos (Keeling Island)	28	3,066
2-22 Aug 1985	Cocos Island to Mauritius Island	20	2,376
15-16 Oct 1985	Mauritius Island to Reunion Island	1	145
1-15 Nov 1985	Reunion Island to Durban, South Africa	14	1,473
30 Jan-8 Feb 1986	Durban to Cape Town, South Africa	10	866
21 Feb-9 Mar 1986	Cape Town to St. Helena Island	17	1,711
16 Mar-19 Apr 1986	St. Helena to Martinique, French West Indies	34	3,842
14-26 May 1986	Martinique to Ft. Lauderdale, Florida	13	1333
Average speed:	**106 miles per day** **Total:**	**243**	**25,643**